1,000,000 Books

are available to read at

—◆—

www.ForgottenBooks.com

—◆—

Read online
Download PDF
Purchase in print

ISBN 978-1-330-98425-3
PIBN 10129814

1 MONTH OF
FREE
READING

at
www.ForgottenBooks.com

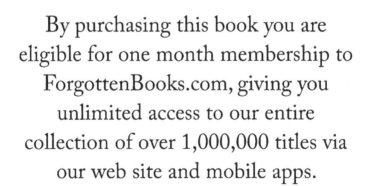

By purchasing this book you are eligible for one month membership to ForgottenBooks.com, giving you unlimited access to our entire collection of over 1,000,000 titles via our web site and mobile apps.

To claim your free month visit:
www.forgottenbooks.com/free129814

English
Français
Deutsche
Italiano
Español
Português

www.forgottenbooks.com

Mythology Photography **Fiction**
Fishing Christianity **Art** Cooking
Essays Buddhism Freemasonry
Medicine **Biology** Music **Ancient
Egypt** Evolution Carpentry Physics
Dance Geology **Mathematics** Fitness
Shakespeare **Folklore** Yoga Marketing
Confidence Immortality Biographies
Poetry **Psychology** Witchcraft
Electronics Chemistry History **Law**
Accounting **Philosophy** Anthropology
Alchemy Drama Quantum Mechanics
Atheism Sexual Health **Ancient History**
Entrepreneurship Languages Sport
Paleontology Needlework Islam
Metaphysics Investment Archaeology
Parenting Statistics Criminology
Motivational

Books for Teachers.

IN PREPARATION :

D. C. HEATH & CO., Publishers,
BOSTON.

HISTORY OF PEDAGOGY.

BY

GABRIEL COMPAYRÉ,

DEPUTY, DOCTOR OF LETTERS, AND PROFESSOR IN THE NORMAL SCHOOL
OF FONTENAY-AUX-ROSES.

*TRANSLATED, WITH AN INTRODUCTION,
NOTES, AND AN INDEX,*

BY

W. H. PAYNE, A.M.,

PROFESSOR OF THE SCIENCE AND THE ART OF TEACHING IN THE UNIVERSITY
OF MICHIGAN ; AUTHOR OF " CHAPTERS ON SCHOOL SUPERVISION,"
AND " OUTLINES OF EDUCATIONAL DOCTRINE."

BOSTON:
D. C. HEATH & COMPANY.
1886.

J. S. CUSHING & CO.. PRINTERS, B

TABLE OF CONTENTS.

TRANSLATOR'S PREFACE.

THE two considerations that have chiefly influenced me in making this translation are the following: —

1. Of the three phases of educational study, the practical, the theoretical, and the historical, the last, as proved by the number of works written on the subject, has received but very little attention from English and American teachers; and yet, if we allow that a teacher should first of all be a man of culture, and that an invaluable factor in his professional education is a knowledge of what has hitherto been done within his field of activity, there are the best of reasons why the claims of this study should be urged upon the teaching profession. For giving breadth of view, judicial candor, and steadiness of purpose, nothing more helpful can be commended to the teacher than a critical survey of the manifold experiments and experiences in educational practice. The acutest thinkers of all the ages have worked at the solution of the educational problem, and the educating art has been practised under every variety of conditions, civil, social, religious, philosophic, and ethnic. Is it not time for us to review these experiments, as the very best condition for advancing surely and steadily?

2. The almost complete neglect of this study among us has been due, in great measure, to the fact that there have

been no books on the subject at all adapted to the ends to
be attained. A dry, scrappy, and incomplete narration of
facts can end only in bewilderment and in blunting the taste
for this species of inquiry. The desirable thing has been
a book that is comprehensive without being tedious, whose
treatment is articulate and clear, and that is pervaded by 'a
critical insight at once catholic and accurate. Some years
ago I read with the keenest admiration, the *Histoire Critique
des Doctrines de l'Éducation en France depuis le Seizième
Siècle*, by Gabriel Compayré (Paris, 1879) ; and it seemed
to me a model, in matter and method, for a general history
of education. Within a recent period Monsieur Compayré
has transformed this *Histoire Critique* into such a general
history of education, under the title *Histoire de la Pédagogie*.
In this book all the characteristics of the earlier work have
been preserved, and it represents to my own mind very
nearly the ideal of the treatise that is needed by the teaching profession of this country.

The reader will observe the distinction made by Monsieur
Compayré between *Pedagogy* and *Education*. Though our
nomenclature does not sanction this distinction, and though
I prefer to give to the term *Pedagogy* a different connota-
tion, I have felt bound on moral grounds to preserve Monsieur Compayré's use of these terms wherever the context
would sanction it.

It seems mere squeamishness to object to the use of .the
word *Pedagogy* on account of historical associations. The
fact that this term is in reputable use in German, French,

and Italian educational literature, is a sufficient guaranty that we may use it without danger. With us, the term *Pedagogics* seems to be employed as a synonym for *Pedagogy*. It would seem to me better to follow continental usage, and restrict the term *Pedagogy* to the art or practice of education, and *Pedagogics* to the correlative science.

I feel under special obligations to Monsieur Compayré, and to his publisher, Monsieur Paul Delaplane, for their courteous permission to publish this translation. I am also greatly indebted to my friend, Mr. C. E. Lowrey, Ph.D., for material aid in important details of my work.

W. H. PAYNE.

UNIVERSITY OF MICHIGAN,
Jan. 4, 1886.

The issue of a second edition has permitted a careful revision of the translation and the correction of several verbal errors. In subsequent editions, no effort will be spared by the translator and his publishers to make this volume worthy of the favor with which it has been received by the educational public.

W. H. P.

AUG. 1, 1886.

INTRODUCTION.

WHAT A COMPLETE HISTORY OF EDUCATION WOULD BE. — In writing an elementary history of pedagogy, I do not pretend to write a history of education. Pedagogy and education, like logic and science, or like rhetoric and eloquence, are different though analogous things.

What would a complete history of education not include? It would embrace, in its vast developments, the entire record of the intellectual and moral culture of mankind at all periods and in all countries. It would be a *résumé* of the life of humanity in its diverse manifestations, literary and scientific, religious and political. It would determine the causes, so numerous and so diverse, which act upon the characters of men, and which, modifying a common endowment, produce beings as different as are a contemporary of Pericles and a modern European, a Frenchman of the middle ages and a Frenchman subsequent to the Revolution.

In fact, there is not only an education, properly so called, that which is given in schools and which proceeds from the direct action of teachers, but there is a natural education, which we receive without our knowledge or will, through the influence of the social environment in which we live. There are what a philosopher of the day has ingeniously called the *occult coadjutors* of education, — climate, race, manners, social condition, political institutions, religious beliefs. If a man of the nineteenth century is very unlike a man of the seventeenth century, it is not merely because the first was educated in a Lycéc of the University and the other in a college of the Jesuits ; it is also because in the atmosphere in which they have been enveloped they have contracted different habits of mind and heart; it is because they have grown up under different laws, under a different social and political *régime;* because they have been nurtured by a different philosophy and a different religion. Upon that delicate and variable composition known as the human soul, how many forces which we do not suspect have left their imprint! How many unobserved and latent causes are involved in our virtues and in our faults! The conscious and determined influence of the teacher is not, perhaps, the most potent. In conjunction with him are at work, obscurely but effectively, innumerable agents, besides personal effort and what is produced by the original energy of the individual.

We see what a history of education would be : a sort of philosophy of history, to which nothing would be foreign, and which would scrutinize in its most varied and most trifling causes, as well as in its most profound sources, the moral life of humanity.

WHAT AN ELEMENTARY HISTORY OF PEDAGOGY SHOULD
BE. — Wholly different is the limited and modest purpose
of a history of pedagogy, which proposes merely to set
forth the doctrines and the methods of educators properly
so called. In this more limited sense, education is reduced
to the premeditated action which the will of one man
exercises over other men in order to instruct them and
train them. It is the reflective auxiliary of the natural
development of the human soul. To what can be done
by nature and by the blind and fatal influences which
sport with human destiny, education adds the concurrence
of art, that is, of the reason, attentive and self-possessed,
which voluntarily and consciously applies to the training
of the soul principles whose truth has been recognized,
and methods whose efficiency has been tested by expe-
ricuce.

Even thus limited, the history of pedagogy still presents
to our inquiry a vast field to be explored. There is scarcely
a subject that has provoked to the same degree as education the best efforts of human thinking. Note the catalogue of educational works published in French, which
Buisson has recently prepared.[1] Though incomplete, this
list contains not less than two thousand titles; and probably educational activity has been more fruitful, and has
been given a still greater extension in Germany than in
France. \This activity is due to the fact, first of all, that

---

[1] See the *Dictionnaire de Pédagogie*, by F. Buisson, Article *Bibliogra-*
phie.

educational questions, brought into fresh notice with each generation, exercise over the minds of men an irresistible and perennial attraction ; and also to the fact that parenthood inspires a taste for such inquiries, and, a thing that is not always fortunate, leads to the assumption of some competence in such matters ; and finally to the very nature of educational problems, which are not to be solved by abstract and independent reasoning, after the fashion of mathematical problems, but which, vitally related to the nature and the destiny of man, change and vary with the fluctuations of the psychological and the moral doctrines of which they are but the consequences. To different systems of psychology correspond different systems of education. An idealist, like Malebranche, will not reason upon education after the manner of a sensationalist like Locke. In the same way there is in every system of morals the germ of a characteristic and original system of education. A mystic, like Gerson, will not assign to education the same end as a practical and positive writer like Herbert Spencer. Hence a very great diversity in systems, or at least an infinite variety in the shades of educational opinion.

Still farther, educational activity may manifest itself in different ways, either in doctrines and theories or in methods and practical applications. The historian of pedagogy has not merely to make known the general conceptions which the philosophers of education have in turn submitted to the approbation of men. If he wishes to make his work complete, he must give a detailed account of what has been accomplished, and make an actual study of the educational establishments which have been founded at different periods by those who have organized instruction.

Pedagogy is a complex affair, and there are many ways of writing its history. One of these which has been too little considered, and which would surely be neither the least interesting nor the least fruitful, would consist in studying, not the great writers on education and their doctrines, not the great teachers and their methods, but pupils themselves. If it were possible to relate in minute detail, supposing that history would furnish us the necessary information on this point, the manner in which a great or a good man has been educated; if an analysis could be made of the different influences which have been involved in the formation of talent or in the development of virtue in the case of remarkable individuals; if it were possible, in a word, to reproduce through exact and personal biographies the toil, the slow elaboration whence have issued at different periods solidity of character, rectitude of purpose, and minds endowed with judicial fairness; the result would be a useful and eminently practical work, something analogous to what a history of logic would be, in which there should be set forth not the abstract rules and the formal laws for the search after truth, but the successful experiments and the brilliant discoveries which have little by little constituted the patrimony of science. This perhaps would be the best of logics because it is real and in action; and also the best of treatises on pedagogy, since there might be learned from it, not general truths, which are often of difficult application and of uncertain utility, but practical means and living methods whose happy and efficient applications would be seen in actual use.

We have just traced the imaginary plan of a history of pedagogy rather than the exact outline of the series of lessons which this book contains. However, we have approached this ideal as nearly as we have been able, by attempting to group about the principal philosophical and moral ideas the systems of education which they have inspired; by endeavoring to retain whatever is essential; by adding to the first rapid sketches studied and elaborate portraits; by ever mingling with the expositions of doctrines and the analysis of important works the study of practical methods and the examination of actual institutions; and, finally, by penetrating the thought of the great educators, to learn from them how they became such, and by following them, as they have united practice with theory, in the particular systems of education which they have directed with success.[1]

DIVISION OF THE HISTORY OF PEDAGOGY. — The abundance and the variety of pedagogical questions, the great number of thinkers who have written upon education, in a word, the complexity of the subject, might inspire the

---

[1] The book now offered to the public was taught before it was written. It is the result of the lectures given for three years past, either at the higher normal school of Fontenay-aux-Roses, or in the normal courses for men at Sèvres and at Saint Cloud.

historian of pedagogy with the idea of dividing his work, and of distributing his studies into several series. For example, it would be possible to write the history of education in general by itself, and then the history of instruction, which is but an element of education. As education itself comprises three parts, physical education, intellectual education, and moral education, there would be an opportunity for three series of distinct studies on these different subjects. But these divisions would present grave inconveniences. In general, the opinions of an educator are not susceptible of division; there is a connection between his manner of regarding the matter of instruction and the solution he gives to educational questions proper. One mode of thinking pervades his theories or his practice in the matter of moral discipline, and his ideas on intellectual education. It is, then, necessary to consider each of the different systems of education as a whole.

Perhaps a better order of division would be that which, without regard to chronological order, should distinguish all pedagogical doctrines and applications into a certain number of schools, and connect all educators with certain general tendencies: as the ascetic tendency, that of the fathers of the church, for example, and of the middle ages; the utilitarian tendency of Locke, and of a great number of moderns; the pessimism of Port Royal, the optimism of Fénelon; the literary school of the humanists of the Renaissance, and the scientific school of Diderot and of Condorcet. Such a mode of procedure would have its interest, because in the manifestations of educational thought so apparently different it would sharply distinguish certain uniform principles which reappear at all periods of history; but this would be rather a philosophy of the history of education than a simple history of pedagogy.

The best we can do, then, is to follow the chronological order and to study in turn the educators of antiquity, those of the middle ages, of the Renaissance, and of modern times. We shall interrogate in succession those who have become eminent as teachers and educators, and ask of each how he has solved for himself the various portions of the problems of education. Besides being more simple and more natural, this order has the advantage of showing us the progress of education as it has gradually risen from instinct to reflection, from nature to art, and after long periods of groping and many halts, ascending from humble beginnings to a complete and definite organization. This plan also exhibits to us the beautiful spectacle of a humanity in a state of ceaseless growth. At first, instruction comprised but few subjects, at the same time that only a select few participated in it. Then there was a simultaneous though gradual extension of the domain of knowledge which must be acquired, of the moral qualities demanded by the struggle for existence, and of the number of men who are called to be instructed and educated, — the ideal being, as Comenius has said, that all may learn and that everything may be taught.

Utility of the History of Pedagogy. — The history of pedagogy is henceforth to form a part of the course of study for the primary normal schools of France. It has been included in the prescribed list of subjects for the third year, under this title: *History of Pedagogy, — Principal educators and their doctrines; Analysis of the most important works.*[1]

Is argument necessary to justify the place which has been assigned to this study? In the first place, the history of pedagogy possesses great interest from the fact that it is closely connected with the general history of thought and also with the philosophic explication of human actions. Certainly, pedagogical doctrines are neither fortuitous opinions nor events without significance. On the one hand, they have their causes and their principles in moral, religions, and political beliefs, of which they are the faithful image; on the other, they are instrumental in the training of mind and in the formation of manners. Back of the *Ratio Studiorum* of the Jesuits, back of the *Émile* of Rousseau, there distinctly appears a complete religion, a complete philosophy. In the classical studies organized by the humanists of the Renaissance we see the dawn of that literary brilliancy which distinguished the century of Louis XIV., and so in the scientific studies preached a hundred years ago by Diderot and by Condorcet there was a preparation for the positive spirit of our time. The education of the people is at once the consequence

---

[1] Resolution of Aug. 3, 1881.

of all that it believes and the source of all that it is destined to be.

But there are other reasons which recommend the study of educators and the reading of their works. The history of pedagogy is a necessary introduction to pedagogy itself. It should be studied, not for purposes of erudition or for mere curiosity, but with a practical purpose for the sake of finding in it the permanent truths which are the essentials of a definite theory of education. The desirable thing just now is not perhaps so much to find new ideas, as properly to comprehend those which are already current; to choose from among them, and, a choice once having been made, to make a resolute effort to apply them to use. When we consider with impartiality all that has been conceived or practised previous to the nineteenth century, or when we see clearly what our predecessors have left us to do in the way of- consequences to deduce, of incomplete or obscure ideas to generalize or to illustrate, and especially of opposing tendencies to reconcile, we may well inquire what they have really left us to discover.

It is profitable to study even the chimeras and the educational errors of our predecessors. In fact, these are so many marked experiments which contribute to the progress of our methods by warning us of the rocks which we should shun. A thorough analysis of the paradoxes of Rousseau, and of the absurd consequences to which the abuse of the principle of nature leads us, is no less instructive than meditation on the wisest precepts of Montaigne or of Port Royal.

In truth, for him who has an exact knowledge of the educators of past centuries, the work of constructing a system of education is more than half done. It remains only to co-ordinate the scattered truths which have been collected from their works by assimilating them through personal reflection, and by making them fruitful through psychological analysis and moral faith.

Let it be observed that as studied by the men who first conceived and practised them, pedagogical methods present themselves to our examination with a sharpness of outline that is surprising. Innovators lend to whatever they invent a personal emphasis, something life-like and occasionally extravagant; but it is exactly this which permits us the better to comprehend their thought, and the more completely to discover its truth or its falsity.

However, it is not alone the intellectual advantage · which recommends the history of pedagogy; it is also the moral stimulus which will be derived from the study. For the sake of encouraging to noble efforts the men and women who are our teachers, is it of no moment to present to them the names of Comenius, Rollin, and Pestalozzi as men who have attained such high excellence in their profession? Will not the teacher who each day resumes his heavy burden be revived and sustained? Will he not enter his class-room, where so many difficulties and toils await him, a better and a stronger man if his imagination teems with articulate memories of those who, in the past, have opened for him the way, and shown him by their example how to walk in it? By the marvellous agency of electricity we are now able to transport material and mechanical power, and to cause its transfer across space without regard to distance. But by reading and by meditation we are able to do something analogous to this in the moral world; we are able to borrow from the ancients, across the centuries, something of the moral energy that inspired them, and to make live again in our own hearts some of their virtues of devotion and faith. Doubtless a brief history of pedagogy could not, from this point of view, serve as a substitute for the actual reading of the authors in question; but it is a preparation for this work and inspires a taste for it.

We are warranted in saying, then, that the utility of the history of pedagogy blends with the utility of pedagogy itself. To-day it is no longer necessary for us to offer any proof on this point. Pedagogy, long neglected even in our country, has regained its standing; nay more, it has become the fashion. "France is becoming addicted to pedagogy" was a remark recently made by one of the men who, of our day, will have contributed most to excite and also to direct the taste for pedagogical studies.[1] The words *pedagogue*, *pedagogy*, have

---

[1] See the Article of M. Pécaut in the *Revue Pédagogique*, No. 2, 1882.

encountered dangers in the history of our language. Littré tells us that the word *pedagogue* "is most often used in a bad sense." On the other hand, we shall see, if we consult his dictionary, that several years ago the sense of the word *pedagogy* was not yet fixed, since it is there defined as "the moral education of children." To-day, not only in language, but in facts and in institutions, the fate of pedagogy is settled. Of course we must neither underrate it nor attribute to it a sovereign and omnipotent efficiency that it does not have. We might freely say of pedagogy what Sainte-Beuve said of logic: The best is that which does not argue in its own favor; which is not enamoured of itself, but which modestly recognizes the limits of its power. The best is that which we make for ourselves, not that which we learn from books.

Even with this reserve, the teaching of pedagogy is destined to render important services to the cause of education, and education, let us be assured, is in the way of acquiring a fresh importance day by day. This is due to the fact, first, that under a liberal govern-ment, and in a republican society, it is more and more necessary that the citizens shall be instructed and enlightened. Liberty is a dangerous thing unless it has instruction for a counterpoise. Moreover, we must rec-ollect that in our day, among those *occult coadjutors* of which we have spoken, and which at all times add their action to that of education proper, some have lost their influence, while others, so far from co-operating in this movement, oppose it and compromise it. On the one hand, religion has seen her influence curtailed. She is no longer, as she once was, the tutelary power under whose shadow the rising generations peacefully matured. It is necessary that education, through the progress of the reason and through the reflective development of morality, should compensate for the waning influence of religion.

On the other hand, social conditions, the very progress of civil and political liberty, the growing independence accorded the child in the family, the multiplication of books, good and bad, all these collateral agents of education are not always compliant and useful aids. They would prove the accomplices of a moral decadence did not our teachers make an effort as much more vigorous to affect the will and the heart, as well as the mind, in order to establish character, and thus assure the recuperation of our country.

A SKETCH OF THE LIFE OF GABRIEL COMPAYRÉ.[1]

GABRIEL COMPAYRÉ was born Jan. 2, 1843, at Albi, a city of Southern France, containing about fifteen thousand inhabitants, and the capital of the province of Tarn. His early education was received from his father, a man of sterling character, and the author of a book entitled, *Historical Studies Concerning the Albigenses.*

He passed from his father's care to the *collège* of Castres, then to the *lycée* of Toulouse, and finally to the *lycée Louis-le-Grand* at Paris. His fellow-pupils recall with pleasure his triumphs at these institutions of learning. His brilliant intellectual powers, his vivid imagination, his well-stored memory, and his unwearied industry, marked him as destined to render signal services to his race.

He entered the *École Normale Supérieure* in 1862. His tastes led him to philosophical studies; indeed, he had already manifested a strong tendency to moral and intellectual science. Yet his intensely practical nature could not long remain satisfied with metaphysical subtleties where he found no sure foot-hold. He became a warm advocate of experimental methods, and of the Baconian philosophy. He set himself to a study of man as he appears in society

---

[1] Furnished by Mr. Geo. E. Gay, Principal of the Malden High School.

and in the family; to the analysis of his emotions and his acts, and to the deduction, from these analyses, of those rules which ought to preside over his conduct and his intellectual and moral development.

He graduated from the normal school in 1865, and was immediately appointed professor of philosophy at the *lycée* of Pau. A lecture upon Rousseau, which he delivered here, brought upon him the severe condemnation of the ultramontane party, and involved him in a controversy which has continued to the present time.

In 1868, having been made a fellow of the University, he was sent to the *lycée* of Poitiers. At this place he manifested his sympathy for the common people by a course of lectures to workmen on moral subjects. About this time he received honorable mention from the Academy for an eloquent eulogy upon Rousseau, in which he carefully portrayed the influence of Rousseau upon the government of his country and upon methods of school instruction, giving him full credit for the reform in both.

From this time forward Compayré's life has been filled with labors and with honors. In addition to his professional duties and philosophical writings, he has made careful study of the social and political questions of his country.

Promoted from one post of honor to another, on the 14th of July, 1880, he was appointed Chevalier of the Legion of Honor.

In 1874 he presented his theme for his doctor's degree upon the *Philosophy of David Hume*, a work of the highest philosophical thought and language, which received a prize from the Academy.

Between 1874 and 1880 his lectures were largely devoted to the subjects most closely connected with modern thought. *A Study of Darwinism*, *The Psychology of a Child*, *Educational Principles*, are subjects that indicate the sweep of his investigations. The brilliancy of his style, the liberality of his opinions, and the extent of his learning have exposed him to bitter attacks from those who envy his powers and disbelieve his doctrines; yet his popularity has continually increased, and the young professor has become a great power in the party of the republic, to whose cause he early devoted himself.

The works which he published during this period were numerous. He translated with great care, adding valuable matter of his own: Bain's *Inductive and Deductive Logic*, Huxley's *Hume, His Life and Philosophy*, and Locke's *Thoughts on Education*. His most considerable work is his *History of the Doctrine of Education in France since the Sixteenth Century*, a work of two volumes, published in 1879, which reached its fourth edition in France in 1883, has been translated entire into German, and from which numerous extracts have been made for the educational journals of England and America. If we add to these labors his work upon the *Revue Philosophique*, and the *Dictionnaire de Pédagogie*, we shall understand why he was called to Paris in 1881, by the Minister of Public Instruction, to aid in founding the *École Normale Supérieure des Institutrices, de Fontenay-aux-Roses.* He successfully arranged the course of instruction for this school. In the same year he assisted in the organization of a new school at Sèvres, which prepares young teachers for the course of instruction in the normal schools.

In 1880 he published his *Manual of Civil and Moral Instruction*, in two courses, or parts. This book has had a remarkable career. In less than three years more than three hundred thousand copies of the first part, and over five hundred thousand of the second part, were sold.

In 1882, in conjunction with a friend, M. A. Delplan, an author of merit, he published his *Civil and Moral Lectures*. In 1883 he published a *Course of Civil Instruction* for normal schools.

Compayré entered political life in 1881, having been elected deputy from the arrondissement of Lavaur in Tarn. He occupies a distinguished position among the men of to-day; his character, his talents, his popularity, and his devotion to the cause of civil and intellectual freedom, give him the assurance of a place no less important among the men of the future.

In his personal appearance Compayré combines the scholar and the man of the world. His dark hair, parted in the middle, is combed back from a forehead very high and very broad. His eye is bright and piercing, and his face, clean shaven except upon the upper lip, bears the impress of both his ingenuousness and his indomitable perseverance.

THE

HISTORY OF PEDAGOGY.

———◆———

CHAPTER I.

EDUCATION IN ANTIQUITY.

PRELIMINARY CONSIDERATIONS; EDUCATION AMONG THE HINDOOS;
POLITICAL CASTE AND RELIGIOUS PANTHEISM; EFFECTS ON EDUCA-
TION; BUDDHISTIC REFORM; CONVERSATION OF BUDDHA AND
PURNA; EDUCATIONAL USAGES; EDUCATION AMONG THE ISRAEL-
ITES; PRIMITIVE PERIOD; RELIGIOUS AND NATIONAL EDUCATION;
PROGRESS OF POPULAR INSTRUCTION; ORGANIZATION OF SCHOOLS;
RESPECT FOR TEACHERS; METHODS AND DISCIPLINE; EXCLUSIVE
AND JEALOUS SPIRIT; EDUCATION AMONG THE CHINESE; FORMAL-
ISM; LÂO-TSZE AND KHUNG-TSZE (CONFUCIUS); EDUCATION AMONG
OTHER PEOPLE OF THE EAST; THE EGYPTIANS AND THE PERSIANS;
ANALYTICAL SUMMARY.

1. PRELIMINARY CONSIDERATIONS. — A German historian of
philosophy begins his work by asking this question: " Was
Adam a philosopher?" In the same way certain historians
of pedagogy begin by learned researches upon the education
of savages. We shall not carry our investigations so far
back. Doubtless from the day when a human family began
its existence, from the day when a father and a mother began
to love their children, education had an existence. But there
is very little practical interest in studying these obscure beginnings of pedagogy. It is a matter of erudition and curi-

osity.[1] Besides the difficulty of gathering up the faint traces of primitive education, there would be but little profit in painfully following the slow gropings of primeval man. In truth, the history of pedagogy dates but from the period relatively recent, when human thought, in the matter of education, substituted reflection for instinct, art for blind nature. So we shall hasten to begin the study of pedagogy among the classical peoples, the Greeks and the Romans, after having thrown a rapid glance over some Eastern nations considered either in their birthplace and remote origin, or in their more recent development.

2. THE PEDAGOGY OF THE HINDOOS. — It would not be worth our while to enter into details respecting a civilization so different from our own as that of the Hindoos. But we should not forget that we are in part the descendants of that people, and that we belong to the same ethnic group, and that the European languages are derived from theirs.

3. POLITICAL CASTE AND RELIGIOUS PANTHEISM. — The spirit of caste, from the social point of view, and pantheism, from the religious point of view, are the characteristics of Hindoo society. The Indian castes constituted hereditary

---

[1] A knowledge of the mental and moral condition of savages serves the invaluable purpose of showing what education has accomplished for the human race. There would be much less grumbling at the tax-gatherer if men could clearly conceive the condition of societies where no taxes are levied. To know what education has actually done we need to know the condition of societies unaffected by systematic education. Such a book as Lubbock's *Origin of Civilization* is a helpful introduction to the history of education. Whoever reads such a book carefully will be confronted with this problem: How is it that intellectual inertness, amounting almost to stupidity, is frequently the concomitant of an acute and persistent sense-training? Besides, savage tribes are historical illustrations of what has been produced on a large scale by " following Nature." (P.)

classes where social rank and special vocation were determined, not by free choice, but by the accident of birth. The
consequence of this was an endless routine, with no care
either for the individuality, or the personal talents, or the
inclination of children, and without the possibility of rising
by personal effort above one's rank in life.[1] On the other
hand, religious ideas came to restrict, within the limits where
it was already imprisoned, the activity of the young Hindoo.
God is everywhere present; he manifests himself in all the
phenomena of heaven and earth, in the sun and in the stars,
in the Himalayas and in the Ganges; he penetrates and animates everything; the things of sense are but the changing
and ephemeral vestments of the unchangeable being. "With
this pantheistic conception of the world and of life, the
thought and the will of the Hindoo perished in the mystic
contemplation of the soul. To become master of one's inclinations; to abandon every terrestrial thought; after this
life to lose one's identity, and to be annihilated by absorption in the divine nature; to prepare one's self by macera-
tions and expiations for complete submersion in the original
principle of all being, — this is the highest wisdom, the true
happiness of the Hindoo, the ideal of all serious education."[2]

---

[1] There is an argument for caste in the modern fiction of a "beautiful
economy of Nature," which plants human beings in society as it does trees
in the earth, and thus makes education consist in the action of environment
upon man and in the reaction of man upon his environment. To support
existence, man needs certain endowments; but the force of circumstances
creates these very endowments. One man is predestined to be a Red
Indian, another a Bushman, and still another an accountant; and in each
case the function of education is to adapt the man to the place where
Nature has fixed him. This modern justification of caste is adroitly
worked out by Mr. Spencer in the first chapter of his *Education*. (P.)

[2] Dittes, *Histoire de l'éducation et de l'instruction*, translated by Redolfi,
1880, p. 38.

4. EFFECTS ON EDUCATION. — It is easy to predict what
education would become under the weight of these double
chains, social and religious.   While the ideal in our modern
societies is more and more to enfranchise the individual, and
to create for him personal freedom and self-consciousness,
the effort of the Hindoo Brahmins consisted above all in
crushing out all spontaneity, in abolishing individual predi-
lections, by preaching the doctrine of absolute self-renuncia-
tion, of voluntary abasement, and of contempt for life.
Man was thus born doubly a slave, — by his social condition,
which predestinated him to the routine apprenticeship of his
ancestral caste, and by his mysterious dependence on the
divine being who absorbed in himself all real activity, and
left to human beings only the deceptive and frail appearance
of it.

5. BUDDHIST REFORM. — The Buddhist reform, which so
profoundly affected Brahmanism at about the sixth century
B.C., did not sensibly modify, from the educational point of
view, the ideas of the Hindoos.   Buddha also taught that
the cause of evil resides in the passions of men, and that in
order to attain moral peace, there is no other means to be
employed than that of self-abnegation and of the renounce-
ment of everything selfish and personal.

6. CONVERSATION OF BUDDHA AND PURNA. — One of the
traditions which permit us the better to appreciate the original character, at once affecting and ingenuous, of Indian
thought, is the conversation of Buddha with his disciple
Purna about a journey the latter was going to undertake to
the barbarians for the purpose of teaching them the new
religion : —

"They are men," said Buddha, "who are fiery in temper,
passionate, cruel, furious, insolent.   If they openly address

you in words which are malicious and coarse, and become angry with you, what will you think?"

" If they address me to my face in coarse and insolent terms, this is what I shall think: they are certainly good men who openly address me in malicious terms, but they will neither strike me with their hands nor stone me."

" But should they strike you with their hands and stone you, what will you think?"

" I shall think that they are good men, gentle men, who strike me with their hands and stone me, but do not beat me with a club nor with a sword."

" But if they beat you with a club and with a sword?"

" They are good men, gentle men, who beat me with a club and with a sword, but they do not completely kill me."

" But if they were really to kill you?"

" They are good men, gentle men, who deliver me with so little pain from this body encumbered with defilements."

" Very good, Purna! You may live in the country of those barbarians. Go, Purna! Being liberated, liberate; being consoled, console; having reached Nirvâna thus made perfect, cause others to go there." [1]

Whatever there is to admire in such a strange system of morals should not blind us to the vices which resulted from its practical consequences: such as the abuse of passive resignation, the complete absence of the idea of right and of justice, and no active virtues.

7. EFFECTS ON EDUCATION. — Little is known of the actual state of educational practice among the Hindoos. It may be said, however, that the Brahmins, the priests, had the exclusive charge of education. Woman, in absolute subjection to man, had no share whatever in instruction.

---

[1] Burnouf, *Introduction à l'histoire du Bouddhisme,* p. 252.

As to boys, it seems that in India there were always schools for their benefit; schools which were held in the open country under the shade of trees, or, in case of bad weather, under sheds. Mutual instruction has been practised in India from the remotest antiquity; it is from here, in fact, that Andrew Bell, at the close of the eighteenth century, borrowed the idea of this mode of instruction. Exercises in writing were performed first upon the sand with a stick, then upon palm leaves with an iron style, and finally upon the dry leaves of the plane-tree with ink. In discipline there was a resort to corporal punishment; besides the rod the teacher employed other original means of correction; for example, he threw cold water on the offender. The teacher, moreover, was treated with a religious respect; the child must respect him as he would Buddha himself.

The higher studies were reserved for the priestly class, who, long before the Christian era, successfully cultivated rhetoric and logic, astronomy and the mathematics.

8. EDUCATION AMONG THE ISRAELITES. — "If ever a people has demonstrated the power of education, it is the people of Israel."[1] In fact, what a singular spectacle is offered us by that people, which, dispossessed of its own country for eighteen hundred years, has been dispersed among the nations without losing its identity, and has maintained its existence without a country, without a government, and without a ruler, preserving with perennial energy its habits, its manners, and its faith! Without losing sight of the part of that extraordinary vitality of the Jewish people, which is due to the natural endowments of the race, its tenacity of temperament, and its wonderful activity of intelligence, it is just to attribute another part of it to the sound education,

[1] Dittes, p. 49.

at once religious and national, which the ancient Hebrews have transmitted by tradition to their descendants.

9. EDUCATION, RELIGIOUS AND NATIONAL, DURING THE PRIMITIVE PERIOD. — The chief characteristic of the education of the Hebrews in the earliest period of their history is that it was essentially domestic. During the whole Biblical period there is no trace of public schools, at least for young children. Family life is the origin of that primitive society where the notion of the state is almost unknown, and where God is the real king.

The child was to become the faithful servant of Jehovah. To this end it was not needful that he should be learned. It was only necessary that he should learn through language and the instructive example of his parents the moral precepts and the religious beliefs of the nation. It has been very justly said[1] that "Among all nations the direction impressed on education depends on the idea which they form of the perfect man. Among the Romans it is the brave soldier, inured to fatigue, and readily yielding to discipline; among the Athenians it is the man who unites in himself the happy harmony of moral and physical perfection; among the Hebrews the perfect man is the pious, virtuous man, who is capable of attaining the ideal traced by God himself in these terms: 'Ye shall be holy, for I the Lord your God am boly!'" J. Simon.

The discipline was harsh, as is proved by many passages in the Bible: "He that spareth his rod, hateth his son," say the Proverbs; "but he that loveth him chasteneth him betimes."[3] "Withhold not correction from the child, for if

---

[1] *L'éducation et l'instruction chez les anciens Juifs*, by J. Simon, Paris, 1879, p. 16.
[2] Levit. xix. 2.   [3] Prov. xiii. 24.

thou beatest him with the rod, he shall not die. Thou shalt
beat him with the rod, and shalt deliver his soul from hell." [1]
And still more significant: " Chasten thy son while there is
hope, and let not thy soul spare for his crying." [2]

Only boys, it seems, learned to read and write. As to
girls, they were taught to spin, to weave, to prepare food for
the table, to superintend the work of the household, and
also to sing and to dance.

In a word, intellectual culture was but an incident in the
primitive education of the Hebrews ; the great thing, in their
eyes, was moral and religious instruction, and education in
love of country. Fathers taught their children the nation's
history, and the great events that had marked the destiny
of the people of God. That series of events celebrated
by the great feasts which were often renewed, and in which
the children participated, served at once to fill their hearts
with gratitude to God and with love for their country.

10. PROGRESS OF POPULAR INSTRUCTION. — It is not easy
to conceive to what extent the zeal for instruction was developed among the ancient Jews in the years that followed the
advent of Christianity. From being domestic, as it had been
up to that time, Jewish education became public. Besides,
it was no longer sufficient to indoctrinate children with good
principles and wholesome moral habits ; they must also be
instructed. From the first centuries of the Christian era,
the Israelites approached our modern ideal, with respect to
making education obligatory and universal. Like every
brave nation that has been vanquished, whose energy has
survived defeat, like the Prussians after Jena, or the
French after 1870, the Jews sought to defend themselves
against the effects of conquest by a great intellectual effort,

---

[1] Prov. xxiii. 13, 14.   [2] Prov. xix. 18.

and to regain their lost ground by the development of popular instruction.

11. ORGANIZATION OF SCHOOLS. — In the year 64, the high priest, Joshua Ben Gamala, imposed on each town, under pain of excommunication, the obligation to support a school. If the town is cut in two by a river, and there is no means of transit by a safe bridge, a school must be established on each side. Even to-day we are far from having realized, as regards the number of schools and of teachers, this rule stated in the Talmud: If the number of children does not exceed twenty-five, the school shall be conducted by a single teacher; for more than twenty-five, the town shall employ an assistant; if the number exceeds forty, there shall be two masters.

12. RESPECT FOR TEACHERS. — In that ancient time, what an exalted and noble conception men had of teachers, "those true guardians of the city"! Even then, how exacting were the requirements made of them! But, on the other hand, how they were esteemed and respected! The Rabbins required that the schoolmaster should be married; they mistrusted teachers who were not at the same time heads of families. Is it possible to enforce the advantages of maturity and experience more delicately than in this beautiful language? "He who learns of a young master is like a man who eats green grapes, and drinks wine fresh from the press; but he who has a master of mature years is like a man who eats ripe and delicious grapes, and drinks old wine." Mildness, patience, and unselfishness were recommended as the ruling virtues of the teacher. "If your teacher and your father," says the Talmud, "have need of your assistance, help your teacher before helping your father, for the latter has given you only the life of this

world, while the former has secured for you the life of the world to come." [1]

13. METHOD AND DISCIPLINE. — The child entered school at the age of six. "If a child below the age of six is brought to your school," says the Talmud, "you need not receive him"; and to indicate that after that age it is proper to regain the lost time, the Talmud adds, "After the age of six, receive the child, and *load him like an ox.*" On the contrary, other authorities of the same period, more judicious and far-seeing, recommend moderation in tasks, and say that it is necessary to treat "the young according to their strength, and the grown-up according to theirs."

There was taught in the Jewish schools, along with reading and writing,[2] a little of natural history, and a great deal of geometry and astronomy. Naturally, the Bible was the first book put in the hands of children. The master interspersed moral lessons with the teaching of reading. He made a special effort to secure a correct pronunciation, and multiplied his explanations in order to make sure of being understood, repeating his comments even to the *four-hundredth time* if it were necessary. It seems that the methods were suggestive and attractive, and the discipline relatively mild. There were but few marks of the proverbial severity of the ancient times. "Children," says the Talmud, "should be punished with one hand, and caressed with two." The Christian spirit, the spirit of him who had said "suffer the

---

[1] On similar grounds, Alexander declared that he owed more to Aristotle his teacher, than to Philip his father. (P.)

[2] What were the methods followed in teaching reading and writing? We are told by Renan in his *Vie de Jésus* that "Jesus doubtless learned to read and write according to the method of the East, which consists in putting into the hands of the child a book which he repeats in concert with his comrades till he knows it by heart."

little children to come unto me," had affected the Jews themselves. However, corporal punishment was tolerated to a
certain extent, but, strange to say, only for children above
the age of eleven. In case of disobedience, a pupil above
that age might be deprived of food, and even struck with a
strap of shoe-leather.

14. EXCLUSIVE AND JEALOUS SPIRIT. — Some reservation
must accompany the encomiums justly due Jewish education.
With respect to the rest of the human race, the Jewish spirit
was mean, narrow, and malevolent. The Israelites of this
day have retained something of these jealous and exclusive
tendencies. At the beginning of the Christian era, the fierce
and haughty patriotism of the Jews led them to proscribe
whatever was of Gentile origin, whatever had not the
sanction of the national tradition. Nothing of Greek or
Roman culture penetrated this closed world.[1] The Jewish
doctors covered with the same contempt him who raises
hogs and him who teaches his son Greek science.

15. EDUCATION AMONG THE CHINESE. — We have attempted to throw into relief the educational practices of
two Eastern nations to which the civilization of the
West is most intimately related. A few words will suffice for the other primitive societies whose history is too
little known, and whose civilization is too remote from
our own, to make their plans of education anything more
than an object of curiosity.

---

[1] This statement needs qualifying. "In nearly all the families of high
rank," says the *Dictionnaire de Pédagogie* (1ᵉʳᵉ Partie, Article JUIFS), the
daughters spoke Greek. The Rabbins did not look with any favor upon
the study of profane philosophy; but notwithstanding their protests, there
were many devoted readers of Plato and Aristotle. It is said that among
the pupils of the celebrated Gamaliel there were five hundred who studied
the philosophy and the literature of Greece." (P.)

China has been civilized from time immemorial, and at every period of her long history she has preserved her national characteristics. For more than three thousand years an absolute uniformity has characterized this immobile people. Everything is regulated by tradition. Education is mechanical and formal. The preoccupation of teachers is to cause their pupils to acquire a mechanical ability, a regular and sure routine. They care more for appearances, for a decorous manner of conduct, than for a searching and profound morality. Life is but a ceremonial, minutely determined and punctually followed. There is no liberty, no glow of spontaneity. Their art is characterized by conventional refinement and by a prettiness that seems mean ; there is nothing of the grand and imposing. By their formalism, the Chinese educators are the Jesuits of the East.

16. Lâo-tsze and Khung-tsze. — Towards the sixth century B.C. two reformers appeared in China, Lâo-tsze and Khung-tsze. The first represents the spirit of emancipation, of progress, of the pursuit of the ideal, of protest against routine. He failed. The second, on the contrary, who became celebrated under the name of Confucius, and to whom tradition ascribes more than three thousand personal disciples, secured the triumph of his ideas of practical, utilitarian morality, founded upon the authority of the State and that of the family, as well as upon the interest of the individual.

A quotation from Lâo-tsze will prove that human thought, in the sixth century B.C., had reached a high mark in China : —

" Certain bad rulers would have us believe that the heart and the spirit of man should be left empty, but that instead his stomach should be filled; that his bones should be strengthened rather than the power of his will; that we should always desire to have the people remain in a state of ignorance, for then their demands would be few. It is difficult, they say, to govern a people that are too wise.

"These doctrines are directly opposed to what is due to humanity. Those in authority should come to the aid of the people by means of oral and written instruction; so far from oppressing them and treating them as slaves, they should do them good in every possible way."

In other words, it is by enlightening the people, and by an honest devotion to their interests, that one becomes worthy to govern them.

If the Chinese have not fully profited by these wise and exalted counsels, it appears that at least they have attempted to make instruction general. Huc, a Chinese missionary, boldly declares that China is the country of all countries where primary instruction is most widely diffused. To the same effect, a German writer affirms that in China there is not a village so miserable, nor a hamlet so unpretending, as not to be provided with a school of some kind.[1] In a country of tradition, like China, we can infer what once existed from what exists to-day. But that instruction which is so widely diffused is wholly superficial and tends merely to an exterior culture. As Dittes says, the educational method of the Chinese consists, not in *developing*, but in *communicating*.[2]

---

[1] For a series of interesting documents on the actual state of education in China, consult the article CHINE, in Buisson's *Dictionnaire de Pédagogie.*

[2] Dittes, *op. cit.*, p. 32.

17. EDUCATION AMONG THE OTHER NATIONS OF THE
EAST. — Of all the oriental nations, Egypt is the one in
which intellectual culture seems to have reached the highest point, but only among men of a privileged class.
Here, as in India, the priestly class monopolized the
learning of the day; it jealously guarded the depository
of mysterious knowledge which it communicated only to
the kings. The common people, divided into working
classes, which were destined from father to son to the
same social status, learned scarcely more than was necessary in order to practise their hereditary trades and
to be initiated into the religious beliefs.

In the more military but less theocratic nation, the
Persian, efforts were made in favor of a general education. The religious dualism which distinguished Ormuzd,
the principle of good, from Ahriman, the principle of
evil, and which promised the victory to the former, made
it the duty of each man to contribute to this final victory by devoting himself to a life of virtue. Hence arose
noble efforts to attain physical and moral perfection. The
education of the Persians in temperance and frugality has
excited the admiration of certain Greek writers, especially
Xenophon, and there will be found in his *Cyropœdia* a thrill-
ing picture of the brave and noble manners of the ancient
Persians.[1]

---

[1] On a recent occasion Archdeacon Farrar referred to Persian education as follows : " We boast of our educational ideal. Is it nearly
as high in some essentials as that even of some ancient and heathen
nations long centuries before Christ came? The ancient Persians were
worshippers of fire and of the sun ; most of their children would have
been probably unable to pass the most elementary examination in
physiology, but assuredly the Persian ideal might be worthy of our
study. (At the age of fourteen — the age when we turn our children
adrift from school, and do nothing more for them — the Persians gave

On the whole, the history of pedagogy among the people of \
the East offers us but few examples to follow. That which,
in different degrees, characterizes primitive education is that
it is the privilege of certain classes ; that woman is most generally excluded from its benefits ; that in respect of the common people it is scarcely more than the question of an
apprenticeship to a trade, or of the art of war, or of a
preparation for the future life ; that no appeal is made to
the free energy of individuals, but that the great masses of
the people in antiquity have generally lived under the har-
assing oppression of religious conceptions, of fixed traditions, and of political despotism.

[18. ANALYTICAL SUMMARY.—Speaking generally, the education of the primitive nations of the East had the following
characteristics : —

1. It was administered by the hieratic class. This was
due to the fact that the priests were the only men of learning, and consequently the only men who could teach.

2. The knowledge communicated was in the main relig- |
ious, ethical, and prudential, and the final purpose of instruction was good conduct.

3. As the matter of instruction was knowledge bearing
the sanction of authority, the learner was debarred from free
inquiry, and the general tendency was towards immobility.

4. As the knowledge of the day was embodied in language, the process of learning consisted in the interpretation
of speech, and so involved a large and constant use of the

---

their young nobles the four best masters whom they could find to
teach their boys wisdom, justice, temperance, and courage — wisdom
including worship, justice including the duty of unswerving truthful-
ness through life, temperance including mastery over sensual tempta-
tions, courage including a free mind opposed to all things coupled
with guilt." (P.) *Archdeacon* ./. / / . /

memory; and this literal memorizing of the principles and
rules of conduct promoted stability of character.

5. As the purpose of instruction was guidance, there was
no appearance of the conception that one main purpose of
education is discipline or culture.

6. The conception of education as a means of national
regeneration had a distinct appearance among the Jews; and
among this people we find one form of compulsion, — the
obligation placed on towns to support schools.

7. In Persia, the State appears for the first time as a distinct agency in promoting education.

8. In China, from time immemorial, scholarship has been
made the condition for obtaining places in the civil service,
and in consequence education has been made subordinate to
examinations.

9. Save to a limited extent among the Jews, woman was
debarred from the privileges of education.

10. In the main, education was administered so as to
perpetuate class distinctions. There was no appearance of
the conception that education is a universal right and a
universal good.]

CHAPTER II.

EDUCATION AMONG THE GREEKS.

GREEK PEDAGOGY; ATHENIAN AND SPARTAN EDUCATION; THE SCHOOLS
OF ATHENS; SCHOOLS OF GRAMMAR; SCHOOLS OF GYMNASTICS; THE
PALESTRA; SCHOOLS OF MUSIC; THE SCHOOLS OF RHETORIC AND OF
PHILOSOPHY; SOCRATES AND THE SOCRATIC METHOD; SOCRATIC
IRONY; MAIEUTICS, OR THE ART OF GIVING BIRTH TO IDEAS;
EXAMPLES OF IRONY AND OF MAIEUTICS BORROWED FROM THE
MEMORABILIA OF XENOPHON; PLATO AND THE REPUBLIC; THE EDU-
CATION OF WARRIORS AND MAGISTRATES; MUSIC AND GYMNASTICS;
RELIGION AND ART IN EDUCATION; THE BEAUTIFUL AND THE GOOD;
HIGH INTELLECTUAL EDUCATION; THE LAWS; DEFINITION OF EDUCA-
TION; DETAILED PRECEPTS; XENOPHON; THE ECONOMICS AND THE
EDUCATION OF WOMAN; THE CYROPÆDIA; PROTESTS OF XENOPHON
AGAINST THE DEGENERATE MANNERS OF THE GREEKS; ARISTOTLE;
GENERAL CHARACTER OF HIS PLAN OF EDUCATION; PUBLIC EDUCA-
TION; PROGRESSIVE DEVELOPMENT OF HUMAN NATURE; PHYSICAL
EDUCATION; INTELLECTUAL AND MORAL EDUCATION; DEFECTS IN
THE PEDAGOGY OF ARISTOTLE, AND IN GREEK PEDAGOGY IN GEN-
ERAL; ANALYTICAL SUMMARY.

19. GREEK PEDAGOGY. — Upon that privileged soil of
Greece, in that brilliant Athens abounding in artists, poets,
historians, and philosophers, in that rude Sparta celebrated
for its discipline and manly virtues, education was rather the
spontaneous fruit of nature, the natural product of diverse
manners, characters, and races, than the premeditated result
of a reflective movement of the human will. Greece, however, had its pedagogy, because it had its legislators and its
philosophers, the first directing education in its practical
details, the second making theoretical inquiries into the
essential principles underlying the development of the human

soul. In respect of education, as of everything else, the higher spiritual life of modern nations has been developed under the influence of Grecian antiquity.[1]

20. ATHENIAN AND SPARTAN EDUCATION. — In the spectacle presented to us by ancient Greece, the first fact that strikes us by its contrast with the immobility and unity of the primitive societies of the East, is a freer unfolding of the human faculties, and consequently a diversity in tendencies and manners. Doubtless, in the Greek republics, the individual is always subordinate to the State. Even in Athens, little regard is paid to the essential dignity of the human person. But the Athenian State differs profoundly from the Spartan, and consequently the individual life is differently understood and differently directed in these two great cities. At Athens, while not neglecting the body, the chief preoccupation is the training of the mind; intellectual culture is pushed to an extreme, even to over-refinement; there is such a taste for fine speaking that it develops an abuse of language and reasoning which merits the disreputable name of sophistry. At Sparta, mind is sacrificed to body; physical strength and military skill are the qualities most desired; the sole care is the training of athletes and soldiers. Sobriety and courage are the results of this one-sided education, but so are ignorance and brutality. Montaigne has thrown into relief, not without some partiality for Sparta, these two contrasted plans of education.

"Men went to the other cities of Greece," he says, "to find rhetoricians, painters, and musicians, but to Lacedæmon for legislators, magistrates, and captains; at Athens fine speaking was taught; but here, brave acting; there, one

---

[1] Upon this subject consult the excellent study of Alexander Martin, entitled *Les Doctrines Pédagogiques des Grecs.* Paris, 1881.

learned to unravel a sophistical argument and to abate the imposture of insidiously twisted words ; here, to extricate one's self from the enticements of pleasure and to overcome the menaces of fortune and death by a manly courage.   The Athenians busied themselves with words, but the Spartans with things ; with the former, there was a continual activity of the tongue ; with the latter, a continual activity of the soul."[1]

The last remark is not just.   The daily exercises of the young Spartans, — jumping, running, wrestling, playing with lances and at quoits, — could not be regarded as intellectual occupations.   On the other hand, in learning to talk, the young Athenians learned also to feel and to think.

21. THE SCHOOLS OF ATHENS. — The Athenian legislator, Solon, had placed physical and intellectual training upon the same footing.   Children, he said, ought, above everything else, to learn " to swim and to read."   It seems that the education of the body was the chief preoccupation of the Athenian republic.   While the organization of schools for grammar and music was left to private enterprise, the State took a part in the direction of the gymnasia.   The director of the gymnasium, or the gymnasiarch, was elected each year by the assembly of the people.   Nevertheless, Athenian education became more and more a course in literary training, especially towards the sixth century B.C.

The Athenian child remained in the charge of a nurse and an attendant up to his sixth or seventh year.   At the age of seven, a pedagogue, that is, a " conductor of children," usually a slave, was charged with the oversight of the child. Conducted by his pedagogue, the pupil attended by turns the school for grammar, the *palestra*,[2] or school for gymnastics,

---

[1] Montaigne, *Essais*, I. i. chap. XXIV.

[2] The *palestra* was the school of gymnastics for children; the *gymnasium* was set apart for adults and grown men.

and the school for music. The grammarian, who sometimes gave his lessons in the open air, in the streets and on the public squares, taught reading, writing, and mythology. Homer was the boy's reading-book. Instruction in gymnastics was given in connection with instruction in grammar. It was begun in the palestra and continued in the gymnasium. Instruction in music succeeded the training in grammar and gymnastics. The music-master, or *citharist*, first taught his pupils to sing, and then to play upon the stringed instruments, the lyre and the cithara. We know what value the Athenians attributed to music. Plato and Aristotle agree in thinking that the rhythm and harmony of music inspire the soul with the love of order, with harmoniousness, regularity, and a soothing of the passions. We must recollect, moreover, that music held a large place in the actual life of the Greeks. The laws were promulgated in song. It was necessary to sing in order to fulfil one's religious duties. It was held that the education of Themistocles had been neglected because he had not learned music. "We must regard the Greeks," says Montesquieu, "as a race of athletes and fighters. Now those exercises, so proper to make men hardy and fierce, had need of being tempered by others which could soften the manners. Music, which affected the soul through the organs of the body, was exactly adapted to this purpose." [1]

In the elementary schools of Athens, at least at the first, the current discipline was severe. Aristophanes, bewailing the degeneracy of his time, recalls in these terms the good order that reigned in the olden school: [2]—

" I will relate what was the ancient education in the happy time when I taught (it is Justice who speaks) and when modesty was the rule. Then the boys came out of each

---

[1] Montesquieu, *Esprit des lois*, I. IV. chap. VIII.

[2] Aristophanes, *Clouds*.

street with bare heads and feet, and, regardless of rain and snow, went together in the most perfect order towards the school for music. There they were seated quietly and modestly. They were not permitted to cross their legs, and they learned some good songs. The master sang the song for them slowly and with gravity. If some one took a notion to sing with soft and studied inflections, he was severely flogged."

22. THE SCHOOLS OF RHETORIC AND PHILOSOPHY. — Grammar, gymnastics, and music proper, represented the elementary instruction of the young Athenian. But this instruction was reserved for citizens in easy circumstances. (The poor, ~~according to the intentions of Solon,~~ were to learn only *reading, swimming,* and a trade.) The privilege of instruction became still more exclusive in the case of the schools of rhetoric and philosophy frequented by those of adult years.

It would be beside our purpose to speak in this place of the courses in literature, or to make known the methods of those teachers of rhetoric who taught eloquence to all who presented themselves for instruction, either in the public squares or in the gymnasia. The sophists, those itinerant philosophers who went from city to city offering courses at high rates of tuition, and teaching the art of speaking on every subject, and of making a plea for error and injustice just as skilfully as for justice and truth, at the same time made illustrious and disgraceful the teaching of eloquence.[1] The philosophers were more worthy of their task. Socrates,

---

[1] The reputation of the sophists has been considerably raised by Mr. Grote (*History of Greece*, vol. VIII.). For an entertaining account of a sophist of a later age, see Pliny's *Letters*, Melmoth's translation, Book II., Letter III. See also Blackie's *Four Phases of Morals*, and Ferrier's *Greek Philosophy*. (P.)

Plato, and Aristotle were illustrious professors of ethics. Socrates had no regular school, but he grouped about him distinguished young men and initiated them into learning and virtue. The *Academy* of Plato and the *Lyceum* of Aristotle were great schools of philosophy, real private universities, each directed by a single man. The teaching given in these schools has traversed the ages, and has been preserved in imperishable books. Moreover, those illustrious spirits of Greece have transmitted to us either methods or general ideas which the history of pedagogy should reverently collect, as the first serious efforts of human reflection on the art of education.

23. SOCRATES : THE SOCRATIC METHOD. — Socrates spent his life in teaching, and in teaching according to an original method, which has preserved his name. He had the genius of interrogation. To question all whom he met, either at the gymnasium or in the streets ; to question the sophists in order to convince them of their errors and to confound their arrogance, and presumptuous young men in order to teach them the truth of which they were ignorant ; to question great and small, statesmen and masons, now Pericles and now a shopkeeper ; to question always and everywhere in order to compel every one to form clear ideas ; such was the constant occupation and passion of his life. When he allowed himself to dream of the future life, he said smilingly that he hoped to continue in the Elysian Fields the habits of the Athenian Agora, and still to interrogate the shades of the mighty dead. With Socrates, conversation became an art, and the dialogue a method. He scarcely ever employed the didactic form, or that of direct teaching. He addressed himself to his interlocutor, urged him to set forth his ideas, harassed him with questions often somewhat subtile, skilfully led him to recognize the truth which he himself had in

mind, or the rather permitted him to go off on a false route
in order finally to discover to him his error and to sport with
his confusion ; and all this with an art of wonderful analysis,
with a subtilty of reasoning pushed almost to an extreme,
and also with a great simplicity of language, and with
examples borrowed from common life, such as we are accustomed to call intuitive examples.

24. THE SOCRATIC IRONY. — To form an intelligible account of the Socratic method, it is necessary to distinguish
its two essential phases.   Socrates followed a double method
and sought a double end.

In the first case, he wished to make war against error and
to refute false opinions.   Then he resorted to what has been
called the Socratic *irony*.[1]   He raised a question as one
who simply desired to be instructed.   If there was the
statement of an error in the reply of the respondent, Socrates made no objection to it, but pretended to espouse the
ideas and sentiments of his interlocutor.   Then, by questions
which were adroit and sometimes insidious, he forced him to
develop his opinions, and to display, so to speak, the whole
extent of his folly, and the next instant slyly brought him
face to face with the consequences, which were so absurd and
contradictory that he ended in losing confidence, in becoming
involved in his conclusions, and finally in making confession
of his errors.

25. MAIEUTICS, OR THE ART OF GIVING BIRTH TO IDEAS. —
Analogous processes constituted the other part of the Socratic method, that which he himself called *maieutics*, or the
art of giving birth to ideas.

---

[1] The primitive meaning of the Greek word εἰρωνεία, irony, is interrogation.   Socrates gave a jeering, ironical turn to his questions, and in consequence this word lost its primary meaning, and took the one which we
give it at this time.

Socrates was convinced that the human mind in its normal condition discovers certain truths through its own energies, provided one knows how to lead it and stimulate it; and so be here appealed to the spontaneity of his auditor, to his innate powers, and thus gently led him on his way by easy transitions to the opinion which he wished to make him admit. However, he applied this method only to the search for truths which could either be suggested by the intuitions of reason and common sense, or determined by a natural induction, that is, psychological, ethical, and religious truths.[1]

26. Examples of Irony and Maieutics. — We can best give an exact idea of the Socratic method by means of examples. These examples are to be found in the writings of the disciples of Socrates, as in the *Dialogues* of Plato, such as the *Gorgias*, the *Euthydemus*, etc., and still better in the *Memorabilia* of Xenophon, where the thought of the master and his manner of teaching are more faithfully reproduced than in the bold and original compositions of Plato. While recognizing the insufficiency of these extracts, we shall here make two quotations, in which is displayed either his incisive, critical spirit, or his suggestive and fruitful method: "The thirty tyrants had put many of the most distinguished citizens to death, and had encouraged others to acts of injustice. 'It would surprise me,' said Socrates one day, 'if the keeper of a flock, who had killed one part of it and had made the

---

[1] The Socratic method for the discovery of truth can be employed only in those cases where the pupil has the crude materials of the new knowledge actually in store. Psychology, logic, ethics, mathematics, and perhaps grammar and rhetoric, fall within the sphere of the Socratic method; but to apply this method of instruction to geography, history, geology, and, in general, to subjects where the material is inaccessible, is palpably absurd. The Socratic dialogue, in its negative phase, is aimed at presumption, arrogance, and pretentious ignorance; but it is sometimes misused to badger and bewilder an honest and docile pupil. (P.)

other part poor, would not confess that he was a bad herdsman; but it would surprise me still more if a man standing
at the head of his fellow-citizens should destroy a part of
them and corrupt the rest, and were not to blush at his conduct and confess himself a bad magistrate.' This remark
having come to the ears of the Thirty, Critias and Charicles
sent for Socrates, showed him the law, and forbade him to
hold conversation with the young.

"Socrates inquired of them if he might be permitted to ask
questions touching what might seem obscure to him in this
prohibition. Upon their granting this permission: 'I am
prepared,' he said, 'to obey the laws, but that I may not
violate them through ignorance, I would have you clearly inform me whether you interdict the art of speaking because it
belongs to the number of things which are good, or because
it belongs to the number of things which are bad. In the
first case, one ought henceforth to abstain from speaking
what is good; in the second, it is clear that the effort should
be to speak what is right.'

"Thereupon Charicles became angry, and said: 'Since
you do not understand us, we will give you something easier
to comprehend: we forbid you absolutely to hold conversation with the young.' 'In order that it may be clearly seen,'
said Socrates, 'whether I depart from what is enjoined, tell
me at what age a youth becomes a man.' 'At the time
when he is eligible to the senate, for he has not acquired
prudence till then; so do not speak to young men who are
below the age of thirty.'

"'But if I wish to buy something of a merchant who is
below the age of thirty, may I ask him at what price he sells
it?'

"'Certainly you may ask such a question; but you are
accustomed to raise inquiries about multitudes of things

which are perfectly well known to you; it is this which is forbidden.'

" ' So I must not reply to a young man who asks me where Charicles lives, or where Critias is.' 'You may reply to such questions,' said Charicles. 'But recollect, Socrates,' added Critias, 'you must let alone the shoemakers, and smiths, and other artisans, for I think they must already be very much worn out by being so often in your mouth.'

" ' I must, therefore,' said Socrates, 'forego the illustrations I draw from these occupations relative to justice, piety, and all the virtues.' "[1]

In the final passage of this cutting dialogue, observe the elevation of tone and the gravity of thought. So Socrates had marvellous skill in allying enthusiasm with irony.

Here is an extract in which Socrates applies the maieutic art to the establishment of a moral truth, the belief in God:

"I will mention a conversation he once had in my presence with Aristodemus, surnamed the Little, concerning the gods. He knew that Aristodemus neither sacrificed to the gods, nor consulted the oracles, but ridiculed those who took part in these religious observances. 'Tell me, Aristodemus,' said he, 'are there men whose talents you admire?' 'There are,' he replied. 'Then tell us their names.' said Socrates. 'In epic poetry I especially admire Homer; in dithyrambic, Melanippides; in tragedy, Sophocles; in statuary, Polycletus; in painting, Zeuxis.' 'But what artists do you think most worthy of admiration, those who form images destitute of sense and movement, or those who produce animated beings, endowed with the faculty of thinking and acting?' 'Those who form animated beings, for these are the work of intelligence and not of chance.' 'And which do you regard

---

[1] *Memorabilia*, I. II.

as the creation of intelligence, and which the product of chance, those works whose purpose cannot be recognized, or those whose utility is manifest?' 'It is reasonable to attribute to an intelligence the works which have some useful purpose.'"[1]

Socrates then points out to Aristodemus how admirably the different organs of the human body are adapted to the functions of life and to the use of man. And so proceeding from example to example, from induction to induction, always keeping the mind of his auditor alert by the questions he raises, and the answers that he suggests, forcing him to do his share of the work, and giving him an equal share in the train of reasoning, he finally brings him to the goal which is to make him recognize the existence of God.

27. THE REPUBLIC OF PLATO. — "Would you form," said J. J. Rousseau, "an idea of public education? read the *Republic* of Plato. It is the finest treatise on education ever written." For truth's sake we must discount the enthusiasm of Rousseau. The *Republic* doubtless contains some elements of a wise and practical scheme of education; but, on the whole, it is but an ideal creation, a compound of paradoxes and chimeras. In Plato's ideal commonwealth, the individual and the family itself are sacrificed to the State. Woman becomes so much like man as to be subjected to the same gymnastic exercises; she too must be a soldier as he is. Children know neither father nor mother. From the day of their birth they are given in charge of common nurses, veritable public functionaries. In that common fold, " care shall be taken that no mother recognize her offspring." We may guess that in making this pompous eulogy of the *Republic*, the paradoxical author of the *Émile* hoped to prepare

---

[1] *Memorabilia*, I. IV.

the reader for giving a complaisant welcome to his own
dreams.

28. THE EDUCATION OF WARRIORS AND MAGISTRATES. —
Plato, by some unexplained recollection of the social constitution of the Hindoos, established three castes in his ideal
State, — laborers and artisans, warriors, and magistrates.
There was no education for laborers and artisans ; it was
sufficient for men of this caste to learn a trade. In politics,
Plato is an aristocrat ; he feels a disdain for the people,
" that robust and indocile animal." It should be observed,
however, that the barriers which he set up between these
three social orders are not insuperable. If a child of the
inferior class gives evidence of exceptional qualities, he must
be admitted to the superior class ; and so if the son of a
warrior or of a magistrate is notably incompetent and unworthy of his rank, he must suffer forfeiture, and become
artisan or laborer.

As to the education which he designs for the warriors and
the magistrates, Plato is minutely careful in regulating it.
The education of the warriors comprises two parts, — music
and gymnastics. The education of the magistrates consists
of a training in philosophy of a high grade ; they are initiated into all the sciences and into metaphysics. Plato's
statesmen must be, not priests, as in the East, but scholars
and philosophers.

29. MUSIC AND GYMNASTICS. — Although Plato attaches a
high value to gymnastics, he gives precedence to music.
Before forming the body, Plato, the idealist, would form
the soul, because it is the soul, according to him, which, by
its own virtue, gives to the body all the perfection of which
it is capable. Even in physical exercises, the purpose should
be to give increased vigor to the soul : " In the training cf

the body, our young men shall aim, above everything else, at augmenting moral power." Note this striking picture of the man who trains only his body :—"Let a man apply himself to gymnastics, and become trained, and eat much, and wholly neglect music and philosophy, and at first his body will become strengthened ; but if he does nothing else, and holds no converse with the Muses, though his soul have some natural inclination to learn, yet if it remains uncultivated by acquiring knowledge, by inquiry, by discourse, in a word, by some department of music, that is, by intellectual education, it will insensibly become weak, deaf, and blind. Like a wild beast, such a man will live in ignorance and rudeness, with neither grace nor politeness." However, Plato is far from despising health and physical strength. On the contrary, it is a reproach to him that he has imposed on the citizens of his Republic the obligation of being physically sound, and of having excluded from it all those whose infirmities and feeble constitution condemn them to "drag out a dying life." The right to live, in Plato's city, as in the most of ancient societies, belonged only to men of robust health. The weak, the ailing, the wretched, all who are of infirm constitution, — Plato does not go so far as ordering such to be killed, but, what amounts almost to the same thing, — "they shall be exposed," that is, left to die. The good of the State demands that every man be sacrificed whose health renders him unfit for civil duties. This cruel and implacable doctrine shocks us in the ease of him whom Montaigne calls the divine Plato, and shocks us even more when we discover it among contemporary philosophers, whom the inspirations of Christian charity or the feeling of human fraternity should have preserved from such rank heartlessness. Is it not Herbert Spencer who blames modern societies for nourishing the diseased and assisting the infirm?

30. RELIGION AND ART IN EDUCATION. — Plato had formed a high ideal of the function of art in education, but this did not prevent him from being severe against certain forms of art, particularly comedy and tragedy, and poetry in general. He would have the poets expelled from the city and conducted to the frontier, though paying them homage with perfumes which will continue to be shed upon their heads, and with flowers with which they will ever be crowned. He admits no other poetry than that which reproduces the manners and discourse of a good man, and celebrates the brave deeds of the gods, or chants their glory. As a severe moralist and worshipper of the divine goodness, he condemns the poets of his time, either because they attribute to the divinity the vices and passions of men, or because they invest the imagination with base fears as they speak of Cocytus and the Styx, and portray a frightful hell and gods always mad with desire to persecute the human race. Elsewhere, in the *Laws*, Plato explains his conception of religion. He says that the religious books placed in the hands of children should be selected with as much care as the milk of a nurse. God is an infinite goodness who watches over men, and he should be honored, not by sacrifices and vain ceremonies, but by lives of justice and virtue.

⟋ For making men moral, Plato counts more upon art than upon religious feeling. To love letters, to hold converse with the Muses, to cultivate music and dancing, such, in the opinion of the noble spirits of Athens, is the natural route towards moral perfection. In their view, moral education is above all an education in art. The soul rises to the good through the beautiful. " Beautiful and good " (καλὸς καὶ ἀγαθός) are two words constantly associated in the speech of the Greeks. Even to-day we have much to learn from reflections like these : " We ought," says Plato, " to seek out artists who by the power of genius can trace out the nature of the fair and the graceful, that our young men, dwelling, as it were, in a healthful region, may drink in good from every quarter, whence any emanation from noble works may strike upon their eye or their ear, like a gale wafting health from salubrious lands, and win them imperceptibly from their earliest years into resemblance, love, and harmony with the true beauty of reason.

" Is it not, then, on these accounts that we attach such supreme importance to a musical education, because rhythm and harmony sink most deeply into the recesses of the soul, bringing gracefulness in their train, and making a man graceful if he be rightly nurtured ; but if not, the reverse? and also because he that has been duly nurtured therein will have the keenest eye for defects, whether in the failures of art, or in the misgrowths of nature ; and feeling a most just disdain for them, will commend beautiful objects, and gladly receive them into his soul, and feed upon them, and grow to be noble and good ; whereas he will rightly censure and hate all repulsive objects, even in his childhood, before he is able to be reasoned with ; and when reason comes, he will welcome her most cordially who can recognize her by the instinct of relationship, and because he has been thus nurtured? " [1]

31. HIGH INTELLECTUAL EDUCATION. — In the *Republic* of Plato the intellectual education of the warrior class remains exclusively literary and æsthetic. In addition to this, the education of the ruling class is to be scientific and philosophic. The future magistrate, after having received the ordinary instruction up to the age of twenty, is to be initiated into the abstract sciences, mathematics, geometry,

---

[1] *Republic*, 401, 402. I have quoted from the version of Vaughan and Davies. (P.)

and astronomy. To this scientific education, which is to continue for ten years, there will succeed for five years the study of dialectics,[1] or philosophy, which develops the highest faculty of man, the reason, and teaches him to discover, through and beyond the fleeting appearances of the world of sense, the eternal verities and the essence of things. But Plato prolongs the education of his magistrates still further. After having given them the nurture of reason and intellectual insight, he sends them back to the cavern[2] at the age of thirty-five, that is, calls them back to public life, and makes them pass through all kinds of civil and military employments, until finally, at the age of fifty, in possession of all the endowments assured by consummate experience superadded to profound knowledge, they are fitted to be charged with the burdens of office. In the *Republic* of Plato statesmen are not improvised. And yet in this elaborate system of instruction Plato omits two subjects of great importance. On the one hand, he entirely omits the physical and natural sciences, because, in his mystic idealism, things of sense are delusive and unreal images, and so did not appear to him worthy of arresting the attention of the mind; and on the other, though coming after Herodotus, and though a con-

---

[1] Dialectic, as used in the *Republic*, is neither philosophy nor logic. I doubt whether it can be considered a subject of instruction at all.* It is rather a method or an exercise, the purpose of which is to subject received opinions, formulated knowledge, current beliefs, etc., to a sifting or analysis for the purpose of distinguishing the real from the apparent, the true from the false. The Socratic dialogues are examples of the dialectic method. Dialectic might be defined as the *method of thought proper* or the *discursive reason in act.* (P.)

[2] See the allegory of the cavern, *Republic*, Book VII. In Plato's scheme of education, knowing is to precede doing, thus following Socrates (*Memorabilia*, IV. chap. II.) and Bias (Γνῶθι καὶ τότε πράττε), and anticipating Bacon ("studies perfect nature, and are perfected by experience"). (P.)

temporary of Thucydides, he makes no mention of history, doubtless through a contempt for tradition and the past.

32. THE LAWS. — In the *Laws*, the work of his old age, Plato disavows in part the chimeras of the *Republic*, and qualifies the radicalism of that earlier work. The philosopher descends to the earth and really condescends to the actual state of humanity. He renounces the distinction of social castes, and his very practical and very minute precepts are applied without distinction to children of all classes.[1]

First note this excellent definition of the end of education: " A good education is that which gives to the body and to the soul all the beauty and all the perfection of which they are capable." As to methods, it seems that Plato hesitates between the doctrine of effort and the doctrine of attractive toil. In fact, he says on the one hand that education is a very skilful discipline which, *by way of amusement*,[2] leads the mind of the child to love that which is to make it finished. On the other hand, he protests against the weakness of those parents who seek to spare their children every trouble and every pain. " I am persuaded," he says, " that the inclination to humor the likings of children is the surest of all ways to spoil them. We should not make too much haste in our search after what is pleasurable, especially as we shall never be wholly exempt from what is painful."

Let us add this definition of a good education: " I call education the virtue which is shown by children when the feelings of joy or of sorrow, of love or of hate, which arise in their souls, are made conformable to order."

---

[1] See especially Book VII. of the *Laws*.

[2] Compare also this quotation: "A free mind ought to learn nothing as a slave. The lesson that is made to enter the mind by force, will not remain there. Then use no violence towards children; the rather, cause them to learn while playing."

With the statement of these principles, Plato enters into details. For children up to the age of six, he recommends the use of swaddling-clothes. The habit of rocking, the natural plays which children find out for themselves, the separation of the sexes ; swimming, the bow, and the javelin, for boys ; wrestling for giving bodily vigor, and dancing, for graceful movement; reading and writing reserved till the tenth year and learned for three years.

It would require too much time to follow the philosopher to the end. In the rules he proposes, he makes a near approach to the practices followed by the Athenians of his day. The *Republic* was a work of pure imagination. The *Laws* are scarcely more than a commentary on the actual state of practice. But here we still find what was nearest the soul of Plato, the constant search for a higher morality.

33. XENOPHON. — As an educator, Xenophon obeyed two different influences. His master, Socrates, was his good genius. That graceful and charming book, the *Economics*, was written under the benign and tempered inspiration of the great Athenian sage. But Xenophon also had his evil genius, — the immoderate enthusiasm which he felt for Sparta, her institutions and her laws. The first book of the *Cyropœ-dia*, which relates the rules of Persian education, is an unfortunate imitation of the laws of Lycurgus.

34. THE ECONOMICS, AND THE EDUCATION OF WOMAN. — All should read the *Economics*, that charming sketch of the education of woman. We may say of this little work what Renan has said of the writings of Plutarch on the same subject : " Where shall we find a more charming ideal of family life? What good nature ! What sweetness of manners ! What chaste and lovable simplicity ! " Before her marriage, the Athenian maiden has learned only to spin wool, to be

discreet, and to ask no questions, — virtues purely negative. Xenophon assigns to her husband the duty of training her mind and of teaching her the positive duties of family life, — order, economy, kindness to slaves, and tender care of children. As a matter of fact, the Athenian woman was still held in a position of inferiority. Shut up in her own apartments, it was an exception that she learned to read and write; it was very rare that she was instructed in the arts and sciences. The idea of human dignity and of the value of the human person had not yet appeared. Man had value only in proportion to the services which he could render the State, or commonwealth, and woman formed no part of the commonwealth. Xenophon has the merit of rising above the prejudices of his time, and of approaching the ideal of the modern family, in calling woman to participate more intimately in the affairs of the house and in the occupations of the husband.[1]

35. THE CYROPÆDIA. — The *Cyropœdia* is not worthy of the same commendation. Under the pretext of describing the organization of the Persian State, Xenophon here traces, after his manner, the plan of an education absolutely uniform and exclusively military. There is no domestic education, no individual liberty, no interest in letters and arts. When the period of infancy is over, the young Persian is made subject to military duty, and must not leave the encampment, even at night. The state is but a camp, and human existence a perpetual military parade. Montaigne praises Xenophon for having said that the Persians taught their children virtue " as other nations do letters." But it is difficult to form an estimate of the methods which were followed in these schools of justice and temperance, and we

---

[1] See particularly Chaps. VII. and VIII.

may be allowed to suspect the efficiency of the means proposed by Xenophon; for example, that which consisted in
transforming the petty quarrels of the scholars into regular
trials which were followed by sentences, acquittals, or convictions. The author of the *Cyropœdia* is on surer ground
when, recollecting his own studies, he recommends the study
of history to those who would become just. He teaches
temperance by practice rather than by precept; his pupils
have only bread for their food, only cresses for seasoning,
and only water for their drink.

Whatever may be the faults and the fancies of the *Cyropœdia*, we must recollect, as a partial excuse for them, that
the purpose of the writer in tracing this picture of a simple,
frugal, and courageous life, was to induce a reaction against
the excesses of the fashionable and formal life of the
Athenians. As Rousseau, in the middle of the eighteenth
century, protested against the license and the artificial
manners of his time by advising an imaginary return to
nature, so Xenophon, a contemporary of the sophists, held
forth the sturdy virtues of the Persians in opposition to the
degenerate manners of the Greeks and the refinements of an
advanced civilization.

36. ARISTOTLE: GENERAL CHARACTER OF HIS PLAN OF
EDUCATION. — By his vast attainments, by his encyclopædic
knowledge, by the experimental nature of his researches, and
by the positive and practical tendencies of his genius,
Aristotle was enabled to excel Plato in clearness of insight
into pedagogical questions. He had another advantage over
Plato in having known and enjoyed the delights of family
life, and in having loved and trained his own children, of
whom he said, "parents love their children as a part of
themselves." Let us add, finally, that he was a practical
teacher, since he was the preceptor of Alexander from 343

to 340 B.C. Such opportunities, superadded to the force of the most mighty genius the world has ever seen, give promise of a competent and clear-sighted educator. Unfortunately, we have lost the treatise, *On Education* ($\pi\epsilon\rho\grave{\iota}$ $\pi\alpha\iota\delta\epsilon\acute{\iota}\alpha\varsigma$), which on the authority of Diogenes Laertius, Aristotle is said to have composed; and to form some conception of his ideas on education, we have at our disposal only some imperfect sketches, some portions, and those in an imperfect state, of his treatises on ethics and politics.[1]

Whoever labors to give stability to the family, and to tighten its bond of union, labors also for the promotion of education. Even in this respect, education is under great obligations to Aristotle. In him the communism of Plato finds an able critic. That feeling of affection which we of to-day would call charity or fraternity, he declared to be the guaranty and the foundation of social life. Now, communism weakens this feeling by diluting it, just as a little honey dropped into a large quantity of water thereby loses all its sweetness. "There are two things which materially contribute to the rise of interest and attachment in the hearts of men, — property and the feeling of affection." It was thus in the name of good sense, and in opposition to the distempered fancies of Plato, that Aristotle vindicated the rights of the family and the individual.

37. PUBLIC EDUCATION. — But Aristotle does not go so far as his premises would seem to lead him, and relinquish to parents the care of educating their children. In accordance with the general tendencies of antiquity, he declares himself the partisan of an education that is public and common. He commends the Spartans for having ordained that " education should be the same for all." " As there is one end

---

[1] See especially the *Politics*, Books IV., V.

in view in every city," he says, " it is evident that education
ought to be one and the same in all, and that this should be
a common care, and not of each individual. . . . It is the
duty of the legislator to regulate this interest for all the
citizens." There must, therefore, be the intervention of
the State, not from the day of birth, as Plato would have it,
for the nursing of infants, but only at the age of seven, for
instructing and training them in the habits of virtue.

What, then, should be the training of the child, and upon
what subjects would Aristotle direct his studies?

38. The Progressive Development of Human Nature.
— An essential and incontrovertible distinction is taken by
the Greek philosopher as his starting-point. (There are, he
says, three moments, three stages, in human development:
first, there is the physical life of the body ; then, instinct and
sensibility, or the irrational part of the soul ; and finally, the
intelligence, or the reason.) From this, Aristotle concludes
that the course of discipline and study should be graduated
according to these three degrees of life. (The first care
should necessarily be given to the body rather than to the
mind ; and then to that part of the spiritual nature which is
the seat of the desires.) But he adds this important observation, which is a refutation of Rousseau in advance : (In the
care which we give to the sensibilities, we must not leave out
of account the intelligence ; and in our care of the body, we
must not forget the soul.) Aristotle.

39. Physical Education. — The son of a physician of the
Macedonian court, and well versed in the natural sciences,
Aristotle is very happy in his treatment of physical education. It begins before the child is born, even before it has
been conceived. Consequently he enjoins a legal regulation
of marriages, interdicts unions that are too early or too late,

indicates the climatic conditions most favorable for marriage, and gives mothers wise counsels on matters of hygiene, recommending them to nurse their own children, and prescribing cold baths. Such, in outline, is a plan which a modern hygienist would not disavow.

40. INTELLECTUAL AND MORAL EDUCATION. — It was the opinion of Aristotle that intellectual education should not begin before the age of five. But, in accordance with the principle stated above, this period of waiting should not be the occasion of loss to the intelligence of the child; even his play should be a preparation for the work to which he will apply himself at a later period. On the other hand, Aristotle strongly insists on the necessity of shielding the child from all pernicious influences, such as those which come from association with slaves, or from immoral plays.

In accord with all his contemporaries, Aristotle includes grammar, gymnastics, and music, among the elements of instruction. To these he adds drawing. But he is chiefly preoccupied with music, by reason of the moral influence which he attributes to it. He shared the prepossession which caused the Greeks to say, that to relax or to reform the manners of a people, it suffices to add a string to the lyre or to take one from it.[1]

Aristotle was strongly preoccupied with moral education. Like Plato, he insists on the greatest care in forming the moral habits of early life. In his different writings on ethics he has discussed different human virtues in a spirit at once wise, practical, and liberal. No one has better sung the

---

[1] It seems impossible to comprehend the almost sovereign power which the Greeks ascribed to music, unless we conceive that the Greek was endowed with peculiar and extreme sensitiveness. Perhaps there is special significance in the story of Orpheus and his lyre. (P.)

praises of justice, of which he says, "Neither the evening nor the morning star inspires as much respect as justice."

It would do Aristotle injustice to seek for a complete expression of his thoughts on education in the incomplete and curtailed statements of theory which are found in his *Politics*. In connection with these, we should recall the admirable instruction which he himself gave in the Lyceum, and which embraced almost all the sciences in its vast programme. He excluded from it only the sciences and the arts which have a mechanical and utilitarian character. Enslaved on this point to the prejudices of antiquity, he regarded as servile and unworthy of a free man whatever has a direct bearing on the practical and material utilities of life. He recommended to his hearers only studies of the intellectual type, those whose sole purpose is to elevate the mind and to fill it with noble thoughts.[1]

41. FAULTS IN THE PEDAGOGY OF ARISTOTLE, AND IN GREEK PEDAGOGY IN GENERAL. — It must be said in conclusion, that whatever admiration we may feel for the pedagogy of Aristotle, it was wrong, like that of all the Greek writers, in being but an aristocratic system of education. The education of which Plato and Aristotle dreamed was restricted to a small minority, and was even made possible only because the majority was excluded from it. The slaves, charged with the duty of providing for the sustenance of their superiors, and of creating for them the leisure claimed by Aristotle, had no more participation in education than in liberty or in property. In the century of Pericles,

---

[1] I think it may be doubted whether the disfavor shown by Plato and Aristotle to practical studies was merely a mean prejudice. Preoccupied as they were with the disciplinary value of studies, they may have seen that the culture aim and the utilitarian aim are in some sort antagonistic. (P.)

at the most glorious period of the Athenian republic, let us not forget that there were at Athens nearly four hundred thousand slaves to do the bidding of twenty thousand free citizens. To indulge in an easy admiration for Greek peda- gogy, we must detach it from its setting, and consider it in itself, apart from the narrow plan on which the Greek states were constructed, and apart from that social *régime* which assured the education of some, only by perpetuating the oppression of the many.

[42. ANALYTICAL SUMMARY. — 1. A leading conception in Greek education is that of symmetry, or harmony; the ideal man, in Plato's phrase, must be "harmoniously constituted"; all opposing tendencies must be reconciled; and while the physical, the intellectual, and the moral must each be made the subject of systematic training, there must be no dispro- portionate development in either direction.

2. The preoccupation of the Greek teacher was discipline or culture, rather than the communication of useful knowl- edge; and the final aim was a life of contemplation, rather than a life of action; ethical rather than practical; "good conduct" rather than mastery over what is material.

3. Physical training received great emphasis, not as an end in itself, but as a means towards mental and spiritual health; and knowledge was valued chiefly as the means for attaining moral excellence.

4. The staple of instruction was *wisdom*, *i.e.*, ethical and prudential knowledge, which was the basis of right action; and teaching, especially according to the Socratic conception of it, consisted in causing the pupil's mind to react on the materials supplied by his own mind. Socrates, says Lewes, " believed that in each man lay the germs of wisdom. He believed that no science could be *taught;* only *drawn out*."

5. The great teaching intrument was dialectic, *i.e.*, discussion, resolution, or analysis. Its use assumed that the subject-matter of instruction was already in the pupil's possession, and that the highest office of the teacher was to liberate the thought which had been formed by the active energies of the pupil's own mind. This is the maieutic art of Socrates.

6. The mode of mental activity which was chiefly brought into requisition was the reason; in a secondary degree the imagination and the emotions; and in a still lower degree, the memory.

7. The large place assigned to music by Plato and Aristotle shows that the culture of the emotions was an important element in Greek education. Æsthetic training was not only an end in itself, but was regarded as the basis of moral and religious culture.

8. In the writings of Socrates, Plato, and Aristotle, we see the first attempt to formulate a body of educational doctrine; we have the germs of a science of education based on psychology, ethics, and politics.

9. In the *Republic*, we see the theory of compulsion in both its phases: the State must provide an education suitable for State needs; and the young must accept this education because the State has ordained it. For the first time in the history of thought, the State appears distinctly and avowedly as an educator.

10. Practically, education was administered on the basis of caste; though in the construction of his ideal State, Plato made it possible for talent, industry, and worth, to find their proper level.]

CHAPTER III.

EDUCATION AT ROME.

TWO PERIODS IN ROMAN EDUCATION; EDUCATION OF THE PRIMITIVE
ROMANS; PHYSICAL AND MILITARY EDUCATION; ROME AT SCHOOL IN
GREECE; WHY THE ROMANS HAD NO GREAT EDUCATORS; VARRO;
CICERO; QUINTILIAN; THE INSTITUTES OF ORATORY; GENERAL
PLAN OF EDUCATION; THE CHILD'S FIRST EDUCATION; READING AND
WRITING; PUBLIC EDUCATION; THE DUTIES OF TEACHERS; GRAMMAR
AND RHETORIC; THE SIMULTANEOUS STUDY OF THE SCIENCES;
SCHOOLS FOR PHILOSOPHY; SENECA; PLUTARCH; THE LIVES OF
ILLUSTRIOUS MEN; THE TREATISE ON THE TRAINING OF CHILDREN;
A CHARMING PICTURE OF FAMILY LIFE; THE EDUCATION OF WOMEN;
THE FUNCTION OF POETRY IN EDUCATION; THE TEACHING OF
MORALS; MARCUS AURELIUS AND PERSONAL EDUCATION; CONCLU
SION; ANALYTICAL SUMMARY.

43. TWO PERIODS IN ROMAN EDUCATION. — In Greece, as
we have seen, there were two essentially different systems of
education in use : at Sparta, a one-sided education, wholly
military, with no regard for intellectual culture ; at Athens,
a complete education, which brought into happy harmony
the training of the body and the development of the mind,
and by means of which, as Thucydides observed, "men
philosophized without becoming effeminate."

Rome, in the long course of her history, followed these
two systems in succession. Under the Republic, down to
the conquest of Greece, preference was given to education
after the Spartan type ; while under the emperors, Athenian
education was dominant, with a very marked tendency to
give the first place to an education in literature and oratory.

44. The Education of the Early Romans. — The first
schools were not opened at Rome till towards the end of the
third century B.C. Till then, the Romans had no teachers
save their parents and nature. Education was almost exclusively physical and moral, or rather, military and religious.
On the one hand, there were the gymnastic exercises on the
Campus Martius, and on the other, the recitation of the
Salian hymns, a sort of catechism containing the names of
the gods and goddesses. Besides this, there was the study
of the Twelve Tables, that is, of the Roman Law. Men the
most robust, the most courageous, the best disciplined, and
the most patriotic that ever lived, were the fruit of this
natural education. Rome was the great school of the civic and
military virtues. The Romans did not imitate the Athenians
in a disinterested pursuit of a perfect physical and intellectual
development. Rome worked for practical ends ; she was
guided only by considerations of utility ; she had no regard
for ideals ; her purpose was simply the education of soldiers
and citizens who should be obedient and devoted. She did
not know man in the abstract ; she knew only the Roman
citizen.

These high qualities of the early Romans were marred by
a sort of brutal insensibility and a contempt for the graces
of intellect and heart ; and leaving out of account the circumstances of environment and race, their practical virtues
may be ascribed to three or four principal causes. First
among these was a firm family discipline. The authority
of the father was absolute, and answering to this excessive
power, there was blind obedience. Another cause was the
position of the mother in the family. At Rome, woman was
held in higher esteem than at Athens. She became almost
the equal of man. She was the guardian of the family circle
and the teacher of her children. The very name *matron*

inspires respect. Coriolanus, who took up arms against his country, could not withstand the tears of his mother Veturia. The noble Cornelia was the teacher of her sons, the Gracchi, whom she was accustomed to call "her fairest jewels." Besides, the influence of religion was made to supplement the active efforts of the family. The Roman lived surrounded by deities. When a child was weaned, tradition would have it that one goddess taught him to eat, and another to drink. Later on, four goddesses guided his first steps and held his two hands. All these superstitions imposed regularity and exactness on the most ordinary acts of daily life. Men breathed, as it were, a divine atmosphere. Finally, the young Roman learned to read in the laws of the Twelve Tables, that is, in the civil code of his country. He was thus accustomed from infancy to consider the law as something natural, inviolable, and sacred.

45. ROME AT SCHOOL IN GREECE. — The primitive state of manners did not last. Under Greek influence, Roman simplicity suffered a change, and, as Horace says, Greece, in being conquered, conquered in turn her rude victor. The taste for letters and arts was introduced at Rome towards the close of the third century B.C., and transformed the austere and rude education of the primitive era. The Romans, in their turn, acquired a liking for fine phrases and subtile dialectics. Schools were opened, and the rhetoricians and philosophers took up the business of education. Parents no longer charged themselves with the instruction of their children. Following the fashion at Athens, they entrusted them to slaves, without troubling themselves about the faults or even the vices of these common *pedagogues*.

" For if any of their servants," says Plutarch, " be better than the rest, they dispose some of them to follow husbandry, some to navigation, some to merchandise, some to be stewards in their houses, and some, lastly, to put out their money to use for them. But if they find any slave that is a drunkard or a glutton, and unfit for any other business, to him they assign the government of their children; whereas, a good pedagogue ought to be such a one in his disposition as Phœnix, tutor to Achilles, was."[1]

46. WHY ROME HAD NO GREAT EDUCATORS. — In the age of Augustus, when Latin literature was in all its glory, we are astonished not to find, as in the century of Pericles, some great thinker like Plato or Aristotle, who presents general views on education, and makes himself famous by a remarkable work on pedagogy. This is due to the fact that the Romans never formed a taste for disinterested science and speculative inquiry. They reached distinction only in the practical sciences; in the law, for example, in which they excelled. Now pedagogy, while in one sense a practical science, nevertheless reposes upon philosophical principles, upon a knowledge of human nature, and upon a theoretical conception of human destiny, — questions which had no living interest for the Roman mind, and which even Cicero has noticed only in passing, in the course of his translation of Plato, made with his usual magnificence of literary style.

It is to be noted, moreover, that the Romans seem never to have considered education as a national undertaking, as an affair of the State. The Law of the Twelve Tables is silent upon the education of children. Up to the time of Quintilian there were at Rome no public schools, no professional teachers. In the age of Augustus each teacher had his own method. "Our ancestors," says Cicero, "did not wish that children should be educated by fixed rules, determined by the laws, publicly promulgated and made uniform for all."[2]

---

[1] Plutarch, *Morals*, vol. I. p. 9.   [2] Cicero, *De Republica*, IV. 115.

And he does not seem to disapprove of this neglect, even while noting the fact that Polybius saw in this an important defect in Roman institutions.

47. CICERO. — In all Cicero's works we find scarcely a line relative to education. And yet the great orator exclaims : " What better, what greater service can we of to-day render the Republic than to instruct and train the young?"[1] But he was content with writing fine discourses on philosophy for his country, abounding more in eloquence than in originality.

48. VARRO. — A less celebrated writer, Varro, seems to have had some pedagogic instinct. He wrote real educational works on grammar, rhetoric, history, and geometry. Most of these have been lost ; but if we may trust his contemporaries, they were instrumental in the education of several generations.

49. QUINTILIAN (35–95 A.D.). — After the age of Augustus, education became more and more an affair of oratory. The chief effort in the way of education was a preparation for a career in the Forum. But from these vulgar rhetoricians, occupied with the exterior artifices of style, these " traffickers in words," as Saint Augustine called them, we must distinguish a rhetorician of a higher order, who does not separate rhetoric from a general culture of the intelligence. This is Quintilian, the author of the *Institutes of Oratory*.

Appointed at the age of twenty-six to a chair of eloquence, the first that was established by the Roman state, and called at a later period by the Emperor Domitian to direct the education of his grand-nephews, Quintilian was practically acquainted with both public and private instruction.

---

[1] Cicero, *De Divinatione*, II. 2.

50. THE INSTITUTES OF ORATORY. — This work, under the form of a treatise on rhetoric, is in parts a real treatise on education. The author, in fact, begins the training of the future orator from the cradle ; he gives counsel to its nurse, and " not blushing to descend to petty details," he follows step by step the education of his pupil. Let us add, that in the noble ideal which he conceives, eloquence never being considered apart from wisdom, Quintilian was led by his very subject to treat of moral education.

51. HIS GENERAL PLAN OF EDUCATION. — The first book entire is devoted to education in general, and its teachings might be applied indifferently to all children, whether destined or not to the practice of oratory.

" Has a son been born to you? From the first conceive the highest hopes of him." Thus Quintilian begins. He thinks that we cannot have too high an opinion of human nature, nor propose for it too high a purpose. Minds that rebel against all instruction are unnatural. Most often it is the training which is at fault ; it is not nature that is to blame.

52. THE EARLY EDUCATION OF THE CHILD. — The child's nurses should be virtuous and prudent. Quintilian does not demand that they shall be learned, as the stoic Chrysippus would have them ; but he requires that their language shall be irreproachable. The first impressions of the child are very durable : " New vases preserve the taste of the first liquor that is put into them : and wool, once colored, never regains its primitive whiteness."

By an illusion analogous to that of the literary men of the sixteenth and seventeenth centuries, who would have the little French boy first learn Latin, Quintilian teaches his pupil Greek before making him study his native tongue.

Studies, moreover, should begin betimes: "Turn to account the child's first years, especially as the elements of learning demand only memory, and the memory of children is very tenacious."

We seem to be listening to a modern teacher when Quintilian recommends the avoidance of whatever might ruffle the spirits of the child. "Let study be to him a play; ask him questions; commend him when he does well; and sometimes let him enjoy the consciousness of his little gains in wisdom."

53. READING AND WRITING. — The passage relative to reading deserves to be quoted in full. It is wrong, says Quintilian, to teach children the names of the letters, and their respective places in the alphabet, before they know their shapes. He recommends the use of letters in ivory, which children take pleasure in handling, seeing, and naming.

As to writing, Quintilian recommends, for the purpose of strengthening the child's hand, and of preventing it from making false movements, that he should practise on wooden tablets on which the letters have been traced by cutting.[1] Later on, the copies shall contain, "not senseless maxims, but moral truths." The Roman teacher did not counsel haste in any case. "We can scarcely believe," he says, "how progress in reading is retarded by attempting to go too fast."

54. PUBLIC EDUCATION. — Quintilian has made an unsurpassed plea for public education and its advantages, which

---

[1] In principle, this is the same as the system of writing commended by Locke: "Get a plate graved with the Characters of such a Hand as you like best . . . let several sheets of good Writing-paper be printed off with red Ink, which he has nothing to do but go over with a good Pen fill'd with black Ink, which will quickly bring his Hand to the Formation of those Characters, being first shewed where to begin, and how to form every Letter." (*On Education*, § 160.) (P.)

Rollin has reproduced almost entire.[1] From this we shall quote only the following passage, which proves how far the contemporaries of Quintilian had already departed from the manly habits of the early ages ; and the truth which is herein expressed will always be applicable to parents who are inclined to be over-indulgent : " Would that we ourselves did not corrupt the morals of our children ! We enervate their very infancy with luxuries. That delicacy of education, which we call fondness, weakens all the powers, both of body and mind. . . . We form the palate of our children before we form their pronunciation. They grow up in sedan chairs ; if they touch the ground, they hang by the hands of attendants supporting them on each side. We are delighted if they utter anything immodest. Expressions which would not be tolerated even from effeminate youths, we hear from them with a smile and a kiss. Need we be astonished at this behavior? We ourselves have taught them." [2]

55. DUTIES OF TEACHERS. — There was at Rome, in the first century of the Christian era, a high conception of the duties of a teacher : " His first care should be to ascertain with all possible thoroughness the mind and the character of the child." Judicious reflections on the memory, on the faculty of imitation, and on the dangers of precocious mental development, are proofs of the fine psychological discernment of Quintilian. His insight is no less accurate when he sketches the rules for moral discipline. " Fear," he says, " restrains some and unmans others. . . . For my part, I prefer a pupil who is sensitive to praise, whom glory animates, and from whom defeat draws tears."

---

[1] " Quintilian has treated this question with great breadth and eloquence." (Traité des Études, Liv. IV. Art. 2.)

[2] Quintilian, Institutes of Oratory, Watson's Translation, Book I. chap. II. 6, 7.

Quintilian expresses himself decidedly against the use of the rod, "although custom authorizes it," he says, "and Chrysippus does not disapprove of it."

56. GRAMMAR AND RHETORIC. — Like his contemporaries, Quintilian distinguishes studies into two grades, — Grammar and Rhetoric. "As soon as the child is able to read and write, he must be placed in the hands of the grammarian." Grammar was divided into two parts, — the art of speaking correctly and the explication of the poets. Exercises in composition, development lessons called *Chriæ*, and narratives, accompanied the theoretical study of the rules of grammar.[1] It is to be observed that Quintilian gives a high place to etymological studies, and that he attaches great importance to reading aloud. "That the child may read well, let him have a good understanding of what he reads. . . . When he reads the poets, let him shun affected modulations. It is with reference to this manner of reading that Cæsar, still a young man, made this excellent observation : 'If you are singing, you sing poorly ; if you are reading, why do you sing?'"

57. THE SIMULTANEOUS STUDY OF THE SCIENCES. — Quintilian is very far from confining his pupil within the narrow circle of grammatical study. Persuaded that the child is capable of learning several things at the same time, he would have him taught geometry, music, and philosophy simultaneously : —

"Must he learn grammar alone, and then geometry, and in the meanwhile forget what he first learned? As well advise a farmer not to cultivate, at the same time, his fields, his vines, his olive trees, and his orchards, and not to give his

---

[1] *Institutes*, Book I. chap. IX.

thought simultaneously to his meadows, his cattle, his gardens, and his bees." [1]

Of course Quintilian considers the different studies which he sets before his pupil only as the instruments for an education in oratory. Philosophy, which comprises dialectics or logic, physics or the science of nature, and lastly morals, furnish the orator with ideas, and teach him the art of distributing them into a consecutive line of argument. And so geometry, a near relative of dialectics, disciplines the mind, and teaches it to distinguish the true from the false. Lastly, music is an excellent preparation for eloquence; it cultivates the sense of harmony and a taste for number and measure.

58. THE SCHOOLS OF PHILOSOPHY. — By the side of the schools of rhetoric, in which the art of speech was cultivated, imperial Rome saw flourish in great numbers schools of philosophy, whose purpose was the formation of morals. It was through no lack of moral sermonizing that there was a degeneration in the virtues of the Romans. All the schools of Greece, especially the Stoics and the Epicureans, and also the schools of Pythagoras, of Socrates, of Plato, and of Aristotle, had their representatives at Rome; but their obscure names have scarcely survived.

59. SENECA. — Among these philosophers and these moralists of the first century of the Christian era, Seneca has the distinction of standing in the front rank. It is true that he was not the founder of a school, but by his numerous writings he succeeded in maintaining among his contemporaries at least some vestiges of the ancient virtues. His *Letters to Lucilius*, letters abounding in real intellectual and moral insight, also contain some pedagogical precepts.

---

[1] *Institutes*, Book I. chap. XII.

Seneca attempts to direct school instruction to practical ends, in following out the thought of this famous precept: "We should learn, not for the sake of the school, but for the purposes of life" (*Non scholæ, sed vitæ discimus*). Moreover, he criticises confused and ill-directed reading that does not enrich the understanding, and concludes by recommending the profound study of a single book (*timeo hominem unius libri*). In another letter he remarks that the best means for giving clearness to one's own ideas is to communicate them to others ; the best way of being taught is to teach (*docendo discimus*). Let us quote this other maxim so often repeated : "The end is attained sooner by example than by precept" (*longum iter per præcepta, breve per exempla*).

60. PLUTARCH (50–138 A.D.). — In the last period of Roman civilization two names deserve to arrest the attention of the educator, — Plutarch and Marcus Aurelius. Although he was born in Bœotia, and wrote in Greek, Plutarch belongs to the Roman world. He lived at Rome at several different times, and there opened a school in the reign of Domitian, where he lectured on philosophy, literature, and history. Numerous works have transmitted to us the substance of that instruction which had such an extraordinary success.

61. THE LIVES OF ILLUSTRIOUS MEN. — Translated in the fifteenth century by Amyot, the *Parallel Lives* of Plutarch were for our fathers a true code of morals founded on history. How many of our great men, or how many of our men of worth, have drawn from this book, at least in part, the material which has nurtured their virtues ! L'Hôpital and d'Aubigné enriched their lives from this source. Henry IV. said of this book : " It has been to me as my conscience, and has whispered in my ear many virtuous suggestions and

excellent maxims for my own conduct and for the management of my affairs."[1]

62. The Essay on the Training of Children. — The
celebrated essay entitled *Of the Training of Children*,[2] is the
first treatise, especially devoted to education, that antiquity
has bequeathed to us. Its authenticity has been called in
question by German critics ; but this is of little moment, since
these critics are the first to recognize the fact that the author
of this essay, whoever he might have been, was intimately
acquainted with Plutarch, and has given us a sufficiently
exact summary of the ideas which are more fully developed
in others of his works.[3]

We shall not give an analysis of this work, which, however, abounds in interesting reflections on the primary period
of education. We shall simply note the fundamental thought
of the essay, its salient and original characteristic, which is
its warm appreciation of the family. In society, as Plutarch
conceives it, the State no longer exercises absolute sover-
eignty. Upon the ruins of the antique commonwealth
Plutarch builds the family. It is to the family that he
addresses himself in order to assure the education of
children.[4] On this point he is not in accord with Quintilian.

---

[1] Equally great has been Plutarch's influence on English thought and
life. Sir Thomas North's translation of Amyot's version appeared in 1579,
and furnished Shakespeare with the materials for his *Coriolanus, Julius
Cæsar*, and *Antony and Cleopatra*. Milton, Wordsworth, and Browning
are also debtors to the *Parallel Lives*. (P.)

[2] "Comment il faut nourrir les enfants," in the translation by Amyot.
"Of the Training of Children," in Goodwin's edition of the *Morals* (Vol. I.).

[3] The references that follow are to Plutarch's *Morals*. The first translation into English was by Philemon Holland, in 1603. The American
edition in five volumes (Boston, 1871) is worthy of all commendation.
The references I make are to this edition. (P.)

[4] Of course Plutarch, like all the writers of antiquity, writes only in be-

What he recommends is an education that is domestic and individual. He scarcely admits the need of public schools save for the higher instruction. At a certain age a young man, already trained by the watchful care of a preceptor under the supervision of his parents, shall go abroad to hear the lectures of the moralists and the philosophers, and to read the poets.

63. THE EDUCATION OF WOMEN. — One of the consequences of the exalted function which Plutarch ascribes to the family is that by this single act he raises the material and moral condition of woman. In his essay entitled *Conjugal Precepts*, which recalls the *Economics* of Xenophon, he restores to the wife her place in the household. He associates her with the husband in the material support of the family, as well as in the education of the children. The mother is to nurse her offspring. " Providence," he naively says, " hath also wisely ordered that women should have two breasts, that so, if any of them should happen to bear twins, they might have two several springs of nourishment ready for them."[1] The mother shall also take part in the instruction of her children, and so she must herself be educated. Plu-

---

half of free-born children in good circumstances. "He abandons," as he himself admits, "the education of the poor and the lowly."

Plutarch seems to aim at what appears to him to be *practicable*. That he was liberal in his opinions must be evident, I think, from this extract : " It is my desire that all children whatsoever may partake of the benefits of education alike ; but if yet any persons, by reason of the narrowness of their estates, cannot make use of my precepts, let them not blame me that give them, but Fortune, which disableth them from making the advantage by them they otherwise might. Though even poor men must use their utmost endeavor to give their children the best education ; or, if they can not, they must bestow upon them the best that their abilities will reach." (*Morals*, vol. I. pp. 19, 20.) (P.)

[1] *Of the Training of Children*, § 6.

tarch proposes for her the highest studies, such as mathematics and philosophy. But he counts much more upon her natural qualities, than upon the science that she may acquire. "With women," he says, "tenderness of heart is enhanced by a pleasing countenance, by sweetness of speech, by an affectionate grace, and by a high degree of sensitiveness."

64. The Function of Poetry in Education. — In the essay entitled *How a Young Man Ought to Hear Poems*, Plutarch has given his opinion as to the extent to which poetry should be made an element in education. More just than Plato, he does not condemn the reading of the poets. He simply demands that this reading should be done with discretion, by choosing those who, in their compositions, mingle moral inspiration with poetic inspiration. "Lycurgus," he says, "did not act like a man of sound reason in the course which he took to reform his people that were much inclined to drunkenness, by traveling up and down to destroy all the vines in the country; whereas he should have ordered that every vine should have a well of water near it, that (as Plato saith) the drunken deity might be reduced to temperance by a sober one."[1]

65. The Teaching of Morals. — Plutarch is above all else a moralist. If he adds nothing in the way of theory to the lofty doctrines of the Greek philosophers from whom he catches his inspiration, at least he enters more profoundly into the study of practical methods which insure the efficacy of fine precepts and exalted doctrines. "That contemplation which is dissociated from practice," he says, "is of no utility." He would have young men come from lectures on

---

[1] *Morals*, vol. II. p. 44.

morals, not only better instructed, but more virtuous. Of what consequence are beautiful maxims unless they are embodied in action? The young man, then, shall early accustom himself to self-government, to reflection upon his own conduct, and to taking counsel of his own reason. . Moreover, Plutarch gives him a director of conscience, a philosopher, whom he will go to consult in his doubts, and to whom he will entrust the keeping of his soul. But that which is of most consequence in his eyes is personal effort, reflection always on the alert, and that inward effort which causes our soul to assimilate the moral lessons which we have received, and which causes them to enter into the very structure and fibre of our personality.

" As it would be with a man who, going to his neighbor's to borrow fire, and finding there a great and bright fire, should sit down to warm himself and forget to go home ; so is it with the one who comes to another to learn, if he does not think himself obliged to kindle his own fire within, and influence his own mind, but continues sitting by his master as if he were enchanted, delighted by hearing." [1]

So are those who are not striving to have a personal morality, but who, incapable of self-direction, are always in · need of the tutorship of another.

The great preoccupation of Plutarch — and by this trait he has a legitimate place among the great educators of the world — was to awaken, to excite, the interior forces of the conscience, and to stimulate the intelligence to a high state of activity. When he wrote this famous maxim, " The soul is not a vase to be filled, but is rather a hearth which is to be

---

[1] *Morals*, I. p. 463. This language directly follows the quotation given in the note (1) at the close of this paragraph. (P.)

made to glow,"[1] he was not thinking alone of moral education, but also of a false intellectual education which, instead
of training the mind, is content with accumulating in the
memory a mass of indigested materials.[2]

66. MARCUS AURELIUS. — The wisest of the Roman emperors, the author of the book entitled *To Myself*, better
known as *Meditations*, Marcus Aurelius deserves mention
in the history of pedagogy. He is perhaps the most perfect
representative of Stoic morality, which is itself the highest
expression of ancient morality. He is the most finished type
of what can be effected in the way of soul-culture by the influence of home-training and the personal effort of the conscience. His teacher of rhetoric was the celebrated Fronto,
of whose character we may judge from this one characteristic :
"I toiled hard yesterday," he wrote to his pupil ; "I composed
a few figures of speech, with which I am pleased." On the
other hand, Marcus Aurelius found examples for imitation in
his own family. "My uncle," he says reverently, "taught
me patience. . . . From my father I inherited modesty. . . .
To my mother I owe my feelings of piety." Notwithstanding
the modesty that led him to attribute to others the whole of
his moral worth, it is especially to himself, to a persistent ·
effort of his own will, and to a ceaseless examination of his
own conscience, that he is indebted for becoming the most
virtuous of men, and the wisest and purest, next to Socrates,
of the moralists of antiquity. His *Meditations* show us in

[1] The exact reading is as follows : "For the mind requires not like an
earthen vessel to be filled up ; convenient fuel and aliment only will influence it with a desire of knowledge and ardent love of truth." (*Morals*, I.
p. 463.) This makes the author's meaning more apparent. (P.)

[2] This does not mean that Plutarch sets a low value on memory, for he
says : "Above all things, we must exercise the memory of children, for it
is the treasury of knowledge."

action that self-education which in our time has suggested such beautiful reflections to Channing.

67. Conclusion. — Finally, it must be admitted that Roman literature is poor in material for educational study. Some passages, scattered here and there in the classical authors, nevertheless prove that they were not absolutely strangers to pedagogical questions.

Thus Horace professed independence of mind; he declares that he is not obliged to swear by the " words of any master."[1] On the other hand, Juvenal defined the ideal purpose of life and of education when he said that the desirable thing above all others is " a sound mind in a sound body."[2] Finally, Pliny the Younger, in three words, *multum, non multa*, " much, not many things," fixes one essential point in educational method, and recommends the thorough study of one single subject in preference to a superficial study which extends over too many subjects.

While by their taste, their accuracy of thought, and the perfection of their style, the Latin writers are worthy of being placed by the side of the Greeks as proficients in education of the literary type, they at the same time deserve to be regarded as reputable guides in moral education. At Rome, as at Athens, that which formed the basis of instruction was the search after virtue. That which preoccupied Cicero as well as Plato, Seneca as well as Aristotle, was not so much the extension of knowledge and the development of instruction as the progress of manners and the moral perfection of man.

[68. Analytical Summary. — 1. In contrast with Greek education, the chief characteristic of which was intellectual

---

[1] " *Nullius addictus jurare in verba magistri.*"
[2] " *Orandum est ut sit mens sana in corpore sano.*" (Sat. x. 356.)

discipline or culture, Roman education may be called *practical*. Greece and Rome have thus furnished the world with two distinct types of education, and their modern representatives are seen in our classical and scientific courses respectively.

2. The disinclination of the Roman mind to speculative inquiry, was a bar to the production of any contributions to the theory of education.

3. In the *Institutes* of Quintilian we see the first attempt to expound the art of teaching ; and in the *Morals* of Plutarch we have the first formal treatise on the education of children.

4. In the later period of Roman education, we see a higher appreciation of woman, and a nobler conception of the family life.

5. In common with all the systems of education thus far studied, Roman education is essentially literary, ethical, and prudential, as distinguished from an education in science. The conception of the money value of knowledge had not yet appeared.]

CHAPTER IV.

THE EARLY CHRISTIANS AND THE MIDDLE AGE.

THE NEW SPIRIT OF CHRISTIANITY; THE POVERTY OF THE EARLY
CHRISTIAN CENTURIES IN RESPECT OF EDUCATION; THE FATHERS
OF THE CHURCH; SAINT JEROME AND THE EDUCATION OF GIRLS;
PHYSICAL ASCETICISM; INTELLECTUAL AND MORAL ASCETICISM; PER-
MANENT TRUTHS; INTELLECTUAL FEEBLENESS OF THE MIDDLE AGE;
CAUSES OF THE IGNORANCE OF THE MIDDLE AGE; THE THREE RENA-
SCENCES; CHARLEMAGNE; ALCUIN; THE SUCCESSORS OF CHARLE-
MAGNE; SCHOLASTICISM; ABELARD; THE SEVEN LIBERAL ARTS;
METHODS AND DISCIPLINE; THE UNIVERSITIES; GERSON; VITTORINO
DA FELTRE; OTHER TEACHERS AT THE CLOSE OF THE MIDDLE AGE;
RECAPITULATION; ANALYTICAL SUMMARY.

---

69. THE NEW SPIRIT OF CHRISTIANITY. — By its dogmas,
by the conception of the equality of all human creatures, by
its spirit of charity, Christianity introduced new elements
into the conscience, and seemed called to give a powerful
impetus to the moral education of men. The doctrine of
Christ was at first a reaction of free will and of personal
dignity against the despotism of the State. "A full half of
man henceforth escaped the action of the State. Christianity taught that man no longer belonged to society except in
part; that he was under allegiance to it by his body and his
material interests; that being subject to a tyrant, he must
submit; that as a citizen of a republic, he ought to give his
life for it; but that in respect of his soul, he was free, and
owed allegiance only to God."[1]   Henceforth it was not simply a question of training citizens for the service of the State;

---

[1] Fustel de Coulanges, *La Cité antique*, p. 476.

but the conception of a disinterested development of the
human person made its appearance in the world. On the
other hand, in proclaiming that all men had the same destiny,
and that they were all equal in the sight of God, Christianity
raised the poor and the disinherited from their condition of
misery, and promised them all the same instruction. To the
idea of liberty was added that of equality; and equal justice for all, and participation in the same rights, were contained in germ in the doctrine of Christianity.

70. POVERTY OF THE FIRST CHRISTIAN CENTURIES IN RE-
SPECT OF EDUCATION. — Nevertheless, the germs contained
in the doctrines of the new religion did not bear fruit at
once. It is easy to analyze the causes which led to the poverty of educational thought during the first centuries of the
Christian era.

In the first place, the Christian instruction was addressed
to barbarous peoples who could not at once rise to a high
intellectual and moral culture. According to the celebrated
comparison of Jouffroy, the invasion of the barbarians into
the midst of ancient society was like an armful of green
wood thrown upon a blazing fire; at first there could issue
from it only a mass of smoke.

Moreover, we must take into account the fact that the
early Christians, in order to establish their faith, had to
struggle against difficulties which were ever being renewed.
The first centuries were a period of struggle, of conquest,
and of organization, which left but little opportunity for the
disinterested study of education. In their contests with the
ancient world, the early Christians came to include in a common hatred classical literature and pagan religion. Could
they receive with sympathy the literary and scientific inheritance of a society whose morals they repudiated, and whose
beliefs they were bent on destroying?

On the other hand, the social, condition of the men who
first attached themselves to the new religion turned them
aside from the studies which are a preparation for real life.
Obliged to conceal themselves, to betake themselves to the
desert, true Pariahs of the pagan world, they lived a life of
contemplation; they were naturally led to conceive an ascetic and monastic existence as the ideal of education.

Moreover, by its mystical tendencies, Christianity at the
first could not be a good school for a practical and humane
system of education.   The Christian was detached from the
commonwealth of man, only to enter into the commonwealth
of God. ' He must break with a corrupt and perverse world.
By privations, and by the renunciation of every pleasure, he
must react against the immorality of Græco-Roman society.
Man must aspire to imitate God; and God is absolute holiness, the very negation of all the conditions of earthly life,—
supreme perfection.   The very disproportion between such an
ideal and human weakness as an actual fact must have be-
trayed the early Christians into leading a mystical life which
was but a preparation for death.   And the consequence of
these doctrines was to make of the Church the exclusive
mistress of education and instruction.   Individual initiative,
if called into play, on the one hand, by the fundamental doctrines of Christianity, was stifled, on the other, under the
domination of the Church.

71. THE FATHERS OF THE CHURCH. — Of the celebrated
doctors who, by their erudition and eloquence, if not by
their taste, made illustrious the beginning of Christianity,
some were jealous mystics and sectaries, in whose eyes philosophical curiosity was a sin, and the love of letters a heresy;
and others were Christians of 'a conciliatory temperament,
who, in a certain measure, allied religious faith and literary
culture.

Tertullian rejected all pagan education. He saw in classical culture only a robbery from God ; a road to the false and arrogant wisdom of the ancient philosophers. Even Saint Augustine, who in his youth could not read the fourth book of the Æneid without shedding tears, and who had been devotedly fond of ancient poetry and eloquence, renounced, after his conversion, his literary tastes as well as the mad passions of his early manhood. It was by his influence that the Council of Carthage forbade the bishops to read the pagan authors.

This was not the course of Saint Basil, who demands, on the contrary, that the young Christian shall be conversant with the orators, poets, and historians of antiquity ; who thinks that the poems of Homer inspire a love for virtue ; and who desires, finally, that full use should be made of the treasures of ancient wisdom in the training of the young.[1] Nor was this the thought of Saint Jerome, who said he would be none the less a Ciceronian in becoming a Christian.

72. SAINT JEROME AND THE EDUCATION OF GIRLS. — The letters of Saint Jerome on the education of girls form the most valuable educational document of the first centuries of Christianity.[2] They have excited high admiration. Erasmus knew them by heart, and Saint Theresa read selections from them every day. It is impossible, to-day, while admiring certain parts of them, not to condemn the general spirit which pervades them, — a narrow spirit, distrustful of the world, which pushes the religious sentiment even to mysticism, and disdain for human affairs to asceticism.

---

[1] See the Homily of Saint Basil *On the Utility which the young can derive from the reading of profane authors.*

[2] *Letter to Læta on the education of her daughter Paula* (403). *Letter to Gaudentius on the education of the little Pacatula.* The letter to Gaudentius is far inferior to the other by reason of the perpetual digressions into which the author permits himself to be drawn.

73. PHYSICAL ASCETICISM. — It is no longer the question of giving power to the body, and thus of making of it the robust instrument of a cultured spirit, as the Greeks would have it. The body is an enemy that must be subdued by fasting, by abstinence, and by mortifications of the flesh.

" Do not allow Paula to eat in public, that is, do not let her take part in family entertainments, for fear that she may desire the meats that may be served there. Let her learn not to use wine, for it is the source of all impurity. Let her food be vegetables, and only rarely of fish ; and let her eat so as always to be hungry."

Contempt for the body is carried so far that cleanliness is almost interdicted.

" For myself, I entirely forbid a young girl to bathe."

It is true that, alarmed at the consequences of such austerity, Saint Jerome, by way of exception, permits children the use of the bath, of wine, and of meat, but only " when necessity requires it, and lest the feet may fail them before having walked."

74. INTELLECTUAL AND MORAL ASCETICISM. — For the mind, as well as for the body, we may say of Saint Jerome what Nicole wrote to a nun of his time : " You feed your pupils on bread and water." The Bible is the only book recommended, and this is little ; but it is the Bible entire, which is too much. *The Song of Songs*, with its sensual imagery, would be strange reading for a young girl. The arts, like letters, find no favor with the mysticism of Saint Jerome.

" Never let Paula listen to musical instruments ; let her even be ignorant of the uses served by the flute and the harp."

As for the flute, which the Greek philosophers also did not like, let it be so ; but what shall we say of this condemnation of the harp, the instrument of David and the angels, and of religious music itself! How far we are, in common with Saint Jerome, from that complete life, from that harmonious development of all the faculties, which modern educators, Herbert Spencer, for example, present to us with reason as the ideal of education! Saint Jerome goes so far as to proscribe walking : —

"Do not let Paula be found in the ways of the world (emphatic paraphrase for *streets*), in the gatherings and in the company of her kindred; let her be found only in retirement."

The ideal of Saint Jerome is a monastic and cloistered life, even in the world. But that which is graver still, that which is the fatal law of mysticism, is that Saint Jerome, after having proscribed letters, arts, and necessary and legitimate pleasures, even brings his condemnation to bear on the most honorable sentiments of the heart. The heart is human also, and everything human is evil and full of danger :

"Do not allow Paula to feel more affection for one of her companions than for others; do not allow her to speak with such a one in an undertone." And as he held in suspicion even the affections of the family, the Doctor of the Church concludes thus : —

"Let her be educated in a cloister, where she will not know the world, where she will live as an angel, having a body but not knowing it, and where, in a word, you will be spared the care of watching over her. . . . If you will send us Paula, I will charge myself with being her master and nurse; I will give her my tenderest care; my old age will not prevent me from untying her tongue, and I shall be more renowned than the philosopher Aristotle, since I shall instruct, not a mortal and perishable king, but an immortal spouse of the Heavenly King."

75. PERMANENT TRUTHS. — The pious exaggerations of Saint Jerome only throw into sharper relief the justice and the excellence of some of his practical suggestions, — upon the teaching of reading, for example, or upon the necessity of emulation : —

"Put into the hands of Paula letters in wood or in ivory, and teach her the names of them. She will thus learn while playing. But it will not suffice to have her merely memorize the names of the letters, and call them in succession as they stand in the alphabet. You should often mix them, putting the last first, and the first in the middle.

"Induce her to construct words by offering her a prize, or by giving her, as a reward, what ordinarily pleases children of her age. . . . Let her have companions, so that the commendation she may receive may excite in her the feeling of emulation. Do not chide her for the difficulty she may have in learning. On the contrary, encourage her by commendation, and proceed in such a way that she shall be equally sensible to the pleasure of having done well, and to the pain of not having been successful. . . . Especially take care that she do not conceive a dislike for study that might follow her into a more advanced age."[1]

76. INTELLECTUAL FEEBLENESS OF THE MIDDLE AGE. — If the early doctors of the Church occasionally expressed some sympathy for profane letters, it is because, in their youth, before having received baptism, they had themselves attended the pagan schools. But these schools once closed, Christianity did not open others, and, after the fourth century, a profound night enveloped humanity. The labor of the Greeks and the Romans was as though it never had

---

[1] For writing, Saint Jerome. like Quintilian, recommends that children first practise on tablets of wood on which letters have been engraved.

been. The past no longer existed. Humanity began anew. In the fifth century, Apollinaris Sidonius declares that " the young no longer study, that teachers no longer have pupils, and that learning languishes and dies." Later, Lupus of Ferrières, the favorite of Louis the Pious and Charles the Bald, writes that the study of letters had almost ceased. In the early part of the eleventh century, the Bishop of Laon, Adalberic, asserts that " there is more than one bishop who cannot count the letters of the alphabet on his fingers." In 1291, of all the monks in the convent of Saint Gall, there was not one who could read and write. It was so difficult to find notaries public, that acts had to be passed verbally. The barons took pride in their ignorance. Even after the efforts of the twelfth century, instruction remained a luxury for the common people ; it was the privilege of the ecclesiastics, and even they did not carry it very far. The Benedictines confess that the mathematics were studied only for the purpose of calculating the date of Easter.

77. Causes of the Ignorance of the Middle Age. — What were the permanent causes of that situation which lasted for ten centuries? The Catholic Church has sometimes been held responsible for this. Doubtless the Christian doctors did not always profess a very warm sympathy for intellectual culture. Saint Augustine had said: " It is the ignorant who gain possession of heaven (*indocti cœlum rapiunt*)." Saint Gregory the Great, a pope of the sixth century, declared that he would blush to have the holy word conform to the rules of grammar. Too many Christians, in a word, confounded ignorance with holiness. Doubtless, towards the seventh century, the darkness still hung thick over the Christian Church. Barbarians invaded the Episcopate, and carried with them their rude manners. Doubtless,

also, during the feudal period the priest often became soldier, and remained ignorant. It would, however, be unjust to bring a constructive charge against the Church of the Middle Age, and to represent it as systematically hostile to instruction. Directly to the contrary, it is the clergy who, in the midst of the general barbarism, preserved some vestiges of the ancient culture. The only schools of that period are the episcopal and claustral schools, the first annexed to the bishops' palaces, the second to the monasteries. The religious orders voluntarily associated manual labor with mental labor. As far back as 530, Saint Benedict founded the convent of Monte Cassino, and drew up statutes which made reading and intellectual labor a part of the daily life of the monks.

In 1179, the third Lateran Council promulgated the following decree: —

" The Church of God, being obliged like a good and tender mother to provide for the bodily and spiritual wants of the poor, desirous to procure for poor children the opportunity for learning to read, and for making advancement in study, orders that each cathedral shall have a teacher charged with the gratuitous instruction of the clergy of that church, and also of the indigent scholars, and that he be assigned a benefice, which, sufficient for his subsistence, may thus open the door of the school to the studious youth. A tutor [1] shall be installed in the other churches and in the monasteries where formerly there were funds set apart for this purpose."

It is not, then, to the Church that we must ascribe the

---

[1] *Écolâtre.* The history of this word, as given by Littré, is instructive. "There was no cathedral church (sixteenth century) in which a sum was not appropriated for the salary of one who taught the ordinary subjects, and another for one who had leisure for teaching Theology. The first was called *cscolastre* (*écolâtre*), the second *theologal.*" Pasquier. (P.)

general intellectual torpor of the Middle Age. Other causes explain that long slumber of the human mind. The first is the social condition of the people. Security and leisure, the indispensable conditions for study, were completely lacking to people always at war, overwhelmed in succession by the barbarians, the Normans, the English, and by the endless struggles of feudal times. The gentlemen of the time aspired only to ride, to hunt, and to figure in tournaments and feats of arms. Physical education was above all else befitting men whose favorite vocation, both by habit and necessity, was war. On the other hand, the enslaved people did not suspect the utility of instruction. In order to comprehend the need of study, that great liberator, one must already have tasted liberty. In a society where the need of instruction had not yet been felt, who could have taken the initiative in the work of instructing the people?

Let us add that the Middle Age presented still other conditions unfavorable for the propagation of instruction, in particular, the lack of national languages, those necessary vehicles of education. The vernacular languages are the instruments of intellectual emancipation. Among a people where a dead language is supreme, a language of the learned, accessible only to the select few, the lower classes necessarily remain buried in ignorance. Moreover, Latin books themselves were rare. Lupus of Ferrières was obliged to write to Rome, and to address himself to the Pope in person, in order to procure for his use a work of Cicero's. Without books, without schools, without any of the indispensable implements of intellectual labor, what could be done for the mental life? It took refuge in certain monasteries; erudition flourished only in narrow circles, with a privileged few, and the rest of the nation remained buried in an obscure night.

78. THE THREE RENASCENCES. — It has been truly said
that there were three Renascences : the first, which owed its
beginning to Charlemagne, and whose brilliancy did not last ;
the second, that of the twelfth century, the issue of which
was Scholasticism ; and the third, the great Renaissance of
the sixteenth century, which still lasts, and which the French
Revolution has completed.

79. CHARLEMAGNE. — Charlemagne undoubtedly formed the
purpose of diffusing instruction about him. He ardently
sought it for himself, drilled himself in writing, and learned
Latin and Greek, rhetoric and astronomy. He would have
communicated to all who were about him the same ardor for
study. " Ah ! that I had twelve clerics," he exclaimed, " as
perfectly instructed as were Jerome and Augustine ! " It
was naturally upon the clergy that he counted, to make of
them the instruments of his plans ; but, as one of his
capitularies of 788 shows, there was need that the clergy
themselves should be reminded of the need of instruction :
" We have thought it useful that, in the bishops' residences,
and in the monasteries, care be taken not only to live according to the rules of our holy religion, but, in addition, to teach
the knowledge of letters to those who are capable of learning
them by the aid of our Lord. Although it avails more to
practise the law than to know it, it must be known before it
can be practised. Several monasteries having sent us
manuscripts, we have observed that, in the most of them,
the sentiments were good, but the language bad. We
exhort you, then, not only not to neglect the study of letters,
but to devote yourselves to them with all your power."

On the other hand, the nobles did not make any great
effort to justify their social rank by the degree of their
knowledge. One day, as Charlemagne entered a school,

displeased with the indolence and the ignorance of the young
barons who attended it, he addressed them in these severe
terms: "Do you count upon your birth, and do you feel a
pride in it? Take notice that you shall have neither government nor bishoprics, if you are not better instructed than
others."

80. ALCUIN (735–804). — Charlemagne was seconded in
his efforts by Alcuin of England, of whom it might be said,
that he was the first minister of public instruction in France.
It is he who founded the Palatine school, a sort of imperial
and itinerant academy which followed the court on its
travels. It was a model school, where Alcuin had for his
pupils the four sons and two daughters of Charlemagne, and
Charlemagne himself, always eager to be instructed.

Alcuin's method was not without originality, but it is a
great mistake to say that it resembles the method of Socrates.
Alcuin doubtless proceeds by interrogation; but here it is
the pupil who interrogates, and the teacher who responds.

"What is speech? asks Pepin, the eldest son of Charlemagne. It is the interpreter of the soul, replies Alcuin.
What is life? It is an enjoyment for some, but for the
wretched it is a sorrow, a waiting for death. What is
sleep? The image of death. What is writing? It is the
guardian of history. What is the body? The tenement
of the soul. What is day? A summons to labor."[1]

All this is either commonplace or artificial. The senten-
tious replies of Alcuin may be fine maxims, fit for embellish-
ing the memory; but in this procedure of the mere scholar,
affected by the over-refinements of his time, there is nothing
which can call into activity the intelligence of the pupil.

---

[1] For other examples, see the *Life of Alcuin*, by Lorenz; and for Middle
Age education in general, consult *Christian Schools and Scholars*, by
Augusta Theodosia Drane. (P.)

Nevertheless the name of Alcuin marks an era in the history of education. His was the first attempt to form an alliance between classical literature and Christian inspiration, — to create a " Christian Athens," according to the emphatic / phrase of Alcuin himself.

81. THE SUCCESSORS OF CHARLEMAGNE. — It had been the ambition of Charlemagne to reign over a civilized society, rather than over a barbarous people. Convinced that the only basis of political unity is a unity of ideas and of morals, he thought to find the basis of that moral unity in religion, and religion itself he purposed to establish upon a more widely diffused system of instruction. But these ideas were too advanced for the time, and their execution too difficult for the circumstances then existing. A new decadence followed the era of Charlemagne. The clergy did not respond to the hopes which the great emperor had placed on them. As far back as 817, the Council of Aix-la-Chapelle decided that henceforth no more day-pupils should be received into the conventual schools, for the reason that too large a number of pupils would make impossible the maintenance of the monastic discipline. No one of Charlemagne's successors seems to have taken up the thought of the great emperor; no one of them was preoccupied with the problems of education. It is upon despotic authority, and not upon the intellectual progress of their subjects, that those unintelligent rulers wished to found their power. Under Louis the Pious and Charles the Bald there were constructed more castles than schools.

The kings of France were far from imitating the Anglo-Saxon king, Alfred the Great (849–901), to whom tradition ascribes these two sayings : " The English ought always to be free, as free as their own thoughts "; " Free-born sons should know how to read and write."

82. SCHOLASTICISM. — It was not till the twelfth century that the human mind was awakened. That was the age of Scholasticism, the essential character of which was the study of reasoning, and the practice of dialectics, or syllogistic reasoning. The syllogism, which reaches necessary conclusions from given premises, was the natural instrument of an age of faith, when men wished simply to demonstrate immutable dogmas, without ever making an innovation on established beliefs. It has often been observed that the art of reasoning is the science of a people still in the early stage of its progress ; we might almost say of a barbarous people. A subtile dialectic is in perfect keeping with manners still rude, and with a limited state of knowledge. It is only an intellectual machine. It was not then a question of original thinking. All that was necessary was simply to reason upon conceptions already acquired, and the sacred depository of these was kept in charge by Theology. Consequently, there was no independent science. Philosophy, according to the language of the times, was but the humble servant of Theology. The dialectics of the doctors of the Middle Age was but a subtile commentary on the sacred books and on the doctrines of Aristotle.[1] It seems, says Locke, to see the inertness of the Middle Age, that God was pleased to make of man a two-footed animal, while leaving to Aristotle the task of making him a thinking being. From his point of view, an able educator of the seventeenth century, the Abbé Fleury, pronounces this severe judgment on the scholastic method : —

---

[1] The following quotation illustrates this servile dependence on authority: "At the time when the discovery of spots on the sun first began to circulate, a student called the attention of his old professor to the rumor, and received the following reply: 'There can be no spots on the sun, for I have read Aristotle twice from beginning to end, and he says the sun is incorruptible. Clean your lenses, and if the spots are not in the telescope, they must be in your eyes!'" Naville, *La Logique de l'Hypothèse.* (P.)

" This way of philosophizing on words and thoughts, without examining the things themselves, was certainly an easy way of getting along without a knowledge of facts, which can be acquired only by reading " (Fleury should have added *and by observation*) ; " and it was an easy way of dazzling the ignorant laics by peculiar terms and vain subtilties."

But Scholasticism had its hour of glory, its erudite doctors, its eloquent professors, chief among whom was Abelard.

83. ABELARD (1079–1142). — A genuine professor of higher instruction, Abelard, by the prestige of his eloquence, gathered around him at Paris thousands of students. Human speech, the living words of the teacher, had then an authority, an importance, which it has lost in part since books; everywhere distributed, have, to a certain extent, superseded oral instruction. At a time when printing did not exist, when manuscript copies were rare, a teacher who combined knowledge with the gift of speech was a phenomenon of incomparable interest, and students flocked from all parts of Europe to take advantage of his lectures. Abelard is the most brilliant representative of the scholastic pedagogy, with an original and personal tendency towards the emancipation of the mind. " It is ridiculous," he said, " to preach to others what we can neither make them understand, nor understand ourselves." With more boldness than Saint Anselm, he applied dialectics to theology, and attempted to reason out the grounds of his faith.

84. THE SEVEN LIBERAL ARTS. — The seven liberal arts constituted what may be called the secondary instruction of the Middle Age, such as was given in the claustral or conventual schools, and later, in the universities. The liberal arts were distributed into two courses of study, known as the *trivium* and the *quadrivium*. The *trivium* comprised grammar (Latin grammar, of course), dialectics, or logic, and

rhetoric; and the *quadrivium*, music, arithmetic, geometry, and astronomy. It is important to note the fact that this programme contains only abstract and *formal* studies, — no real and concrete studies. The sciences which teach us to know man and the world, such as history, ethics, the physical and natural sciences, were omitted and unknown, save perhaps in a few convents of the Benedictines. Nothing which can truly educate man, and develop his faculties as a whole, enlists the attention of the Middle Age. From a course of study thus limited there might come skillful reasoners and men formidable in argument, but never fully developed men.[1]

85. METHODS AND DISCIPLINE. — The methods employed in the ecclesiastical schools of the Middle Age were in accord with the spirit of the times, when men were not concerned about liberty and intellectual freedom; and when they thought more about the teaching of dogmas than about the training of the intelligence. The teachers recited or read their lectures, and the pupils learned by heart. The discipline was harsh. Corrupt human nature was distrusted. In 1363, pupils were forbidden the use of benches and chairs, on the pretext that such high seats were an encouragement to pride. For securing obedience, corporal chastisements were used and abused. The rod is in fashion in the fifteenth as it was in the fourteenth century.

" There is no other difference," says an historian, " except that the rods in the fifteenth century are twice as long as those in the fourteenth."[2]   Let us note, however, the protest of Saint Anselm, a protest that pointed out the evil rather than cured it. "Day and night," said an abbot to

---

[1] This is no exception to the rule that the education of an age is the exponent of its real or supposed needs. (P.)

[2] Monteil, *Histoire des Français des divers états.*

Saint Anselm, "we do not cease to chastise the children confided to our care, and they grow worse and worse." Anselm replied, "Indeed! You do not cease to chastise them! And when they are grown up, what will they become? Idiotic and stupid. A fine education that, which makes brutes of men! . . . If you were to plant a tree in your garden, and were to enclose it on all sides so that it could not extend its branches, what would you find when, at the end of several years, you set it free from its bands? A tree whose branches would be bent and crooked; and would it not be your fault, in having so unreasonably confined it?"

86. THE UNIVERSITIES. — Save claustral and cathedral schools, to which must be added some parish schools, the earliest example of our village schools, the sole educational establishment of the Middle Age was what is called the *University*. Towards the thirteenth and fourteenth century we see multiplying in the great cities of Europe those centres of study, those collections of students which recall from afar the schools of Plato and Aristotle. Of such establishments were the university which opened at Paris for the teaching of theology and philosophy (1200); the universities of Naples (1224), of Prague (1345), of Vienna (1365), of Heidelberg (1386), etc.[1] Without being completely affranchised from sacerdotal control, these universities were a first expansion of free science. As far back as the ninth century, the Arabs had given an example to the rest of Europe by founding at Salamanca, at Cordova, and in other cities of Spain, schools where all the sciences were cultivated.

87. GERSON (1363-1429). — With the gentle Gerson, the supposed author of the *Imitation*, it seems that the dreary dia-

---

[1] Cambridge (1109), Oxford (1140).

lectics disappear to let the heart speak and make way for feeling. The Chancellor of the University of Paris is distinguished from the men of his time by his love for the people. He wrote in the common tongue little elementary treatises for the use and within the comprehension of the *plain people.* His Latin work, entitled *De parvulis ad Christum trahendis* ("Little children whom we must lead to Christ"), gives evidence of a large spirit of sweetness and goodness. It abounds in subtile and delicate observations. For example, Gerson demands of teachers patience and tenderness: "Little children," he says, "are more easily managed by caresses than by fear." For these frail creatures he dreads the contagion of example. "No living being is more in danger than the child of allowing himself to be corrupted by another child." In his eyes, the little child is a delicate plant that must be carefully protected against every evil influence, and, in particular, against pernicious literature, such as the *Roman de la Rose.* Gerson condemns corporal punishment, and requires that teachers shall have for their pupils the affection of a father: —

"Above all else, let the teacher make an effort to be a father to his pupils. Let him never be angry with them. Let him always be simple in his instruction, and relate to his pupils that which is wholesome and agreeable." Tenderhearted and exalted spirit, Gerson is a precursor of Fenelon.[1]

88. VITTORINO DA FELTRE (1379–1446). — It is a pleasure to place beside Gerson one of his Italian contemporaries, the celebrated Vittorino da Feltre, a professor in the University of Padua. It was as preceptor to the sons of the

---

[1] In the *Traité de la visite des diocèses*, in 1400, he directed the bishops to inquire whether each parish had a school, and, in case there were none, to establish one.

Prince of Gonzagas, and as founder of an educational establishment at Venice, that Vittorino found occasion to show his aptitude for educational work. With him, education again became what it was in Greece, — the harmonious development of mind and body. Gymnastic exercises, such as swimming, riding, fencing, restored to honor ; attention to the exterior qualities of fine bearing ; an interesting and agreeable method of instruction ; a constant effort to discover the character and aptitudes of children ; a conscientious preparation for each lesson ; assiduous watchfulness over the work of pupils ; such are the principal features of the pedagogy of Vittorino da Feltre, a system of teaching evidently in advance of his time, and one which deserves a longer study.

89. OTHER TEACHERS AT THE CLOSE OF THE MIDDLE AGE. — Were we writing a work of erudition, there would be other thinkers to point out in the last years of the Middle Age, in that uncertain and, so to speak, twilight period which serves as a transition from the night of the Middle Age to the full day of the Renaissance. Among others, let us notice the Chevalier de la Tour-Landry and Æneas Sylvius Piccolomini.

The Chevalier de la Tour-Landry, in the work which he wrote for the education of his daughters (1372), scarcely rises above the spirit of his time. Woman, as he thinks, is made to pray and to go to church. The model which he sets before his daughters is a countess, who " each day wished to hear three masses." He recommends fasting three times a week in order " the better to subdue the flesh," and to prevent it " from diverting itself too much." There is neither responsibility nor proper dignity for the wife, who owes obedience to her husband, her lord, and " should do his will, whether wrong or right; if wrong, she is absolved from blame, as the blame falls on her lord."

Æneas Sylvius, the future Pope Pius II., in his tract on *The Education of Children* (1451), is already a man of the Renaissance, since he recommends with enthusiasm the reading and study of most of the classical authors. However, he traces a programme of studies relatively liberal. By the side of the humanities he places the sciences of geometry and arithmetic, "which are necessary," he says, "for training the mind and assuring rapidity of conceptions"; and also history and geography. He had himself composed historical narratives accompanied by maps. The distrusts of an overstrained devotion were no longer felt by a teacher who wrote, "There is nothing in the world more precious or more beautiful than an enlightened intelligence."

90. RECAPITULATION. — It is thus that the Middle Age in drawing to a close came nearer and nearer, in the way of continuous progress, to the decisive emancipation which the Renaissance and the Reformation were soon to perpetuate. But the Middle Age, in itself, whatever effort may be put forth at this day to rehabilitate it, and to discover in it the golden age of modern societies, remains an ill-starred epoch. A few virtues, negative for the most part, virtues of obedience and consecration, cannot atone for the real faults of those rude and barbarous centuries. A higher education reserved to ecclesiastics and men of noble rank; an instruction which consisted in verbal legerdemain, which developed only the mechanism of reasoning, and made of the intelligence a prisoner of the formal syllogism ; agreeably to the barbarism of primitive times, a fantastic pedantry which lost itself in superficial discussions and in verbal distinctions ; popular education almost null, and restricted to

the teaching of the catechism in Latin; finally, a Church, absolute and sovereign, which determined for all, great and small, the limits of thought, of belief, and of action; such was, from our own point of view, the condition of the Middle Age. It was time for the coming of the Renaissance to affranchise the human mind, to excite and to reveal to itself the unconscious need of instruction, and by the fruitful alliance of the Christian spirit and profane letters, to prepare for the coming of modern education.

[91. ANALYTICAL SUMMARY. — 1. The fundamental characteristic of Middle Age education was the domination of religious conceptions. The training was for the life to come, rather than for this life; it was almost exclusively religious and moral; was based on authority; and included the whole human race.

2. This alliance of church and school, while giving an exclusive aim to education, also gave it a spirit of intense seriousness and earnestness. The survivals of this historical alliance are church and parish schools, and a disposition of the modern Church to dispute the right of the State to educate.

3. The supreme importance attached to the Scriptures made education literary; made instruction dogmatic and arbitrary; exalted words over things; inculcated a taste for abstract and formal reasoning; made learning a process of memorizing; and stifled the spirit of free inquiry.

4. The inclusion of the whole world in one Christian Commonwealth, led to the intellectual enfranchisement of woman and to the rise of primary education proper.

5. The general tendency was towards harshness in discipline, coarseness in habits and manners, and a contempt for the amenities of life.

6. Scholasticism erred by exaggeration ; but its effect was to develop the power of deductive reaso teach the use of language as the instrument of thou to make apparent the need of nice discriminations in of words.

7. The great intellectual lesson taught is the difficulty of attaining compass, symmetry, and mode

CHAPTER V.

THE RENAISSANCE AND THE THEORIES OF EDUCATION IN THE SIXTEENTH CENTURY.

GENERAL CHARACTERISTICS OF THE EDUCATION OF THE SIXTEENTH CENTURY; CAUSES OF THE RENAISSANCE IN EDUCATION; THE THEORY AND THE PRACTICE OF EDUCATION IN THE SIXTEENTH CENTURY; ERASMUS (1467-1536); EDUCATION OF ERASMUS; THE JEROMITES; PEDAGOGICAL WORKS OF ERASMUS; JUVENILE ETIQUETTE; EARLY EDUCATION; THE INSTRUCTION OF WOMEN; RABELAIS (1483-1553); CRITICISM OF THE OLD EDUCATION; GARGANTUA AND EUDEMON; THE NEW EDUCATION; PHYSICAL EDUCATION; INTELLECTUAL EDUCATION; THE PHYSICAL AND NATURAL SCIENCES; OBJECT LESSONS; ATTRACTIVE METHODS; RELIGIOUS EDUCATION; MORAL EDUCATION; MONTAIGNE (1533-1592) AND RABELAIS; THE PERSONAL EDUCATION OF MONTAIGNE; EDUCATION SHOULD BE GENERAL; THE PURPOSE OF INSTRUCTION; EDUCATION OF THE JUDGMENT; EDUCATIONAL METHODS; STUDIES RECOMMENDED; MONTAIGNE'S ERRORS; INCOMPLETENESS OF HIS VIEWS ON THE EDUCATION OF WOMEN; ANALYTICAL SUMMARY.

92. GENERAL CHARACTERISTICS OF THE EDUCATION OF THE SIXTEENTH CENTURY. — Modern education begins with the Renaissance. The educational methods that we then begin to discern will doubtless not be developed and perfected till a later period; the new doctrines will pass into practice only gradually, and with the general progress of the times. But from the sixteenth century education is in possession of its essential principles. The education of the Middle Age, over-rigid and repressive, which condemned the body to a régime too severe, and the mind to a discipline too narrow, is to be succeeded,

at least in theory, by an education broader and more liberal; which will give due attention to hygiene and physical exercises; which will enfranchise the intelligence, hitherto the prisoner of the syllogism; which will call into play the moral forces, instead of repressing them; which will substitute real studies for the verbal subtilties of dialectics; which will give the preference to things over words; which, finally, instead of developing but a single faculty, the reason, and instead of reducing man to a sort of dialectic automaton, will seek to develop the whole man, mind and body, taste and knowledge, heart and will.

93. Causes of the Renaissance in Education. — The men of the sixteenth century having renewed with classical antiquity an intercourse that had been too long interrupted, it was natural that they should propose to the young the study of the Greeks and the Romans. What is called secondary instruction really dates from the sixteenth century. The crude works of the Middle Age are succeeded by the elegant compositions of Athens and Rome, henceforth made accessible to all through the art of printing; and, with the reading of the ancient authors, there reappear through the fruitful effect of imitation, their qualities of correctness in thought, of literary taste, and of elegance in form. In France, as in Italy, the national tongues, moulded, and, as it were, consecrated by writers of genius, become the instruments of an intellectual propaganda. Artistic taste, revived by the rich products of a race of incomparable artists, gives an extension to the horizon of life, and creates a new class of emotions. Finally, the Protestant Reform develops individual thought and free inquiry, and at the same time, by its success, it imposes still greater efforts on the Catholic Church.

This is not saying that everything is faultless in the educational efforts of the sixteenth century. First, as is natural for innovators, the thought of the teachers of this period is marked by enthusiasm rather than by precision. They are more zealous in pointing out the end to be attained, than exact in determining the means to be employed. Besides, some of them are content to emancipate the mind, but forget to give it proper direction. Finally, others make a wrong use of the ancients ; they are too much preoccupied with the form and the purity of language ; they fall into *Ciceromania*, and it is not their fault if a new superstition, that of rhetoric, does not succeed the old superstition, that of the syllogism.

94. The Theory and the Practice of Education in the Sixteenth Century. — In the history of education in the sixteenth century, we must, moreover, carefully distinguish the theory from the practice. The theory of education is already boldly put forward, and is in advance of its age ; while the practice is still dragging itself painfully along on the beaten road, notwithstanding some successful attempts at improvement.

The theory we must look for in the works of Erasmus, Rabelais, and Montaigne, of whom it may be said, that before pretending to surpass them, even at this day, we should rather attempt to overtake them, and to equal them in the most of their pedagogical precepts.

The practice is, first, the development of the study of the humanities, particularly in the early colleges of the Jesuits, and, before the Jesuits, in certain Protestant colleges, particularly in the college at Strasburg, so brilliantly administered by the celebrated Sturm (1507–1589). Then it is the revival of higher instruction, denoted particularly by the foundation of the College of France (1530), and by the brilliant lectures of Ramus. Finally, it is the progress, we might almost say the birth, of primary instruction, through the efforts of the Protestant reformers, and especially of Luther.

Nevertheless, the educational thought of the sixteenth century is in advance of educational practice; theories greatly anticipate applications, and constitute almost all that is deserving of special note.

95. ERASMUS (1467–1536). — By his numerous writings, translations, grammars, dictionaries, and original works, Erasmus diffused about him his own passionate fondness for classical literature, and communicated this taste to his contemporaries. Without having a direct influence on education, since he scarcely taught himself, he encouraged the study of the ancients by his example, and by his active propagandism. The scholar who said, " When I have money, I will first buy Greek books and then clothes," deserves to be placed in the first rank among the creators of secondary instruction.

96. THE EDUCATION OF ERASMUS: THE JEROMITES. — Erasmus was educated by the monks, as Voltaire was by the Jesuits, a circumstance that has cost these liberal thinkers none of their independent disposition, and none of their satirical spirit. At the age of twelve, Erasmus entered the college of Deventer, in Holland. This college was conducted by the Jeromites, or *Brethren of the Common Life.* Founded in 1340 by Gerard Groot, the association of the Jeromites undertook, among other occupations, the instruction of children. Very mystical, and very ascetic at first, the disciples of Gerard Groot restricted themselves to teaching the Bible, to reading, and writing. They proscribed, as useless to piety, letters and the sciences. But in the fifteenth century, under the influence of John of Wessel and

Rudolph Agricola, the Jeromites became transformed; they were the precursors of the Renaissance, and the promoters of the alliance between profane letters and Christianity. "We may read Ovid once," said John of Wessel, "but we ought to read Virgil, Horace, and Terence, with more attention." Horace and Terence were precisely the favorite authors of Erasmus, who learned them by heart at Deventer. Agricola, of whom Erasmus speaks only with enthusiasm, was also the zealous propagator of the great works of antiquity, and, at the same time, the severe critic of the state of educational practice of the time when the school was too much like a prison.

"If there is anything which has a contradictory name," he said, "it is the school. The Greeks called it $\sigma\chi o\lambda\dot{\eta}$, which means *leisure, recreation;* and the Latins, *ludus,* that is, *play.* But there is nothing farther removed from recreation and play. Aristophanes called it $\phi\rho o\nu\tau\iota\sigma\tau\dot{\eta}\rho\iota o\nu$, that is, *place of care, of torment,* and this is surely the designation which best befits it."

Erasmus then had for his first teachers enlightened men, who, notwithstanding their monastic condition, both knew and loved antiquity. But, as a matter of fact, Erasmus was his own teacher. By personal effort he put himself at the school of the ancients. He was all his life a student. Now he was a foundation scholar at the college of Montaigu, in Paris, and now preceptor to gentlemen of wealth. He was always in pursuit of learning, going over the whole of Europe, that he might find in each cultivated city new opportunities for self-instruction.

97. PEDAGOGICAL WORKS OF ERASMUS. — Most of the works written by Erasmus relate to instruction. Some of them are fairly to be classed as text-books, elementary treatises on practical education, as, for example, his books

On the Manner of writing Letters, Upon Rules of Etiquette for the Young, etc. We may also notice his *Adages*, a vast repertory of proverbs and maxims borrowed from antiquity; his *Colloquies*, a collection of dialogues for the use of the young, though the author here treats of many things which a pupil should never hear spoken of. Another category should include works of a more theoretical character, in which Erasmus sets forth his ideas on education. In the essay *On the Order of Study* (*de Ratione Studii*), he seeks out the rules for instruction in literature, for the study of grammar, for the cultivation of the memory, and for the explication of the Greek and Latin authors. Another treatise, entitled *Of the First Liberal Education of Children* (*De pueris statim ac liberaliter instituendis*), is still more important, and covers the whole field of education. Erasmus here studies the character of the child, the question of knowing whether the first years of child-life can be turned to good account, and the measures that are to be taken with early life. He also recommends methods that are attractive, and heartily condemns the barbarous discipline which reigned in the schools of his time.

98. JUVENILE ETIQUETTE. — Erasmus is one of the first educators who comprehended the importance of politeness. In an age still uncouth, where the manners of even the cultivated classes tolerated usages that the most ignorant rustic of to-day would scorn, it was good to call the attention to outward appearances and the duties of politeness. Erasmus knew perfectly well that politeness has a moral side, that it is not a matter of pure convention, but that it proceeds from the inner disposition of a well-ordered soul. So he assigns it an important place in education :

" The duty of instructing the young," he says, " includes several elements, the first and also the chief of which is, that the tender mind of the child should be instructed in piety; the second, that he love and learn the liberal arts; the third, that he be taught tact in the conduct of social life; and the fourth, that from his earliest age he accustom himself to good behavior, based on moral principles."

We need not be astonished, however, to find that the civility of Erasmus is still imperfect, now too free, now too exacting, and always ingenuous. "It is a religious duty," he says, "to salute him who sneezes." "Morally speaking, it is not a proper thing to throw the head back while drinking, after the manner of storks, in order to drain the last drop from the glass." "If one let bread fall on the ground, he should kiss it after having picked it up." On the other hand, Erasmus seems to allow that the nose may be wiped with the fingers, but he forbids the use of the cap or the sleeve for this purpose. He requires that the face shall be bathed with pure water in the morning; "but," he adds, "to repeat this afterwards is nonsense."

99. EARLY EDUCATION. — Like Quintilian, by whom he is often inspired, Erasmus does not scorn to enter the primary school, and to shape the first exercises for intellectual culture. Upon many points, the thought of the sixteenth century scholar is but an echo of the *Institutes of Oratory*, or of the educational essays of Plutarch. Some of his maxims deserve to be reproduced: "We learn with great willingness from those whom we love;" "Parents themselves cannot properly bring up their children if they make themselves only to be feared;" "There are children who would be killed sooner than made better by blows: by mildness and kind admonitions, one may make of them whatever he will;" "Children will learn to speak their native tongue without any weariness, by usage and practice;" "Drill in reading and writing is a little bit tiresome, and the teacher

will ingeniously palliate the tedium by the artifice of an attractive method;" "The ancients moulded toothsome dainties into the forms of the letters, and thus, as it were, made children swallow the alphabet;" "In the matter of grammatical rules, instruction should at the first be limited to the most simple;" "As the body in infant years is nourished by little portions distributed at intervals, so should the mind of the child be nurtured by items of knowledge adapted to its weakness, and distributed little by little."

From out these quotations there appears a method of instruction that is kindly, lovable, and full of tenderness for the young. Erasmus claims for them the nourishing care and caresses of the mother, the familiarity and goodness of the father, cleanliness, and even elegance in the school, and finally, the mildness and indulgence of the teacher.

100. The Instruction of Women. — The scholars of the Renaissance did not exclude women from all participation in the literary treasures that a recovered antiquity had disclosed to themselves. Erasmus admits them to an equal share.

In the *Colloquy of the Abbé and the Educated Woman*, Magdala claims for herself the right to learn Latin, " so that she may hold converse each day with so many authors who are so eloquent, so instructive, so wise, and such good counsellors." In the book called *Christian Marriage*, Erasmus banters young ladies who learn only to make a bow, to hold the hands crossed, to bite their lips when they laugh, to eat and drink as little as possible at table, after having taken ample portions in private. More ambitious for the wife, Erasmus recommends her to pursue the studies which will assist her in educating her own children, and in taking part in the intellectual life of her husband.

Vives, a contemporary of Erasmus (1492–1540), a Spanish teacher, expressed analogous ideas in his books on the education of women, in which he recommends young women to read Plato and Seneca.

To sum up, the pedagogy of Erasmus is not without value; but with him, education ran the risk of remaining exclusively Greek and Latin. A humanist above everything else, he granted but very small place to the sciences, and to history, which it sufficed to skim over, as he said ; and, what reveals his inmost nature, he recommended the study of the physical sciences for this reason in particular, that the writer will find in the knowledge of nature an abundant source of metaphors, images, and comparisons.

101. RABELAIS (1483–1553). — Wholly different is the spirit of Rabelais, who, under a fanciful and original form, has sketched a complete system of education. Some pages of marked gravity in the midst of the epic vagabondage of his burlesque work, give him the right to appear in the first rank among those who have reformed the art of training and developing the human soul.[1]

The pedagogy of Rabelais is the first appearance of what may be called *realism* in instruction, in distinction from the scholastic *formalism*. The author of *Gargantua* turns the mind of the young man towards objects truly worthy of occupying his attention. He catches a glimpse of the future reserved to scientific education, and to the study of nature. He invites the mind, not to the labored subtilties and complicated tricks which scholasticism had brought into fashion, but to manly efforts, and to a wide unfolding of human nature.

---

[1] See especially the following chapters: Book I. chaps. xiv., xv., xxl, xxii., xxiv.; Book II. chaps. v., vi., vii., viii.

102. CRITICISM OF THE OLD EDUCATION: GARGANTUA AND
EUDEMON. — In the manners of the sixteenth century, the
keen satire of Rabelais found many opportunities for dis-
porting itself ; and his book may be regarded as a collection
of pamphlets. But there is nothing that he has pursued
with more sarcasms than the education of his day.

At the outset, Gargantua is educated according to the
scholastic methods. He works for twenty years with all his
might, and learns so perfectly the books that he studies that
he can recite them by heart, backwards and forwards, "and
yet his father discovered that all this profited him nothing ;
and what is worse, that it made him a madcap, a ninny,
dreamy, and infatuated."

To that unintelligent and artificial training which surcharges the memory, which holds the pupil for long years
over insipid books, which robs the mind of all independent
activity, which dulls rather than sharpens the intelligence, —
to all this Rabelais opposes a natural education, which appeals
to experience and to facts, which trains the young man, not
only for the discussions of the schools, but for real life, and
for intercourse with the world, and which, finally, enriches
the intelligence and adorns the memory without stifling the
native graces and the free activities of the spirit.

Eudemon, who, in Rabelais' romance, represents the pupil
trained by the new methods, knows how to think with accuracy and speak with facility ; his bearing is without boldness, but with confidence. When introduced to Gargantua,
he turns towards him, "cap in hand, with open countenance,
ruddy lips, steady eyes, and with modesty becoming a
youth"; he salutes him elegantly and graciously. To all
the pleasant things which Eudemon says to him, Gargantua
finds nothing to say in reply: "His countenance appeared
as though he had taken to crying immoderately ; he hid his

face in his cap, and not a single word could be drawn from him."

In these two pupils, so different in manner, Rabelais has personified two contrasted methods of education : that which, by mechanical exercises of memory, enfeebles and dulls the intelligence ; and that which, with larger grants of liberty, develops keen intelligences, and frank and open characters.

103. THE NEW EDUCATION. — Let us now notice with some detail how Rabelais conceives this new education.[1] After having thrown into sharp relief the faults contracted by Gargantua in the school of his first teachers, he entrusts him to a preceptor, Ponocrates, who is charged with correcting his faults, and with re-moulding him ; he is to employ his own principles in the government of his pupil.

Ponocrates proceeds slowly at first ; he considers that " nature does not endure sudden changes without great violence." He studies and observes his pupil ; he wishes to judge of his natural disposition. Then he sets himself to work ; he undertakes a general recasting of the character and spirit of Gargantua, while directing, at the same time, his physical, intellectual, and moral education.

104. PHYSICAL EDUCATION. — Hygiene and gymnastics, cleanliness which protects the body, and exercise which strengthens it, — these two essential parts of physical edu-

---

[1] The contrast between the general system of education that culminated with the Reformation, and the system that had its rise at the same period, is so marked that there is an historical propriety in calling the first the old education, and the second, or later, the new education. Recollecting the tendency of the human mind to pass from one extreme to an opposite extreme, we may suspect that the final state of educational thought and practice will represent a mean between these two contrasted systems: it is inconceivable that the old was wholly wrong, or that the new is wholly right. (P.)

cation receive equal attention from Rabelais. Erasmus thought it was nonsense (" *ne rime à rien* ") to wash more than once a day. Gargantua, on the contrary, after eating, bathes his hands and his eyes in fresh water. Rabelais does not forget that he has been a physician ; he omits no detail relative to the care of the body, even the most repugnant. He is far from believing, with the mystics of the Middle Age, that it is permissible to lodge knowledge in a sordid body, and that a foul or neglected exterior is not unbefitting virtuous souls. The first preceptors of Gargantua said that it sufficed to comb one's hair " with the four fingers and the thumb ; and that whoever combed, washed, and cleansed himself otherwise, was losing his time in this world." With Ponocrates, Gargantua reforms his habits, and tries to re-semble Eudemon, " whose hair was so neatly combed, who was so well dressed, of such fine appearance, and was so modest in his bearing, that he much more resembled a little angel than a man."

Rabelais attaches equal importance to gymnastics, to walk-ing, and to active life in the open air. He does not allow Gargantua to grow pale over his books, and to protract his study into the night. After the morning's lessons, he takes him out to play. Tennis and ball follow the application to books : " He exercises his body just as vigorously as he had before exercised his mind." And so, after the study of the afternoon till the supper hour, Gargantua devotes his time to physical exercises. Riding, wrestling, swimming, every species of physical recreation, gymnastics under all its forms, — there is nothing which Gargantua does not do to give agility to his limbs and to strengthen his muscles. Here, as in other places, Rabelais stretches a point, and purposely resorts to exaggeration in order to make his thought better compre-hended. It would require days of several times twenty-four hours, in order that a real man could find the time to do all that the author of Gargantua requires of his giant. In contrast with the long asceticism of the Middle Age, he proposes a real revelry of gymnastics for the colossal body of his hero. We will not forget that here, as in all the other parts of Rabelais' work, fiction is ever mingled with fact. Rabelais wrote for giants, and it is natural that he should demand gigantesque efforts of them. In order to comprehend the exact thought of the author, it is necessary to reduce his fantastic exaggerations to human proportions.

105. INTELLECTUAL EDUCATION. — For the mind, as for the body, Rabelais requires prodigies of activity. Gargantua rises at four in the morning, and the greater part of the long day is filled with study. For the indolent contemplations of the Middle Age, Rabelais substitutes an incessant effort and an intense activity of the mind. Gargantua first studies the ancient languages, and the first place is given to Greek, which Rabelais rescues from the long discredit into which it had fallen in the Middle Age, as is proved by the vulgar adage, " *Græcum est, non legitur.*"

" Now, all disciplines are restored, and the languages reinstated, — Greek (without which it is a shame for a person to call himself learned), Hebrew, Chaldean, Latin. There are very elegant and correct editions in use, which have been invented in my age by divine inspiration, as, on the other hand, artillery was invented by diabolic suggestion. The whole world is full of wise men, of learned teachers, and of very large libraries, and it is my opinion that neither in the time of Plato nor in that of Cicero, nor in that of Papinian, were there such opportunities for study as we see to-day."

Like all his contemporaries, Rabelais is an enthusiast in classical learning ; but he is distinguished from them by a very decided taste for the sciences, and in particular for the natural sciences.

106. THE PHYSICAL AND NATURAL SCIENCES. — The Middle Age had completely neglected the study of nature. The art of observing was ignored by those subtile dialecticians, who would know nothing of the physical world except through the theories of Aristotle or the dogmas of the sacred books ; who attached no value to the study of the material universe, the transient and despised abode of immortal souls ; and who, moreover, flattered themselves that they could discover at the end of their syllogisms all that was necessary to know about it. Rabelais is certainly the first, in point of time, of that grand school of educators who place the sciences in the first rank among the studies worthy of human thought.

The scholar of the Middle Age knew nothing of the world. Gargantua requires of his son that he shall know it under all its aspects :

" As to the knowledge of the facts of nature," he writes to Pantagruel, " I would have you devote yourself to them with great care, so that there shall be neither sea, river, nor fountain, whose fish you do not know. All the birds of the air, all the trees, shrubs, and fruits of the forests, all the grasses of the earth, all the metals concealed in the depths of the abysses, the precious stones of the entire East and South, — none of these should be unknown to you. By frequent dissections, acquire a knowledge of the other world, which is man. In a word, I point out a new world of knowledge."

Nothing is omitted, it is observed, from what constitutes the science of the universe or the knowledge of man.

It is further to be noticed, that Rabelais wishes his pupil not only to know, but to love and experience nature. He recommends his pupils to go and read the *Georgics* of Virgil in the midst of meadows and woods. The precursor of Rousseau on this point as upon some others, he thinks there is a gain in spiritual health by refreshing the imagination and giving repose to the spirit, through the contemplation of the beauties of nature.

Ponocrates, in order to afford Gargantua distraction from his extreme attention to study, recommended once each month some very clear and serene day, on which they set out at an early hour from the city, and went to Chantilly, or Boulogne, or Montrouge, or Pont Charenton, or Vannes, or Saint Cloud. And there they passed the whole day in playing, singing, dancing, frolicking in some fine meadow, hunting for sparrows, collecting pebbles, fishing for frogs and crabs.[1]

107. OBJECT LESSONS. — In the scheme of studies planned by Rabelais, the mind of the pupil is always on the alert, even at table. There, instruction takes place while talking. The conversation bears upon the food, upon the objects which attract the attention of Gargantua, upon the nature and properties of water, wine, bread, and salt. Every sensible object becomes material for questions and explanations. Gargantua often takes walks across fields, and he studies botany in the open country, " passing through meadows or other grassy places, observing trees and plants, comparing them with ancient books where they are described, . . . and taking handfuls of them home." There are but few didactic lessons ; intuitive instruction, given in the presence of the objects themselves, such is the method of Rabelais. It is in the same spirit that he sends his pupil to visit the stores of the silversmiths, the founderies, the alchemists' labora-

---

[1] Book I. chap. xxiv.

tories, and shops of all kinds, — real scientific excursions, such as are in vogue to-day. Rabelais would form a complete man, skilled in art and industry, and also capable, like the *Émile* of Rousseau, of devoting himself to manual labor. When the weather is rainy, and walking impracticable, Gargantua employs his time in splitting and sawing wood, and in threshing grain in the barn.

108. ATTRACTIVE METHODS. — By a reaction against the irksome routine of the Middle Age, Rabelais would have his pupil study while playing, and even learn mathematics " through recreation and amusement." It is in handling playing-cards that Gargantua is taught thousands of " new inventions which relate to the science of numbers." The same course is followed in geometry and astronomy. The accomplishments are not neglected, especially fencing. Gargantua is an enormous man, who is to be developed in all directions. The fine arts, music, painting, and sculpture, are not strangers to him. The hero of Rabelais represents, not so much an individual man, as a collective being who personifies the whole of society, with all the variety of its new aspirations, and with all the intensity of its multiplied needs. While the Middle Age, through a narrow spirit, left in inaction certain natural tendencies, Rabelais calls them all into life, without choice, it is true, and without discrimination, with the whole ardor of an emancipated imagination.

109. RELIGIOUS EDUCATION. — In respect of religion as of everything else, Rabelais is the adversary of an education wholly exterior and of pure form. He ridicules his Gargantua, who, before his intellectual conversion, when he was still at the school of " his preceptors, the sophists," goes to church, after a hearty dinner, to hear twenty-six or thirty masses. What he substitutes for this exterior devotion, for

this abuse of superficial practices, is a real feeling of piety, and the direct reading of the sacred texts: " It is while Gargantua was being dressed that there was read to him a page of Divine Scripture."[1] Still more, it is the intimate and personal adoration " of the great psalmodist of the universe," excited by the study of the works of God. Gargantua and his master, Ponocrates, have scarcely risen when they observe the state of the heavens, and admire the celestial vault. In the evening they devote themselves to the same contemplation. After his meals, as before going to sleep, Gargantua offers prayers to God, to adore Him, to confirm his faith, to glorify Him for His boundless goodness, to thank Him for all the time past, and to recommend himself to Him for the time to come. The religious feeling of Rabelais proceeds at the same time, both from the sentiment which provoked the Protestant Reformation, of which he came near being an adherent, and from tendencies still more modern, — those, for example, which animate the deistic philosophy of Rousseau.

110. MORAL EDUCATION. — Those who know Rabelais only by reputation, or through some of his innumerable drolleries, will perhaps be astonished that the jovial author can be counted a teacher of morals. It is impossible, however, to misunderstand the sincere and lofty inspiration of such passages as this :

" Because, according to the wise Solomon, wisdom does not enter into a malevolent soul, and knowledge without conscience is but the ruin of the soul ; it becomes you to serve, to love, and to fear God, and to place on Him all your thoughts,

---

[1] Rabelais recommends the study of Hebrew, so that the sacred books may be known in their original form. In some place he says: " I love much more to hear the Gospel than to hear the life of Saint Margaret or some other cant."

all your hopes. . . . Be suspicious of the errors of the world. Apply not your heart to vanity, for this life is transitory; but the word of God endures forever. Be useful to all your neighbors, and love them as yourself. Revere your teachers, flee the company of men whom you would not resemble; and the grace which God has given you receive not in vain. And when you think you have all the knowledge that can be acquired by this means, return to me, so that I may see you, and give you my benediction before I die."[1]

111. MONTAIGNE (1533–1592) AND RABELAIS. — Between Erasmus, the learned humanist, exclusively devoted to belles-lettres, and Rabelais, the bold innovator, who extends as far as possible the limits of the intelligence, and who causes the entire encyclopædia of human knowledge to enter the brain of his pupil at the risk of splitting it open, Montaigne occupies an intermediate place, with his circumspect and conservative tendencies, with his discreet and moderate pedagogy, the enemy of all excesses. It seemed that Rabelais would develop all the faculties equally, and place all studies, letters, and sciences upon the same footing. Montaigne demands a choice. Between the different faculties he attempts particularly to train the judgment; among the different knowledges, he recommends by preference those which form sound and sensible minds. Rabelais overdrives mind and body. He dreams of an extravagant course of instruction where every science shall be studied exhaustively.[2]

---

[1] Book II. chap. VIII.

[2] This pansophic scheme of Rabelais has been revived in later times by Bentham, in his *Chrestomathia*, and still later by Spencer, in his *Education*. It seems to have been forgotten that the division of labor affects education in much the same way as it affects all other departments of human activity: that there is no more need of having as a personal possession all the knowledge we need for guidance, than for owning all the agencies we need for locomotion or communication. (P.)

Montaigne simply demands that "one taste the upper crust of the sciences"; that one skim over them without going into them deeply, "in French fashion." In his view, a well-made head is worth more than a head well filled. It is not so much to accumulate, to amass, knowledge, as to assimilate as much of it as a prudent intelligence can digest without fatigue. In a word, while Rabelais sits down, so to speak, at the banquet of knowledge with an avidity which recalls the gluttony of the Pantagruelian repasts, Montaigne is a delicate connoisseur, who would only satisfy with discretion a regulated appetite.

112. THE PERSONAL EDUCATION OF MONTAIGNE. — One often becomes teacher through recollection of his personal education. This is what happened to Montaigne. His pedagogy is at once an imitation of the methods which a father full of solicitude had himself applied to him, and a protest against the defects and the vices of the college of Guienne, which he entered at the age of six years. The home education of Montaigne affords the interesting spectacle of a child who develops freely. My spirit, he himself says, was trained with all gentleness and freedom, without severity or constraint. His father, skilful in his tender care, had him awakened each morning at the sound of musical instruments, so as to spare him those brusque alarms that are bad preparations for toil. In a word, he applied to him that tempered discipline, at once indulgent and firm, equally removed from complacency and harshness, which Montaigne has christened with the name of *severe mildness*. Another characteristic of Montaigne's education is, that he learned Latin as one learns his native tongue. His father had surrounded him with domestics and teachers who conversed with him only in Latin. The result of this was, that at the age of six he was so proficient in the language of Cicero, that the best

Latinists of the time feared to address him (*craignissent à l'accoster*). On the other hand, he knew no more of French than he did of Arabic.[1] It is evident that Montaigne's father had taken a false route, but at least Montaigne derived a just conception from this experience, namely, that the methods ordinarily pursued in the study of the dead languages are too slow and too mechanical; that an abuse is made of rules, and that sufficient attention is not given to practice: " No doubt but *Greek* and *Latin* are very great ornaments, and of very great use, but we buy them too dear."[2]

At the college of Guienne, where he passed seven years, Montaigne learned to detest corporal chastisements and the hard discipline of the scholars of his day : " . . . Instead of tempting and alluring children to letters by apt and gentle ways, our pedants do in truth present nothing before them but rods and ferules, horror and cruelty. Away with this violence ! away with this compulsion ! than which, I certainly believe, nothing more dulls and degenerates a well-descended nature. . . . The strict government of most of our colleges has evermore displeased me. . . . 'Tis the true house of correction of imprisoned youth. . . . Do but come in when they are about their lesson, and you shall hear nothing but the outcries of boys under execution, with the thundering noise of their *Pedagogues*, drunk with fury, to make up the consort. A pretty way this ! to tempt these tender and timorous souls to love their book, with a furious countenance, and a rod in hand. A cursed and pernicious way of

---

[1] " I was above six years of age before I understood either *French* or *Perigordian* any more than Arabic, and without art, book, grammar, or precept, whipping, or the experience of a tear, had by that time learned to speak as pure *Latin* as my master himself." *Essays*, Book I. chap. xxv. In this chapter I have several times quoted from Cotton's translation. (London: 1711.) (P.)

[2] Book I. chap. xxv.

proceeding. . . . How much more decent would it be to see their classes strewed with green leaves and fine flowers, than with bloody stumps of birch and willows? Were it left to my ordering, I should paint the school with the pictures of Joy and Gladness, Flora and the Graces . . . that where their profit is, they might have their pleasure too." [1]

113. IMPORTANCE OF A GENERAL RATHER THAN A SPECIAL EDUCATION. — If Montaigne, in different chapters of his essays,[2] has given passing attention to pedagogical questions, it is not only through a recollection of his own years of apprenticeship, but also because of his judgment as a philosopher, that " the greatest and most important task of human understanding is in those matters which concern the nurture and instruction of children."

For him, education is the art of forming men, and not specialists. This he explains in his original manner under the form of an anecdote :

" Going to Orleans one day, I met in that plain this side Clery, two pedants who were going towards Bordeaux, about fifty paces distant from one another. Still further back of them, I saw a troop of horse, and at their head a gentleman who was the late Count de la Rochefoucault. One of my company inquired of the foremost of these dominies, who that gentleman was who was following him. He had not observed the train that was following after, and thought that the question related to his companion ; and so he replied pleasantly, ' He is not a gentleman, but a grammarian, and I am a logician.' Now, as we are here concerned in the training, not of a grammarian, or of a logician, but of a

---

[1] Book I. chap. xxv.

[2] See particularly Chap. xxiv. of Book I., *Of Pedantry ;* Chap. xxv. Book I., *Of the Education of Children ;* Chap. viii. Book II., *Of the Affection of Fathers to their Children.*

complete gentleman, we will let those who will abuse their leisure ; but we have business of another nature." [1]

It is true that Montaigne says gentleman, and not simply man ; but in reality his thought is the same as that of Rousseau and of all those who require a general education of the human soul.

114. THE PURPOSE OF INSTRUCTION. — From what has now been said, it is easy to comprehend that, in the opinion of Montaigne, letters and other studies are but the means or instrument, and not the aim and end of instruction. The author of the *Essays* does not yield to the literary craze, which, in the sixteenth century, took certain scholars captive, and made the ideal of education to consist of a knowledge of the ancient languages. It is of little consequence to him that a pupil has learned to write in Latin ; what he does require, is that he become better and more prudent, and have a sounder judgment. " If his soul be not put into better rhythm, if the judgment be not better settled, I would rather have him spend his time at tennis." [2]

115. EDUCATION OF THE JUDGMENT. — Montaigne has expressed his dominant thought on education in a hundred different ways. He is preoccupied with the training of the judgment, and on this point we might quote whole pages :

" . . . According to the fashion in which we are instructed, it is not singular that neither scholars nor masters become more able, although they become more wise. In fact, our parents devote their care and expense to furnishing our heads with knowledge ; but to judgment and virtue no additions are made. Say of a passer-by to people, ' O what a learned man ! ' and of another, ' O what a good man goes there ! ' and they will not fail to turn their eyes and attention towards

---

[1] Book I. chap. xxv.   [2] Book I. chap. xxiv.

the former. There should be a third to cry, 'O the block-heads!' Men are quick to inquire, 'Does he know Greek or Latin? Does he write in verse or in prose?' But whether he has become better or more prudent, which is the principal thing, this receives not the least notice; whereas we ought to inquire who is the better learned, rather than who is the more learned?"

"We labor only at filling the memory, and leave the understanding and the conscience void. Just as birds sometimes go in quest of grain, and bring it in their bills without tasting it themselves, to make of it mouthfuls for their young; so our pedants go rummaging in books for knowledge, only to hold it at their tongues' end, and then distribute it to their pupils."[1]

116. STUDIES RECOMMENDED. — The practical and utilitarian mind of Montaigne dictates to him his programme of studies. With him it is not a question of plunging into the depths of the sciences; disinterested studies are not his affair. If Rabelais proposed to develop the speculative faculties, Montaigne, on the contrary, is preoccupied with the practical faculties, and he makes everything subordinate to morals. For example, he would have history learned, not for the sake of knowing the facts, but of appreciating them. It is not so necessary to imprint in the memory of the child "the date of the fall of Carthage as the character of Hannibal and Scipio, nor so much where Marcellus died as why it was unworthy of his duty that he died there."[2]

And so in philosophy, it is not the general knowledge of man and nature that Montaigne esteems and recommends; but only those parts that have a direct bearing on morals and active life.

---

[1] Book I. chap. xxiv.   [2] Book I. chap. xxv.

" It is a pity that matters should be at such a pass as they are in our time, that philosophy, even with people of understanding, should be looked upon as a vain and fanciful name, a thing of no use and no value, either for opinion or for action. I think that it is the love of quibbling that has caused things to take this turn. . . . Philosophy is that which teaches us to live." [1]

117. EDUCATIONAL METHODS. — An education purely bookish is not to Montaigne's taste. He counts less upon books than upon experience and mingling with men ; upon the observation of things, and upon the natural suggestions of the mind :

" For learning to judge well and speak well, whatever presents itself to our eyes serves as a sufficient book. The knavery of a page, the blunder of a servant, a table witticism, — all such things are so many new things to think about. And for this purpose conversation with men is wonderfully helpful, and so is a visit to foreign lands . . . to bring back the customs of those nations, and their manners, and to whet and sharpen our wits by rubbing them upon those of others."

". . . The lesson will be given, sometimes by conversation, sometimes by book. . . . Let the child examine every man's talent, a peasant, a mason, a passer-by. Put into his head an honest curiosity in everything. Let him observe whatever is curious in his surroundings, — a fine house, a delicate fountain, an eminent man, the scene of an ancient battle, the routes of Cæsar, or of Charlemagne. . . ." [1]

Things should precede words. On this point Montaigne anticipates Comenius, Rousseau, and all modern educators.

---

[1] Book I. chap. xxv.

" Let our pupil be provided with things; words will follow only too fast."[1]

" The world is given to babbling ; I hardly ever saw a man who did not rather prate too much, than speak too little. Yet the half of our life goes in that way ; we are kept four or five years in learning words. . . ."[2]

" This is not saying that it is not a fine and good thing to speak well; but not so good as it is made out to be. I am vexed that our life is so much occupied with all this."

118. How we should read. — Montaigne has keenly criticised the abuse of books : " I would not have this boy of ours imprisoned, and made a slave to his book. . . . I would not have his spirit cow'd and subdu'd by applying him to the rack, and tormenting him, as some do, fourteen or fifteen hours a day, and so make a pack-horse of him. Neither should I think it good, when, by a solitary and melancholic complexion, he is discovered to be much addicted to his book, to nourish that humor in him, for that renders them unfit for civil conversation, and diverts them from better employments."[3]

But while he advises against excess in reading, he has admirably defined the manner in which we ought to read. Above all, he says, let us assimilate and appropriate what we read. Let the work of the reader resemble that of bees, that, on this side and on that, tap the flowers for their sweet

---

[1] Has not this extravagant preference for things, as distinguished from words, become a new superstition in educational theory? Considering the misuse made of words by Scholasticism, it was time for Montaigne to summon the attention outwards to sensible realities; but it is more than doubtful whether there is any valid ground for the absolute rule of modern pedagogy, " first the idea, then the term." In actual experience, there is no invariable sequence. The really important thing is, that *terms be made significant.* (P.)

[2] Book I. chap. xxv.

[3] Book I. chap. xxv.

juices, and make them into honey, which is no longer thyme nor marjoram. In other terms, we should read with reflection, and with a critical spirit, while mastering the thoughts of the author by our personal judgment, without ever becoming slaves to them.

119. MONTAIGNE'S ERRORS. — Montaigne's greatest fault, it must be confessed, is that he is somewhat heartless. Somewhat of an egoist and Epicurean, he celebrates only the easy virtues that are attained " by shady routes through green meadows and fragrant flowers." Has he himself ever performed painful duties that demand effort? To love children, he waits till they are amiable ; while they are small, he disdains them, and keeps them at a distance from him :

" I cannot entertain that passion of dandling and caressing an infant, scarcely born, having as yet neither motion of soul nor shape of body distinguishable, by which they can render themselves amiable ; and have not suffered them to be nursed near me. . . ." [1] " Never take, and, still less, never give, to the women of your household the care of the feeding of your children ! "

Montaigne joined precept to example. He somewhere says unfeelingly : " My children all died while at nurse." [2] He goes so far as to say that a man of letters ought to prefer

---

[1] Book II. chap. VIII.

[2] I am not sure that this remark does not do Montaigne injustice, especially when we consider the connection in which the original remark is made: " I am of opinion that what is not to be done by reason, prudence, and address, is never to be effected by force. I myself was brought up after that manner; and they tell me that, in all my first age, I never felt the rod but twice, and then very easily. I have practised the same method with my children, who all of them dy'd at nurse; but Leonora, my only daughter, is arrived to the age of six years and upwards without other correction for her childish faults than words only, and those very gentle." Book II. chap. VIII. (P.)

his writings to his children : " The births of our intelligence are the children the most truly our own." [1]

120. INCOMPLETENESS OF HIS VIEWS ON THE EDUCATION OF WOMEN. — Another mental defect in Montaigne is, that, by reason of his moderation and conservatism, he remains a little narrow. High conceptions of human destiny are not to be expected of him ; his manner of conceiving of it is mean and commonplace. This lack of intellectual breadth is especially manifest in his reflections on the education of women. Montaigne is of that number, who, through false gallantry, would keep woman in a state of ignorance on the pretext that instruction would mar her natural charms. In their case, he would prohibit even the study of rhetoric, because, he says, that would " conceal her charms under borrowed charms." Women should be content with the advantages which their sex assures to them. With the knowledge which they naturally have, " they command with the switch, and rule both the regents and the schools." However, he afterwards thinks better of it ; but in his concessions there is more of contempt than in his prohibitions : " If, however, it displeases them to make us any concessions whatever, and they are determined, through curiosity, to know something of books, poetry is an amusement befitting their needs ; for it is a wanton, crafty art, disguised, all for pleasure, all for show, just as they are." [2]

The following passage may also be quoted : —

" When I see them tampering with rhetoric, law, logic, and the like, so improper and unnecessary for their business, I begin to suspect that the men who inspire them with such things do it that they may govern them upon that account." [3]

---

[1] Book III. chap. XIII.   [2] Book III. chap. III.
[3] Book III. chap. III.

It is impossible to express a greater contempt for women. Montaigne goes so far as to deny her positive qualities of heart. He chances to say, with reference to Mlle. de Gournay, his adopted daughter: "The perfection of the most saintly affection has been attained when it does not exhibit the least trace of sex."

To conclude: notwithstanding some grave defects, the pedagogy of Montaigne is a pedagogy of good sense, and certain parts of it will always deserve to be admired. The Jansenists, and Locke, and Rousseau, in different degrees, draw their inspiration from Montaigne. In his own age, it is true, his ideas were accepted by scarcely any one save his disciple Charron, who, in his book of *Wisdom*,[1] has done scarcely more than to arrange in order the thoughts that are scattered through the *Essays*. But if he had no influence upon his own age, Montaigne has at least remained, after three centuries, a sure guide in the matter of intellectual education.

[121. ANALYTICAL SUMMARY. — 1. The dominant characteristic of education during the Renaissance period is the reaction which it exhibits against certain errors in Middle Age education.

2. A second characteristic is a disposition to conciliate or harmonize principles and methods whose fault is exaggeration.

3. Against instruction based almost wholly on authority, there is a reaction in favor of free inquiry.

4. Opposed to an education of the professional or technical type, there is proposed an education of the general or liberal type.

---

[1] See particularly Chap. XIV. of Book III.

5. From being almost exclusively ethical and religious, education tends to become secular.

6. Didactic, formal instruction out of books, dealing in second-hand knowledge, is succeeded by informal, intuitive instruction from natural objects, dealing in knowledge at first hand.

7. The conception that education is a process of manufacture begins to give place to the conception that it is a process of growth.

8. Teaching whose purpose was information is succeeded by teaching whose purpose is formation, discipline, or training.

9. A discipline that was harsh and cruel is succeeded by a discipline comparatively mild and humane; and manners that were rude and coarse, are followed by a finer code of civility.]

CHAPTER VI.

PROTESTANTISM AND PRIMARY INSTRUCTION. — LUTHER AND COMENIUS.

122. ORIGIN OF PRIMARY INSTRUCTION. — With La Salle and the foundation of the Institute of the Brethren of the Christian Schools, the historian of education recognizes the Catholic origin of primary instruction; in the decrees and laws of the French Revolution, its lay and philosophical origin; but it is to the Protestant Reformers, — to Luther in the sixteenth century, and to Comenius in the seventeenth — that must be ascribed the honor of having first organized schools for the people. In its origin, the primary school is the child of Protestantism, and its cradle was the Reformation.

123. SPIRIT OF THE PROTESTANT REFORM. — The development of primary instruction was the logical consequence of the fundamental principles of the Protestant Reform. As Michel Bréal has said: "In making man responsible for his own faith, and in placing the source of that faith in the Holy Scriptures, the Reform contracted the obligation to put each one in a condition to save himself by the reading and the understanding of the Bible. . . . The necessity of explaining the Catechism, and making comments on it, was for teachers an obligation to learn how to expound a thought, and to decompose it into its elements. The study of the mother tongue and of singing, was associated with the reading of the Bible (translated into German by Luther) and with religious services." The Reform, then, contained, in germ, a complete revolution in education; it enlisted the interests of religion in the service of instruction, and associated knowledge with faith. This is the reason that, for three centuries, the Protestant nations have led humanity in the matter of primary instruction.

124. CALVIN (1509–1564), MELANCTHON (1497–1560), ZWINGLI (1484–1532). — However, all the Protestant Reformers were far from exhibiting the same zeal in behalf of primary instruction. Calvin, absorbed in religious struggles and polemics, was not occupied with the organization of schools till towards the close of his life, and even the college that he founded at Geneva, in 1559, was scarcely more than a school for the study of Latin. Melancthon, who has been called "the preceptor of Germany," worked more for high schools than for schools for the people. He was above all else a professor of Belles-Lettres; and it was with chagrin that he saw his courses in the University of Wittenberg deserted by students when he lectured on the *Olynthiacs* of

Demosthenes. Before Calvin and Melancthon, the Swiss reformer Zwingli had shown his great interest in primary teaching, in his little book " upon the manner of instructing and bringing up boys in a Christian way " (1524). In this he recommended natural history, arithmetic, and also exercises in fencing, in order to furnish the country with timely defenders.

125. LUTHER (1483-1546). The German reformer Luther is, of all his co-religionists, the one who has served the cause of elementary instruction with the most ardor. He not only addressed a pressing appeal to the ruling classes in behalf of founding schools for the people, but, by his influence, methods of instruction were improved, and the educational spirit was renewed in accordance with the principles of Protestantism. " Spontaneity," it has been said, not without some exaggeration, " free thought, and free inquiry, are the basis of Protestantism ; where it has reigned, there have disappeared the method of repeating and of learning by heart without reflection, mechanism, subjection to authority, the paralysis of the intelligence oppressed by dogmatic instruction, and science put in tutelage by the beliefs of the Church." [1]

126. APPEAL ADDRESSED TO THE MAGISTRATES AND LEGISLATORS OF GERMANY. — In 1524, Luther, in a special document addressed to the public authorities of Germany, forcibly expressed himself against the neglect into which the interests of instruction had fallen. This appeal has this characteristic, that the great reformer, while assuming that the Church is the mother of the school, seems especially to count on the secular arm, upon the power of the people, to serve his pur-

---

[1] Dittes, *op. cit.* p. 127.

poses in the cause of universal instruction. "Each city," he said, "is subjected to great expense every year for the construction of roads, for fortifying its ramparts, and for buying arms and equipping soldiers. Why should it not spend an equal sum for the support of one or two school-masters? The prosperity of a city does not depend solely on its natural riches, on the solidity of its walls, on the elegance of its mansions, and on the abundance of arms in its arsenals ; but the safety and strength of a city reside above all in a good education, which furnishes it with instructed, reasonable, honorable, and well-trained citizens."[1]

127. DOUBLE UTILITY OF INSTRUCTION. — A remarkable fact about Luther is, that as a preacher of instruction, he does not speak merely from the religious point of view. After having recommended schools as institutions auxiliary to the Church, he makes a resolute argument from the human point of view. "Were there neither soul, heaven, nor hell," he says, "it would still be necessary to have schools for the sake of affairs here below, as the history of the Greeks and the Romans plainly teaches. The world has need of educated men and women, to the end that the men may govern the country properly, and that the women may properly bring up their children, care for their domestics, and direct the affairs of their households."

128. NECESSITY OF PUBLIC INSTRUCTION. — The objection will perhaps be made, says Luther, that for the education of

---

[1] Luther's argument for compulsion should not be omitted: "It is my opinion that the authorities are bound to force their subjects to send their children to school. . . . If they can oblige their able-bodied subjects to carry the lance and the arquebuse, to mount the ramparts, and to do complete military service, for a much better reason may they, and ought they, to force their subjects to send their children to school, for here it is the question of a much more terrible war with the devil." (P.)

children the home is sufficient, and that the school is useless. " To this I reply : We clearly see how the boys and girls are educated who remain at home." He then shows that they are ignorant and " stupid," incapable of taking part in conversation, of giving good advice, and without any experience of life ; while, if they had been educated in the schools, by teachers who could give instruction in the languages, in the arts, and in history, they might in a little time gather up within themselves, as in a mirror, the experience of whatever has happened since the beginning of the world ; and from this experience, he adds, they would derive the wisdom they need for self-direction and for giving wise counsel to others.

129. CRITICISM OF THE SCHOOLS OF THE PERIOD. — But since there must be public schools, can we not be content with those which already exist? Luther replies by proving that parents neglect to send their children to them, and by denouncing the uselessness of the results obtained by those who attend them. " We find people," he says, " who serve God in strange ways. They fast and wear coarse clothing, but they pass blindly by the true divine service of the home, — they do not know how to bring up their children. . . . Believe me, it is much more necessary to give attention to your children and to provide for their education than to purchase indulgencies, to visit foreign churches, or to make solemn vows. . . . All people, especially the Jews, oblige their children to go to school more than Christians do. This is why the state of Christianity is so low, for all its force and power are in the rising generation ; and if these are neglected, there will be Christian churches like a garden that has been neglected in the spring-time. . . . Every day children are born and are growing up, and, unfortunately, no one cares for the poor young people, no one thinks to train them ;

they are allowed to go as they will. Was it not lamentable to see a lad study in twenty years and more only just enough bad Latin to enable him to become a priest, and to go to mass? And he who attained to this was counted a very happy being! Right happy the mother who bore such a child! And he has remained all his life a poor unlettered man. Everywhere we have seen such teachers and masters, who knew nothing themselves and could teach nothing that was good and useful; they did not even know how to learn and to teach. Has anything else been learned up to this time in the high schools and in the convents except to become asses and blockheads? . . . "

130. ORGANIZATION OF THE NEW SCHOOLS. — So Luther resolves on the organization of new schools. The cost of their maintenance he makes a charge on the public treasury; he demonstrates to parents the moral obligation to have their children instructed in them; to the duty of conscience he adds civil obligation; and, finally, he gives his thought to the means of recruiting the teaching service. '' Since the greatest evil in every place is the lack of teachers, we must not wait till they come forward of themselves; we must take the trouble to educate them and prepare them." To this end Luther keeps the best of the pupils, boys and girls, for a longer time in school; gives them special instructors, and opens libraries for their use. In his thought he never distinguishes women teachers from men teachers; he wants schools for girls as well as for boys. Only, not to burden parents and divert children from their daily labor, he requires but little time for school duties. '' You ask: Is it possible to get along without our children, and bring them up like gentlemen? Is it not necessary that they work at home? I reply: I by no means approve of those schools where a child was accustomed to pass twenty or thirty years

in studying Donatus or Alexander[1] without learning anything. Another world has dawned, in which things go
differently. My opinion is that we must send the boys to
school one or two hours a day, and have them learn a trade
at home for the rest of the time. It is desirable that these
two occupations march side by side. As it now is, children
certainly spend twice as much time in playing ball, running
the streets, and playing truant. And so the girls can
equally well devote nearly the same time to school, without
neglecting their home duties ; they lose more time than this
in over-sleeping and in dancing more than is meet."

131. PROGRAMME OF STUDIES. — Luther gives the first
place to the teaching of religion : " Is it not reasonable that
every Christian should know the Gospel at the age of nine
or ten ? "

Then come the languages, not, as might be hoped, the
mother tongue, but the learned languages, Latin, Greek, and
Hebrew. Luther had not yet been sufficiently rid of the old
spirit to comprehend that the language of the people ought
to be the basis of universal instruction. He left to Comenius
the glory of making the final separation of the primary
school from the Latin school. But yet, Luther gave excellent advice for the study of languages, which must be
learned, he said, less in the abstract rules of grammar than
in their concrete reality.

Luther recommends the mathematics, and also the study
of nature ; but he has a partiality for history and historians,

---

[1] Names for treatises on grammar and philosophy respectively. Donatus
was a celebrated grammarian and rhetorician who taught at Rome in the
middle of the fourth century A.D.; and Alexander, a celebrated Greek com-
mentator on the writings of Aristotle, who taught the Peripatetic philosophy at Athens in the end of the second and the beginning of the third centuries A.D. (P.)

who are, he says, "the best people and the best teachers," on the condition that they do not tamper with the truth, and that "they do not make obscure the work of God."

Of the liberal arts of the Middle Age, Luther does not make much account. He rightly says of dialectics, that it is no equivalent for real knowledge, and that it is simply "an instrument by which we render to ourselves an account of what we know."

Physical exercises are not forgotten in Luther's pedagogical regulations. But he attaches an especial importance to singing. "Unless a schoolmaster know how to sing, I think him of no account." "Music," he says again, "is a half discipline which makes men more indulgent and more mild."

132. PROGRESS IN METHODS. — At the same time that he extends the programme of studies, Luther introduces a new spirit into methods. He wishes more liberty and more joy in the school.

"Solomon," he says, "is a truly royal schoolmaster. He does not, like the monks, forbid the young to go into the world and be happy. Even as Anselm said: 'A young man turned aside from the world is like a young tree made to grow in a vase.' The monks have imprisoned young men like birds in their cage. It is dangerous to isolate the young. It is necessary, on the contrary, to allow young people to hear, see, and learn all sorts of things, while all the time observing the restraints and the rules of honor. Enjoyment and recreation are as necessary for children as food and drink. The schools till now were veritable prisons and hells, and the schoolmaster a tyrant. . . . A child intimidated by bad treatment is irresolute in all he does. He who has trembled before his parents will tremble all his life at the sound of a leaf which rustles in the wind."

These quotations will suffice to make appreciated the large and liberal spirit of Luther, and the range of his thought as an educator. No one has more extolled the office of the teacher, of which he said, when comparing it to preaching, it is the work of all others the noblest, the most useful, and the best; " and yet," he added, " I do not know which of these two professions is the better."

Do not let ourselves imagine, however, that Luther at once exercised a decisive influence on the current education of his day. A few schools were founded, called writing schools; but the Thirty Years' War, and other events, interrupted the movement of which Luther has the honor of having been the originator.

133. THE STATES GENERAL OF ORLEANS (1560). — While in Germany, under the impulse of Luther, primary schools began to be established, France remained in the background. Let us note, however, the desires expressed by the States General of Orleans, in 1560 : —

" May it please the king," it was said in the memorial of the nobility, " to levy a contribution upon the church reve- nues for the reasonable support of teachers and men of learning in every city and village, for the instruction of the needy youth of the country ; and let all parents be required, under penalty of a fine, to send their children to school, and let them be constrained to observe this law by the lords and the ordinary magistrates."

It was demanded, in addition, that public lectures be given on the Sacred Scriptures in *intelligible language*, that is, in the mother tongue. But these demands, so earnest and democratic, of the Protestant nobility of sixteenth century France, were not regarded. With the fall of Protestantism, the cause of primary instruction in France was doomed to a long eclipse. The nobles of the seventeenth and eighteenth

centuries did not think of petitioning again for the education
of the people, and Diderot could truthfully say of them:
" The nobility complain of the farm laborers who know how
to read.   Perhaps the chief grievance of the nobility reduces
itself to this : that a peasant who knows how to read is more
difficult to oppress than another."

134.   RATICH (1571–1635). — In the first half of the
seventeenth century, Ratich, a German, and Comenius, a
Slave, were, with very different degrees of merit, the heirs
of the educational thought of Luther.

With something of the charlatan and the demagogue,
Ratich devoted his life to propagating a novel art of teaching,
which he called *didactics*, and to which he attributed marvels.
He pretended, by his *method of languages*, to teach Hebrew,
Greek, and Latin, in six months.   But nevertheless, out of
many strange performances and lofty promises, there issue
some thoughts of practical value.   The first merit of Ratich
was to give the mother tongue, the German language, the
precedence over the ancient languages.   An English educational writer, Mr. R. H. Quick, in his *Essays on Educational
Reformers* (1874), has thus summed up the essential principles of the pedagogy of Ratich: 1. Everything should be
taught in its own time and order, and according to the natural
method, in passing from the more easy to the more difficult.
2. Only one thing should be learned at a time.   " We do not
cook at the same time in one pot, soup, meat, fish, milk, and
vegetables."   3. The same thing should be repeated several
times.   4. By means of these frequent repetitions, the pupil
will have nothing to learn by heart.   5. All school-books
should be written on the same plan.   6. The thing as a whole
should be made known before the thing in its details, and
the sequence should be from the general to the special.
7. In every case we should proceed by induction and experi-

ment. Ratich especially means by this that we must make an end of mere authority, and of the testimony of the ancients, and must appeal to individual reason. 8. Finally, everything should be learned without coercion. Coercion and the rod are contrary to nature, and disgust the young with study. The human understanding learns with pleasure all that it ought to retain. It does not seem that Ratich knew how to draw from these principles, which, by the way, are not true save under certain corrections, all the happy results that are contained in them. He left to Comenius the glory of applying the new spirit to actual practice.

135. COMENIUS (1592–1671). — For a long time unknown and unappreciated, Comenius has finally received from our contemporaries the admiration that is due him. Michelet speaks of him with enthusiasm as " that rare genius, that gentle, fertile, universal scholar " ;[1] and he calls him the first evangelist of modern pedagogy, Pestalozzi being the second. It is easy to justify this appreciation. The character of Comenius equals his intelligence. Through a thousand obstacles he devoted his long life to the work of popular instruction. With a generous ardor he consecrated himself to infancy. He wrote twenty works and taught in twenty cities. Moreover, he was the first to form a definite conception of what the elementary studies should be. He determined, nearly three hundred years ago, with an exactness that leaves nothing to be desired. the division of the different grades of instruction. He exactly defined some of the essential laws of the art of teaching. He applied to pedagogy, with remarkable insight, the principles of modern logic. Finally, as Michelet has said, he was the Galileo, we would rather say, the Bacon, of modern education.

---

[1] Michelet, *Nos fils*, p. 175 *et seq.*

136. BACONIAN INSPIRATION. — The special aims of pedagogy are essentially related to the general aims of science.
All progress in science has its corresponding effects on education. When an innovator has modified the laws for the
discovery of truth, other innovators appear, who modify, in
their turn, the rules for instruction. To a new logic almost
necessarily corresponds a new pedagogy.

Now Bacon, at the opening of the seventeenth century,
had opened unknown routes to scientific investigation. For
the abstract processes of thought, for the barren comparison
of propositions and words, in which the whole art of the
syllogism consisted, the author of the *Novum Organum* had
substituted the concrete study of reality, the living and
fruitful observation of nature. The mechanism of deductive reasoning was replaced by the slow and patient interpretation of facts. It no longer answered to analyze with
docile spirit principles that were assumed, right or wrong, as
absolute truths ; nor to become expert in handling the syllogism, which, like a mill running dry, often produced but
little flour. It was now necessary to open the eyes to the
contemplation of the universe, and by sense intuition, by
observation, by experiment, and by induction, to penetrate
its secrets, and determine its laws. It was necessary to
ascend, step by step, from the knowledge of the simplest
things to the discovery of the most general laws ; and,
finally, to demand of nature herself to reveal all that the
human intelligence, in its solitary meditations, is powerless
to discover.

Looking at this subject more closely, this revolution in
science, so important from the point of view of speculative
inquiry, and destined to change the aspect of the sciences,
also contained in itself a revolution in education. For this
purpose, all that was needed was to apply to the develop-

ment of the intelligence and to the communication of knowledge the rules proposed by Bacon for the investigation of
truth. The laws of scientific induction might become the
laws for the education of the soul. No more setting out
with abstract principles, imposed by authority; but facts
intuitively apprehended, gathered by observation and veri-
fied by experiment; the order of nature faithfully followed;
a cautious progression from the simplest and most elementary ideas to the most difficult and most complex truths;
the knowledge of things instead of an analysis of words, —
such was to be the character of the new system of instruction. In other terms, it was possible to make the child follow, in order to lead him to know and to comprehend the
capitalized truths that constitute the basis of elementary
instruction, the same method that Bacon recommended to
scholars for the discovery of unknown truths.[1]

It is this conversion, or, as we might say, this translation,
of the maxims of the Baconian logic into pedagogical rules,
that Comenius attempted, and this is why he has been called
"the father of the intuitive method." He was nourished,
intellectually, by the reading of Bacon, whom he resembles,
not only in his ideas, but also in his figurative and often
allegorical language. Even the title of one of his books,
Didactica Magna, recalls the title of Bacon's *Instauratio
Magna*.

---

[1] This is, perhaps, the earliest appearance of the conception that learning should be a process of discovery or of re-discovery. Condillac (1715–
1780) has elaborated this idea in the introduction to his *Grammaire*, and
Spencer (*Education*, p. 122) makes it a fundamental law of teaching. If
this assumed principle were to be rigorously applied, as, fortunately, it
cannot be, progress in human knowledge would be impossible. Mr. Bain's
comment on this doctrine (*Education as a Science*, p. 94) is as follows:
"This bold fiction is sometimes put forward as one of the regular arts of
the teacher; but I should prefer to consider it as an extraordinary device,
admissible only on special occasions." (P.)

137. The Life of Comenius. — To know Comenius and
the part he played in the seventeenth century, to appreciate
this grand educational character, it would be necessary to
begin by relating his life ; his misfortunes ; his journeys to
England, where Parliament invoked his aid ; to Sweden,
where the Chancellor Oxenstiern employed him to write
manuals of instruction ; especially his relentless industry, his
courage through exile, and the long persecutions he suffered
as a member of the sect of dissenters, the Moravian Brethren ; and the schools he founded at Fulneck, in Bohemia, at
Lissa and at Patak, in Poland. But it would require too
much of our space to follow in its incidents and catastro-
phes that troubled life, which, in its sudden trials. as in the
firmness that supported them, recalls the life of Pestalozzi.[1]

138. His Principal Works. — Comenius wrote a large
number of books in Latin, in German, and in Czech ; but
of these only a few are worthy to engage the attention of
the educator. In his other works he allows himself to go off
on philosophic excursions, and to indulge in mystic reveries,
led by his ardor to find what he called *pansophia*, wisdom or
universal knowledge. In this wilderness of publications
destined to oblivion, we shall notice only three works, which

---

[1] It may not be generally known that Comenius was once solicited to
become the President of Harvard College. The following is a quotation
from Vol. II., p. 14, of Cotton Mather's *Magnalia :* "That brave old man,
Johannes Amos Commenius, the fame of whose worth hath been *trumpetted*
as far as more than three languages (whereof every one is indebted unto
his *Janua*) could carry it, was indeed agreed withal, by our Mr. Winthrop
in his travels through the *low countries*, to come over into New England,
and illuminate this Colledge and *country*, in the quality of a President,
which was now become vacant. But the solicitations of the Swedish Am-
bassador diverting him another way, that incomparable Moravian became
not an American." This was on the resignation of President Dunster, in
1654. (P.)

contain the general principles of the pedagogy of Comenius, and the applications which he has made of his method : —

1. The *Didactica Magna*, the *Great Didactics* (written in Czech at about 1630, and rewritten in Latin at about 1640). In this work Comenius sets forth his principles, his general theories on education, and also his peculiar views on the practical organization of schools. It is to be regretted that a French translation has not yet popularized this important book, that would be worthy a place beside the *Thoughts* of Locke and the *Émile* of Rousseau.[1]

2. The *Janua linguarum reserata*, the *Gate of Tongues Unlocked* (1631). In the thought of the author, this was a new method of learning the languages. Comenius, led astray on this point by his religious prejudices, wished to banish the Latin authors from the schools, "for the purpose," he said, "of reforming studies in the true spirit of Christianity." Consequently, in order to replace the classical authors, which he repudiated for this further reason, that the reading of them is too difficult, and to make a child study them "is to wish to push out into the vast ocean a tiny bark that should be allowed only to sport on a little lake," he had formed the idea of composing a collection of phrases distributed into a hundred chapters. These phrases, to the number of a thousand, at first very simple, and of a single member, then longer and more complicated, were formed of two thousand words, chosen from among the most common and the most useful. Moreover, the hundred chapters of the *Janua* taught the child, in succession and in a methodical order, all the things in the universe, — the elements, the metals, the stars, the animals, the organs of the body, the arts

---

[1] The most complete account ever written of Comenius and his writings is, "John Amos Comenius," by S. S. Laurie (Boston: 1885). It is an invaluable contribution to the philosophy and the history of education. (P.)

CII.

Geometria

Die Erdmeßkunst.

Geómetra m. 1.	Der Erdmeſſer	
métitur	miſſet	
altitúdinem	die Höbe	Altitudo, f. 3. die Höhe.
turris, 1—2	eines Thurns, 1—2	Turris, f. 3. der Thurn.
aut *diſtantiam*	oder die Weite, Diſtanz	Diſtantia, f. 1. die Weite.
locorum, 3—4	der Oerter, 3—4	Locus, m. 2. der Ort.
ſive *quadrante,* 5	entweder mit dem Qua= (drat, 5	Quadrans, m. 3. der Quadrat.
ſive *radio.* 6	oder mit dem Meßſtab. (6	Rádius, m. 2. der Meß= ſtab.
Figuram rerum	Die Abriſſe der Din= (ge	Figúra, f. 1. der Abriß. Res, f. 5. das Ding.
deſignat	zeichnet er ab	
lineis, 7	mit Linien, (Gleich= (zügen,) 7	Linea, f. 1. die Linien/ (der Gleichzug.)
angulis, 8	Winckel, (Eckzügen) 8	Angulus, m. 2. der Win= ckel/ (Eckzug.)
& *circulis,* 9	und Kreiſen, Ringen, (Rundzügen) 9	Circulus, m. 2. der Kreiß/ (Ring/ Rundzug.)
ad *regulam,* 10	nach dem Linial, Richt= (ſcheit, 10	Regula, f. 1. das Linial. (Richtſcheit.)
normam, 11	Winckelmaß, 11	Norma, f. 1. das Win= ckelmas.
& *circinum.* 12	und Circkel, Ringmaß. (12	Circinus, m. 2. der Cir= ckel/ das Ringmas.)
Ex his	Aus dieſen	
oriuntur	entſtehen	
cylindrus, 13 m. 2.	das Oval, langrund. 13	
trigonus, 14 m. 2.	der Triangel, (Drey= (eck,) 14	
tetragonus, 15 m. 2.	der Quadrat, (Vier= (eck,) 15	
& aliæ figuræ.	und andere Figuren.	Alius, a, ud, Andere.

and trades, etc., etc.   In other terms, the *Janua linguarum* is a nomenclature of ideas and words designed to fix the attention of the child upon everything he ought to know of the world.   Divested of the Latin text that accompanies it, the *Janua* is a first reading-book, very defective doubtless, but it gives proof of a determined effort to adapt to the intelligence of the child the knowledge that he ought to acquire.

3. The *Orbis sensualium pictus*, the *Illustrated World of Sensible Objects*, the most popular of the author's works (1658).   It is the *Janua linguarum* accompanied with pictures, in lieu of real objects, representing to the child the things that he hears spoken of, as fast as he learns their names.   The *Orbis pictus*, the first practical application of the intuitive method, had an extraordinary success, and has served as a model for the innumerable illustrated books which for three centuries have invaded the schools.

139. THE FOUR GRADES OF INSTRUCTION. — We must not require a man of the seventeenth century to abjure Latin studies.   Comenius prizes them highly ; but at least he is wise enough to put them in their place, and does not confound them, as Luther did, with elementary studies.

Nothing could be more exact, more clearly cut, than the scholastic organization proposed by Comenius.   We shall find in it what the experience of three centuries has finally sanctioned and established, the distribution of schools into these grades, — infant schools, primary schools, secondary schools, and higher schools.

The first grade of instruction is the *maternal school*, the school *by the mother's knee*, *materni gremii*, as Comenius calls it.   The mother is the first teacher.   Up to the age of six the child is taught by her ; he is initiated by her into those branches of knowledge that he will pursue in the primary school.

The second grade is the *elementary public school*.   All the children, girls and boys, enter here at six, and leave at twelve.   The characteristic of this school is that the instruction there given is in the mother tongue, and this is why Comenius calls it the " common" school, *vernacula*, a term given by the Romans to the language of the people.

The third grade is represented by the *Latin school* or *gymnasium*.   Thither are sent the children from twelve to eighteen years of age for whom has been reserved a more complete instruction, such as we would now call secondary instruction.

Finally, to the fourth grade correspond the *academies*, that is, institutions of higher instruction, opened to young men from eighteen to twenty-four years of age.

The child, if he is able, will traverse these four grades in succession ; but, in the thought of Comenius, the studies should be so arranged in the elementary schools, that in leaving them, the pupil shall have a general education which makes it unnecessary for him to go farther, if his condition in life does not destine him to pursue the courses of the Latin School.

"We pursue," says Comenius, "a general education, the teaching to all men of all the subjects of human concern. . . . The purpose of the people's school shall be that all children of both sexes, from the tenth to the twelfth or the thirteenth year, may be instructed in that knowledge which is useful during the whole of life."

This was an admirable definition of the purpose of the primary school.   A thing not less remarkable is that Comenius establishes an elementary school in each village : —

" There should be a maternal school in each family ; an elementary school in each district ; a gymnasium in each city ; an academy in each kingdom, or even in each considerable province."

140. ELEMENTARY INITIATION INTO ALL THE STUDIES. — One of the most novel and most original ideas of the great Slavic educator is the wish that, from the earliest years of his life, the child may acquire some elementary notions of all the sciences that he is to study at a later period. From the cradle, the gaze of the infant, guided by the mother, should be directed to all the objects that surround him, so that his growing powers of reflection will be brought into play in working on these sense intuitions. "Thus, from the moment he begins to speak, the child comes to know himself, and, by his daily experience, certain general and abstract expressions; he comes to comprehend the meaning of the words *something, nothing, thus, otherwise, where, similar, different;* and what are generalizations and the categories expressed by these words but the rudiments of metaphysics? In the domain of physics, the infant can learn to know water, earth, air, fire, rain, snow, etc., as well as the names and uses of the parts of his body, or at least of the external members and organs. He will take his first lesson in optics in learning to distinguish light, darkness, and the different colors; and in astronomy, in noticing the sun, the moon, and the stars, and in observing that these heavenly bodies rise and set every day. In geography, according to the place where he lives, he will be shown a mountain, a valley, a plain, a river, a village, a hamlet, a city, etc. In chronology, he will be taught what an hour is, a day, a week, a year, summer, winter, yesterday, the day before yesterday, to-morrow, the day after to-morrow, etc. History, such as his age will allow him to conceive, will consist in recalling what has recently passed, in taking account of it, and in noting the part that this one or that has taken in such or such an affair. Arithmetic, geometry, statistics, mechanics, will not remain strangers to him. He will acquire the elements of these sciences in distinguishing

the difference between little and much, in learning to count up
to ten, in observing that three is more than two; that one
added to three makes four; in learning the sense of the
words *great* and *small, long* and *short, wide* and *narrow,
heavy* and *light;* in drawing lines, curves, circles, etc.; in
seeing goods measured with a yard-stick; in weighing an
object in a balance; in trying to make something or to take it
to pieces, as all children love to do.

" In this impulse to construct and destroy, there is but the
effort of the little intelligence to succeed in making or building something for himself; so that, instead of opposing the
child in this, he should be encouraged and guided."

" The grammar of the first period will consist in learning
to pronounce the mother tongue correctly. The child may
receive elementary notions even of politics, in observing
that certain persons assemble at the city hall, and that they
are called councillors; and that among these persons there
is one called mayor, etc. "[1]

141. THE PEOPLE'S SCHOOL. — Divided into six classes,
the people's school should prepare the child either for active
life or for the higher courses. Comenius sends here not
only the sons of peasants and workmen, but the sons of the
middle class or of the nobility, who will afterwards enter
the Latin school. In other terms, the study of Latin is
postponed till the age of twelve; and up to that period all
children must receive a thorough primary education, which
will comprise, with the mother tongue, arithmetic, geometry,
singing, the salient facts of history, the elements of the natural sciences, and religion. The latest reforms in secondary
instruction, which, only within a very late period, have post-

---

[1] Buisson's *Dictionnaire de Pédagogie*, Article COMENIUS.

poned the study of Latin till the sixth year,[1] and which till then keep the pupil upon the subjects of primary instruction, —what are they but the distant echo of the thought of Comenius? Let it be noted, too, that the plan of Comenius gave to its primary school a complete encyclopædic course of instruction, which was sufficient for its own ends, but which, while remaining elementary, was a whole, and not a beginning.[2]

Surely, the programme of studies devised by Comenius did not fail in point of insufficiency; we may be allowed, on the contrary, to pronounce it too extended, too crowded, conformed rather to the generous dreams of an innovator than to a prudent appreciation of what is practically possible; and we need not be astonished that, to lighten in part the heavy burden that is imposed on the teacher, Comenius had the notion of dividing the school into sections which assistants, chosen from among the best pupils, should instruct under the supervision of the master.

142. SITE OF THE SCHOOL. — One is not a complete educator save on the condition of providing for the exterior and material organization of the school, as well as for its moral administration. In this respect, Comenius is still deserving of our encomiums. He requires a yard for reere-

---

[1] In the French Lycées and Colleges the grades are named as follows, beginning with the lowest: "ninth, eighth, seventh, sixth, fifth, fourth, third, second, rhetoric, philosophy, preparatory mathematics, elementary mathematics, special mathematics." Latin was formerly begun in an earlier grade.

[2] The public school of the European type may be represented by a series of (3) pyramids, the second higher than the first, and the third higher than the second, each independent and complete in itself; while the public school of the American type is represented by a single pyramid in three sections. While in an English, French, or German town, public education is administered in three separate establishments, in an American town there is a single graded school that fulfills the same functions. (P.)

ation, and demands that the school-house have a gay and cheerful aspect. The question had been discussed before him by Vives (1492–1540).

"There should be chosen," says the Spanish educator, "a healthful situation, so that the pupils may not one day have to take their flight, dispersed by the fear of an epidemic. Firm health is necessary to those who would heartily and profitably apply themselves to the study of the sciences. And the place selected should be isolated from the crowd, and especially at a distance from occupations that are noisy, such as those of smiths, stone-masons, machinists, wheelwrights, and weavers. However, I would not have the situation too cheerful and attractive, lest it might suggest to the scholars the taking of too frequent walks."

But these considerations that do honor to Vives and to Comenius, were scarcely in harmony with the resources then at the disposal of the friends of instruction. There was scarcely occasion seriously to consider how school-houses should be constructed and situated, at a period when the most often there were no school-houses existing. "In winter," says Platter, "we slept in the school-room, and in summer in the open air."[1]

143. Sense Intuitions. — If Comenius has traced with a master hand the general organization of the primary school, he has no less merit in the matter of methods.

When they recommend the observation of sensible things as the first intellectual exercise, modern educators do but repeat what Comenius said three centuries ago.

"In the place of dead books, why should we not open the living book of nature? . . . To instruct the young is not to beat into them by repetition a mass of words, phrases, sen-

---

[1] Platter, a Swiss teacher of the sixteenth century (1499–1582).

tences, and opinions gathered out of authors; but it is to open their understanding through things. . . .

" The foundation of all knowledge consists in correctly representing sensible objects to our senses, so that they can·be comprehended with facility. I hold that this is the basis of all our other activities, since we could neither act nor speak wisely unless we adequately comprehended what we were to do and say. Now it is certain that *there is nothing in the understanding that was not first in the senses*, and, consequently, it is to lay the foundation of all wisdom, of all eloquence, and of all good and prudent conduct, carefully to train the senses to note with accuracy the differences between natural objects; and as this point, important as it is, is ordinarily neglected in the schools of to-day, and as objects are proposed to scholars that they do not understand because they have not been properly represented to their senses or to their imagination, it is for this reason, on the one hand, that the toil of teaching, and on the other, that the pain of learning, have become so burdensome and so unfruitful. . . .

" We must offer to the young, not the shadows of things, but the things themselves, which impress the senses and the imagination. Instruction should commence with a real observation of things, and not with a verbal description of them."

We see that Comenius accepts the doctrine of Bacon, even to his absolute sensationalism. In his pre-occupation with the importance of instruction through the senses, he goes so far as to ignore that other source of knowledge and intuitions, the inner consciousness.

144. SIMPLIFICATION OF GRAMMATICAL STUDY. — The first result of the experimental method applied to instruction, is to simplify grammar and to relieve it from the abuse of ab-

stract rules. "Children," says Comenius, "need examples and things which they can see, and not abstract rules."

And in the *Preface* of the *Janua linguarum*, he dwells upon the faults of the old method employed for the study of languages.

"It is a thing self-evident, that the true and proper way of teaching languages has not been recognized in the schools up to the present time. The most of those who devoted themselves to the study of letters grew old in the study of words, and upwards of ten years was spent in the study of Latin alone ; indeed, they even spent their whole life in the study, with a very slow and very trifling profit, which did not pay for the trouble devoted to it."[1]   It is by use and by reading that Comenius would abolish the abuse of rules. Rules ought to intervene only to aid use and give it surety. The pupil will thus learn language, either in speaking, or in reading a book like the *Orbis Pictus*, in which he will find at the same time all the words of which the language itself is composed, and examples of all the constructions of its syntax.

145. NECESSITY OF DRILL AND PRACTICE. — Another essential point in the new method, is the importance attributed by Comenius to practical exercises : "Artisans," he said, "understand this matter perfectly well. Not one of them will give an apprentice a theoretical course on his trade. He is allowed to notice what is done by his master, and then the tool is put in his hands : it is in smiting that one becomes a smith."[2]

---

[1] For this quotation, as for all those which we borrow from the preface of the *Janua linguarum*, a French edition of which (in three languages: Latin, German, and French) appeared in 1643, we copy from the authentic text.

[2] There is a misleading fallacy in all such illustrations. What analogy is there between the learning of history or geology and the learning of a trade

It is no longer the thing to repeat mechanically a lesson learned by heart. There must be a gradual habituation to action, to productive work, to personal effort.

146. GENERAL BEARING OF THE WORK OF COMENIUS. — How many other new and judicious ideas we shall have to gather from Comenius! The methods which we would be tempted to consider as wholly recent, his imagination had already suggested to him. For example, preceding the *Orbis Pictus*, we find an alphabet, where to each letter corresponds the cry of an animal, or else a sound familiar to the child. Is not this already the very essence of the phononimic processes [1] brought into fashion in these last years? But what is of more consequence with Comenius than a few happy discoveries in practical pedagogy, is the general inspiration of his work. He gives to education a psychological basis in demanding that the faculties shall be developed in their natural order : first, the senses, the memory, the imagination, and lastly the judgment and the reason. He is mindful of physical exercises, of technical and practical instruction, without forgetting that in the primary schools, which he calls the "studios of humanity," there must be trained, not only strong and skilful artisans, but virtuous and religious men, imbued with the principles of order and justice. If he has stepped from theology to pedagogy, and if he permits himself sometimes to be borne along by his artless bursts of mysticism, at least he does not forget the necessities of the real condition,

---

like carpentry? Should a physician and a blacksmith be educated on the same plan? In every case knowledge should precede practice; and the liberal arts are best learned by first learning their correlative sciences. (P.)

[1] " A process of instruction which consists in placing beside the elements of human speech thirty-three onomatopoetic gestures, which recall to the sight the same ideas that the sounds and the articulations of the voice recall to the ear."— GROSSELIN. (P.)

and of the present life of men. "The child," he says, "shall learn only what is to be useful to him in this life or in the other." Finally, he does not allow himself to be absorbed in the minute details of school management. He has higher views, — he is working for the regeneration of humanity. Like Leibnitz, he would freely say: "Give me for a few years the direction of education, and I agree to transform the world!"

[147. ANALYTICAL SUMMARY. — 1. Decisive changes in human opinion, political, religious, or scientific, involve corresponding changes in the purposes and methods of education.

2. The Reformation was a breaking with authority in matters of religion, as the Baconian philosophy was a breaking with authority in matters of science; and their joint effect on education was to subject matters of opinion, belief, and knowledge to the individual reason, experience, and observation.

3. In holding each human being responsible for his own salvation, the Reformation made it necessary for every one to read, and the logical consequence of this was to make instruction universal; and as schools were multiplied, the number of teachers must be increased, and their grade of competence raised.

4. The conception that ignorance is an evil, and a constant menace to spiritual and temporal safety, led to the idea of compulsory school-attendance.

5. In the recoil from the intuitions of the intellect sanctioned by Socrates, to the intuitions of the senses sanctioned by Bacon, education passed from an extreme dependence on reflection and reason, to an extreme dependence on sense and observation; so that inference has been thrown into dis-

credit, and the verdict of the senses has been made the test
of knowledge.

6. In adapting the conception of universal education to
the social conditions of his time, Comenius was led to a gradation of schools that underlies all modern systems of public
instruction.]

CHAPTER VII.

THE TEACHING CONGREGATIONS. — JESUITS AND JANSENISTS.

148. THE TEACHING CONGREGATIONS.[1]— Up to the French
Revolution, up to the day when the conception of a public
and national education was embodied in the legislative acts

---

[1] Religious congregations, as known in France, are associations of persons who, consecrating themselves to the service of God, make a vow to
live in common under the same rule. Many of these congregations devote
themselves to the work of teaching, and these are of two classes, the
authorized and the unauthorized. For example, the "Brethren of the
Christian Schools," founded by La Salle. is an *authorized*, and the "Society
of Jesus" an *unauthorized*, congregation. From statistics published in
1878. it appears that there were then in France, 24 congregations of men
authorized to teach, and controlling 3096 establishments; and 528 similar
congregations of women, controlling 16.478 establishments. At the same
time there were 85 unauthorized congregations of men, and 260 unauthorized
congregations of women, devoted to teaching. (P.)

of our assembled rulers, education remained almost exclusively an affair of the Church. The universities themselves were dependent in part on religious authority. But especially the great congregations assumed a monopoly of the work of teaching, the direction and control of which the State had not yet claimed for her right.

Primary instruction, it is true, scarcely entered at first into the settled plans of the religious orders. The only exception to this statement that can properly be made, is the congregation of the *Christian Doctrine*, which a humble priest, Cæsar de Bus, founded at Avignon in 1592, the avowed purpose of which was the religious education of the children of the company.[1] But, on the other hand, secondary instruction provoked the greatest educational event of the sixteenth century, the founding of the company of Jesus, and this movement was continued and extended in the seventeenth century, either in the colleges of the Jesuits, ever growing in number, or in other rival congregations.

149. JESUITS AND JANSENISTS. — Among the religious orders that have consecrated their efforts to the work of teaching, the first place must be assigned to the Jesuits and the Jansenists. Different in their statutes, their organization, and their destinies, these two congregations are still more different in their spirit. They represent, in fact, two opposite, and, as it were, contrary phases of human nature and of the Christian spirit. For the Jesuits, education is reduced to a superficial culture of the brilliant faculties of the intelligence ; while the Jansenists, on the contrary, aspire to develop the solid faculties, the judgment, and the reason.

---

[1] The congregation of the *Doctrinaries* founded at a later period establishments of secondary instruction. Maine de Biran, Laromiguière, and Lakanal were pupils of the *Doctrinaries*.

In the colleges of the Jesuits, rhetoric is held in honor; while in the Little Schools of Port Royal, it is rather logic and the exercise of thought. The shrewd disciples of Loyola adapt themselves to the times, and are full of compassion for human weakness; the solitaries of Port Royal are exacting of others and of themselves. In their suppleness and cheerful optimism, the Jesuits are almost the Epicureans of Christianity; with their austere and somewhat sombre doctrine, the Jansenists would rather be the Stoics. The Jesuits and the Jansenists, those great rivals of the seventeenth century, are still face to face as enemies at the present moment. While the inspiration of the Jesuits tries to maintain the old worn-out exercises, like Latin verse, and the abuse of the memory, the spirit of the Jansenists animates and inspires the reformers, who, in the teaching of the classics, break with tradition and routine, to substitute for exercises aimed at elegance, and for a superficial instruction, studies of a greater solidity and an education that is more complete.

The merit of institutions ought not always to be measured by their apparent success. The colleges of the Jesuits, during three centuries, have had a countless number of pupils; the Little Schools of Port Royal did not live twenty years, and during their short existence they enrolled at most only some hundreds of pupils. And yet the methods of the Jansenists have survived the ruin of their colleges and the dispersion of the teachers who had applied them. Although the Jesuits have not ceased to rule in appearance, it is the Jansenists who triumph in reality, and who to-day control the secondary instruction of France.

150. FOUNDATION OF THE SOCIETY OF JESUS. — In organizing the Society of Jesus, Ignatius Loyola, that compound of the mystic and the man of the world, purposed to establish,

not an order devoted to monastic contemplation, but a real
fighting corps, a Catholic army, whose double purpose was to
conquer new provinces to the faith through missions, and to
preserve the old through the control of education.   Solemnly
consecrated by the Pope Paul III., in 1540, the congregation
had a rapid growth.   As early as the middle of the sixteenth
century, it had several colleges in France, particularly those
of Billom, Mauriac, Rodez, Tournon, and Pamiers.   In 1561
it secured a footing in Paris, notwithstanding the resistance
of the Parliament, of the university, and of the bishops themselves.   A hundred years later it counted nearly fourteen
thousand pupils in the province of Paris alone.   The college
of Clermont, in 1651, enrolled more than two thousand young
men.   The middle and higher classes assured to the colleges
of the society an ever-increasing membership.   At the end
of the seventeenth century, the Jesuits could inscribe on the
roll of honor of their classes a hundred illustrious names,
among others, those of Condé and Luxembourg, Fléchier and
Bossuet, Lamoignon and Séguier, Descartes, Corneille, and
Molière.   In 1710 they controlled six hundred and twelve
colleges and a large number of universities.   They were the
real masters of education, and they maintained this educational
supremacy till the end of the eighteenth century.

151. DIFFERENT JUDGMENTS ON THE EDUCATIONAL MERITS
OF THE JESUITS. — Voltaire said of these teachers : " The
Fathers taught me nothing but Latin and nonsense."   But
from the seventeenth century, opinions are divided, and the
encomiums of Bacon and Descartes must be offset by the
severe judgment of Leibnitz.   " In the matter of education," says this great philosopher, " the Jesuits have remained
below mediocrity." [1]   Directly to the contrary, Bacon had

---

[1] *Leibnitii Opera*, Genevæ, 1768, Tome VI. p. 65.

written : " As to whatever relates to the instruction of the young, we must consult the schools of the Jesuits, for there can be nothing that is better done." [1]

152. AUTHORITIES TO CONSULT. — The Jesuits have never written anything on the principles and objects of education. We must not demand of them an exposition of general views, or a confession of their educational faith. But to make amends, they have drawn up with precision, with almost infinite attention to details, the rules and regulations of their course of study. Already, in 1559, the *Constitutions*, probably written by Loyola himself, devoted a whole book to the organization of the colleges of the society.[2] But in particular, the *Ratio Studiorum*, published in 1599, contains a complete scholastic programme, which has remained for three centuries the invariable educational code of the congregation. Without doubt, the Jesuits, always ready to make apparent concessions to the spirit of the times, without sacrificing anything of their own spirit, and without renouncing their inflexible purpose, have introduced modifications into their original rules ; but the spirit of their educational practice has remained the same, and, in 1854, Beckx, the actual general of the order, could still declare that the *Ratio* is the immutable rule of Jesuit education.

153. PRIMARY INSTRUCTION NEGLECTED. — A permanent and characteristic feature of the educational policy of the Jesuits is, that, during the whole course of their history, they have deliberately neglected and disdained primary instruction. The earth is covered with their Latin colleges ; and wherever they have been able, they have put their hands

[1] *Bacon de Augmentis Scientiarum*, Lib. VI. chap. IV.
[2] See the fourth book of the *Constitutions*.

on the institutions for university education; but in no instance have they founded a primary school. Even in their establishments for secondary instruction, they entrust the lower classes to teachers who do not belong to their order, and reserve to themselves the direction of the higher classes. Must we believe, as they have declared in order to explain this negligence, that the only reason for their reserve and their indifference is to be sought for in the insufficiency of their teaching force? No; the truth is that the Jesuits neither desire nor love the instruction of the people. To desire and to love this, there must be faith in conscience and reason; there must be a belief in human equality. Now the Jesuits distrust the human intelligence, and administer only the aristocratic education of the ruling classes, whom they hope to retain under their own control. They wish to train amiable gentlemen, accomplished men of the world; they have no conception of training men. Intellectual culture, in their view, is but a convenience, imposed on certain classes of the nation by their rank. It is not a good in itself; it may even become an evil. In certain hands it is a dangerous weapon. The ignorance of a people is the best safeguard of its faith, and faith is the supreme end. So we shall not be astonished to read this in the *Constitutions:* —

"None of those who are employed in domestic service on account of the society, ought to learn to read and write, or, if they already know these arts, to learn more of them. They shall not be instructed without the consent of the General, for it suffices for them to serve with all simplicity and humility our Master, Jesus Christ."

154. CLASSICAL STUDIES: LATIN AND THE HUMANITIES. — It is only in secondary instruction that the Jesuits have taken position with marked success. The basis of their teaching is the study of Latin and Greek. Their purpose is

to monopolize classical studies in order to make them serve
for the propagation of the Catholic faith. To write in Latin
is the ideal which they propose to their pupils. The first
consequence of this is the proscription of the mother tongue.
The *Ratio* forbids the use of French even in conversation;
it permits it only on holidays. Hence, also, the importance
accorded to Latin and Greek composition, to the explication
of authors, and to the study of grammar, rhetoric, and
poetry. It is to be noted, besides, that the Jesuits put
scarcely more into the hands of their pupils than select
extracts, expurgated editions. They wish, in some sort, to
efface from the ancient books whatever marks the epoch and
characterizes the time. They detach fine passages of eloquence and beautiful extracts of poetry; but they are afraid,
it seems, of the authors themselves; they fear lest the pupil
find in them the old human spirit, — the spirit of nature.
Moreover, in the explication of authors, they pay more
attention to words than to things. They direct the pupil's
attention, not to the thoughts, but to the elegancies of language, to the elocutionary effect; in a word, to the form,
which, at least, has no religious character, and can in no-
wise give umbrage to Catholic orthodoxy. They fear to
awaken reflection and individual judgment. As Macaulay
has said, they seem to have found the point up to which
intellectual culture can be pushed without reaching intellectual emancipation.

155. DISDAIN OF HISTORY, OF PHILOSOPHY, AND OF THE
SCIENCES IN GENERAL. — Preoccupied before all else with
purely formal studies, and exclusively devoted to the exercises which give a training in the use of elegant language,
the Jesuits leave real and concrete studies in entire neglect.
History is almost wholly banished from their programme.
It is only with reference to the Greek and Latin texts that

the teacher should make allusion to the matters of history which are necessary for the understanding of the passage under examination. No account is made of modern history, nor of the history of France. "History," says a Jesuit Father, "is the destruction of him who studies it." This systematic omission of historical studies suffices to put in its true light the artificial and superficial pedagogy of the Jesuits, admirably defined by Beckx, who expresses himself thus : —

" The gymnasia will remain what they are by nature, a gymnastic for the intellect, which consists far less in the assimilation of real matter, in the acquisition of different knowledges, than in a culture of pure form."

The sciences and philosophy are involved in the same disdain as history. Scientific studies are entirely proscribed in the lower classes, and the student enters his year in philosophy,[1] having studied only the ancient languages. Philosophy itself is reduced to a barren study of words, to subtile discussions, and to commentaries on Aristotle. Memory and syllogistic reasoning are the only faculties called into play ; no facts, no real inductions, no care for the observation of nature. In all things the Jesuits are the enemies of progress. Intolerant of everything new, they would arrest the progress of the human mind and make it immovable.

156. DISCIPLINE. — Extravagant statements have been made relative to the reforms in discipline introduced by the Jesuits into their educational establishments. The fact is, that they have caused to prevail in their colleges more of order and of system than there was in the establishments of the University. On the other hand, they have attempted to please their pupils, to gild for them, so to speak, the bars of

---

[1] See note to § 141.

the prison which confined them.   Theatrical representations, excursions on holidays, practice in swimming, riding, and fencing, — nothing was neglected that could render their residence at school endurable.

But, on the other hand, the Jesuits have incurred the grave fault of detaching the child from the family.   They wish to have absolute control of him.   The ideal of the perfect scholar is to forget his parents.   Here is what was said by a pupil of the Jesuits, who afterwards became a member of the Order, J. B. de Schultaus : —

"His mother paid him a visit at the College of Trent. He refused to take her hand, and would not even raise his eyes to hers.   The mother, astonished and grieved, asked her son the cause of such a cold greeting.   'I refuse to notice you,' said the pupil, 'not because you are my mother, but because you are a woman.'   And the biographer adds: 'This was not excessive precaution; woman preserves to-day the faults she had at the time of our first father; it is always she who drives man from Paradise.'   When the mother of Schultaus died, he did not show the least emotion, having long ago adopted the Holy Virgin for his true mother."

157. EMULATION ENCOURAGED. — The Jesuits have always considered emulation as one of the essential elements of discipline.   "It is necessary," says the *Ratio*, "to encourage an honorable emulation; it is a great stimulus to study. Superior on this point, perhaps on this alone, to the Jansenists, who through mistrust of human nature feared to excite pride by encouraging emulation, the Jesuits have always counted upon the self-love of the pupil.   The *Ratio* multiplies rewards, — solemn distributions of prizes, crosses, ribbons, decorations, titles borrowed from the Roman Republic, such as *decurions* and *prœtors;* all means, even

the most puerile, were invented to nourish in pupils an ardor for work, and to incite them to surpass one another. Let us add that the pupil was rewarded, not only for his own good conduct, but for the bad conduct of his comrades if he informed against them. The *decurion* or the *prætor* was charged with the police care of the class, and, in the absence of the official disciplinarian, he himself chastised his comrades; in the hands of his teacher, he became a spy and an informer. Thus a pupil, liable to punishment for having spoken French contrary to orders, will be relieved from his punishment if he can prove by witnesses that one of his comrades has committed the same fault on the same day.

158. OFFICIAL DISCIPLINARIAN. — The rod is an element, so to speak, of the ancient pedagogical régime. It holds a privileged place both in the colleges and in private education. Louis XIV. officially transmits to the Duke of Montausier the right to correct his son. Henry IV. wrote to the governor of Louis XIII. : " I complain because you did not inform me that you had whipped my son; for I desire and order you to whip him every time that he shall be guilty of obstinacy or of anything else that is bad; for I well know that there is nothing in the world that can do him more good than that. This I know from the lessons of experience, for when I was of his age, I was soundly flogged." [1]

The Jesuits, notwithstanding their disposition to make discipline milder, were careful not to renounce a punishment that was in use even at court. Only, while the Brethren of the Christian Schools, according to the regulations of La Salle, chastised the guilty pupil themselves, the Jesuits did not think it becoming the dignity of the master to apply the correction himself. They reserved to a laic the duty of

---

[1] Letter to Madame Montglat, Nov. 14, 1607.

handling the rods. An official disciplinarian, a domestic, a porter, was charged in all the colleges with the functions of chief executioner. And while the *Ratio Studiorum* recommends moderation, certain witnesses prove that the special disciplinarian did not always carry a discreet hand. Here, for example, is an account given by Saint Simon : —

" The eldest son of the Marquis of Boufflers was fourteen years old. He was handsome, well formed, was wonderfully successful, and full of promise. He was a resident pupil of the Jesuits with the two sons of d'Argenson. I do not know what indiscretion he and they were guilty of. The Fathers wished to show that they neither feared nor stood in awe of any one, and they flogged the boy, because, in fact, they had nothing to fear of the Marquis of Boufflers ; but they were careful not to treat the two others in this way, though equally culpable, because every day they had to count with d'Argenson, who was lieutenant of police. The boy Boufflers was thrown into such mental agony that he fell sick on the same day, and within four days was dead. . . . There was a universal and furious outcry against the Jesuits, but nothing ever came of it." [1]

159. GENERAL SPIRIT OF THE PEDAGOGY OF THE JESUITS. — The general principles of the doctrine of the Jesuits are completely opposed to our modern ideas. Blind obedience, the suppression of all liberty and of all spontaneity, such is the basis of their moral education.

" To renounce one's own wishes is more meritorious than to raise the dead ; " " We must be so attached to the Roman Church as to hold for black an object which she tells us is black, even when it is really white ; " " Our confidence in God should be strong enough to force us, in the lack of a

---

[1] Saint Simon, *Mémoires*, Tome IX. 83.

boat, to cross the ocean on a single plank ; " "If God should appoint for our master an animal deprived of reason, you should not hesitate to render it obedience, as to a master and a guide, for this sole reason, that God has ordered it thus ; " "One must allow himself to be governed by divine Providence acting through the agency of the superiors of the Order, just as if he were a dead body that could be put into any position whatever, and treated according to one's good pleasure ; or as if one were a bâton in the hands of an old man who uses it as he pleases."

As to intellectual education, as they understand it, it is wholly artificial and superficial. To find for the mind occupations that absorb it, that soothe it like a dream, without wholly awakening it ; to call attention to words, and to niceties of expression, so as to reduce by so much the opportunity for thinking ; to provoke a certain degree of intellectual activity, prudently arrested at the place where the reflective reason succeeds an embellished memory ; in a word, to excite the spirit just enough to arouse it from its inertia and its ignorance, but not enough to endow it with a real self-activity by a manly display of all its faculties, — such is the method of the Jesuits. "As to instruction," says Bersot, "this is what we find with them : history reduced to facts and tables, without the lesson derived from them bearing on the knowledge of the world ; even the facts suppressed or altered when they say too much ; philosophy reduced to what is called empirical doctrine, and what de Maistre called the philosophy of the nothing, without danger of one's acquiring a liking for it ; physical science reduced to recreations, without the spirit of research and liberty ; literature reduced to the complaisant explication of the ancient authors, and ending in innocent witticisms. . . . With respect to letters, there are two loves which have nothing iu common save their name; one of them makes men, the other, great boys. It is the last that we find with the Jesuits; they amuse the soul."

160. THE ORATORIANS. — Between the Jesuits, their adversaries, and the Jansenists, their friends, the Oratorians occupy an intermediate place. They break already with the over-mechanical education, and with the wholly superficial instruction which Ignatius Loyola had inaugurated. Through some happy innovations they approach the more elevated and more profound education of Port Royal. Founded in 1614, by Bérulle, the Order of the Oratory soon counted quite a large number of colleges of secondary instruction, and, in partienlar, in 1638, the famous college of Juilly. While with the Jesuits it is rare to meet the names of celebrated professors, several renowned teachers have made illustrious the Oratory of the seventeenth century. We note the Père Lamy, author of *Entretiens sur les Sciences* (1683) ; the Père Thomassin, whom the Oratorians call the "incomparable theologian," and who published, from 1681 to 1690, a series of *Methods* for studying the languages, philosophy, and letters ; Mascaron and Massillon, who taught rhetoric at the Oratory ; the Père Lecointe and the Père Lelong, who taught history there. All these men unite, in general, some love of liberty to ardor of religious sentiment ; they wish to introduce more air and more light into the cloister and the school; they have a taste for the facts of history and the truths of science ; finally, they attempt to found an education at once liberal and Christian, religious without abuse of devotion, elegant without refinement, solid without excess of erudition, worthy, finally, to be counted as one of the first practical tentatives of modern pedagogy.

The limits of this study forbid our entering into details. Let us merely note a few essential points. That which distinguishes the Oratorians, is, first, a sincere and disinterested love of truth.

" We love the truth," says the Père Lamy ; " the days do not suffice to consult her as long as we would wish ; or, rather, we never grow weary of the pleasure we find in studying her. There has always been that love for letters in this House : those who have governed it have tried to nourish it. When there is found among us some penetrating and liberally endowed spirit who has a rare genius for the sciences, he is discharged from all other duties." [1]

Nowhere have ancient letters been more loved than at the Oratory.

" In his leisure hours the Père Thomassin read only the authors of the humanities ; " and yet French was not there sacrificed to Latin. The use of the Latin language was not obligatory till after the fourth year, and even then not for the lessons in history, which, till the end of the courses, had to be given in French. History, so long neglected even in the colleges of the University, particularly the history of France, was taught to the pupils of the Oratory. Geography was not separated from it ; and the class-rooms were furnished with large mural maps. On the other hand, the sciences had a place in the course of study. A Jesuit father would not have expressed himself as the Père Lamy has done : —

" It is a pleasure to enter the laboratory of a chemist. In the places where I have happened to be, I did not miss an opportunity to attend the anatomical lectures that were given, and to witness the dissection of the principal parts of the human body. . . . I know of nothing of greater use than algebra and arithmetic."

Finally, philosophy itself, — the Cartesian philosophy, so mercilessly decried by the Jesuits, — was in vogue at the Ora-

---

[1] *Entretiens sur les Sciences*, p. 197.

tory. "If Cartesianism is a pest," wrote the regents of the College of Angers, " there are more than two hundred of us who are infected with it." ... "They have forbidden the Fathers of the Oratory to teach the philosophy of Descartes, and, consequently, the blood to circulate," wrote Madame de Sévigné, in 1673.

Let us also furnish proof of the progress and amelioration of the discipline at the Oratory : —

"There are many other ways besides the rod," says the Père Lamy; "and, to lead pupils back to their duty, a caress, a threat, the hope of a reward, or the fear of a humiliation, has greater efficiency than whips."

The ferule, it is true, and whips also, were not forbidden, but made part of the *legitima pœnarum genera.* But it does not appear that use was often made of them ; either through a spirit of mildness, or through prudence, and through the fear of exasperating the child.

"There is needed," says the Père Lamy again, "a sort of politics to govern this little community, — to lead them through their inclinations ; to foresee the effect of rewards and punishments, and to employ them according to their proper use. There are times of stubbornness when a child would sooner be killed than yield."

"What made it easier at the Oratory to maintain the authority of the master without resorting to violent punishments, is that the same professor accompanied the pupils through the whole series of their classes. The Père Thomassin, for example, was, in turn, professor of grammar, rhetoric, philosophy, mathematics, history, Italian, and Spanish, — a touching example, it must be allowed, of an absolute devotion to scholastic labor. But this universality, somewhat superficial, served neither the real interests of the masters nor those of their pupils. The great pedagogical law is the division of labor.

161. FOUNDATION OF THE LITTLE SCHOOLS. — From the very organization of their society, the Jansenists gave evidences of an ardent solicitude for the education of youth. Their founder, Saint Cyran, said : " Education is, in a sense, the *one thing necessary*. . . . I wish you might read in my heart the affection I feel for children. . . . You could not deserve more of God than in working for the proper bringing up of children." It was in this disinterested feeling of charity for the good of the young, in this display of sincere tenderness for children, that the Jansenists, in 1643, founded the Little Schools at Port Royal in the Fields, in the vicinity, and then in Paris.[1] They received into those schools only a small number of pupils, preoccupied as they were, not with dominating the world and extending their influence, but with doing modestly and obscurely the good they could. Persecution did not long grant them the leisure to continue the work they had undertaken. By 1660 the enemies of Port Royal had triumphed ; the Jesuits obtained an order from the king closing the schools and dispersing the teachers. Pursued, imprisoned, expatriated, the solitaries of Port Royal had but the opportunity to gather up in memorable documents the results of their educational experience all too short.[2]

162. THE TEACHERS AND THE BOOKS OF PORT ROYAL. — Singular destiny, — that of those teachers whom a relentless

---

[1] For the Little Schools of Port Royal, see a recent account by Carré (*Revue Pédagogique*, 1883, Nos. 2 and 8).

[2] No more pathetic piece of history has ever been written than that which relates the vindictive and relentless persecution of the peaceful and pious solitaries of Port Royal: " The house was razed to the ground, and even the very foundations ploughed up. The gardens and walks were demolished; and the dead were even torn from their graves, that not a vestige might be left to mark the spot where this celebrated institution had stood." — *Lancelot's Tour to La Grande Chartreuse*, p. 243. See also *Narrative of the Demolition of Port Royal* (London, 1816). (P.)

fate permitted to exercise their functions for only five years, yet who, through their works, have remained perhaps the best authorized exponents of French education! The first of these is Nicole, the moralist and logician, one of the authors of the Port Royal *Logic*, who taught philosophy and the humanities in the Little Schools, and who published in 1670, under the title, *The Education of a Prince*, a series of reflections on education, applicable, as he himself says, to children of all classes. Another is Lancelot, the grammarian, the author of the *Methods* for learning the Latin, Greek, Italian, and Spanish languages. Then there is Arnauld, the great Arnauld, the ardent theologian, who worked on the *Logic*, and the *General Grammar*, and who finally composed the *Regulation of Studies in the Humanities*. In connection with these celebrated names, we must mention other Jansenists not so well known, such as De Sacy and Guyot, both of whom were the authors of a large number of translations; Coustel, who published the *Rules for the Education of Children* (1687) ; Varet, the author of *Christian Education* (1668). Let us add to this list, still incomplete, the *Regimen for Children*, by Jacqueline Pascal (1657), and we shall have some idea of the educational activity of Port Royal.

163. THE STUDY OF THE FRENCH LANGUAGE. — As a general rule, we may have a good opinion of the teachers who recommend the study of the mother tongue. In this respect, the solitaries of Port Royal are in advance of their time. "We first teach to read in Latin," said the Abbé Fleury, "because, compared with French, we pronounce it more as it is written." [1] A curious reason, which did not satisfy Fleury himself; for he acknowledged the propriety of putting, as soon as possible, into the hands of children, the French

---

[1] *Du choix et de la méthode des études.*

books that they can understand.   This was what was done at Port Royal.   With their love of exactness and clearness, with their disposition, wholly Cartesian, to make children study only the things they can comprehend, the Jansenists saw at once the great absurdity of choosing Latin works as the first reading-books.   " To learn Latin before learning the mother tongue," said Comenius, wittily, " is like wishing to mount a horse before knowing how to walk."   And again, as Sainte-Beuve says, "It is to compel unfortunate children to deal with the unintelligible in order to proceed towards the unknown."   For these unintelligible texts, the Jansenists substituted, not, it is true, original French works, but at least good translations of Latin authors.   For the first time in France, the French language was made the subject of serious study.   Before being made to write in Latin, pupils were drilled in writing in French.   They were set to compose little narratives, little letters, the subjects of which were borrowed from their recollections, by being asked to relate on the spot what they had retained of what they had read.

164. NEW SYSTEM OF SPELLING. — In their constant preoccupation to make study easier, the Jansenists reformed the current method of learning to read.   " What makes reading more difficult," says Arnauld in Chapter VI. of the *General Grammar*, "is that while each letter has its own proper name, it is given a different name when it is found associated with other letters.   For example, if the pupil is made to read the syllable *fry*, he is made to say *ef, ar, y*, which invariably confuses him.   It is best, therefore, to teach children to know the letters only by the names of their real pronunciation, to name them only by their natural sounds."   Port Royal proposes, then, " to have children pronounce only the vowels and the diphthongs, and not the consonants, which they need not

pronounce, except in the different combinations which they form with the same vowels or diphthongs, in syllables and words.

This method has become celebrated under the name of the Port Royal Method ; and it appears, from a letter of Jacqueline Pascal, that the original notion was due to Pascal himself.[1]

165. DISCIPLINÉ IN PERSONAL REFLECTION. — That which profoundly distinguishes the method of the Jansenists from the method of the Jesuits, is that at Port Royal the purpose is less to make good Latinists than to train sound intelligences. The effort is to call into activity the judgment and personal reflection. As soon as the child is capable of it, he is made to think and comprehend. In the lessons of the class-room, not a word is allowed to pass till the child has understood its meaning. Only those tasks are proposed to the child which are adapted to his childish intelligence. His attention is occupied only with the things that are within the compass of his powers.

The grammars of Port Royal are written in French, " because it is ridiculous," says Nicole, " to teach the principles of a language in the very language that is to be learned, and that for the present is unknown." Lancelot, in his *Methods*, abbreviates and simplifies grammatical studies : —

" I have found out, at last, how useful this maxim of Ramus is, — *Few precepts and much practice :* and, also, that as soon as children begin to know these rules somewhat, it is well to make them observe them in practice."

It is by the reading of authors that the grammar of Port Royal completes the theoretical study of the rules that are rigidly reduced to their minimum. The professor, with ref-

---

[1] See Cousin, *Jacqueline Pascal*, p. 262.

erence to such or such a passage of an author, will make appropriate oral remarks. In this way the example, not the dry and uninteresting one of the grammar, but the living example, expressive, and, drawn from a writer that is being read with interest, will precede or accompany the rule, and the particular case will explain the general law. This is an excellent method, because it accords with the real movement of the mind, and adapts the sequence of studies to the progress of the intelligence, and also because, according to the advice of Descartes, the child in this way proceeds from the known to the unknown, from the simple to the complex.

166. GENERAL SPIRIT OF THE INTELLECTUAL EDUCATION AT PORT ROYAL. — Without doubt, we need not expect to find among the solitaries of Port Royal a disinterested devotion to science. In their view, instruction is but a means of forming the judgment. " The sciences should be employed," says Nicole, " only as an instrument for perfecting the reason." Historical, literary, and scientific knowledge has no intrinsic value. The thing required is simply to employ those subjects for educating just, equitable, and judicious men. Nicole declares that it would be better absolutely to ignore the sciences than to become absorbed in the useless portions of them. Speaking of astronomical researches, and of the works of those mathematicians who believe that " it is the finest thing in the world to know whether there is a bridge and an arch suspended around the planet Saturn," he concludes that it is preferable to be ignorant of those things than to be ignorant that they are vain.

But, on the other hand, the Jansenists have struck from their programme of studies everything that is merely sterile verbiage, exercises of memory or of artificial imagination. Little attention is given to Latin verse at Port Royal. Ver-

sion takes precedence of the theme,[1] and the oral theme
often replaces the written. The pupil is to be taught, " not
to be blinded by a vain flash of words void of sense, not to
rest satisfied with mere words or obscure principles, and
never to be satisfied till he has gained a clear insight into
things."

167. PEDAGOGICAL PRINCIPLES OF NICOLE. — In his treatise on the *Education of a Prince*, Nicole has summarized,
under the form of aphorisms, some of the essential principles of his system of education.

Let us first notice this maxim, a true pedagogical axiom :
" The purpose of instruction is to carry forward intelligences
to the farthest point they are capable of attaining." This
is saying that every child, whether of the nobility or of the
people, has the right to be instructed according to his aptitude and ability.

Another axiom : We must proportion difficulties to the
growing development of the child's intelligence. " The
greatest minds have but a limited range of intelligence. In
all of them there are regions of twilight and shadow ; but
the intelligence of the child is almost wholly pervaded by
shadows ; he catches glimpses of but few rays of light. So
everything depends on managing these rays, on increasing
them, and on exposing to them whatever we wish to have the
child comprehend."

A corollary to the preceding axiom is, that the first
appeal must be made to the senses. " The intelligence of
children always being very dependent on the senses, we
must, as far as possible, address our instruction to the
senses, and cause it to reach the mind, not only through

---

[1] *Version:* translation from Latin or Greek into French. *Theme:*
translation of French into Latin or Greek. (P.)

hearing, but also through seeing." Consequently, geography is a study well adapted to early years, provided we employ books in which the largest cities are pictured. If children study the history of a country, we must not neglect to show them the situation of places on the map. Nicole also recommends that they be shown pictures that represent the machines, the arms, and the dress of the ancients, and also the portraits of kings and illustrious men.

168. MORAL PESSIMISM. — Man is wicked, human nature is corrupt: such is the cry of despair that comes to our ears from all the writings of the Jansenists.

"The devil," says Saint Cyran, "already possesses the soul of even the unborn child." . . .

And again: "We must always pray for souls, and always be on the watch, standing guard as in a city menaced by an enemy. On the outside the devil makes his rounds." . . .

"As soon as children begin to have reason," says another Jansenist, "we observe in them only blindness and weakness. Their minds are closed to spiritual things, and they cannot comprehend them. But, on the contrary, their eyes are open to evil; their senses are susceptible to all sorts of corruption, and they have a natural inertia that inclines them to it."

"You ought," writes Varet, "to consider your children as wholly inclined to evil, and carried forward towards it. All their inclinations are corrupt, and, not being governed by reason, they will permit them to find pleasure and diversion only in the things that carry them towards vice."

169. EFFECTS ON DISCIPLINE. — The doctrine of the original perversity of man may produce contrary results, and direct the practical conduct of those who accept it in two opposite directions. They are either inspired with severity

toward beings deeply tainted and vicious, or they are excited to pity and to tenderness for those fallen creatures who suffer from an incurable evil. The solitaries of Port Royal obeyed the second tendency. They were as affectionate and good to the children confided to their care as, in theory, they were harsh and rigorous towards human nature. In the presence of their pupils they felt touched with an infinite tenderness for those poor sick souls, whom they would willingly cure of their ills, and raise from their fall, at the cost of any and every sacrifice.

The conception of the native wickedness of man had still another result at Port Royal. It increased the zeal of the teachers. It prompted them to multiply their assiduity and vigilance in order to keep guard over young souls, and there destroy, whenever possible, the seeds of evil that sin had sown in them. When one is charged with the difficult mission of moral education, it is, perhaps, dangerous to have too much confidence in human nature, and to form too favorable an opinion of its qualities and dispositions ; for then one is tempted to accord to the child too large a liberty, and to practise the maxim, " Let it take its own course, let it pass " (*Laissez faire, laissez passer*). It is better to err on the other side, in excess of mistrust ; for, in this case, knowing the dangers that menace the child, we watch over him with more attention, abandon him less to the inspiration of his caprices, and expect more of education ; we demand of effort and labor what we judge nature incapable of producing by herself.

Vigilance, patience, mildness, — these are the instruments of discipline in the schools of Port Royal. There were scarcely any punishments in the Little Schools. " To speak little, to tolerate much, to pray still more," — these are the three things that Saint Cyran recommended. The threat to send children home to their parents sufficed to maintain order in a flock somewhat small. In fact, all whose example would have proved bad were sent away; an excellent system of elimination when it is practicable. The pious solitaries endured without complaint, faults in which they saw the necessary consequences of the original fall. Penetrated, however, as they were, with the value of human souls, their tenderness for children was mingled with a certain respect; for they saw in them the creatures of God, beings called from eternity to a sublime destiny or to a terrible punishment.

170. FAULTS IN THE DISCIPLINE OF PORT ROYAL. — The Jansenists did not shun the logical though dangerous consequences that were involved, in germ, in their pessimistic theories of human nature. They fell into an excess of prudence or of rigidity. They pushed gravity and dignity to a formalism that was somewhat repulsive. At Port Royal pupils were forbidden to thee and thou one another. The solitaries did not like familiarities. faithful in this respect to the *Imitation of Jesus Christ*, in which it is somewhere said that it does not become a Christian to be on familiar terms with any one whatever. The young were thus brought up in habits of mutual respect, which may have had their good side, but which had the grave fault of being a little ridlenlous in children, since they forced them to live among themselves as *little gentlemen*, while at the same time they oppose the development of those intimate friendships, of those lasting attachments of which all those who have lived at college know the sweetness and the charm.

The spirit of asceticism is the general character of all the Jansenists. Varet declares that balls are places of infamy. Pascal denies himself every agreeable thought, and what he called an agreeable thought was to reflect on geometry.

Lancelot refuses to take to the theatre the princes of Conti, of whom he was the preceptor.

But perhaps a graver fault at Port Royal was, that through fear of awakening self-love, the spirit of emulation was purposely suppressed. It is God alone, it was said, who is to be praised for the qualities and talents manifested by men. " If God has placed something of good in the soul of a child, we must praise Him for it and keep silent. " By this deliberate silence men put themselves on guard against pride; but if pride is to be feared, is indolence the less so? And when we purposely avoid stimulating self-love through the hope of reward, or through a word of praise given in due season, we run a great risk of not overcoming the indolenee that is natural to the child, and of not obtaining from him any serious effort. Pascal, the greatest of the friends of Port Royal, said : " The children of Port Royal, who do not feel that stimulus of envy and glory, fall into a state of indifference."

171. General Judgment on Port Royal. — After all has been said, we must admire the teachers of Port Royal, who were doubtless deceived on some points, but who were animated by a powerful feeling of their duty to educate, and by a perfect charity. Ardor and sincerity of religious faith; a great respect for the human person; the practice of piety held in honor, but kept subordinate to the reality of the inner feeling; devotion advised, but not imposed; a marked mistrust of nature, corrected by displays of tenderness and tempered by affection; above all, the profound, unwearied devotion of Christian souls who give themselves wholly and without reserve to other souls to raise them up and save them, — this is what was done by the discipline of Port Royal. But it is rather in the methods of teaching, and in the administration of classical studies, that we must look for

the incontestable superiority of the Jansenists. The teachers of the Little Schools were admirable humanists, not of form, as the Jesuits were, but of judgment. They represent, it seems to us, in all its beauty and in all its force, that intellectual education, already divined by Montaigne, which prepares for life men of sound judgment and of upright conscience. They founded the teaching of the humanities. "Port Royal," says an historian of pedagogy, Burnier, " simplifies study without, however, relieving it of its wholesome difficulties; it strives to make it interesting, while it does not convert it into child's play; it purposes to confide to the memory only what has first been apprehended by the intelligence. . . . It has given to the world ideas that it has not again let go, and fruitful principles from which we have but to draw their logical consequences."

[172. Analytical Summary. 1. In the history of the three great teaching congregations we have an illustration of the supposed power of education over the destinies of men.

2. To resist the encroachments of Protestantism that followed the diffusion of instruction among the people, Loyola organized his teaching corps of Catholic zealots; and this mode of competition for purposes of moral, sectarian, and political control has covered the earth, in all Christian countries, with institutions of learning.

3. The tendency towards extremes, and the difficulty of attaining symmetry and completeness, are seen in the preference of the Jesuits for form, elegance, and mere discipline, in their excessive use of emulation; and in the pessimism of the Jansenists, their distrust of human nature, and their fear of human pride.]

CHAPTER VIII.

FÉNELON.

173. EDUCATION IN THE SEVENTEENTH CENTURY. — Outside of the teaching congregations, the seventeenth century counts a certain number of independent educators, isolated thinkers, who have transmitted to us in durable records the results of their reflection or of their experience. The most of these belong to the clergy, — they are royal preceptors. In a monarchical government there is no grander affair than the education of princes. Some others are philosophers, whom the general study of human nature has led to reflect on the principles of education. Without pretending to include everything within the narrow compass of this elementary history, we would make known either the fundamental doctrines or the essential methods which have been concerned in the education of the seventeenth century, and

which, at the same time, have made a preparation for the educational reforms of the succeeding centuries.

174. FÉNELON (1651–1715). — Fénelon holds an important place in French literature ; but it seems that of all the varied aspects of his genius, the part he played as an educator is the most important and the most considerable. Fénelon wrote the first classical work of French pedagogy, and it may be said, considering the great number of authors who have been inspired by his thoughts, that he is the head of a school of educators.

175. HOW FÉNELON BECAME A TEACHER. — It is well known that the valuable treatise, *On the Education of Girls*, was written in 1680, at the request of the Duke and the Duchess of Beauvilliers. These noble friends of Fénelon, besides several boys, had eight girls to educate. It was to assist, by his advice, in the education of this little family school, that Fénelon wrote his book which was not designed at first for the public, and which did not appear till 1687. The young Abbé who, in 1680, was but thirty years old, had already had experience in educational matters in the management of the Convent of the *New Catholics* (1678). This was an institution whose purpose was to retain young Protestant converts in the Catholic faith, or even to call them there by mild force. It would have been better, we confess, for the glory of Fénelon, if he had gained his experience elsewhere than in that mission of fanaticism, where he was the auxiliary of the secular arm, the accomplice of dragoons, and where was prepared the Revocation of the Edict of Nantes. We would have preferred that the *Education of Girls* had not been planned in a house where were violently confined girls torn from their mothers, and wives stolen from their husbands. But if the first source of Fénelon's educa-

tional inspiration was not as pure as one could wish, at least in the book there is nothing that betrays the spirit of intoler_ance and violence with which the author was associated. On the contrary, *The Education of Girls* is a work of gentleness and goodness, of a complaisant and amiable grace, which is pervaded by a spirit of progress.

Fénelon soon had occasion to apply the principles that he had set forth in his treatise. August 16, 1689, he was chosen preceptor of the Duke of Bourgogne,[1] with the Duke of Beauvilliers for governor, and the Abbé Fleury for sub_preceptor. From 1689 to 1695, he directed with marvellous success the education of a prince, " a born terror," as Saint Simon expressed it, but who, under the penetrating influence of his master, became an accomplished man, almost a saint. It was for his royal pupil that he composed, one after another, a large number of educational works, such as the *Collection of Fables*, the *Dialogues of the Dead*, the treatise on *The Existence of God*, and especially the *Telemachus*, one of the most popular works in French literature.

In furnishing occasion for the exercise of his educational activity, events served Fénelon according to his wish. We may say that his nature predestinated him to the work of education. With his tender soul, preserving its paternal instincts even in his celibate condition, with his admirable grace of spirit, with his various erudition and profound knowledge of antiquity, with his competence in the studies of grammar and history, attested by different passages in his *Letter to the Academy;* finally, with his temperate disposition and his inclinations towards liberalism in a century of absolute monarchy, he was made to become one of the guides, one of the masters, of French education.

---

[1] Son of Louis XIV., born Aug. 6, 1682; died Feb. 18, 1712.

176. ANALYSIS OF THE TREATISE ON THE EDUCATION OF
GIRLS. — This charming masterpiece of Fénelon's should be
read entire. A rapid analysis would not suffice, as it is
difficult to reduce to a few essential points the flowing
thought of our author. With a facility in expression inclining to laxness, and with a copiousness of thought somewhat
lacking in exactness, Fénelon easily repeats himself; he
returns to thoughts which have already been elaborated, and
does not restrict his easy flowing thought to a rigorous and
methodical plan. We may, however, distinguish three principal parts in the thirteen chapters composing the work.
Chapters I. and II. are critical, and in these the ordinary
faults in the education of women are brought into sharp outline; then in chapters III. to VIII. we have general
observations, and the statement of the principles and
methods that should be followed and applied in the education
of boys as in the education of girls; and finally, from chapter IX. to the end of the book, are all the spécial reflections
which relate exclusively to the merits and demerits, the
duties and the studies, of women.

177. CRITICISM ON MONASTIC EDUCATION. — In the opening of the treatise, as in another little essay [1] that is usually
included in this volume, Fénelon expresses a preference for
a liberal and humane education, where the light of the world
penetrates, and which is not confined to the shadow of a
monastery : —

" I conclude that it is better for your daughter to be with
you than in the best convent that you could select. . . . If
a convent is not well governed, she will see vanity honored,
which is the most subtile of all the poisons that can affect a

---

[1] See the *Advice* of Fénelon, Archbishop Cambray, to a lady of quality
on the education of her daughter.

young girl. She will there hear the world spoken of as a sort of enchanted place, and nothing makes a more pernicions impression than that deceptive picture of the world, which is seen at a distance with admiration, and which exaggerates all its pleasures without showing its disappointments and its sorrows. . . . So I would fear a worldly convent even more than the world itself. If, on the contrary, a convent conforms to the fervor and regularity of its constitution, a girl of rank will grow up there in a profound ignorance of the world. . . . She leaves the convent like one who had been confined in the shadows of a deep cavern, and who suddenly returns to the full light of day. Nothing is more dazzling than this sudden transition, than this glare to which one has never been accustomed."

178. REFUTATION OF THE PREJUDICES RELATIVE TO THE EDUCATION OF WOMEN. — It is, then, for mothers that Fénelon writes his book, still more than for the convents that he does not love. Woman is destined to play a grand part in domestic life. "Can men hope for any sweetness in life, if their most select companionship, which is that of marriage, is turned into bitterness?" Then let us cease to neglect the education of women, and renounce the prejudices by which we pretend to justify this neglect. A learned woman, it is said, is vain and affected! But it is not proposed that women shall engage in useless studies which would make ridiculous pedants of them; it is simply a question of teaching them what befits their position in the household. Woman, it is said again, ordinarily has a weaker intellect than man! But this is the best of reasons why it is necessary to strengthen her intelligence. Finally, woman should be brought up in ignorance of the world! But, replies Fénelon, the world is not a phantom; "it is the aggregate of all the

families"; and women have duties to fulfill in it which are scarcely less important than those of men. "Virtue is not less for women than for men."

179. GOOD OPINION OF HUMAN NATURE. — There are two categories of Christians : the first dwell particularly on the original fall ; and the others attach themselves by preference to the doctrine of redemption. For the first, the child is deeply tainted with sin ; his only inclinations are those towards evil ; he is a child of wrath, who must be severely punished. For the others, the child, redeemed by grace, " has not yet a fixed tendency towards any object"; his instincts have no need of being thwarted ; all they need is direction. Fénelon follows this last mode of thinking, which is the correct one. He does not fear self-love, and does not interdict deserved praise. He counts upon the spontaneity of nature. He regrets the education of the ancients, who left more liberty to children. Finally, in his judgments on human nature, he is influenced by a cheerful and amiable optimism, and sometimes by an excess of complacency and approbation.

180. FEEBLENESS OF THE CHILD. — But if Fénelon believes in the innocence of the child, he is not the less convinced of its feebleness. Hence the measures he recommends to those who have in charge the bringing up of children : " The most important thing in the first years of infancy is the management of the child's health. Through the selection of food and the régime of a simple life, the body should be supplied with pure blood. . . . Another thing of great importance is to allow the organs to strengthen by holding instruction in abeyance. . . ." The intellectual weakness of the child comes for the most part from his inability to fix his attention. " The mind of the child is like a lighted taper in

a place exposed to the wind, whose flame is ever unsteady."
Hence the urgent necessity of not pressing children beyond
measure, of training them little by little as occasion permits,
" of serving and assisting Nature, without urging her."

181. INSTRUCTIVE CURIOSITY; OBJECT LESSONS. — If the
inattention of the child is a great obstacle to his progress,
his natural curiosity, by way of compensation, is a potent
auxiliary. Fénelon knows the aid that can be derived from
this source, and we shall quote entire the remarkable passage
in which he indicates the means of calling it into exercise
through familiar lessons which are already real lessons on
objects : —

" Curiosity in children is a natural tendency which comes
as the precursor of instruction. Do not fail to take advantage of it. For example, in the country they see a mill, and
they wish to know what it is. They should be shown the
manner of preparing the food that is needed for human use.
They notice harvesters, and what they are doing should be
explained to them ; also, how the wheat is sown, and how it
multiplies in the earth. In the city, they see shops where
different arts are practised, and where different wares are
sold. You should never be annoyed by their questions ;
these are so many opportunities offered you by nature for
facilitating the work of instruction. Show that you take
pleasure in replying to such questions, and by this means
you will insensibly teach them how all the things are made
that serve human needs, and that give rise to commercial
pursuits."

182. INDIRECT INSTRUCTION. — Even when the child has
grown up, and is more capable of receiving direct instruction, Fénelon does not depart from his system of mild management and precaution. There are to be no didactic lessons,

but as far as possible the instruction shall be indirect. This is the great educational method of Fénelon, and we shall soon see how he applied it to the education of the Duke of Bourgogne. "The less formal our lessons are, the better." However, there is need of discretion and prudence in the choice of the first ideas, and the first pictures that are to be impressed on the child's mind.

"Into a reservoir so little and so precious only exquisite things should be poured." The absence of pedantry is one of the characteristics of Fénelon. "In rhetoric," he says, "I will give no rules at all; it is sufficient to give good models." As to grammar, "I will give it no attention, or, at least, but very little." Instruction must be insinuated, not imposed. We must resort to unexpected lessons, — to such as do not appear to be lessons. Fénelon here antici- pates Rousseau, and suggests the system of pre-arranged scenes and instructive artifices, similar to those invented for Émile.[1]

183. ALL ACTIVITY MUST BE PLEASURABLE. — One of the best qualities of Fénelon as a teacher is that of wishing that study should be agreeable ; but this quality becomes a fault with him, because he makes an abuse of attractive instruc- tion. We can but applaud him when he criticises the harsh and crabbed pedagogy of the Middle Age, and depicts to us those tiresome and gloomy class-rooms, where teachers are ever talking to children of words and things of which they understand nothing. "No liberty," he says, "no enjoy- ment; but always lessons, silence, uncomfortable postures, correction. and threats." And so there is nothing more just than this thought: "In the current education, all the pleas-

---

[1] For an example of this "artifice" carried to the extreme of absurdity, see Miss Worthington's translation of the Émile, p. 133. (P.)

ure is put on one side, and all that is disagreeable on the other; the disagreeable is all put into study, and all the pleasure is found in the diversions." Fénelon would change all this. For study, as for moral discipline, " pleasure must do all."

First, as to study, seek the means of making agreeable to children whatever you require of them. " We must always place before them a definite and agreeable aim to sustain them in their work." " Conceal their studies under the appearance of liberty and pleasure." Let their range of vision extend itself a little, and their intelligence acquire more breadth." " Mingle instruction with play." " I have seen," he says again, " certain children who have learned to read while playing."

For giving direction to the will, as for giving activity to the intelligence, never subject children to cold and absolute authority. Do not weary them by an indiscreet exactness. Let wisdom appear to them only at intervals, and then with a laughing face. Lead them by reason whenever it is possible for you to do it. Never assume, save in case of extreme necessity, an austere, imperious air that makes them tremble.

" You would close their heart and destroy their confidence, without which there is no profit to hope for from education. Make yourself loved by them. Let them feel at ease in your presence, so that they do not fear to have you see their faults."

Such, intellectually and morally, is the amiable discipline dreamed of by Fénelon. It is evident that the imagination of our author conducts him a little too far and leads him astray. Fénelon sees everything on the bright side. In education, such as this too complacent teacher dreams of it, there is no difficulty, nothing laborious, no thorns. " All metals there are gold ; all flowers there are roses." The child is almost exempted from making effort: he shall not be made to repeat the lesson he has heard, "for fear of annoying him." It is necessary that he learn everything while playing. If he has faults, he must not be told of them, save with precaution, " for fear of hurting his feelings." Fénelon is decidedly too good-natured, too much given to cajolery. In his effort to shun whatever is repulsive, he comes to exclude whatever is laborious. He falls into an artless pleasantry when he demands that the books of his pupil shall be " beautifully bound, with gilt edges, and fine pictures."

184. FABLES AND HISTORY. — Fénelon's very decided taste for agreeable studies, determines him to place in the foremost rank of the child's intellectual occupations, fables and history, because narratives please the infant imagination above everything else. It is with sacred history especially that he would have the attention occupied, always selecting from it " that which presents the most pleasing and the most magnificent pictures." He properly demands, moreover, that the teacher "animate his narrative with lively and familiar tones, and so make all his characters speak." By this means we shall hold the attention of children without forcing it ; " for, once more," he says, " we must be very careful not to impose on them a law to hear and to remember these narratives."

185. MORAL AND RELIGIOUS EDUCATION. — Contrary to Rousseau's notions, Fénelon requires that children should early have their attention turned to moral and religious truths. He would have this instruction given in the concrete, by means of examples drawn from experience. We need not fear to speak to them of God as a venerable old man, with white beard, etc. Whatever of the superstitious

there may be in these conceptions adapted to the infant imagination will be corrected afterwards by the reason. It is to be noted, moreover, that a religion of extremes is not what Fénelon desires. He fears all exaggerations, even that of piety. What he demands is a tempered devotion, a reasonable Christianity. He is suspicious of false miracles. "Accustom girls," he says, "not to accept thoughtlessly certain unauthorized narrations, and not to practise certain forms of devotion introduced by an indiscreet zeal." But possibly, without intending it, Fénelon himself is preparing the way for the superstition he combats, when, for the purpose of indoctrinating the child with the first principles of religion, he presents to him the notion of God under sensible forms, and speaks to him of a paradise where all is of gold and precious stones.

186. STUDIES PROPER FOR WOMEN. — So far, we have noted in Fénelon's work only general precepts applicable to boys and girls alike. But in the last part of his work, Fénelon treats especially of women's own work, of the qualities peculiarly their own, of their duties, and of the kind of instruction they need in order to fulfill them.

No one knew better than Fénelon the faults that come to woman through ignorance, — unrest. unemployed time, inability to apply herself to solid and serious duties, frivolity, indolence, lawless imagination, indiscreet curiosity concerning trifles, levity, and talkativeness, sentimentalism, and, what is remarkable with a friend of Madame Guyon, a mania for theology: "Women are too much inclined to speak decisively on religious questions."

What does Fénelon propose as a corrective of these mischievous tendencies? It must be confessed that the plan of instruction which he proposes is still insufficient, and that it scarcely accords with the ideal as we conceive it to-day.

" Keep young girls," he says, " within the common bounds, and teach them that there should be for their sex a modesty with respect to knowledge almost as delicate as that inspired by the horror of vice."

Is not this the same .as declaring that knowledge is not intended for women, and that it is repugnant to their delicate nature?

When Fénelon tells us that a young girl ought to learn to read and write correctly (and observe that account is taken only of the daughters of the nobility and of the wealthy middle classes) ; when he adds, *let her also learn grammar*, we can infer from these puerile prescriptions, that Fénelon does not exact any great things from women in the way of knowledge. And yet, such as it is, this programme surpassed, in the time of Fénelon, the received custom, and constituted a substantial progress. It was to state an excellent principle, whose consequences should have been more fully analyzed, to demand that women should learn all that is necessary for them to know, in order to bring up their children. Fénelon should also be commended for having recommended to young women the reading of profane authors. He who had been nourished on such literature, who was, so to speak, but a Greek turned Christian, who knew Homer so perfectly as to write the *Telemachus*, could not, without belying himself, advise against the studies from which he had derived so much pleasure and profit. He also recognized the utility of history, ancient and modern. He grants a place to poetry and eloquence, provided an elimination be made of whatever would be dangerous to purity of morals. What we comprehend less easily is that he condemns, as severely as he does, music, which, he says, " furnishes diversions that are poisonous."

But these faults, this mistrust of too high an intellectual

culture, ought not to prevent us from admiring the *Education
of Girls.* Let us be grateful to Fénelon for having resisted,
in part, the prejudices of a period when young women were
condemned by their sex to an almost absolute ignorance ; for
having declared that he would follow a course contrary " to
that of alarm and of a superficial culture of the intelligence " ;
and finally, for having written a book, all the generous inspirations of which Madame de Maintenon herself has not
caught ; and of which we may say, finally, that almost everything that it contains is excellent, and that it is defective
only in what it does not contain.

187. Madame de Lambert (1647-1733). — Fénelon, as
an educator of women, was the founder of a school, From
Rollin to Madame de Genlis, how many teachers have been
inspired by him! But in the front rank of his pupils we
must place Madame de Lambert. In her *Counsels to her Son*
(1701), and especially in her *Counsels to her Daughter* (1728),
she has taken up the tradition of Fénelon with greater
breadth and freedom of spirit. " As discreet as he with
respect to works of the imagination, of which she fears that
the reading may inflame the mind ; " more severe, even, than
he towards Racine, whose name she seems to hesitate to
pronounce ; disposed to exclude her daughter from " plays,
representations that move the passions, music, poetry, — all
belonging to the retinue of pleasure, — in other respects,
Madame de Lambert takes precedence and surpasses her
master" (Gréard). She reproaches Molière for having
abandoned women to idleness, pastime, and pleasure. She
loves history, especially the history of France, " which no
one is permitted not to know." Finally, without entering
into the details of her protests, she makes a powerful plea for
the cause of woman's education ; she already belongs to the
eighteenth century.

188. EDUCATION OF THE DUKE OF BOURGOGNE. — Singularly enough, Fénelon did not make an application of his ideas on education till after he had set them forth in a theoretical treatise. The education of the Duke of Bourgogne permitted him to make a practical test of the rules established in the *Education of Girls*. Nothing is of more interest to the historian of pedagogy than the study of that princely education into which Fénelon put all his mind and heart, and which, by its results, at once brilliant and insufficient, exhibits the merits and the faults of his plan of education.

189. HAPPY RESULTS. — The Duke of Bourgogne with his active intelligence, and also with his impetuous, indocile character, and his fits of passion, was just the pupil for the teacher who relied on *indirect instruction*. It would have been unwise to indoctrinate with heavy didactic lessons a spirit so impetuous. Through tact and industry, Fénelon succeeded in captivating the attention of the prince, and in skillfully insinuating into his mind knowledges that he would probably have rejected, had they been presented to it in a scientific and pedantic form. " I have never seen a child," says Fénelon, " who so readily understood the finest things of poetry and eloquence." Doubtless the happy nature of the prince contributed a large part towards these results ; but the art of Fénelon had also its share in the final account.

190. MORAL LESSONS ; THE FABLES. — How shall morals be taught to a violent and passionate child? Fénelon did not think of preaching fine sermons to him ; but presented to him, under the form of *Fables*, the moral precepts that he wished to inculcate. The *Fables* of Fénelon certainly have not, as a whole, a large literary value ; but, to form a just appreciation of them, we must recollect that their merit is

especially to be seen in the circumstances attending their composition. Composed from day to day, they were adapted to the circumstances of the life of the young prince ; they were filled with allusions to his faults and his virtues, and they conveyed to him, at the favorable moment, under the veil of a pleasing fiction, the commendation or the censure that he deserved. "One might," says the Cardinal de Bausset, "follow the chronological order in which these pieces were composed, by comparing them with the progress which age and instruction must have made in the education of the prince." The apologues, even with their very general morals, will always have their value and place in the education of children. What shall be said of the fables in which the moral, wholly individual, was addressed exclusively to the pupil for whom they were written, either on account of some perversity that he let come to the surface, or of a rising virtue that had been manifested in his conduct? It is thus that the fable called *The Capricious* presented to the young duke the picture of his fits of passion, and taught him to correct himself ; that of the *Bee and the Fly* reminded him that the most brilliant qualities serve no good purpose without moderation. One day, in a fit of anger, the prince so far forgot himself as to say to Fénelon, who was reproving him : " *No, no, Sir! I know who I am, and who you are!* " The next day, doubtless in response to this explosion of princely self-conceit, Fénelon had him read the fable entitled *Bacchus and the Faun:* " As Bacchus could not abide a malicious jeerer always ready to make sport of his expressions that were not correct and elegant, he said to him in a fiery and important tone : " How dare you jeer the son of Jupiter? " The Faun replied without emotion : " Alas ! how does the son of Jupiter dare to commit any fault? "

Certain fables, of a more elevated tone than the others,

are not designed simply to correct the faults of children; they prepare the prince for the exercise of government. Thus, the fable of the *Bees* disclosed to him the beauties of an industrious State, and one where order reigns; the *Nile and the Ganges* taught him love for the people, " compassion for humanity, harassed and suffering." Finally, from each of these fables there issued a serious lesson under the pleasing exterior of a witticism; and more than once, in reading them, the prince doubtless felt an emotion of pleasure or of shame, as he recognized himself in a commendation or in a reproof addressed to the imaginary personages of the *Fables*.

191. HISTORICAL LESSONS ; THE DIALOGUES OF THE DEAD.— It is not alone in moral education, but in intellectual education as well, that Fénelon resorts to artifice. The ingenious preceptor has employed fiction in all its forms the better to compass and dominate the spirit of his pupil. There are the fables for moral instruction, the dialogues for the study of history, and finally, the epopee in the *Telemachus*, for the political education of the heir to the throne of France.

The *Dialogues of the Dead* put on the stage men of all countries and conditions, Charles the Fifth and a monk of Saint Just, Aristotle and Descartes, Leonardo da Vinci and Poussin, Cæsar and Alexander. History proper, literature, philosophy, the arts, were the subjects of conversations composed, as in the *Fables*, at different intervals, according to the progress and the needs of the Duke of Bourgogne. These were attractive pictures that came from time to time to be introduced into the scheme for the didactic study of universal history. They should be taken only for what they were intended to be, — the pleasing complement to a regular and consecutive course of instruction. Fénelon knew better than any one else that history is interesting in itself, and that to make the study of it interesting, it is sufficient to present it to the childish imagination with clearness, with vivacity, and with feeling.

192. VARIETY OF DISCIPLINARY AGENTS. — The education of the Duke of Bourgogne is the practical application of Fénelon's principles as to the necessity of employing an insinuating gentleness rather than an authority which dryly commands. There are to be no sermons, no lectures, but indirect means of moral instruction. The Duke of Bourgogne was irascible. Instead of reading to him Seneca's treatise *On Anger*, this is Fénelon's device: One morning he has a cabinet-maker come to his apartments, whom he has instructed for the purpose. The prince enters, stops, and looks at the tools. " Go about your business, Sir," cries the workman, who assumes a most threatening air, " for I am not responsible for what I may do; when I am in a passion, I break the arms and legs of those whom I meet." We guess the conclusion of the story, and how, by this experimental method, Fénelon contrives to teach the prince to guard against anger and its effects.

When indirect means did not answer, Fénelon employed others. It is thus that he made frequent appeals to the self-love of his pupil; he reminded him of what he owed to his name and to the hopes of France. He had him record his word of honor that he would behave well: "I promise the Abbé Fénelon, on the word of a prince, that I will obey him, and that, in case I break my word, I will submit to any kind of punishment and dishonor. Given at Versailles, this 29th day of November, 1689. Signed: Louis." At other times Fénelon appealed to his feelings, and conquered him by his tenderness and goodness. It is in such moments of tender confidence that the prince said to him, " I leave the

Duke of Bourgogne outside the door, and with you I am but the little Louis." Finally, at other times, Fénelon resorted to the harshest punishments; he sequestered him, took away his books, and interdicted all conversation.

193. DIVERSIFIED INSTRUCTION. — By turns serious and tender, mild and severe, in his moral discipline, Fénelon was not less versatile in his methods of instruction. His dominant preoccupation was to *diversify* studies — the term is his own. If a given subject of study was distasteful to his pupil, Fénelon passed to another. Although the success of his tutorship seems to be a justification of his course, there is ground for thinking that, as a general rule, Fénelon's precept is debatable, and that his example should not be followed by making an over-use of amusement and agreeable variety. Fénelon has too often made studies puerile through his attempts to make them agreeable.

194. RESULTS OF THE EDUCATION OF THE DUKE OF BOURGOGNE. — It seems like a paradox to say that Fénelon was too successful in his educational apostleship; and yet this is the truth. Under his hand — "the ablest hand that ever was," says Saint Simon — the prince became in all respects the image of his master. He was a bigot to the extent of being unwilling to attend a royal ball because that worldly entertainment coincided with the religious celebration of the Epiphany; he was rather a monk than a king; he was destitute of all spirit of initiative and liberty, irresolute, absorbed in his pious erudition and mystic prayers; finally, he was another Telemachus, who could not do without his Mentor. Fénelon had monopolized and absorbed the will of his pupil. He had forgotten that the purpose of education is to form, not a pale copy, an image of the master, but a man independent and free, capable of sufficing for himself.

195. The Telemachus. — The *Telemachus*, composed from 1694 to 1698, was designed for the Duke of Bourgogne ; but he was not to read it, and did not read it, in fact, till after his marriage. Through this epopee in prose, this romance borrowed from Homer, Fénelon purposed to continue the moral education of his pupil. But the book abounds in sermons. " I could have wished," said Boileau, " that the Abbé had made his Mentor a little less a preacher, and that the moral of the book could have been distributed a little more imperceptibly, and with more art." At least, they are beautiful and excellent sermons, aimed against luxury, the spirit of conquest, the consequences of absolute power, and against ambition and war. Louis XIV. had probably read the *Telemachus*, and had comprehended the allusions concealed in the description of the Republic of Salentum, when he said of Fénelon that he was " the most chimerical spirit in his kingdom." Besides the moral lesson intended for princes, the *Telemachus* also contains bold reflections on political questions. For example, note the conception of a system of public instruction, very new for the time : " Children belong less to their parents than to the Republic, and ought to be educated by the State. There should be established public schools in which are taught the fear of God, love of country, and respect for the laws."

196. Bossuet and Fénelon. — Bossuet, as preceptor of the Dauphin,[1] was far from having the same success as Fénelon. Nothing was overlooked, however, in the education of the son of Louis XIV. ; and the *Letter to Pope Innocent XI.* (1679), in which Bossuet presents his scheme of study, gives proof of high fitness for educational work.

---

[1] Eldest son of Louis XIV., born Nov. 1, 1661; died April 14, 1711.

He recommends assiduous labor, no leaves of absence, and play mingled with study. "A child must play and enjoy himself," he says. Emulation excited by the presence of other children, who came to compete with the prince; a thorough reading of the Latin authors, explained, not in fragments, as with the Jesuits, but in complete texts; a certain breadth of spirit, since the study of the comic poets — of Terence in particular — was expressly recommended; a familiarity with the Greeks and the Romans, "especially with the divine Homer"; the grammar learned in French; history, "the mistress of human life," studied with ardor, and presented, first, in its particular facts, in the lessons which the Dauphin drew up, and then in its general laws, the spirit of which has been transmitted to us in the *Discourse on Universal History;* geography learned "while playing and making imaginary journeys"; philosophy; and finally the sciences, brilliantly presented, — with such a programme, and under such a master, it seems that the Dauphin ought to have been a student of the highest rank; but he remained a mediocre pupil, "absorbed," to use Saint Simon's expression, "in his own fat and gloom."

It must certainly be acknowledged that, notwithstanding his excellent intentions, Bossuet was in part responsible for the fact that these results were insufficient, or, rather, nil. He did not know how "to condescend," as Montaigne says, "to the boyish ways of his pupil." In dealing with him he proceeded on too high a plane. "The austere genius of Bossuet," says Henry Martin, "did not know how to become small with the small." Bossuet lacked in flexibility and tact, precisely the qualities that characterized Fénelon. Bossuet, in education, as in everything else, is grandeur, noble and sublime bearing; Fénelon, as preceptor, is address, insinuating grace. That which dominates in the one is authority, a majesty almost icy; that which constitutes the charm of the other is versatility, a persuasive gentleness, a penetrating tenderness.

To be just, however, it must be added that the faults were not all on Bossuet's side. In that education, stamped with failure, the pupil was the great culprit, with his ungrateful and rebellious nature. "My lord has much spirit," said a courtier, "but he has it *concealed.*" For one not a courtier, does it not amount to the same thing to have one's spirit concealed and to have none at all?

197. SPHERE AND LIMITS OF EDUCATION. — It seems that, on one page of the *Education of Girls*, Fénelon has traced in advance, and by a sort of divination, the parallels of the two educations of the Dauphin and of the Duke of Bourgogne respectively. How can we fail to recognize the anticipated portrait of Fénelon's future pupil in this passage, written in 1680?

"It must be acknowledged, that of all the difficulties in education, none is comparable to that of bringing up children who are lacking in sensibility. The naturally quick and sensitive are capable of terrible mistakes, — passion and presumption do so betray them! But they have also great resources, and when far gone often come to themselves. Instruction is a germ concealed within them, which starts, and sometimes bears fruit, when experience comes to the aid of knowledge, and the passions lose their power. At least, we know how to make them attentive, and to awaken their curiosity. We have the means of interesting them, and of stimulating them through their sense of honor; but, on the other hand, we can gain no hold on indolent natures."

On the other hand, all that follows applies perfectly to the Dauphin, the indocile pupil of Bossuet : —

" . . . All the thoughts of these are distractions ; they are never where they ought to be ; they cannot be touched to the quick even by corrections ; they hear everything and feel nothing. This indolence makes the pupil negligent, and disgusts him with whatever he does. Under these conditions, the best planned education runs the risk of failure. . . . Many people, who think superficially, conclude from this poor success that nature does all for the production of men of merit, and that education has no part in the result; but the only conclusion to be drawn from the case is, that there are natures like ungrateful soils, upon which culture has but little effect." [1]

Nothing better can be said, and Fénelon has admirably summed up the lesson that should be drawn from these two princely illustrations of the seventeenth century. If the sorry results of Bossuet's efforts should inspire the educator with some modesty, and prove to him that the best grain does not grow in an ingrate soil, is not the brilliant education of the Duke of Bourgogne, which developed almost all the virtues in a soul where nature seemed to have planted the seeds of all the vices, of a nature to increase the confidence of teachers, and show them what can be done by the art of a shrewd and able teacher?

[198. ANALYTICAL SUMMARY. — 1. Education as a plastic art has never been exhibited in a more favorable light than in this history of Fénelon's teaching ; and perhaps the resistance that sometimes sets at defiance the teacher's art could not be better illustrated than in the case of Bossuet's royal pupil.

2. These two historical illustrations also exhibit the play of the two factors that enter into education, — nature and

---

[1] *Education of Girls*, Chap. v.

art. Fénelon's teaching illustrates the potency of human art in controlling, modifying, almost re-creating a work of nature. The Duke of Bourgogne was almost re-made to order.

3. Here is also an illustrious example of the attempt to make education a pastime, to divest it of all constraint, to make learning run parallel with the pupil's inclinations. In the natural recoil from a dry and formal teaching that had to be enforced against the pupil's will, it is sometimes forgotten that a large part of life's duties lie outside of our inclinations.

4. The policy of leading pupils at such a distance that they seem to themselves to be following their own initiative, is one of the highest of the teacher's arts.

5. The inculcation of moral lessons through fables, after Fénelon's plan, is a practice that modern teaching might profitably adopt.]

CHAPTER IX.

THE PHILOSOPHERS OF THE SEVENTEENTH CENTURY. DESCARTES, MALEBRANCHE, LOCKE.

199. DESCARTES, MALEBRANCHE, AND LOCKE. — Descartes, a spiritualist; Malebranche, an idealist; Locke, a sensationalist, — such are the philosophers of the seventeenth century who are related to the history of pedagogy. And yet the first two have only a remote connection with it, through their exposition of some of its general principles. Locke is the only one who has resolutely approached educational questions in a special treatise that has become a classic in English pedagogy.

200. DESCARTES (1596–1650). — Descartes, the father of modern philosophy, does not generally figure in the lists drawn up by the historians of education; and yet, in our

opinion, there is no thinker who has exercised a more decisive influence on the destinies of education. The author of the *Discourse of Method* has, properly speaking, no system of pedagogy, having never directly treated of educational affairs ; but through his philosophical principles he has changed the direction of human thought, and has introduced into the study of known truths, as well as into the search for new truths, a method and a taste for clearness and precision, which have profited instruction in all of its departments. ˙

" We now find, ' says Rollin, " in the discourses from the pulpit and the bar, and in the dissertations on science, an order, an exactness, a propriety, and a solidity, which were formerly not so common. Many believe, and not without reason, that we owe this manner of thinking and writing to the extraordinary progress which has been made within a a century in the study of philosophy." [1]

201. THE DISCOURSE OF METHOD (1637). — Every system of philosophy contains in germ a special system of education. From the mere fact that philosophers define, each in his own way, the nature and the destiny of man, they come to different conclusions as to the aims and methods of education. Only a few of them have taken pains to deduce from their principles the consequences that are involved in them ; but all of them, whether they will or no, are educators.

Such is the case of Descartes. In writing, in the first part of his *Discourse of Method*, his *Considerations Touching the Sciences*, Descartes has written a chapter on practical pedagogy, and through the general rules of his logic, he has, in effect, founded a new theory of education.

---

[1] Rollin, *Traité des études*, Tome IV. p. 335.

202. CRITICISM OF THE CURRENT EDUCATION.—Descartes has given a long account of the education which he had received among the Jesuits, at the college of La Flèche, and this account furnished him occasion, either to criticize the methods in use, or to indicate his personal views and his educational preferences.

"From my infancy letters have been my intellectual nourishment. . . . But as soon as I had completed the course of study required for the·doctor's degree, I found myself embarrassed with so many doubts and errors that it seemed to me that I had received no other profit from my efforts at learning than the discovery of my growing ignorance."

In other terms, Descartes ascertained that his studies, though pursued with ardor for eight years in one of the most celebrated schools of Europe, had not permitted him to acquire " a clear and sure knowledge of all that is useful for living." This was to condemn the barren teaching and the formal instruction of the Jesuits. Passing in review the different parts of the instruction, Descartes first remarks that it was wrong to make an abuse of the reading of ancient books ; for, to hold converse with the men of other centuries " is about the same as travelling ; and when we spend too much time in travelling, we become strangers in our own country." Then he complains that he was not made to know " the true use of mathematics," since he had been shown their application only to the mechanic arts. He nearly condemns rhetoric and poetics, since eloquence and poetry are "intellectual gifts rather than the fruits of study." The ancient languages — and in this he gravely deceives himself — seem to him useful only for the understanding of authors. He does not admit that the study of Latin or Greek can contribute to intellectual development.

From these reflections there seems to issue the notion of an instruction more solid, more positive, more directly useful for the purposes of life, than that which had been brought into fashion by the Jesuits. However, Descartes does not eliminate the ordinary studies, as eloquence, "which has incomparable power and beauty"; poetry, "which has an enchanting tenderness and melody"; the reading of the classics, which is "a studied conversation with the most estimable men of past centuries"; history, "which forms the judgment"; fables, whose "charm arouses the spirit." But he would give to all these exercises a more practical turn, a more utilitarian character, a more positive application.

203. GREAT PRINCIPLES OF MODERN PEDAGOGY. — Without intending it, without any other thought than that of modifying the false direction of the mind in the search for scientific truth, Descartes has stated some of the great principles of modern pedagogy.

The first is the equal aptitude of minds to know and comprehend. "Good sense," says Descartes, "is the thing of all else in this world that is most equally distributed.[1] . . . The latent ability to judge well, to distinguish the true from the false, is naturally equal among all men." What is this but saying that all men are entitled to instruction? In a certain sense, what are the innumerable primary schools scattered over the surface of the civilized globe, but the application and the living commentary of Descartes' ideas on the equal distribution of good sense and reason among men?

---

[1] I am in doubt whether M. Compayré intends to sanction this doctrine or not. This is an anticipation of one of Jacotot's paradoxes: "All human beings are equally capable of learning." The verdict of actual teachers is undoubtedly to the effect that there are manifold differences in the ability of pupils to know, comprehend, and judge. (P.)

But, adds Descartes, "it is not enough to have a sound mind; the principal thing is to make a good use of it." In other words, nature is not sufficient in herself; she needs to be guided and directed. Method is the essential thing; it has a sovereign importance. Success will depend less on natural qualities, such as imagination, memory, quickness of thought, than upon the rules of intellectual direction imposed on the mind. Education has a far greater part than nature in the formation and development of accurate and upright intelligences.

Another Cartesian principle is the substitution of free inquiry and reflective conviction for blind beliefs founded upon authority. Descartes promulgated this famous rule of his method: "The first precept is, never to receive anything for true that I do not know, upon evidence, to be such; . . . and to comprise no more within my judgments than what is presented so clearly and distinctly to my mind that I have no occasion to call it in question." In this declaration he has not only reformed science and revolutionized philosophy, but has banished from the school the old routine, the mechanical processes and exercises of pure memory, and has made a demand for rational methods that excite the intelligence, awaken clear and distinct ideas, and provoke judgment and reflection. Of course, it is not proposed to make a little Descartes out of every child, despoiling him of received beliefs in order to construct personal opinions *de novo;* but the rule of evidence, applied with moderation and discretion, is none the less an excellent pedagogical precept, which will never be disallowed by those who wish to make of the child something more than a mere machine.

204. OBJECTIVE AND SUBJECTIVE PEDAGOGY. — We have now reached a place where we may call into notice two different tendencies, equally legitimate, which we shall find,

with exaggerations that compromise their utility, in the
practice of modern teachers. There are those who wish
above all to develop the intelligence; and there are others
who are preoccupied with furnishing the mind with a stock
of positive knowledge. The first conceive instruction as
taking place, as it were, through what is within, through the
development of the internal qualities of precision and measure; the others are preoccupied only with the instruction
that takes place through what is without, through an extended erudition, through an accumulation of knowledges.
In a word, if I may be allowed the expression, some affect
a subjective pedagogy, and others an objective pedagogy.
Bacon is of the latter number. That which preoccupies the
great English logician above everything else is the extension of observations and experiments. "To reason without
knowing anything of that which we reason upon," he says,
"is as if we were to weigh or measure the wind." Descartes, however, who has never neglected the study of facts,
esteems them less as material to be accumulated in the mind,
than as instruments for training the mind itself. He would
have repudiated those teachers of our day who seem to
think the whole thing is done when there has been made to
pass before the mental vision of the child an interminable
series of object-lessons, without the thought of developing
that intelligence itself.

205. MALEBRANCHE (1638–1715). — We must not expect
great pedagogical wisdom from a mystical dreamer and resolute idealist, who has imagined the vision of all things in
God. Besides, Malebranche has given only a passing attention to things relating to education. The member of a
teaching congregation, the Oratory, he has not taught; and
the whole effort of his mind was spent in the search for
metaphysical truth. Nevertheless, it is interesting to stop

for a moment this visionary who traverses the earth with eyes fixed on the heavens, and inquire of him what he thinks of the very practical question, education.

206. SENSE INSTRUCTION CONDEMNED. — Malebranche will reply to us, with the prejudices of a metaphysician of the idealist type, that the first thing to do is to nourish the child on abstract truths. In his view, souls have no age, so to speak, and the infant is already capable of ideal contemplation. Then let sense instruction be abandoned, "for this is the reason why children leave metaphysical thoughts, to apply themselves to sensations." Is it objected that the child does not seem very well adapted to meditation on abstract truths? It is not so much the fault of nature, Malebranche will reply, as of the bad habits he has contracted. There is a means of remedying this ordinary incapacity of the child.

"If we kept children from fear, from desires, and from hope, if we did not make them suffer pain, if we removed them as far as possible from their little pleasures, then we might teach them, from the moment they knew how to speak, the most difficult and the most abstract things, or at least the concrete mathematics, mechanics."

Does Malebranche hope, then, to suppress, in the life of the child, pleasure and pain, and triumph over the tendencies which ordinary education has developed?

"As an ambitious man who had just lost his fortune and his credit would not be in a condition to resolve questions in metaphysics or equations in algebra, so children, on whose brains apples and sugar-plums make as profound impressions as are made on those of men of forty years by offices and titles, are not in a condition to hear the abstract truths that are taught them."

Consequently, we must declare war against the senses, and

exclude, for example, all sorts of sensible rewards. Only, by a singular contradiction, Malebranche upholds material punishments in the education of children. The only thing of sense he retains is the rod.[1]

207. INFLUENCE OF MATERIAL ENVIRONMENT. — Another contradiction more worthy of note is, that, notwithstanding his idealism, Malebranche believes in the influence of physical conditions on the development of the soul. He does not go so far as to say with the materialists of our time, that "man is what he eats"; but he accords a certain amount of influence to nourishment. He speaks cheerfully of wine and of "those wild spirits who do not willingly submit to the orders of the will." He never applied himself to work without having partaken of coffee. The soul, in his view, is not a force absolutely independent and isolated, which develops through an internal activity: "we are bound," he says, "to everything, and stand in relations to all that surrounds us."

208. LOCKE (1632-1704). — Locke is above all else a psychologist, an accomplished master in the art of analyzing the origin of ideas and the elements of the mental life. He is the head of that school of empirical psychology that rallies around its standard, Condillac in France, Herbart in Germany, and in Great Britain Hume and other Scotchmen, and

---

[1] Is not the antagonism pointed out by Malebranche more serious than M. Compayré seems to think? If the current of mental activity sets strongly towards the feelings, emotions, or senses, it is thereby diverted from the purely intellectual processes, such as reflection and judgment. The mind of the savage is an example of what comes from "following the order of nature" in an extreme training of the senses. On the nature and extent of this antagonism, the following authorities may be consulted: Hamilton, *Metaphysics*, p. 336 ; Mansel, *Metaphysics*, pp. 68, 70, 77 ; Bain, *The Senses and the Intellect*, pp. 392-394 ; Bain, *Education as a Science*, pp. 17, 29, 37 ; Spencer, *Principles of Psychology*, pp. 98-99. (P.)

the most of modern philosophers. But from psychology to pedagogy the transition is easy, and Locke had to make no great effort to become an authority in education after having been an accomplished philosopher.

209. SOME THOUGHTS ON EDUCATION (1693). — The book which he published towards the close of his life, under the modest title *Some Thoughts concerning Education*, was the summing up of a long experience. A studious pupil at Westminster, he conceived from his early years, as Descartes did at La Flèche, a keen sense of repugnance for a purely formal classical instruction, and for language studies in general, in which, nevertheless, he attained distinction. A model student at the University of Oxford, he there became an accomplished humanist, notwithstanding the practical and positive tendency of his mind that was already drawn towards the natural sciences and researches in physics and in medicine. Made Bachelor of Arts in 1656, and Master of Arts in 1658, he passed directly from the student's bench to the professor's chair. He was successively lecturer and tutor in Greek, but this did not prevent him later from eliminating Hellenism almost completely from his scheme of liberal education. Then he became lecturer on rhetoric, and finally on moral philosophy. When, in 1666, he discontinued his scholastic life to mingle in political and diplomatic affairs, he at least carried from his studious residence at Oxford, the germs of the most of his ideas on education. He sought occasion to make an application of them in the education of private indi-´ viduals, of whom he was the inspirer and counsellor, if not the official director. In the families of friends and hosts that he frequented, for example, in that of Lord Shaftesbury, he made a close study of children ; and it is in studying them, and in following with a sagacious eye the successive steps of their improvement in disposition and mind, that he succeeded in

acquiring that educational experience which has left a trace on each page of the *Thoughts concerning Education*. This book, in fact, is the issue of one of Locke's experiences as an assistant in the education of the children of his friends. Towards the year 1684–5, he addressed to his friend Clarke a series of letters which, retouched and slightly modified, have become a classical work, simple and familiar in style, a little disconnected, perhaps, and abounding in repetitious, but the substance of which is excellent, and the ideas as remarkable, in general, for their originality as for their justness. Translated into French in 1695 by P. Coste, and reprinted several times in the lifetime of their author, the *Thoughts concerning Education* have had a universal success. They have exercised an undoubted influence on the educational writings of Rousseau and Helvetius. They have received the enthusiastic praise of Leibnitz, who placed this work above that on the *Human Understanding*. " I am persuaded," said H. Marion recently, in his interesting study on Locke, " that if an edition of the *Thoughts* were to be published to-day in a separate volume, it would have a marked success." [1]

210. ANALYSIS OF THE THOUGHTS CONCERNING EDUCA-
TION. — Without pretending to give in this place a detailed analysis of Locke's book, which deserves to be read entire, and which discusses exhaustively or calls to notice, one after another, almost all important educational questions, we shall attempt to make known the essential principles which are to be drawn from it. These are : 1. in physical education, the *hardening process;* 2. in intellectual education, practical utility ; 3. in moral education, the principle of honor, set up as a rule for the free self-government of man.

---

[1] *John Locke. His Life and his Work.* Paris, 1878.

211. PHYSICAL EDUCATION ; THE HARDENING PROCESS. — The ideal of education, according to Locke, is " a sound mind in a sound body." A physician like Rabelais, the author of the *Thoughts concerning Education* had special competence in questions of physical education. But a love for the paradoxical, and an excessive tendency towards the hardening of the body, have marred, on this point, the reflections of the English philosopher. He has summed up his precepts on this subject in the following lines : —

" The whole is reduced," he says, " to a small number of rules, easy to observe ; much air, exercise, and sleep ; a simple diet, no wine or strong liquors ; little or no medicine at all ; garments that are neither too tight nor too warm ; finally, and above all, the habit of keeping the head and feet cold, of often bathing the feet in cold water and exposing them to dampness."[1] But it is necessary to enter somewhat into details, and to examine closely some of these ideas.

Locke is the first educator to write a consecutive and methodical dissertation on the food, clothing, and sleep of children. It is he who has stated this principle, afterwards taken up by Rousseau : " Leave to nature the care of forming the body as she thinks it ought to be done." Hence, no close-fitting garments, life in the open air and in the sun ; children brought up like peasants, inured to heat and cold, playing with head and feet bare. In the matter of food, Locke forbids sugar, wine, spices, and flesh, up to the age of three or four. As to fruits, which children often crave with an inordinate appetite, a fact that is not surprising, he pleasantly remarks, " since it was for an apple that our first parents lost paradise," he makes a singular choice. He

---

[1] *Thoughts*, translation by G. Compayré, p. 57.

authorizes strawberries, gooseberries, apples, and pears ; but he interdicts peaches, plums, and grapes. To excuse Locke's prejudice against the grapes, it must be recollected that he lived in England, a country in which the vine grows with difficulty, and of which an Italian said, "The only ripe fruit I have seen in England is a baked apple." As to meals, Locke does not think it important to fix them at stated hours. Fénelon, on the contrary, more judiciously requires that the hour for repasts be absolutely determined. But this is not the only instance in which Locke's wisdom is at fault. What shall be said of that hygienic fancy which consists in allowing the child "to have his shoes so thin, that they might leak and let in water, whenever he comes near it"?

It is certain that Locke treats children with an unheard-of severity, all the more surprising in the case of one who had an infirm and delicate constitution that could be kept in repair only through precaution and management. I do not know whether the consequences of the treatment which he proposes, applied to the letter, might not be disastrous. Madame de Sévigné was more nearly right when she wrote : " If your son is very robust, a rude education is good; but if he is delicate, I think that in your attempts to make him robust, you would kill him." The body, says Locke, may be accustomed to everything. We may reply to this by quoting an anecdote of Peter the Great, who one day took it into his head, it is said, that it would be best for all the sailors to form the habit of drinking salt water. Immediately he promulgated an edict which ordered that all naval cadets should henceforth drink only sea-water. The boys all died, and there the experiment stopped.

Still, without subscribing to Locke's paradoxes, which have found no one to approve of them except Rousseau, we should recollect that in his precepts on physical education as a whole, the author of the *Thoughts* deserves our commendation for having recommended a manly course of discipline, and a frugal diet, for having discarded fashionable conventionalities and drawn near to nature, and for having condemned the refinements of an indolent mode of life, and for being inspired by the simple and manly customs of England.

212. MORAL EDUCATION. — In the thought of Locke, moral education takes precedence of instruction properly so called:

"That which a gentleman ought to desire for his son, besides the fortune he leaves him is, 1. virtue; 2. prudence; 3. good manners; 4. instruction."

Virtue and prudence — that is, moral qualities and practical qualities — are of first consideration. "Instruction," says Locke again, "is but the least part of education." In the book of *Thoughts*, where repetitions abound, there is nothing more frequently repeated than the praise of virtue.

Doubtless it may be thought that Locke, like Herbert Spencer in our own day, cherishes prejudices with respect to instruction, and that he does not take sufficient account of the moralizing influence exercised over the heart and will by intellectual enlightenment; but, even with this admission, we must thank Locke for having protested against the teachers who think they have done all when they have embellished the memory and developed the intelligence.

The grand thing in education is certainly to establish good moral habits, to cultivate noble sentiments, and, finally, to form virtuous characters.

213. HONOR, THE PRINCIPLE OF MORAL DISCIPLINE. — But after having placed moral education in its proper rank, which is the first, it remains to inquire what shall be the principles and the methods of this education. Shall it be the maxim of utility, as Rousseau requires? Must the child,

before acting, inquire what is the good of this? *Cui bono?*
No ; utilitarian in instruction and in intellectual education, as
we have just seen, Locke is not so in moral education.
Shall it be fear, shall it be the authority of the teacher or of
parents, founded on punishments, upon the slavish feeling
of terror? Still less. Locke reproves repressive discipline,
and is not inclined to chastisements. Shall it be affection,
the love of parents, the aggregate of tender sentiments?
Locke scarcely speaks of them. Of too little sensibility himself, he does not seem to think of all that can be done through
the sensibility of the child.

Locke, who perhaps is wrong in treating the child too
early, as though he were a man, who does not take sufficient
account of all the feebleness that is in infant nature, appeals
from the first to the sentiment of honor, and to the fear of
shame, that is, to emotions which, I fear, by their very
nobleness, are above the powers of the child. Honor, which
is, in fact, but another name for duty, and the ordinary
synonym of virtue, — honor may assuredly be the guide of
an adult and already trained conscience ; but is it not chimerical to hope that the child, from his earliest years, will be
sensible to the esteem or the contempt of those who surround
him? If it were possible to inspire a child with a regard for
his reputation, I grant with Locke that we might henceforth
" make of him whatever we will, and teach him to love all
the forms of virtue "; but the question is to know whether
we can succeed in this, and I doubt it, notwithstanding the
assurances of Locke.

Kant has very justly said : —

" It is labor lost to speak of duty to children. They comprehend it only as a thing whose transgression is followed by
the ferule. . . . So one ought not to try to call into play with
children the feeling of shame, but to wait for this till the

period of youth comes. In fact, it cannot be developed in them till the idea of honor has already taken root there."

Locke is the dupe of the same illusion, both when he expects of the child enough moral power so that the sense of honor suffices to govern him, and when he counts enough on his intellectual forces to desire to reason with him from the moment he knows how to speak. For forming good habits in the child, and preparing him for a life of virtue, there is full need of all the resources that nature and art put at the disposal of the educator, — sensibility under all its forms, the calculations of self-interest, the lights of the intelligence. It is only little by little, and with the progress of age, that an exalted principle, like the sentiment of honor or the sentiment of duty, will be able to emerge from out the mobile humors of the child, and dominate his actions like a sovereign law. The moral pedagogy of Locke is certainly faulty in that it is not sufficiently addressed to the heart, and to the potency of loving, which is already so great in the child. I add, that in his haste to emancipate the child, to treat him as a reasonable creature, and to develop in him the principles of self-government, Locke was wrong in proscribing almost absolutely the fear of punishment. It is good to respect the liberty and the dignity of the man that is in the child, but it is not necessary that this respect degenerate into superstition ; and it is not sure that to train firm and robust wills, it is necessary to have them early affranchised from all fear and all constraint.

214. CONDEMNATION OF CORPORAL PUNISHMENT. — It is undeniable that Locke has not sufficiently enlarged the bases of his theory of moral discipline ; but if he has rested incomplete in the positive part of his task, if he has not advised all that should be done, he has been more successful in the

negative part, that which consists in eliminating all that ought not to be done. The chapters devoted to punishments in general, and in particular to corporal punishments, count among the best in the *Thoughts*. Rollin and Rousseau have often copied from them. It is true that Locke himself has borrowed the suggestion of them from Montaigne. The "severe mildness" which is the pedagogical rule of the author of the *Essays*, is also the rule of Locke. It is in accordance with this that Locke has brought to bear on the rod the final judgment of good sense : "The rod is a slavish discipline, which makes a slavish temper." He has yielded to the ideas of his time on only one point, when he admits one exception to the absolute interdiction of the rod, and tolerates its use in extreme cases to overcome the obstinate and rebellious resistance of the child. This is going too far without any doubt; but to do justice to the boldness of Locke's views, we must consider how powerful the custom then was, and still is, in England, in a country where the heads of institutions think themselves obliged to notify the public, in the advertisements published in the journals, that the interdiction of corporal punishment counts among the advantages of their schools. "It is difficult to conceive the perseverance with which English teachers cling to the old and degrading customs of corrections by the rod. . . . A more astonishing thing is that the scholars seem to hold to it as much as the teachers." "In 1818," relates one of the former pupils of Charterhouse, "our head master, Doctor Russell, who had ideas of his own, resolved to abolish corporal punishment and substitute for it a fine. Everybody resisted the innovation. The rod seemed to us perfectly consistent with the dignity of a gentleman ; but a fine, for shame ! The school rose to the cry : 'Down with the fine ! Long live the rod !' The revolt triumphed, and the rod was solemnly restored. Then we were glad-hearted over the affair. On the next day after the fine was abolished, we found, on entering the class-room, a superb forest of birches, and the two hours of the session were conscientiously employed in making use of them." [1,2]

215. INTELLECTUAL EDUCATION. — In what concerns intellectual education, Locke manifestly belongs to the school, small in his time, but more and more numerous to-day, of utilitarian teachers. He would train, not men of letters, or of science, but practical men, armed for the battle of life, provided with all the knowledge they will need in order to keep their accounts, administer their fortune, satisfy the requirements of their profession, and, finally, to fulfill their duties as men and citizens. In a word, he wrote for a nation of tradesmen and citizens.

216. UTILITARIAN STUDIES. — An undeniable merit of Locke is that of having reacted against a purely formal instruction, which substitutes for the acquisition of positive and real knowledge a superfluous culture, so to speak, a training in a superficial rhetoric and an elegant verbiage. Locke disdains and condemns studies that do not contribute directly to a preparation for life. Doubtless he goes a little

---

[1] Demogeot et Montucci, de l'Enseignement secondaire en Angleterre, p. 41.

[2] On the question of corporal punishment in school, is not M. Compayré too absolute in his assumptions? On what principle does he base his absolute condemnation of the rod? What is to be done in those cases of revolt against order and decency that occur from time to time in most schools? There is no doubt that the very best teachers can govern without resorting to this hateful expedient ; but what shall be done in extreme cases by the multitude who are not, and never can be, teachers of this ideal type? Nor does this question stand alone. Below, it is related to family discipline ; and above, to civil administration. If corporal punishment is interdicted in the school, should it not be interdicted in the State ? (P.)

too far in his reaction against the current formalism and in his predilection for realism. He is too forgetful of the fact that the old classical studies, if not useful in the positive sense of the term, and not satisfying the ordinary needs of existence, have yet a higher utility, in the sense that they may become, in skillful and discreet hands, an excellent instrument for intellectual discipline and the education of the judgment. But Locke spoke to fanatics and pedants, for whom Latin and Greek were the whole of instruction, and who, turning letters from their true purpose, wrongly made a knowledge of the dead languages the sole end, and not, as should be the case, one of the means of instruction. Locke is by no means a blind utilitarian, a coarse positivist, who dreams of absolutely abolishing disinterested studies. He wishes merely to put them in their place, and to guard against investing them with a sort of exclusive privilege, and against sacrificing to them other branches of instruction that are more essential and more immediately useful.

217. PROGRAMME OF STUDIES. — As soon as the child knows how to read and write, he should be taught to draw. Very disdainful of painting and of the fine arts in general, whose benign and profound influence on the souls of children his colder nature has not sufficiently recognized, Locke, by way of compensation, recommends drawing, because drawing may be practically useful, and he puts it on almost the same footing as reading and writing.

These elements once acquired, the child should be drilled in the mother tongue, first in reading, and afterwards in exercises in composition, in brief narratives, in familiar letters, etc. The study of a living language (Locke recommends French to his countrymen) should immediately follow ; and it is only after this has been acquired that the child shall be put to the study of Latin. Save the omission of the sciences, Locke's plan is singularly like that which for ten years has been in use in the French lycées.

As to Latin, which follows the living language, Locke requires that it shall be learned above all through use, through conversation if a master can be found who speaks it fluently, but if not, through the reading of authors. As little of grammar as possible, no memoriter exercises, no Latin composition, either in prose or verse, but, as soon as possible, the reading of easy Latin texts, — these are the recommendations of Locke that have been too little heeded. The purpose is no longer to learn Latin for the sake of writing it elegantly; the only purpose truly desirable is to comprehend the authors who have written in that language. The obstinate partisans of Latin verse and conversation will not read without chagrin these earnest protests of Locke against exercises that have been too much abused, and that impose on the learner the torment of writing in a language which he handles with difficulty, upon subjects which he but imperfectly understands. As to Greek, Locke proscribes it absolutely. He does not disparage the beauty of a language whose masterpieces, he says, are the original source of our literature and science; but he reserves the knowledge of it to the learned, to the lettered, to professional scholars, and he excludes it from secondary instruction, which ought to be but the school which trains for active life. Thus relieved, classical instruction will more easily welcome the studies that are of real use and of practical application, — geography, which Locke places in the first rank, because it is "an exercise of the eyes and memory"; arithmetic, which "is of so general use in all parts of life and business, that scarce anything can be done without it"; then what he somewhat ambitiously calls astronomy, and which is in reality an elementary cosmography; the parts of geometry which are necessary for

" a man of business"; chronology and history, " the most agreeable and the most instructive of studies"; ethics and common law, which do not yet have a place in French programmes; finally, natural philosophy, that is, the physical sciences; and, to crown all, a manual trade and book-keeping.

218. ATTRACTIVE STUDIES. — Another characteristic of Locke's intellectual discipline is, that, utilitarian in its purpose, the instruction which he organizes shall be attractive in its methods. After hatred for the pedantry which uselessly spends the powers of the learner in barren studies, the next strongest antipathy of Locke is that which is inspired by the rigor of a too didactic system of instruction, where the methods are repulsive, the processes painful, and where the teacher appears to his pupils only as a bugbear and a marplot.

Although he may go to extremes in this, he is partly right in wishing to bring into favor processes that are inviting and methods that are attractive. Without hoping, as he does, without desiring even, that the pupil may come to make no distinction between study and other diversions, we are disposed to believe that something may be done to alleviate for him the first difficulties in learning, to entice and captivate him without constraining him, and, finally, to spare him the disgust which cannot fail to be inspired by studies too severely forced upon him, and which are made the subject of scourges and scoldings. It is especially for reading and the first exercises of the child that Locke recommends the use of instructive plays. " They may be taught to read, without perceiving it to be anything but a sport, and play themselves into that which others are whipped for."

Children of every age are jealous of their independence and eager for pleasure. No one before Locke had so clearly recognized the need of the activity and liberty which are natural to the child, or so strongly insisted on the necessity of respecting his independent disposition and his personal tastes. Here again English pedagogy of the seventeenth century meets its illustrious successor of the nineteenth. Herbert Spencer has thoroughly demonstrated the fact that the mind really appropriates only the knowledge that affords it pleasure and agreeable exercise. Now, there is pleasure and agreeable excitation wherever there is the development of a normal activity corresponding to an instinctive taste and proportioned to the natural powers of the child; and there is no real instruction save at the expense of a real display of activity.[1]

219. SHOULD THERE BE LEARNING BY HEART? — To this question, Should there be learning by heart? Locke gives a resolute reply in the negative. The conclusion is absolute and false; but the premises that he assumes to justify his conclusion are, if possible, falser still. Locke sets out from this psychological idea, that the memory is not susceptible of progress. He brings into the discussion his sensualistic prejudices, his peculiar conception of the soul, which is

---

[1] It is usually said that a pupil's distaste for a study indicates one of two things, either the mode of presenting the subject is bad, or it is presented at an unseasonable period of mental development ; but this distaste is quite as likely to be due to the fact that a certain mode of mental activity has not yet been established ; for until fairly established, its exercise cannot be pleasurable. The assumption that intellectual appetites already exist and are waiting to be gratified, or that they will invariably appear at certain periods of mental development, is by no means a general law of the mental life. In many cases, these appetites must be created, and it may often be that the studies employed for this purpose may not at first be relished. And there are cases where, under the best of skill, this relish may never come ; and still, the knowledge or the discipline is so necessary that the studies may be enforced contrary to the pupil's pleasure. (P.)

but a *tabula rasa*, an empty and inert capacity, and not a congeries of energies and of living forces that are strengthened by exercise. He does not believe that the faculties, whatever they may be, can grow and develop, and this for the good reason, according to his thinking, that the faculties have no existence.

But here let him speak for himself : —

" I hear it is said that children should be employed in getting things by heart, to exercise and improve their memories. I would wish this were said with as much authority and reason as it is with forwardness of assurance, and that this practice were established upon good observation more than old custom. For it is evident that strength of memory is owing to an happy constitution, and not to any habitual improvement got by exercise. 'Tis true what the mind is intent upon, and, for fear of letting it slip, often imprints afresh on itself by frequent reflection, that it is apt to retain, but still according to its own natural strength of retention. An impression made on beeswax or lead will not last so long as on brass or steel. Indeed, if it be renewed often, it may last the longer ; but every new reflecting on it is a new impression, and 'tis from thence one is to reckon, if one would know how long the mind retains it. But the learning pages of Latin by heart no more fits the memory for retention of anything else, than the graving of one sentence in lead makes it the more capable of retaining firmly any other characters." [1]

If Locke were right, education would become wholly impossible ; for, in case of all the faculties, education supposes the existence of a natural germ which exercise fertilizes and develops.

---

[1] *Thoughts*, edited by R. H. Quick (Cambridge, 1880), pp. 153–4.

220. A Trade should be learned. — Locke, like Rousseau, but for other reasons, wishes his pupil to learn a trade: " I can not forbear to say, I would have my gentleman *learn a trade, a manual trade;* nay, two or three, but one more particularly." [1]

Rousseau will say the same: " Recollect that it is not talent that I require of you ; it is a trade, a real trade, a purely mechanical art, in which the hands work more than the head."

But Locke, in having his gentleman learn carpentry or agriculture, especially designed that this physical labor should lend the mind a diversion, an occasion for relaxation and repose, and secure to the body a useful exercise. Rousseau is influenced by totally different ideas. What he wants is, first, that through an apprenticeship to a trade, Émile may protect himself against need in case a revolutionary crisis should deprive him of his wealth. In the second place, Rousseau obeys his social, we might even say his socialistic, preoccupations. Work, in his view, is a strict duty, from which no one can exempt himself. " Rich or poor, every idle citizen is a knave."

221. Working Schools. — Although Locke is almost exclusively preoccupied with classical studies and with a gentleman's education, nevertheless he has not remained completely a stranger to questions of primary instruction. In 1697 he addressed to the English government a remarkable document on the importance of organizing " working schools" for the children of the poor. All children over three and under fourteen years of age are to be collected in homes where they will find labor and food. In this way Locke thought to contend against immorality and pauperism. He would find a remedy for the idleness and vagabondage of

---

[1] *Thoughts*, p. 177.

the child, and lighten the care of the mother who is absorbed in her work. He would also, through habits of order and discipline, train up steady men and industrious workmen. In other terms, he attempted a work of social regeneration, and the tutor of *gentlemen* became the educator of the poor.

222. LOCKE AND ROUSSEAU. — In the *Émile* we shall frequently find passages inspired by him whom Rousseau calls " the wise Locke." Perhaps we shall admire even more the practical qualities and the good sense of the English educator when we shall have become acquainted with the chimeras of his French imitator. In the case of Locke, we have to do, not with an author who wishes to shine, but with a man of sense and judgment who expresses his opinions, and who has no other pretense than to understand himself and to be comprehended by others. To appreciate the *Thoughts* at their full value, they should not be read till after having re-read the *Émile*, which is so much indebted to them. On coming from the reading of Rousseau, after the brilliant glare and almost the giddiness occasioned his reader by a writer of genius whose imagination is ever on the wing, whose passion urges him on, and who mingles with so many exalted truths, hasty paradoxes, and noisy declamations, it is like repose and a delicious unbending to the spirit to go to the study of Locke, and to find a train of thought always equable, a style simple and dispassionate, an author always master of himself, always correct, notwithstanding some errors, and a book, finally, filled, not with flashes and smoke, but with a light that is agreeable and pure.

[223. ANALYTICAL SUMMARY. — 1. This study illustrates the fact that the aims and methods of education are determined by the types of thought, philosophical, political, religious, scientific, and social, that happen to be in the ascendent; and also the tendency of the human mind to adopt extreme views.

2. The subjective tendency of human thought is typified by the Socratic philosophy, and the objective tendency by the Baconian philosophy ; and from these two main sources have issued two distinctive schools of educators, the formalists and the realists, the first holding that the main purpose of education is discipline, training, or formation, and the other, that this purpose is furnishing instruction or information. This line is distinctly drawn in the seventeenth century, and the two schools are typified by Malebranche and Locke.

3. The spirit of reaction is exhibited in the opposition to classical studies, in the effort to convert study into a diversion, in the use of milder means of discipline, and in the importance attached to useful studies. In these particulars the reaction of the sixteenth century is intensified.]

CHAPTER X.

THE EDUCATION OF WOMEN IN THE SEVENTEENTH
CENTURY. — JACQUELINE PASCAL AND MADAME DE
MAINTENON.

224. THE EDUCATION OF WOMEN IN THE SEVENTEENTH
CENTURY. — The *Education of Girls* of Fénelon has shown us
how far the spirit of the seventeenth century was able to go
in what concerns the education of women, as exhibited in
the most liberal theories on the subject; but in practice,
save in brilliant exceptions, even the modest and imperfect
ideal of Fénelon was far from being attained.

Chrysale was not alone of this opinion, when he said in
the *Learned Ladies:* —

"It is not very proper, and for several reasons, that a
woman should study and know so many things. To train the
minds of her children in good morals and manners, to superintend her household, by keeping an eye on her servants,
and to control the expenditures with economy, ought to be

her study and philosophy." [1] It is true that Molière himself
did not sympathize with the prejudices whose expression he
put in the mouth of his comic character, and that he concludes that a woman " may be enlightened on every subject"
(" Je consens qu'une femme ait des clartés de tout "). But
in real fact and in practice, it is the opinion of Chrysale
that prevailed. Even in the higher classes, woman held
herself aloof from instruction, and from things intellectual.
Madame Racine had never seen played, and had probably
never read, the tragedies of her husband.

225. MADAME DE SÉVIGNÉ. — However, the seventeenth
century was not wanting in women of talent or genius, who
might have made an eloquent plea in behalf of their sex ; but
they were content to give personal examples of a high order,
without any anxiety to be imitated. Madame de Lafayette
made beautiful translations from Latin ; Madame Dacier
was a humanist of the first order ; and Madame de Sévigné
knew the modern languages as well as the ancient. No one
has better described the advantage of reading. She recommends the reading of romances in the following terms : —

" I found that a young man became generous and brave
in seeing my heroes, and that a girl became genteel and wise
in reading *Cleopatra*. There are occasionally some who take
things somewhat amiss, *but they would perhaps do scarcely
any better if they could not read*." [2]

Madame de Sévigné had her daughter read Descartes, and
her granddaughter Pauline, the tragedies of Corneille.

" For my part," she said, " if I were to bring up my
granddaughter, I would have her read what is good, but not
too simple. I would reason with her." [3]

---

[1] *Les Femmes Savantes*, Act II. Scene VII., Van Laun's translation.
[2] Letter of Nov. 16, 1689.   [3] Letter of June 1, 1680.

226. THE ABBÉ FLEURY. — But Madame de Sévigné and Madame de Grignan were but brilliant exceptions. If one were to doubt the ignorance of the women of this period, it would suffice to read this striking passage from the Abbé Fleury, the assistant of Fénelon in the education of the Duke of Bourgogne : —

" This, doubtless, will be a great paradox, that women ought to learn anything else than their catechism, sewing, and different little pieces of work, singing, dancing, and dressing in the fashion, and to make a fine courtesy. As things now go, this constitutes all their education." [1]

Fleury desires something else for woman. He demands that she learn to write correctly in French, and that she study logic and arithmetic. But we need not fear lest the liberalism of a thinker of the seventeenth century carry him too far. Fleury admits, for example, that history is absolutely useless to women.

227. EDUCATION IN THE CONVENTS. — It is almost exclusively in convents that young girls then received what passed for an education. The religious congregations that devoted themselves to female education were numberless ; we note, for example, among the most celebrated, the Ursulines, founded in 1537 ; the Association of the Angelics, established in Italy in 1536 ; and the Order of Saint Elizabeth. But, notwithstanding the diversity of names, all the convents for girls resemble one another. In all of them woman was educated for heaven, or for a life of devotion. Spiritual exercises formed the only occupation of the pupils, and study was scarcely taken into account.

228. PORT ROYAL AND THE REGULATIONS OF JACQUELINE PASCAL. — The best means of penetrating into the inner life

---

[1] *Traité du choix et de la méthode des études*, Chap. XXXVIII.

of the convents of the seventeenth century is to read the *Regulations for Children*, written towards 1657 by Jacqueline Pascal, Sister Saint Euphemia. The education of girls interested the Jansenists not less than the education of men; but in this respect, Port Royal is far from deserving the same encomiums in both cases.

229. GENERAL IMPRESSION. — There is nothing so sombre and sad as the interior of their institution for girls, and nothing so austere as the rules of Jacqueline Pascal.

"A strange emotion, even at the distance of centuries, is caused by the sight of those children keeping silent or speaking in a whisper from rising till retiring, never walking except between two nuns, one in front and the other behind, in order to make it impossible, by slackening their pace on the pretext of some indisposition, for them to hold any communication; working in such a way as never to be in companies of two or three; passing from meditation to prayer, and from prayer to instruction; learning, besides the catechism, nothing but reading and writing; and, on Sunday, 'a little arithmetic, the older from one to two o'clock, and the younger from two to half past two'; the hands always busy to prevent the mind from wandering; but without being able to become attached to their work, which would please God as much the more as it pleased themselves the less; opposing all their natural inclinations, and despising the attentions due the body ' destined to serve as food for worms'; doing nothing, in a word, except in the spirit of mortification. Imagine those days of fourteen and sixteen hours, slowly succeeding one another, and weighing down on the heads of those poor little sisters, for six or eight years in that dreary solitude, where there was nothing to bring in the stir of life, save the sound of the bell announc-

ing a change of exercise or of penance, and you will comprehend Fénelon's feeling of sadness when he speaks of the
shadows of that deep cavern in which was imprisoned and,
as it were, buried the youth of girls." [1]

230. SEVERITY AND LOVE. — The severity of the *Regulations* is such that the editor, M. de Pontchartrain, also a
Jansenist, allows that it will be impossible to obtain from
all children " so complete a silence and so formal a life ";
and requires that the mistresses shall try to gain their affections.   Love must be united with severity.   Jacqueline
Pascal does not seem to be entirely of this opinion, since
she declares that only God must be loved.   However, notwithstanding her habitual severity, human tenderness sometimes asserts its rights in the rules which she established.
We feel that she loves more than she confesses, those young
girls whom she calls " little doves."   On the one hand,
the *Regulations* incite the pupils to eat of what is placed
before them indifferently, and to begin with what they like
the least, through a spirit of penitence ; but, on the other
hand, Jacqueline writes : " They must be exhorted to take
sufficient nourishment so as not to allow themselves to
become weakened, and this is why care is taken that they
have eaten enough."   And so there is a touching solicitude
that is almost maternal in this remark : " As soon as they
have retired, each particular bed must be visited, to see
whether all proprieties have been observed, and whether the
children are well covered in winter."   The mystic sister of
the ascetic Pascal has moments of tenderness.   " Nevertheless, we must not cease to feel pity for them, and to
accommodate ourselves to them in every way that we can,
but without letting them know that we have thus conde-

---

[1] Gréard, *Memoire sur l'enseignement secondaire des filles*, p. 55.

scended." However, the dominant conception ever reappearing, is the idea that human nature is evil; that we have to do with rebellious spirits which must be conquered, and that they deserve no commiseration.

There is a deal of anxiety to make study agreeable! Jacqueline directs her pupils to work at the very things that are most repulsive, because the work that will please God the most is that which will please them the least. The exterior manifestations of friendship are forbidden, and possibly friendship itself. " Our pupils shall shun every sort of familiarity one towards another."

Instruction is reduced to the catechism, to the application of the Christian virtues, to reading, and to writing. Arithmetic is not taught save on holidays. It seems that memory is the only faculty that Jacqueline wishes to have developed. " This opens their minds, gives them occupation, and keeps them from evil thoughts." Have we not reason to say that at Port Royal women have less value than men! What a distance between the solid instruction of Lancelot's and Nicole's pupils and the ignorance of Jacqueline Pascal's! Even when the men of Port Royal speak of the education of women, they have more liberal ideas than those which are applied at their side. Nicole declares that books are necessary even in convents for girls, because it is necessary " to sustain prayer by reading."

231. GENERAL CHARACTER OF SAINT CYR. — In leaving Port Royal for Saint Cyr, we seem, on coming out of a profound night, to perceive a ray of light. Without doubt, Madame de Maintenon has not yet, as a teacher, all that breadth of view that could be desired. Her work is far from being faultless, but the founding of Saint Cyr (1686) was none the less a considerable innovation. " Saint Cyr," it has been said, " is not a convent. It is a great establish-

ment devoted to the lay education of young women of
noble birth; it is a bold and intelligent secularization of the
education of women." There is some excess of praise in
this statement, and the lay character of Saint Cyr is very
questionable. Lavallée, an admirer, could write: "The
instructions of Madame de Maintenon are doubtless too
religious, too monastic." Let us grant, however, that
Madame de Maintenon, who, after having founded Saint
Cyr, was the director of it, *extra muros*, and even taught
there, at stated times, is personally the first lay teacher of
France. Let us grant, also, that at least in the beginning,
and up to 1692, the women entrusted with the work of
instruction were not nuns in the absolute sense of the term.
They were not bound by solemn and absolute vows.

But this character relatively laic, and this rupture with
monastic traditions, were not maintained during the whole
life of the institution.

232. Two Periods in the History of Saint Cyr. —
Saint Cyr, in fact, passed, within a few years, through two
very different periods, and Madame de Maintenon followed
in succession two almost opposite currents. For the first
years, from 1686 to 1692, the spirit of the institution is
broad and liberal; the education is brilliant, perhaps too
much so; literary exercises and dramatic representations
have an honored place. Saint Cyr is an institution inclining
to worldliness, better fitted to train women of intellect than
good economists and housewives. Madame de Maintenon
quickly saw that she had taken a false route, and, from
1692, she reacted, not without excess, against the tendencies
which she had at first obeyed. She conceived an extreme
distrust of literary studies, and cut off all she could from the
instruction. in order to give her entire thought to the moral
and practical qualities of her pupils. Saint Cyr became a

convent, with a little more liberty, doubtless, than there was in the other monasteries of the time, but it was a convent still.

233. DRAMATIC REPRESENTATIONS. — It was the notorious success of the performance of *Andromaque* and *Esther* that caused the overthrow of the original intentions of Madame de Maintenon. *Esther*, in particular, was the great event of the first years of Saint Cyr. Racine distributed the parts; Boileau conducted the training in elocution; and the entire Court, the king at the head, came to applaud and entertain the pretty actresses, who left nothing undone to please their spectators. Heads were a little turned by all this; dissipation crept into the school. The pupils were no longer willing to sing in church, for fear of spoiling their voices. Evidently the route was now over a dangerous declivity. The institution had been turned from its purpose. Matters were in a way to establish, under another form, another Hôtel de Rambouillet.[1]

234. REFORM OF 1692. — At the first, as we have seen, the ladies of Saint Louis, charged with the direction of Saint Cyr, did not found a monastic order properly so-called; but, when Madame de Maintenon resolved to reform the general spirit of the house, she thought it necessary to transform Saint Cyr into a monastery, and she founded the Order of Saint Augustine.

[1] " The name generally given to a social circle, which for more than half a century gathered around Catherine de Vivonne, marquise de Rambouillet, and her daughter, Julie d'Angennes, duchess de Montausier, and which exercised a very conspicuous influence on French language, literature, and civilization. . . . Her house soon became the place where all who had genius, wit, learning, talent, or taste, assembled, and from these reunions originated the French Academy, the highest authority of French literature, and the *salons*, the most prominent feature of French civilization."
— Johnson's *Cyclopædia*.

But what she changed in particular was the moral discipline, and the programme of studies.

Madame de Maintenon has herself recited, in a memorable letter,[1] the reasons of that reform which modified so profoundly the character of Saint Cyr: —

" The sorrow I feel for the girls of Saint Cyr," she said, " can be cured only by time and by an *entire change* in the education that we have given them up to this hour. It is very just that I should suffer for this, since I have contributed to it more than any one else. . . . The whole establishment has been the object of my pride, and the ground for this feeling has been so real that it has gone to extremes that I never intended. God knows that I wished to establish virtue at Saint Cyr, but I have built upon the sand. Not having, what alone can make a solid foundation, I wished the girls to be witty, high-spirited, and trained to think ; I have succeeded in this purpose. They have wit, and they use it against us. They are high-spirited, and are more heady and haughty than would be becoming in a royal princess. Speaking after the manner of the world, we have trained their reason, and have made them talkative, presumptuous, inquisitive, bold . . . witty, — such characters as even we who have trained them cannot abide. . . . Let us seek a remedy, for we must not be discouraged. . . . As many little things form pride, many little things will destroy it. Our girls have been treated with too much consideration, have been petted too much, treated too gently. We must now leave them more to themselves in their class-rooms, make them observe the daily regulations, and speak to them of scarcely anything else. . . . Pray to God, and ask Him to change their hearts ; and that He may give to all of them

---

[1] See the Letter to Madame de Fontaine, general mistress of the school, Sept. 20, 1691.

humility. There should not be much conversation with them on the subject. Everything at Saint Cyr is made a matter of discourse. We often speak of simplicity, and try to define it correctly . . . and yet, in practice, the girls make merry in saying : ' Through simplicity I take the best place ; through simplicity I am going to commend myself.' Our girls must be cured of that jesting turn of mind which I have given them. . . . We have wished to shun the pettiness of certain convents, and God has punished us for this haughty spirit. There is no house in the world that has more need of humility within and without than our own. Its situation near the Court ; the air of favor that pervades it ; the favors of a great king ; the offices of a person of consideration, — all these snares, so full of danger, should lead us to take measures directly contrary to those we have really taken. . . ."

235. THE PART PLAYED BY MADAME DE MAINTENON. — Whatever may be the opinion respecting the tone of the educational work at Saint Cyr, there cannot be the least doubt as to the admirable zeal of Madame de Maintenon, and her indefatigable devotion to the success of her favorite undertaking. The vocation of the teacher was evidently hers. For more than thirty years, from 1686 to 1717, she did not cease to visit Saint Cyr every day, sometimes at six in the morning. She wrote for the directresses and for the pupils counsels and regulations that fill several volumes. Nothing which concerns " her children " is a matter of indifference to her. She devotes her attention to their meals, their sleep, their toilet, as well as to their character and their instruction : —

" The affairs we discuss at Court are bagatelles ; those at Saint Cyr are the more important. . . ." " May that establishment last as long as France, and France as long as the world. Nothing is dearer to me than my children of Saint Cyr."

It is not tenderness, it is well known, that characterizes
the soul of Madame de Maintenon; but, at Saint Cyr, from
being formal and cold, which is her usual state, she becomes
loving and tender : —

" Forget nothing that may save the souls of our young
girls, that may fortify their health and preserve their form."

One day, as she had come to the school, as her custom was,
to consult with the nuns, a company of girls passed by raising
a cloud of dust. The nuns, fearing that Madame de Maintenon was annoyed by it, requested them to withdraw.
" Pray, let the dear girls be," replied Madame de Maintenon; " I love them even to the dust they raise." Con-
versely, as it were, the pupils of Pestalozzi, consulted on
the question of knowing whether they were willing always to
be beaten and clawed by their old master, replied. affirm-
atively : they loved him even to his claws !

236. Her Pedagogical Writings. — It is only in our
day that the works of Madame de Maintenon have been
published in the integrity of their text, thanks to the labors
of Théophile Lavallée. For the most part, these long and
interesting letters are devoted to education and to Saint Cyr.
These are, first, the *Letters and Conversations on the Education of Girls.*[1] These letters were written from day to day,
and are addressed, sometimes to the ladies of Saint Cyr, and
sometimes to the pupils themselves. " We find in them,"
says Lavallée, " for all circumstances and for all times, the
most solid teaching, masterpieces of good sense, of natural-
ness, and of truth, and, finally, instructions relative to education that approach perfection. The *Conversations* originated
in the consultations that Madame de Maintenon had during
the recreations or the recitations, either with the ladies or

[1] Two volumes, 2d edition, 1861.

with the young women, who themselves collected and edited the words of their governess."

After the *Letters and Conversations* comes the *Counsels to Young Women who enter Society*,[1] which contain general advice, conversations or dialogues, and, finally, proverbs, that is, short dramatic compositions, designed at once to instruct and amuse the young ladies of Saint Cyr. These essays are not admirable in all respects ; most often they are lacking in imagination ; and Madame de Maintenon, though an imitation of Fénelon, makes a misuse of indirect instruction, of artifice, and of amusement, in order to teach some moral commonplaces by insinuation. Here are the titles of some of these proverbs : *The occasion makes the rogue; Women make and unmake the home; There is no situation more embarrassing than that of holding the handle of the frying-pan.*

Finally, let us note the third collection, the *Historical and Instructive Letters addressed to the Ladies of Saint Cyr.*[2]

It is to be regretted that, out of these numerous volumes, where repetitions abound, there have not been extracted, in a methodical manner, a few hundred pages which should contain the substance of Madame de Maintenon's thinking on educational questions.

237. INTERIOR ORGANIZATION. — The purpose of the founding of Saint Cyr was to assure to the two hundred and fifty daughters of the poor nobility, and to the children of officers dead or disabled, an educational retreat where they would be suitably educated so as to be prepared for becoming either nuns, if this was their vocation, or, the more often, good mothers. As M. Gréard has justly observed, " the very conception of an establishment of this kind, the idea of

---

[1] Two volumes, 1857.   [2] Two volumes, 1860.

making France pay the debt of France, educating the children of those who had given her their blood, proceeds from a feeling up to that time unknown." [1]

Consequently, children of the tenderest years, from six or seven, were received at Saint Cyr, there to be cared for till the age of marriage, till eighteen and twenty.

The young girls were divided into four classes, — the reds, the greens, the yellows, and the blues. The blues were the largest, and they wore the royal colors. Each class was divided into five or six *bands* or *families*, of eight or ten pupils each.

The ladies of Saint Cyr were ordinarily taken from the pupils of the school. They were forty in number, — the superior, the assistant who supplied the place of the superior, the mistress of the novices, the general mistress of the classes, the mistresses of the classes, etc.

The capital defect of Saint Cyr is, that, as in the collèges of the Jesuits, the residence is absolute and the sequestration complete. From her fifth to her twentieth year the young girl belongs entirely to Saint Cyr. She scarcely knows her parents. It will be said, perhaps, that in many cases she has lost them, and that in some cases she could expect only bad examples from them. But no matter ; the general rule, which interrupted family intercourse to the extent of almost abolishing it, cannot obtain our approbation. The girl was permitted to see her parents only three or four times a year, and even then these interviews would last only for a half an hour each time, and in the presence of a mistress. There was permission to write family letters from time to time ; but as though she mistrusted the natural impulses of the heart, and the free outpouring of filial affection, Madame de Maintenon had taken care to compose some models

---

[1] M. Gréard, *Mémoire sur l'enseignement secondaire des filles,* 1882, p. 59.

of these letters. With more of reason than of feeling, Madame de Maintenon is not exempt from a certain coldness of heart. It seems that she would impose on her pupils the extraordinary habits of her own family. She recollected having been kissed only twice by her mother, on her forehead, and then only after a long separation.

238. DISTRUST OF READING. — After the reforms of 1692, the instruction at Saint Cyr became a matter of secondary importance. Reading, writing, and counting were taught, but scarcely anything besides. Reading, in general, was viewed with distrust: " Teach girls to be very sparing as to reading, and always to prefer manual labor instead." Books of a secular nature were interdicted ; only works of piety were put in the hands of pupils, such as the *Introduction to a Devout Life*, by Saint François de Salles, and the *Confessions* of Saint Augustine. " Renounce intellectual culture " is the perpetual injunction of Madame de Maintenon.

" We must educate citizens for citizenship. It is not the question of giving them intellectual culture. We must preach family duties to them, obedience to husband, and care for children. . . . Reading does more harm than good to young girls. . . . Books make witlings and excite an insatiable curiosity."

239. THE STUDY OF HISTORY NEGLECTED. — To judge of the spirit of Saint Cyr, from the point of view of intellectual education, it suffices to note the little importance that was there given to history. This went so far as to raise the question whether it were not best to prohibit the study of French history entirely. Madame de Maintenon consents to have it taught, but only just enough so that " pupils may not confuse the succession of our kings with the princes of other countries, and not take a Roman emperor for an

emperor of China or Japan, a king of Spain or of England for a king of Persia or of Siam." As to the history of antiquity, it must be held in mistrust for the very reason — who would believe it? — of the beautiful examples of virtue that it contains. "I should fear that those grand examples of generosity and heroism would give our young girls too much elevation of spirit, and make them vain and pretentious." Have we not some right to feel surprised that Madame de Maintenon is alarmed at the thought of *raising* the intelligence of woman? It is true that she doubtless thought of the romantic exaggerations produced by the reading of the *Cyrus the Great* and other writings of Mlle. de Scudéry. Let us add, besides, to excuse the shortcomings of the programme of Saint Cyr in the matter of history, that even for boys in the colleges of the University, the order that introduced the teaching of history into the classes dates only from 1695.

240. INSUFFICIENT INSTRUCTION. — "Our day," says Lavallée, "would not accept that education in which instruction properly so-called was but a secondary matter, and entirely sacrificed to the manner of training the heart, the reason, and the character ; and an education, too, that, as a whole and in its details, was wholly religious." The error of Madame de Maintenon consists essentially in the wish to develop the moral virtues in souls scarcely instructed, scarcely enlightened. There was much moral discoursing at Saint Cyr. If it did not always bear fruit, it was because the seed fell into intelligences that were but little cultivated.

" Our young women are not to be made scholarly. Women never know except by halves, and the little that they know usually makes them conceited, disdainful, chatty, and disgusted with serious things."

241. MANUAL LABOR. — If intellectual education was neglected at Saint Cyr, by way of compensation great atten-

tion was paid to manual education. The girls were there taught to sew, to embroider, to knit, and to make tapestry; and there was also made there all the linen for the house, the infirmary, and the chapel, and the dresses and clothing of the ladies and the pupils : —

" But no exquisite productions," says Madame de Maintenon, " nor of very elaborate design ; none of those flimsy edgings in embroidery or tapestry, which are of no use."

With what good grace Madame de Maintenon ever preaches the gospel of labor, of which she herself gave the example ! In the coaches of the king, she always had some work in hand. At Saint Cyr, the young women swept the dormitories, put in order the refectory, and dusted the class-rooms. "They must be put at every kind of service, and made to work at what is burdensome, in order to make them robust, healthy, and intelligent."

" Manual labor is a moral safeguard, a protection against sin."

" Work calms the passions, occupies the mind, and does not leave it time to think of evil."

242. MORAL EDUCATION. — "The Institute," said Madame de Maintenon, " is intended, not for prayer, but for action." What she wished, above all else, was to prepare young women for home and family life. She devoted her thought to the training of wives and mothers. "What I lack most," she said, "is sons-in-law!" Hence she was incessantly preoccupied with moral qualities. One might make a fine and valuable book of selections out of all the practical maxims of Madame de Maintenon ; as her reflections on talkativeness: "There is always sin in a multitude of words;" on indolence : "What can be done in the family of an indolent and fastidious woman?" on politeness, "which consists, above all else, in giving one's thought to others;"

on lack of energy, then too common among women of the world : " The only concern is to eat and to take one's ease. Women spend the day in morning-gowns, reclining in easy-chairs, without any occupation, and without conversation ; all is well, provided one be in a state of repose."

243. DISCREET DEVOTION. — We must not imagine that Saint Cyr was a house of prayer, a place of overdone devotion. Madame de Maintenon held to a reasonable Christianity. Piety, such as was recommended at Saint Cyr, is a piety that is *steadfast, judicious*, and *simple;* that is, conformed to the state in which one ought to live, and exempt from refinements.

" The young women are too much at church, considering their age," she wrote to Madame de Brinon, the first director of the institution. . . . " Consider, I pray you, that this is not to be a cloister." [1]

And later, after the reform had begun, this is what she wrote —:

" Let the piety with which our young girls shall be inspired be cheerful, gentle, and free. Let it consist rather in the innocence of their lives, and in the simplicity of their occupations, than in the austerities, the retirements, and the refinements of devotion. . . . When a girl comes from a convent, saying that nothing ought to interfere with vespers, she is laughed at ; but when an educated woman shall say that vespers may be omitted for the sake of attending her sick husband, everybody will commend her. . . . When a girl shall say that a woman does better to educate her children and instruct her servants than to spend the forenoon in church, that religion will be heartily accepted, and will make itself loved and respected." [2]   Excellent advice, perhaps too

---

[1] *Lettres historiques*, Tome I. p. 48.
[2] *Lettres historiques*, Tome I. p. 89.

little followed! Madame de Maintenon here speaks the language of good sense, and we are wholly surprised to hear it from the lips of a politic woman who, not without reason, and for her part in the Revocation of the Edict of Nantes, has the reputation of being an intolerant fanatic.

244. SIMPLICITY IN ALL THINGS. — The simplicity which she recommended in religion, Madame de Maintenon demanded in everything, — in dress and in language : " Young girls," she says, " must wear as few ribbons as possible."

A class-teacher had given a fine lecture, in which she exhorted her pupils to make an " eternal divorce " with sin. " Very well said, doubtless," remarked Madame de Maintenon ; " but, pray, who among our young ladies knows what divorce is ? "

245. FÉNELON AND SAINT CYR. — Michelet, speaking of Saint Cyr, which he does not love, said : " Its cold governess was much more a man than Fénelon." The fact is, that the author of the *Education of Girls* gives a larger place to sensibility and intelligence. It is not Madame de Maintenon who said : " As much as possible, tenderness of heart must be excused in young girls." It is not at Saint Cyr that these maxims were practised. " Pray let them have Greek and Roman histories. They will find in them prodigies of courage and disinterestedness. Let them not be ignorant of the history of France, which also has its beauty. . . . All this serves to give dignity to the mind, and to lift the soul to noble sentiments." Nevertheless, Fénelon's work was highly esteemed at Saint Cyr. It appeared in 1687, and Saint Cyr was founded in 1686. A great number of its precepts were there observed, such as the following : " Frequent leaves of absence should be avoided ; " " Young girls should not be accustomed to talk much."

246. General Judgment. — In a word, if the ideal proposed to the young women of Saint Cyr by Madame de Maintenon cannot satisfy those who, in our day, conceive "an education broader in its scheme and more liberal in its spirit," at least we must do justice to an institution which was, as its foundress said, "a kind of college," a first attempt at enfranchisement in the education of women. Without demanding of Madame de Maintenon what was not in her age to give, let us be inspired by her in what concerns the changeless education in moral virtues, and in the qualities of discretion, reserve, goodness, and submission. "However severe that education may appear," says Lavallée, "I believe it will suggest better reflections to those who observe the way in which women are educated to-day, and the results of that education in luxury and pleasure, not only on the fireside, but still more on society and political life, and on the future of the men that it is preparing for France. I believe they will prefer that manly education, so to speak, which purified private morals and begot public virtues; and that they will esteem and regret that work of Madame de Maintenon, which for a century prevented the corruption of the Court from extending to the provinces, and maintained in the old country-seats, from which came the greater part of the nobility, the substantial virtues and the simple manners of the olden time."

[247. Analytical Summary.—1. The education of women in the seventeenth century reflects the sentiment of the age as to their relative position in society, their rights, and their destiny. Woman was still regarded as the inferior of man, in the lower classes as a drudge, in the higher as an ornament; in her case, intellectual culture was regarded as either useless or dangerous; and the education that was given her was to fit her for a life of devotion or a life of seclusion from society.

2. The rules of Jacqueline Pascal exhibit the effects of an ascetic belief on education, — human nature is corrupt; all its likes are to be thwarted, and all its dislikes fostered under compulsion.

3. The education directed by Madame de Maintenon is the beginning of a rupture with tradition. It was a movement towards the secularization of woman's education, and towards the recognition of her equality with man, with respect to her grade of intellectual endowments, her intellectual culture, and to her participation in the duties of real life.

4. The type of the higher education was still monastic, both for men and women. No one was able to conceive that both sexes might be educated together with mutual advantage.]

CHAPTER XI.

ROLLIN.

THE UNIVERSITY OF PARIS; STATUTES OF 1598 AND OF 1600; ORGANIZA-
TION OF THE DIFFERENT FACULTIES; DECADENCE OF THE UNIVERSITY
OF PARIS IN THE SEVENTEENTH CENTURY; THE RESTORATION OF
STUDIES AND ROLLIN (1661-1741); THE TREATISE ON STUDIES; DIF-
FERENT OPINIONS; DIVISION OF THE TREATISE ON STUDIES; GENE-
RAL REFLECTIONS ON EDUCATION; STUDIES FOR THE FIRST YEARS;
THE EDUCATION OF GIRLS; THE STUDY OF FRENCH; GREEK AND
LATIN; ROLLIN THE HISTORIAN; THE TEACHING OF HISTORY;
PHILOSOPHY; SCIENTIFIC INSTRUCTION; EDUCATIONAL CHARACTER
OF ROLLIN'S PEDAGOGY; INTERIOR DISCIPLINE OF COLLEGES;
PUBLIC EDUCATION; THE ROD; PUNISHMENTS IN GENERAL; CON-
CLUSION; ANALYTICAL SUMMARY.

248. THE UNIVERSITY OF PARIS. — Since the thirteenth
century, the University of Paris had been a centre of light
and a resort for students. Ramus could say: " This University is not the university of one city only, but of the
entire world." But even in the time of Ramus, in consequence of the civil discords, and by reason also of the progress in the colleges organized by the Company of Jesus, the
University of Paris declined; she saw the number of her
pupils diminish. She persisted, however, in the full light of
the Renaissance, in following the superannuated regulations
which the Cardinal d'Estouteville had imposed on her in 1452 ;
she fell behind in the routine of the scholastic methods. A
reform was necessary, and in 1600 it was accomplished by
Henry IV.

249. STATUTES OF 1600. — The statutes of the new university were promulgated " by the order and the will of the most Christian and most invincible king of France and Navarre, Henry IV." This was the first time that the State directly intervened in the control of education, and that secular power was set up in opposition to the absolute authority of the Church.

In the thirteenth and fourteenth centuries a reform had been made in the University, by the Popes Innocent III. and Urban V. The reformer of 1452, the Cardinal d'Estouteville, acted as the legate of the pontifical power. On the contrary, the statutes of 1600 were the work of a commission named by the king, and there sat at its deliberations, by the side of a few ecclesiastics, magistrates, and even professors.

250. ORGANIZATION OF THE DIFFERENT FACULTIES. — The University of Paris comprised four Faculties : the Faculties of Theology, of Law, and of Medicine, which corresponded to what we to-day call superior instruction, and the Faculty of Arts, which was almost the equivalent of our secondary instruction.[1]

It would take too long to enumerate in this place the different innovations introduced by the statutes of 1600. Let us merely say a word of the Faculty of Arts.

In the Faculty of Arts the door was finally opened to the classical authors. In a certain degree the tendencies of the

---

[1] " Formerly secondary schools were schools in which was given a more advanced instruction then in the primary schools; and they were distinguished into communal secondary schools, or communal colleges, and into private secondary schools or institutions. . . . To-day, secondary instruction includes the colleges and lycées in which are taught the ancient languages, modern languages, history, mathematics, physics, chemistry, and philosophy. Public instruction is divided into primary, secondary, and superior instruction." — LITTRÉ.

Renaissance were obeyed. Nevertheless, the methods and
the general spirit were scarcely changed. Catholicism was
obligatory, and the French language remained under ban.
Frequent exercises in repetition and declamation were maintained. The liberal arts were always considered " the
foundation of all the sciences." Instruction in philosophy
was always reduced to the interpretation of the texts of Aristotle. As to history, and the sciences in general, no account
whatever was taken of them.

251. DECADENCE OF THE UNIVERSITY IN THE SEVENTEENTH
CENTURY. — The reform, then, was insufficient, and the
results were bad. While the colleges of the Jesuits
attracted pupils in crowds, and while the Oratorians and
the Jansenists reformed secondary instruction, the colleges
of the University[1] remained mediocre and obscure. Save
in rare exceptions, there were no professors of distinction ; the education was formal, in humble imitation of that
of the Company of Jesus ; there was an abuse of abstract
rules, of grammatical exercises, of written tasks, and of
Latin composition ; there was no disposition to take an advance step ; but an obstinate resistance to the new spirit,
which was indicated either by the interdiction of the philosophy of Descartes, or by the refusal to teach in the French
language ; in a word, there was complete isolation in im-

---

[1] This refers to the University of Paris, which must be distinguished
from the Napoleonic University. "The latter was founded by a decree of
Napoleon I., March 17, 1808. It was first called the Imperial University,
and then the University of France. It comprises: 1. The faculties;* 2. the
lycées or colleges of the State; 3. the communal colleges; 4. the primary
schools. All these are under the direction of a central administration." —
LITTRÉ.

* There are now five Faculties or institutions for special instruction. —
the Faculties of the Sciences, of Letters, of Medicine, of Law, and of Theology. (P.)

movable routine, and in consequence, decadence, — such is a summary history of the University of Paris up to the last quarter of the seventeenth century.

252. THE RESTORATION OF STUDIES AND ROLLIN (1661–1741). — We must go forward to the time when Rollin taught, to observe a revival in the studies of the University. Several distinguished professors, as his master Hersan, Pourchot, and still others, had prepared the way for him. There was then, from 1680 to 1700, a real rejuvenescence of studies, which was initiated in part by Rollin.

Latin lost a little ground in consequence of a growing recognition of the rights of the French language and the national literature, which had just been made illustrious by so many masterpieces. The spirit of the Jansenist methods penetrated the colleges of the University. The Cartesian philosophy was taught in them, and a little more attention was given to the explication of authors, and a little less to the verbal repetition of lessons. New ideas began to infiltrate into the old citadel of scholasticism. The question came to be asked if celibacy was indeed an indispensable condition of the teaching office. Men began to comprehend that at least marriage was not a reason for exclusion. Finally, real progress was made in discipline as well as in methods, and the indubitable proof of this is the *Treatise on Studies*, by Rollin.

253. THE TREATISE ON STUDIES. — Rollin has summed up his educational experience, an experience of fifty years, in a book which has become celebrated under the title of *Treatise on Studies*. The full title of this work was : *De la manière d'enseigner et d'étudier les belles-lettres par rapport à l'esprit et au cœur*. The first two volumes appeared in 1726, and the other two in 1728.

The *Treatise on Studies* is not like the *Émile*, which was published twenty years later, a work of venturesome inquiry and original novelties ; but is a faithful exposition of the methods in use, and a discreet commentary on them. While this treatise belongs by its date to the eighteenth century, it is the pedagogy of the seventeenth century, and the traditions of the University under the reign of Louis XIV. that Rollin has collected, and of which he has simply wished to be the reporter. In the Latin dedication, which he addresses to the Rector of the University of Paris, he clearly defines his intentions and his purpose : —

" My first design was to put in writing and define the method of teaching which has long been in use among you, and which, up to this time, has been transmitted only by word of mouth, and through a sort of tradition ; and to erect, so far as I am able to do it, a durable monument of the rules and practice which you have followed in the instruction of youth, for the purpose of preserving, in all its integrity, the taste for *belles-lettres*, and to preserve it, if possible, from the injuries and the alterations of time."

254. DIFFERENT OPINIONS. — Rollin has always had warm admirers. Voltaire called the *Treatise* a book " forever useful," and whatever may be our reservations on the deficiences, and on the short and narrow views of certain parts of the pedagogy of Rollin, we must subscribe to this judgment. But we shall not go so far as to accept the enthusiastic declarations of Villemain, who complains that the study of the *Treatise* is neglected in our time, " as if new methods had been discovered for training the intelligence and the heart " ; and he adds, " Since the *Treatise on Studies, not a forward step has been taken.*" This is to undervalue all the earnest efforts that have been made for two centuries by

educators just as profound as was the ever timid and cautious Rollin. When we compare the precepts of the *Treatise* with the reforms which the spirit of progress has already effected, and particularly with those which it will effect, we are astonished to hear Nisard say : " In educational matters, the *Treatise on Studies* is the unique book, or better still, the book."

To put such a burden of pompous praise on Rollin· is to compromise his real worth ; and without ceasing to do justice to his wise and judicious spirit, we wish to employ more discretion in our admiration.

255. DIVISION OF THE TREATISE ON STUDIES. — Before calling attention to the most interesting parts of the *Treatise on Studies*, let us briefly state the object of the eight books of which it is composed.

The *Treatise* opens with a *Preliminary Discourse* which recites the advantages of instruction.

The title of the first book is : *Exercises which are proper for very young children; of the education of girls.* Rollin acknowledges that he treats only very superficially " this double subject," which is foreign to his original plan. In fact, the first edition of his *Treatise on Studies* contained but seven books, and it is only in 1734 that he wrote, " at the urgent requests and prayers of several persons," that short essay on the education of boys and girls which first appeared under the form of a supplement, and which became the first book of the work only in the subsequent editions.

The different subjects proper for training the youth in the public schools, that is, in the colleges, — such is the object of the six books which follow : Book II. *Of the learning of the languages;* that is, the study of Greek and Latin ; Book III. *Of poetry;* Book IV. *Of rhetoric;* Book V. *Of the three kinds of eloquence;* Book VI. *Of history;* Book VII. *Of philosophy.*

Book VIII., the last, -entitled *Of the interior government of schools and colleges,* has a particular character. It does not treat of studies and intellectual exercises, but of discipline and moral education. It is, on all accounts, the most original and interesting part of Rollin's work, and it opens to us the treasures of his experience. This eighth book has been justly called the "Memoirs of Rollin." That which constitutes its merit and its charm is that the author here at last decides to be himself. He does not quote the ancients so much; but he speaks in his own name, and relates what he has done, or what he has seen done.

256. GENERAL REFLECTIONS ON EDUCATION. — There is little to be gathered out of the *Preliminary Discourse* of Rollin. He is but slightly successful in general reflections. When he ventures to philosophize, Rollin easily falls into platitudes. He has a dissertation to prove that "study gives the mind more breadth and elevation; and that study gives capacity for business."

On the purpose of education, Rollin, who copies the moderns when he does not translate from the ancients, is content with reproducing the preamble of the regulations of Henry IV., which assigned to studies three purposes: learning, morals and manners, and religion.

"The happiness of kingdoms and peoples, and particularly of a Christian State, depends on the good education of the youth, where the purpose is to cultivate and to polish, by the study of the sciences, the intelligence, still rude, of the young, and thus to fit them for filling worthily the different vocations to which they are destined, without which they will be useless to the State; and finally, to teach them the sincere religious practices which God requires of them, the inviolable attachment they owe to their fathers and mothers and to their country, and the respect and obedience which they are bound to render princes and magistrates."

257. PRIMARY STUDIES. — Rollin is original when he introduces us to the classes of the great colleges where he has lived; but is much less so when he speaks to us of little children, whom he has never seen near at hand. He has never known family life, and scarcely ever visited public schools; and it is through his recollections of Quintilian that he speaks to us of children.

There is, then, but little to note in the few pages that he has devoted to the studies of the first years, from three to six or seven.

One of the most interesting things we find here, perhaps, is the method which he recommends for learning to read, — "the typographic cabinet of du Mas." "It is a novelty," says the wise Rollin, "and it is quite common and natural that we should be suspicious of this word *novelty*." But after the examination, he decides in favor of the system in question, which consists in making of instruction in reading, something analogous to the work of an apprentice who is learning to print. The pupil has before him a table, and on this table is placed a set of pigeon-holes, "logettes," which contain the letters of the alphabet, printed on cards. The pupil is to arrange on the table the different letters needed to construct the words required of him. The reasons that Rollin gives for recommending this method, successful tests of which he had seen made, prove that he had taken into account the nature of the child and his need of activity: —

"This method of learning to read, besides several other advantages, has one which seems to me very considerable, —

it is that of being amusing and agreeable, and of not having the appearance of study. Nothing is more wearisome or tedious in infancy than severe mental effort while the body is in a state of repose. With this device, the mind of the child is not wearied. He need not make a painful effort at recollection, because the distinction and the name of the boxes strike his senses. He is not constrained to a posture that is oppressive by being always tied to the place where he is made to read. There is free activity for eyes, hands, and feet. The child looks for his letters, takes them out, arranges them, overturns them, separates them, and finally replaces them in their boxes. This movement is very much to his taste, and is exactly adapted to the active and restless disposition of that age."

Rollin seems really to believe that there " is no danger in beginning with the reading of Latin." However, " for the schools of the poor, and for those in the country, it is better," he says, " to fall in with the opinion of those who believe that it is necessary to begin with the reading of French."

It may be thought that Rollin puts a little too much into the first years of the child's course of study. Before the age of six or seven he ought to have learned to read, to write, to be nourished on the *Historical Catechism* of Fleury, to know some of the fables of La Fontaine by heart, and to have studied French grammar, and geography. At least, Rollin requires that " no thought, no expression, which is within the child's range," shall be allowed to be passed by. He requires that the teacher speak little, and that he make the child speak much, " which is one of the most essential duties and one of those that are the least practised." He demands, above all else, clearness of statement, and commends the use of illustrations and pictures in reading books.

"They are very suitable," he says, "for striking the attention of children, and for fixing their memory; this is properly the writing of the ignorant."[1]

258. THE EDUCATION OF GIRLS. — The same reasons explain the shortcomings of Rollin's views on the education of women, and the relative mediocrity of his ideas on the education of children. Living in solitude and in the celibate state, he had no personal information on these subjects, and so he goes back to Fénelon for his ideas on the education of women, and to Quintilian in the case of children.

Is the study of Latin fit for girls? Such is the first question which he raises; but he has the wisdom to answer it in the negative, save for "nuns, and also for Christian virgins and widows." "There is no difference in minds," Rollin emphatically says, "that is due to sex." But he does not extend the consequences of this excellent principle very far.

---

[1] Save once, Rollin has scarcely made an allusion to primary instruction proper. We quote this passage on account of its singularity: "Several years ago there was introduced into most of the schools for the poor in Paris a method which is very useful to scholars, and which spares much trouble to the teachers. The school is divided into several classes. I select only one of them, that composed of children who already know how to write syllables; the others must be judged by this one. I suppose that the subject of the reading lesson is *Dixit Dominus Domino meo: Sede a dextris meis.* Each child pronounces one syllable, as *Di.* His competitor, who stands opposite, takes up the next, *xit,* and so on. The whole class is attentive; for the teacher, without warning, passes at once from the head of the line to the middle, or to the foot, and the recitation must continue without interruption. If a pupil makes a mistake in some syllable, the teacher, without speaking, raps upon the table with his stick, and the competitor is obliged to repeat as it should be the syllable that has been wrongly pronounced. If he fail also, the next, upon a second rap of the stick, goes back to the same syllable, and so on till it has been pronounced correctly. More than thirty years ago, I saw with unusual pleasure this method in successful operation at Orleans, where it originated through the care and industry of M. Garot, who presided over the schools of that city."

He is content to require of women the four rules of arithmetic ; orthography, in which he is not over exacting, for " their ignorance of orthography should not be imputed to them as a crime, since it is almost universal in their sex ; " ancient history and the history of France, " which it is disgraceful to every good Frenchman not to know."[1] As to reading, Rollin is quite as severe as Madame de Maintenon : " The reading of comedies and tragedies may be very dangerous for young ladies." He sanctions only *Esther* and *Athalie.* Music and dancing are allowed, but without enthusiasm and with endless precautions : —

" An almost universal experience shows that the study of music is an extraordinary dissipation."

" I do not know how the custom of having girls learn to sing and play on instruments at such great expense has become so common. . . . I hear it said that as soon as they enter on life's duties, they make no farther use of it."

259. THE STUDY OF FRENCH. — Rollin is chiefly preoccupied with the study of the ancient languages ; but he has the merit, notwithstanding his predilection for exercises in Latin, of having followed the example of the Jansenists so far as the importance accorded to the French language is concerned.

" It is a disgrace," he says, " that we are ignorant of our own language ; and if we are willing to confess the truth, we will almost all acknowledge that we have never studied it."

Rollin admitted that he was " much more proficient in the study of Latin than in that of French." In the opening of his *Treatise,* which he wrote in French only that he might place himself within the reach of his young readers and their parents, he excuses himself for making a trial *in a kind of*

---

[1] Rollin does not require it, however, of young men.

writing which is almost new to him. And in congratulating him on his work, d'Aguesseau wrote, " You speak French as if it were your native tongue." Such was the Rector of the University in France at the commencement of the eighteenth century.

Let us think well of him, therefore, for having so overcome his own habits of mind as to recommend the study of French. He would have it learned, not only through use, but also " through principles," and would have " the genius of the language understood, and all its beauties studied."

Rollin has a high opinion of grammar, but would not encourage a misuse of it: —

" Long-continued lessons on such dry matter might become very tedious to pupils. Short questions, regularly proposed each day after the manner of an ordinary conversation, in which they themselves would be consulted, and in which the teacher would employ the art of having them tell what he wished to make them learn, would teach them in the way of amusement, and, by an insensible progress, continued for several years, they would acquire a profound knowledge of the language."

It is in the *Treatise on Studies* that we find for the first time a formal list of classical French authors. Some of these are now obscure and forgotten, as the *Remarkable Lives* written by Marsolier, and the *History of the Academy of Inscriptions and Belles-Lettres*, by de Boze ; but the most of them have held their place in our programmes, and the judgments of Rollin have been followed for two centuries, on the *Discourse on Universal History*, by Bossuet, on the works of Boileau and Racine, and on the *Logic* of Port Royal.

Like all his contemporaries, Rollin particularly recommends Latin composition to his pupils. However, he has spoken a word for French composition, which should bear, first, on fables and historical narratives, then on exercises in epistolary style, and finally, on common things, descriptions, and short speeches.

260. GREEK AND LATIN. — But it is in the teaching of the ancient languages that Rollin has especially tried the resources of his pedagogic art. For two centuries, in the colleges of the University, his recommendations have been followed. In Greek, he censures the study of themes, and reduces the study of this language to the understanding of authors. More of a Latinist than of a Hellenist, of all the arguments he offers to justify the study of Greek, the best is, that, since the Renaissance, Greek has always been taught; but, without great success, he admits : —

" Parents," he says, " are but little inclined in favor of Greek. They also learned Greek, they claim, in their youth, and they have retained nothing of it; this is the ordinary language which indicates that one has not forgotten much of it."

But Latin, which it does not suffice to learn to read, but which must be written and spoken, is the object of all Rollin's care, who, on this point, gives proof of consummate experience. Like the teachers of Port Royal, he demands that there shall be no abuse of themes in the lower classes, and recommends the use of oral themes, but he holds firmly to version, and to the explication of authors : —

" Authors are like a living dictionary, and a speaking grammar, whereby we learn, through experience, the very force and the true use of words, of phrases, and of the rules of syntax."

This is not the place to analyze the parts of the *Treatise on Studies* which relate to poetics and rhetoric, and which are the code, now somewhat antiquated, of Latin verse and prose. Rollin brings to bear on this theme great professional sagacity, but also a spirit of narrowness. He condemns ancient mythology, and excludes, as dangerous, the French poets, save some rare exceptions. He claims that the true use of poetry belongs to religion. He has no conception of the salutary and wholesome influence which the beauties of poetry and eloquence can exercise over the spirit.

261. ROLLIN THE HISTORIAN. — Rollin has made a reputation as an historian. Frederick II. compares him to Thucydides, and Chateaubriand has emphatically called him the " Fénelon of History." Montesquieu himself has pleasantly said : " A noble man has enchanted the public through his works on history ; it is heart which speaks to heart ; we feel a secret satisfaction in hearing virtue speak ; he is the bee of France."

Modern criticism has dealt justly with these exaggerations. The thirteen volumes of his *Ancient History*, which Rollin published, from 1730 to 1738, are scarcely read to-day. His great defect as an historian is his lack of erudition and of the critical spirit ; he accepts with credulity every fable and every legend.

We are to recollect, however, that as professor of history — and in truth he pretended to be only this — Rollin has greater worth than as an historian. He knew how to introduce into the exposition of facts great simplicity and great facility. And especially he attempted to draw from events their moral lesson. " We ought not to forget," says a German of our time, " that Rollin has never made any personal claim to be considered an investigator in historical study, but that the purpose he had chiefly in view was educational. As he was the first to introduce the study of history into French colleges (this is true only of the colleges of the University), he sought to remedy the complete absence of historical reading adapted to the needs of the young.

This is a great educational feat; for it is undeniable that his works are of a nature to give to the young of all nations a real taste for the study of history, and at the same time a vivid conception of the different epochs, and of the life of nations." [1]

262. THE TEACHING OF HISTORY. — However, considered simply as a professor of history, Rollin is far from being irreproachable. Doubtless it is good to moralize on history, and to make of it, as he says, "a school of enduring glory and real grandeur." But is not historical accuracy necessarily compromised, and is there not danger of making the subject puerile, when the teacher is guided exclusively by the idea of moral edification?

Another graver fault in Rollin is that he systematically omits the history of France, and with it, all modern history. In this respect, he falls below the Oratory, Port Royal, Bossuet, Fénelon, and Madame de Maintenon. It is interesting to observe, moreover, that Rollin recognizes the utility of the study of national history, but his excuse for omitting it is the lack of time : —

"I do not speak of the history of France. . . . I do not think it possible to find time, during the regular course of instruction, to make a place for this study; but I am far from considering it as of no importance, and I observe with regret that it is neglected by many persons to whom, nevertheless, it would be very useful, not to say necessary. When I say this, it is myself that I criticise first, for I acknowledge that I have not given sufficient attention to it, and I am ashamed of being in some sort a stranger in my own country after having traversed so many others."

[1] Doctor Wolker, quoted by Cadet, in his edition of Rollin, Paris, 1882.

263. PHILOSOPHY. — It is moral edification that Rollin seeks in philosophical studies, as in historical studies. With but little competence in these matters, he admits that he has applied himself only very superficially to the study of philosophy. He knows, however, the value of ethics and logic, which govern the morals and perfect the mind; of physics, which furnishes us a mass of interesting knowledge; and finally, of metaphysics, which fortifies the religious sentiment. The ethics of antiquity seems to him worthy of attention; it is, in his view, the introduction to Christian ethics.

264. SCIENTIFIC INSTRUCTION. — Rollin has given us a compendium of astronomy, of physics, and of natural history. Without doubt his essays have but a moderate value. Rollin's knowledge is often inexact, and his general ideas are narrow. He is capable of believing that "nature entire is made for man." But yet he deserves some credit for having comprehended the part that the observation of the sensible world ought to play in education : —

"I call *children's physics* a study of nature which requires scarcely anything but eyes, and which, for this reason, is within the reach of all sorts of persons, and even of children. It consists in making ourselves attentive to the objects which nature presents to us, to consider them with care, and to admire their different beauties; but without searching into their secret causes, which comes within the province of the physics of the scientist.

"I say that even children are capable of this, for they have eyes, and are not wanting in curiosity. They wish to know; they are inquisitive. It is only necessary to awaken and nourish in them the desire to learn and to know, which is natural to all men. This study, moreover, if it may be so called, far from being painful and tedious, affords only pleasure and amusement; it may take the place of recreation, and ordinarily ought not to take place save in playing. It is inconceivable how much knowledge of things children might gain, if we knew how to take advantage of all the occasions which they furnish for the purpose."

265. The Educative Character of Rollin's Pedagogy. — It should not be supposed that Rollin's exclusive purpose was to make Latinists and literary men. I know very well that he himself has said that "to form the taste was his principal aim." Nevertheless, he has thought of other things, — moral qualities not less than intellectual endowments. He wished to train at once "the heart and the intellect." With him, instruction in all its phases takes an educative turn. He esteems knowledge only because it leads to virtue. In the explication of authors, attention should be directed to the morality of their thoughts, at least as much as to their literary beauty. The maxims and examples which their writings contain should be skillfully put in relief, so that these readings may become moral lessons not less than studies in rhetoric. To sum up in a word, Rollin follows the tradition of the Jansenists, and not that of the Company of Jesus.

266. Christianity of Rollin. — Rollin, though persecuted for his Jansenist tendencies, was a fervent Christian. "A Roman probity" did not suffice for him; he desired a Christian virtue. Consequently, he requires that religious instruction should form a part of every lesson. A regulation which dates from his rectorship required that the scholar in each class should learn and recite each day one or more maxims drawn from the Holy Scriptures. This custom has been maintained to this day. Rollin knew, moreover, that

the best means of inspiring piety is to preach by example, and to be pious one's self : —

` ⸤To make true Christians, — this is the end and purpose of ⟩ the education of children ; all the rest but fulfills the pur- ⟩ pose of means. . . . When a teacher has received this spirit,· there is nothing more to say to him. . . ."᷉ {{ ℛollin }}

The religious spirit of Rollin comes to view on each page of his book : —

" It remains for me," he says, in concluding his preface, " to pray God, in whose hands we all are, we and our discourses, to deign to bless my good intentions."

267. INTERIOR DISCIPLINE OF THE COLLEGES. — The part of the *Treatise on Studies* which has preserved the most interest, and which will be studied with the most profit, is certainly that which treats of *the interior government of schools and colleges.* Here, though he does not completely divest himself of his method of borrowings, and references to the authority of others, and though he is especially under the influence of Locke, whose wise advice on rewards and punishments he reproduces almost verbatim, Rollin makes use of a long personal experience. We have charged him with not knowing the little child. On the other hand, he knows exactly what scholars a little older are, — children from ten to sixteen years old. And he not only knows them, but he loves them tenderly. He gives them this testimony, which affection alone can explain, that he has always found them reasonable.

268. ENUMERATION OF THE QUESTIONS TREATED BY ROLLIN. — To give an idea of this part of the *Treatise,* the best way is to reproduce the titles of the thirteen articles composing the chapter entitled *General Counsels on the Education of the Young :* —

I. What end should be proposed in education? II. How to study the character of children in order to become able to instruct them properly. III. How at once to gain authority over children. IV. How to become loved and feared. V. Punishments: 1. Difficulties and dangers in punishments; 2. Rules to be observed in punishments. VI. Reprimands: 1. Occasion for reprimanding; 2. Time for making the reprimand; 3. Manner of reprimanding. VII. Reasoning with children. Stimulating them with the sense of honor. Making use of commendation, rewards, and caresses. VIII. How to train children to be truthful. IX. How to train children to politeness, to cleanliness, and to exactness. X. How to make study attractive. XI. How . to give rest and recreation to children. XII. How to train the young to goodness by instruction and example. XIII. Piety, religion, zeal for the salvation of children.

269. PUBLIC EDUCATION. — Rollin does not definitely express himself on the superiority of public education. He does not dare give formal advice to parents; but he brings forward the advantages of the common life of· colleges with so much force, that it is very evident that he prefers it to a private education. Let it be noted, besides, that he accepts on his own account " the capital maxim of the ancients, that children belong more to the State than to their parents."

270. THE ROD. — In the matter of discipline, Rollin leans rather to the side of mildness. However, he does not dare pronounce himself absolutely against the use of the rod. That which in particular causes him to hesitate, which gives him scruples, which prevents him from expressing a censure which is at the bottom of his heart, but which never rises to his lips, is that there are certain texts of the Bible whose

interpretation is favorable to the use of the rod. It is interesting to notice how, in a strait between his sentiments as a
docile Christian and his instincts towards mildness, the good
and timid Rollin tries to find a less rigorous meaning in the
sacred text, and to convince himself that the Bible does not
say what it seems to say. After many hesitations, he finally
comes to the conclusion that corporal chastisements are permitted, but that they are not to be employed save in extreme and desperate cases; and this is also the conclusion
of Locke.

271. PUNISHMENTS IN GENERAL. — But how many wise
counsels on punishments, and on the precautions that must
be taken when we punish or reprimand! One should refrain
from punishing a child at the moment he commits his fault,
because this might then exasperate him and provoke him to
new breaches of duty. Let the master be cool when he
punishes, and avoid the anger which discredits his authority.
The whole of this excellent code of scholastic discipline might
be quoted with profit. Rollin is reason and good sense itself
when he guides and instructs the teacher as to his relations
with the pupil. Doubtless the most of these precepts are not
new; but when they come from the mouth of Rollin, there
is something added to them which I cannot describe, but
which gives to the most threadbare advice the authority of
personal experience.

272. CONCLUSION. — We shall not dwell on the other
precepts of Rollin. The text must be consulted for his
reflections on plays, recreations, the means of making study
attractive, and on the necessity of appealing to the child's
reason betimes, and of explaining to him why one does this
or that. In this last part of the *Treatise on Studies* there is
a complete infant psychology which is lacking neither in

keenness nor in penetration. In particular, there is a code of moral discipline which cannot be too highly commended to educators, and to all those who desire, in the words of Rollin, " to train at once the heart and the mind " of the young. Rollin has worked for virtue even more than for science. His works are less literary productions than works on morals, and the author himself is the perfect expression of what can be done for the education of the young by the Christian spirit allied to the university spirit.

[273. ANALYTICAL SUMMARY. — 1. The characteristic fact disclosed by this study is the very slow rate at which progress in education takes place. There is also an enforcement of the lesson which has reappeared from time to time, that education follows in the wake of new and general movements in human thought.

2. A more specific fact is the extreme conservatism of universities, or the tenacity with which they hold to traditions. The question is suggested whether, after all, the conservative habit of the university does not best befit its judicial functions.

3. In the elbowing of the classics by history and French, we see the rise of innovations which have become embodied in the modern university.

4. A new factor in the higher education is the intervention of the State, as opposed to the historical domination of the Church. In the reform of the University of Paris the State became an educator.

5. There is evidence of some progress in the historical struggle towards the conception that woman has equal rights with man in the benefits of education.]

CHAPTER XII.

CATHOLICISM AND PRIMARY INSTRUCTION. — LA SALLE
AND THE BRETHREN OF THE CHRISTIAN SCHOOLS.

STATE OF PRIMARY INSTRUCTION IN THE SEVENTEENTH CENTURY;
DÉMIA AND THE INFANT SCHOOLS OF LYONS; CLAUDE JOLY,
DIRECTOR OF THE PRIMARY SCHOOLS OF PARIS; THE BOOK OF
THE PARISH SCHOOL; LA SALLE (1651-1719) AND THE CHRISTIAN
SCHOOLS; LIFE AND CHARACTER OF LA SALLE; ASCETIC TEN-
DENCIES; FOUNDATION OF THE INSTITUTE OF THE BRETHREN
(1684); THE IDEA OF NORMAL SCHOOLS; THE IDEA OF GRATUITOUS
AND COMPULSORY INSTRUCTION; PROFESSIONAL INSTRUCTION;
CONDUCT OF THE CHRISTIAN SCHOOLS; SUCCESSIVE EDITIONS;
ABUSE OF SCHOOL REGULATIONS; DIVISION OF THE CONDUCT;
INTERIOR ORGANIZATION OF THE SCHOOLS; SIMULTANEOUS IN-
STRUCTION; WHAT WAS LEARNED IN THE CHRISTIAN SCHOOLS;
METHOD OF TEACHING; THE CHRISTIAN CIVILITY; CORPORAL
CHASTISEMENTS; REPRIMANDS; PENANCES; THE FERULE; THE
ROD; REWARDS; MUTUAL ESPIONAGE; GENERAL CONCLUSION;
ANALYTICAL SUMMARY.

---

274. THE STATE OF PRIMARY INSTRUCTION IN THE SEVEN-
TEENTH CENTURY. — It does not form a part of our plan to
follow from day to day the small increments of progress and
the slow development of the primary schools of France;
but we must confine ourselves to the essential facts and to
the important dates.

The Catholic Church, in the sixteenth and seventeenth
centuries, did not altogether renounce her interest in popular instruction. She took measures, without doubt, to evan-
gelize the poor people, and sometimes " even to teach them

how to read and write." Nevertheless, up to the organization of the Christian schools, by La Salle, no serious effort was made. Some religious foundations establish gratuitous schools in many places, — *charity schools*, — but no comprehensive purpose directs these establishments. Conflicts of prerogative among certain independent colleagues, as that between the writing-masters and the masters of the infant schools placed under the direct authority of the precentor, or among the rectors and the tutors (*écolâtres*), that is, the assistants of the bishops charged with the supervision of the schools, — such dissensions came still further to defeat the good intentions of individuals, and to embarrass the feeble movement that was exerted in favor of popular instruction. For example, towards 1680, the writing-masters attempted to prevent the masters of the primary schools [1] from giving writing lessons, at least, *from giving their pupils any copies except monosyllables;* and a decree of Parliament is necessary to re-establish the liberty — and then under certain restrictions — of teaching to write.

"Christian instruction was neglected, not to say dishonored," is the statement of contemporaries. The children who attended the schools of the poor were subjected to public contempt. They were obliged to wear on their caps a distinctive badge. In brief, far from progressing, primary instruction was rather in a state of decadence.

275. DÉMIA AND THE PRIMARY SCHOOLS OF LYONS. — Among the progressive men who struggled against this unhappy state of affairs, and who tried to develop the Catholic schools, we must mention, before La Salle, Démia,

---

[1] *Petites écoles.* This is the term commonly applied to primary schools at this period. By the Jansenists this term was used in a more distinctive sense, and for this reason I have translated it "Little Schools" in Chap. VII. (P.)

a priest of Lyons, who, in 1666, founded the Congregation of the Brethren of Saint Charles, for the instruction of poor children. The Institute of La Salle was not organized till eighteen years later, in 1684. In 1668, having addressed to the provosts of the merchants of the city of Lyons a warm appeal, his *Proposals for the establishment of Christian schools for the instruction of the poor*, Démia obtained an annual grant of two hundred livres. In 1675 he was charged by "express command" of the archbishop of Lyons "with the management and direction of the schools of that city and diocese," and drew up a body of school regulations which was quoted as a model.[1] For the method of "teaching to read, of learning the catechism, of correcting children, and similar things," Démia conformed to the book known as the *Parish School* (*École paroissiale*), of which we shall presently say a word. He took it upon himself to proceed "to the examination of the religion, the ability, and the good morals, of the persons who proposed to teach school." But, what was of greater moment, he established, for preparing and training them, a sort of seminary.

A few quotations will give an idea of Démia's zeal in the establishment of Christian schools.

"This establishment is of such importance and of so great utility, that there is nothing in our political organization which is more worthy of the care and the watchfulness of the magistrates, since on it depend our peace and public tranquillity. The poor, not having the means of educating their children, leave them in ignorance of their obligations. . . . Thus we see, with keen displeasure, that such an education of the children of the poor is totally neglected, although it is the most important interest of the State, of

---

[1] See the *Lectures pédagogiques*. Hachette, 1883, p. 420.

which they comprise the largest part; and, although it is quite as necessary, and even more so, to maintain public schools for them, as to support colleges for the children of families in good circumstances. . . ."

276. CLAUDE JOLY.—In 1676, Claude Joly, precentor of Notre Dame, " collator, director, and judge of the primary schools of the city, the suburbs, and the outskirts of Paris," published his *Christian and Moral Counsels for the Instruction of Children.* There is but little to gather from this work, where the author is so forgetful of elementary instruction as to speak only of secondary instruction and of the education of princes. What most concerns Claude Joly is to put in force the regulations which forbid the association of boys and girls in the schools. The separation of the sexes was for a long time an absolute principle in France. Démia, in article nine of his regulations, restores the ordinance of the archbishop of Lyons, " which forbids school-masters to admit girls, and school-mistresses to admit boys." Rollin was of the same opinion. Claude Joly, in the capacity of chief precentor, bluntly claimed his sovereign rights in the matter of primary instruction : —

" We shall contest the power claimed by the rectors of Paris to control the schools, under the name and pretext of charity, without the permission of the chief precentor, to whom alone belongs this power. To him, also, belongs the right of nomination to the schools of the religious and seen-lar communities. We shall disclose, besides, the attempts of writers to interfere with the teaching of orthography, which belongs only to good grammarians, that is, to the masters of the little schools."

We see to what petty questions of prerogative was sacrificed, in the seventeenth century, the great cause of popular instruction.

277. THE BOOK OF THE PARISH SCHOOL. — Under the title, *The Parish School, or the Manner of Properly Instructing the Children in the Little Schools*, a priest of the diocese of Paris had written, in 1655, a school manual, often reprinted,[1] which became the general standard of the schools during the years that followed, and which gives an exact idea of what was narrow and poorly defined in the primary instruction of that period.

The author of the *Parish School* does not have a high opinion of the office of the teacher, which he regards as an employment *without lustre, without pleasure, and without interest.* He does not expect great results from instruction, of which he is pleased to say, that *it is not completely useless.* It is true that instruction is reduced to a very few things, — reading, writing, and counting. To this the author adds religion and politeness.

Let us observe in particular, that the programme of the parish school also comprises the *principles of the Latin language.* The primary school of that period was still confounded with the college of secondary instruction; the ancient languages and rhetoric were taught in it. In the catalogue of the master's books, drawn up by the author of the *Parish School*, we find a Greek grammar. In the classes, the reading of Latin precedes the reading of French.

Some good advice in practical pedagogy might be extracted from the first part of the work, especially on the duties of a school-master, on the power of example, and on the necessity of knowing the disposition of pupils. But how many' artless assertions and mischievous precepts, in that school code of the city of Paris, in the near presence of the grand century! The *Parish School* complains that the scholars eat too much bread: —

---

[1] We have before us the edition of 1722.

" The children of Paris, as a rule, eat a great deal of bread. This food stupefies the mind, and very often makes them, at the age of nine or ten, incapable of learning. *Omnis repletio mala, panis vero pessima.*" A serious matter is that espionage is not only authorized, but is encouraged and organized : —

" The master will select two of the most reliable and intelligent to be on the lookout for the disorders and the improprieties of the school and the church. They shall write the names of the offenders, and of those guilty of improprieties, on pieces of paper or on tablets, to be given to the master. These officers shall be called *observers.*"

278. La Salle (1651–1719) and the Christian Schools. — The reading of the *Parish School* prepares us the better to comprehend the work of La Salle. If one were in any degree tempted to depreciate the Institute of the Brethren of the Christian Schools, it would suffice, to counteract this disposition, to contrast the reforms of La Salle, however insufficient they may be, with the real state of the schools of that period. To be equitably judged, human institutions ought to be replaced in their setting and in their environment. It is easy to-day to formulate charges against the pedagogy of the Brethren of the Christian Schools. But considered in their time, and compared with what existed, or rather with what did *not* exist, the establishments of La Salle deserve the esteem and the gratitude of the friends of instruction. They represent the first systematic effort of the Catholic Church to organize popular instruction. What the Jesuits did in the matter of secondary instruction, with immense resources and for pupils who paid them for their efforts, La Salle attempted in primary instruction, through a thousand obstacles and for pupils who did not pay.

279. LIFE AND CHARACTER OF LA SALLE. — We shall have to criticise in the most of its principles and in many details of its practice, the educational institute of La Salle. But that which merits an admiration without reserve is the professional zeal of the founder of the order, the dauntless spirit of improvement which he displayed ·in the organization of his schools, and in the recruitment of his teachers; it is also his tenacious zeal which was discouraged neither by the jealous opposition of corporations, the writing-masters for example, nor by the inexplicable opposition of the clergy; and, finally, it is the indefatigable devotion of a beautiful life consecrated to the cause of instruction, which was a long series of efforts and sacrifices. At an early hour, La Salle had given proofs of the energy of his character. Weak and sickly, he was obliged to struggle against the infirmities of his constitution. To overcome sleep, and to prolong his studious vigils, he sometimes kneeled on sharp stones, and sometimes he placed in front of him, upon his study-table, a board fitted with iron points, against which his head would strike as soon as fatigue made him doze and he leaned forward. Canon of the chapter of Reims in 1667, ordained priest in 1678, he resigned his prebendship in 1683, and, voluntarily making himself poor, in. order to approach those whose souls he would save, he renounced his whole patrimony, to the great disgust of his friends, who treated him as a madman.

280. ASCETIC TENDENCIES. — But it is not a disinterested love of the people, it is not the thought of their moral regeneration, and of their intellectual progress, which animated and sustained the efforts of La Salle. His purpose was above all else religious. He pushed devotion even to asceticism. In his childhood, while he still lived at home, he

came to have a sense of unrest in the parlors of his mother ; and one evening, as his biographers relate, while those about him were engaged in music, or were talking on worldly matters, he threw himself into the arms of one of his aunts, and said to her, "Madam, relate to me the life of one of the saints." He himself was a saint, though the Church did not think him worthy of this venerable title. In his youth he passed whole nights in prayer, and slept on boards. All his life he was severe to himself and also to others, considering abstinence and privations as the regimen of the Christian. His adversaries, at different times, imputed this to him as a crime. He was represented as a hardened man, pushing his ascetic requirements to the extreme of cruelty. To appease their anger, he removed penances and bodily inflictions from his institution, but he maintained them for himself, and continued his life of voluntary suffering. Heroic virtues, it may be ; but it may be added also, an unfortunate disposition for a teacher of children. We distrust, in advance, a system of teaching whose beginning was so sad, whose founder inclosed his life within so narrow an horizon, and which, at first, was illuminated by no rays of ,gladness and good humor.

281. FOUNDATIONS OF THE INSTITUTE. — The Institute of the Brethren was founded in 1684, but it was not sanctioned by pontifical authority and royal power till forty years later, in 1724.

We shall not recite at full length the vicissitudes of the first years of the Institute. We simply state that La Salle inaugurated his work by offering hospitality in his own house to several poor teachers. In 1679 he opened at Reims a school for boys. In 1684 he imposed on his disciples vows of *stability* and *obedience*, and prescribed their costume. In 1688 he went to Paris in order to found schools there, and

-it was here in particular, as he himself says, that "he saw himself persecuted by the men from whom he expected help." In spite of all these difficulties his enterprise prospered, and when he died, in 1720, the Institute of the Brethren already counted a large number of establishments for primary instruction.

282. THE IDEA OF NORMAL SCHOOLS. — We know how the teaching force was then recruited. In Paris, if we may believe Pourchot, the chief precentor, Claude Joly, was obliged to employ, for the direction of schools, old-clothes-men, innkeepers, cooks, masons, wig-makers, puppet-players — the list might be continued. In 1682 Marie Moreau, a teacher, was sent by Bossuet to keep the school at Ferté-Gaucher. The rector of the place, in his capacity as tutor (écolâtre), wishing to ascertain her competence, subjected her to an examination, of which the following is an account : —

"1. He asked her if she could read, and she replied that she read passably well, but not well enough to teach.

"2. He gave her a pen to mend, and she declared that she could not do it.

"3. He handed her a Latin book and requested her to read it, but she was prevented from making the attempt by sister Remy, who had just prevented her from exhibiting her writing."[1]

Ignorance, and often moral unfitness, was the general character of the teachers of that period. They often entered upon their duties without the least preparation. La Salle had too great an anxiety for the good condition of his schools to accept improvised teachers. So in 1685 he opened at Reims, under the name of *Seminary for Schoolmasters*, a

---

[1] *Histoire d'une école gratuite*, par V. Plessier, p. 15.

real normal school, in which teachers were to be trained for the rural districts. Only Démia had preceded him in this work. Later he founded an establishment of the same kind in Paris, and — a thing worthy of note — he annexed to this normal school a primary school, in which the teaching was done by the students in training under the direction of an experienced teacher.

In the third part of his *Conduct of Schools* La Salle has drawn up the rules for what he calls the *training of new masters*. Here are the faults that he notices in young teachers : —

1. An itching to talk ; 2. too great activity, which degencrates into petulance ; 3. indifference ; 4. preoccupation and embarrassment ; 5. harshness ; 6. spite ; 7. partiality ; 8. slowness and negligence ; 9. pusillanimity and lack of force ; 10. despondency and fretfulness ; 11. familiarity and trifling ; 12. distractions and loss of time ; 13. fickleness ; 14. giddiness ; 15. exclusiveness ; 16. lack of attention to the different characters and dispositions of children.

283. The Idea of Gratuitous and Obligatory Instruction. — The Institute of the Brethren of the Christian Schools, say the statutes of the order in so many words, is a society whose members make a profession to conduct schools *gratuitously*. " La Salle thought only of the children of artisans and of the poor, who, he said, being occupied during the whole day in earning their own livelihood and that of their families, could not give their children the instruction they need, and a respectable and Christian education." In 1694, the founder of the Institute and his first twelve disciples went and kneeled at the foot of the altar, and pledged themselves to " conduct collectively and through organized effort schools of gratuitous instruction, even when, in order

to do this, they might be obliged to ask alms and to live on bread alone."

But a thing still more remarkable than to have popularized gratuitous instruction, already realized in many places through charity schools, is to have formed the conception of obligatory instruction. La Salle, who did not believe that this was any encroachment on the liberty of parents, proposes, in this *Conduct of Schools*, a means for affecting their will: —

"If among the poor there are certain ones who are unwilling to take advantage of the opportunities for instruction, they should be reported to the rectors. The latter will be able to cure them of their indifference by threatening to give them no more assistance till they send their children to school."

284. PROFESSIONAL INSTRUCTION. — Besides primary schools proper, La Salle, who is truly an innovator, inaugurated the organization of a technical and professional instruction. At Saint Yon, near Rouen, he organized a sort of college where was taught "all that a young man can learn, with the exception of Latin, and whose purpose was to prepare the student for commercial, industrial, and administrative occupations."

285. CONDUCT OF THE CHRISTIAN SCHOOLS : SUCCESSIVE EDITIONS. — La Salle took the trouble to draw up for his Institute a very minute code of rules, with this title : *The Conduct of Schools*. The first edition bears the date of 1720. It appeared at Avignon a year after the author's death.[1] Two other editions have since appeared, in 1811 and in 1870, with some important modifications. The sub-

---

[1] We have before us a copy of this Avignon edition: J. Charles Chastanier, printer and bookseller, near the College of the Jesuits.

stance has not been changed, but certain passages relative to discipline, and to the use of the rod, have been suppressed.

" With the view to adapt our education to the mildness of the present state of manners," says the preface of 1811, " we have suppressed or modified whatever includes corporal correction, and have advantageously (*sic*) replaced this, on the one hand, by good marks, by promises and rewards, and on the other by bad marks, by deprivations and tasks."

On the other hand, some additions have been made. The Institute of the Brethren had to yield in part to the demands of the times, and to subtract something from the inflexibility of its government.

" The Brethren," it is said in the preface to the edition of 1870, written by the Frère Philip, " the Brethren have little by little enlarged the original *Conduct*, in proportion as they have perfected their methods. . . . It is plain that a book of this kind cannot receive a final form. New experiments, progress in methods, legislative enactments, new needs, etc., require that it receive divers modifications from time to time."

286. ABUSE OF REGULATIONS. — A feature common to the pedagogy of the Jesuits, and to that of the Brethren of the Christian Schools, is, that everything is regulated in advance with extraordinary exactness. No discretion is left to the teachers. The instruction is but a rule in action. All novelty is interdicted.

"It has been necessary," says the *Preface* of La Salle, to prepare this *Conduct* of the Christian schools, " to the end that there may be uniformity in all the schools, and in all the places where there are Brethren of the Institute, and that the methods employed may always be the same. Man is so subject to slackness, and even to changeableness, that there must be written rules for him, in order to keep him within the bounds of his duty, and to prevent him from introducing something new, or from destroying that which has been wisely established."

Need we be astonished, after this, that the teaching of the Brethren often became a useless routine?

287. DIVISION OF THE CONDUCT. — The *Conduct of the Christian Schools* is divided into three parts. The first treats of all the exercises of the school, and of what is done in it from the time the pupils enter till they leave. The second describes the means for establishing and maintaining order; in a word, the discipline. The third treats of the duties of the inspector of schools, of the qualities of the teachers, and of the rules to be followed in the education of the teachers themselves. This may be called, so to speak, the manual of the normal schools of the Institute.

288. INTERIOR ORGANIZATION OF THE SCHOOLS. — That which first strikes the attention in the Christian Schools, such as La Salle organized, is the complete silence that reigns in them. Nothing is better than silence on the part of pupils, when it can be obtained, but La Salle enjoins silence on teachers as well. The Frère is a professor who does not talk.

"He will watch carefully over himself, to speak very rarely, and very low." " It would be of but little use for the teacher to try to make his pupils keep silence if he does not do this himself." "When necessity obliges him to speak — and he is careful that this necessity is rare — he will always speak in a moderate tone."

It might be said that La Salle fears a strong and sonorous voice.

How, then, shall the teacher communicate with his pupils, since he is almost debarred from the use of speech? La Salle has invented, to supersede language, a complete system of signs, a sort of scholastic telegraphy, a long account of which will be found in several chapters of the *Conduct*. To have prayers repeated, the teacher will fold his hands; to have the catechism repeated, he will make the sign of the cross. In other cases he will strike his breast, will look at the pupil steadily, etc. Besides, he will employ an instrument of iron named a *signal*, which he will raise or lower, and handle in a hundred ways, to indicate his wish, or to announce the beginning or the close of such or such an exercise.

What is the meaning of this distrust of speech? And what are we to think of these schools of mutes where teachers and pupils proceed only by signs? When a scholar asks permission to speak, he will stand erect in his place, with hands crossed and eyes modestly lowered. Doubtless, to attempt to excuse these practices, we must consider the annoyances of a noisy school, and the advantages of a silent school where everything is done discreetly and noiselessly. Is there not, however, in these odd regulations, something besides the desire for order and good conduct, — the revelation of a complete system of pedagogy which is afraid of life and liberty, and which, under the pretext of making the school quiet, deadens the school, and, in the end, reduces teachers and pupils to mere machines?

289. SIMULTANEOUS INSTRUCTION. — By the side of the evil we must note the good. Up to the time of La Salle, the individual method was almost alone in use in primary instruction; but he substituted for this the simultaneous method, that is, teaching given to all the pupils at the same time. For this purpose, La Salle divided each school into

three divisions: "The division of the weakest, that of the mediocres, and that of the more intelligent or the more capable."

"All the scholars of the same order will receive the same lesson together. The instructor will see that all are attentive, and that, in reading for example, all read in a low voice what the teacher reads in a loud voice."

To aid the instructor, La Salle gives him one or two of the better pupils of each division, who become his assistants, and whom he calls *inspectors*. "The more children have taught," said La Salle, "the more they will learn."

To be just, however, we must recognize, in certain recommendations of La Salle, some desire to appeal to the judgment and the reason of the child: —

"The teacher will not speak to the scholars during the catechism, as in preaching, but he will interrogate them almost continually by questions, direct or indirect, in order to make them comprehend that which he is teaching them."

The Frère Luccard, in his *Life of the Venerable J. B. de La Salle*,[1] quotes this still more expressive passage, borrowed from his manuscript *Counsels:* —

"Let the teacher be careful not to lend his pupils too much help in resolving the questions that have been proposed to them. He ought, on the contrary, to invite them not to be discouraged, but to seek with ardor what he knows they will be able to find for themselves. He will convince them that they will the better retain the knowledge they have acquired by a personal and persevering effort."

290. WHAT WAS LEARNED IN THE CHRISTIAN SCHOOLS. — Reading, writing, orthography, arithmetic, and the catechism, — this is the programme of La Salle.

---

[1] Two Volumes, Paris, 1876.

In reading, La Salle, agreeing in this respect with Port Royal, requires that French books be used in the beginning.

"The book in which the pupil will begin to learn Latin is the Psalter ; but this lesson will be given only to those who can readily read in French."

La Salle requires that the pupil shall not be exercised in writing till "he can read perfectly." He attaches, more- over, an extreme importance to calligraphy, and it is known that the Brethren have remained masters in this art. La Salle does not weary in giving advice on this subject: the pens, the knife for mending them, the ink, the paper, the tracing-papers and blotters, round letters and italic letters (a bastard script), — everything is passed in review.[1] The *Conduct* also insists "on the manner of teaching the proper posture of the body" and "on the manner of teaching how to hold the pen and the paper."

"It will be useful and timely in the beginning to give the pupil a stick of the bigness of a pen, on which there are three notches, two on the right and one on the left, to mark the places where his fingers should be put."

The exercises in writing are to be followed by exercises in orthography and in composition : —

"The teacher will require the pupils to compose and write for themselves notes, receipts, bills, etc. He will also require them to write out what they remember of the cate- chism, and of the lectures that they have heard."[2]

As to arithmetic, reduced to the four rules, we must commend La Salle's attempt to have it learned by reason and not by routine. Thus, he requires the teacher to inter- rogate the pupil, in order to make him the better comprehend

---

[1] The use of the round script was in fashion. La Salle introduced the bastard hand.

[2] See Chap. II. of the Second Part.

and retain the rule, or to make sure that he is attentive. He " will give him a complete understanding" of what he teaches ; and, finally, he will require him "to produce a certain number of rules that he has discovered for himself."

Prayers and religious exercises naturally hold a large place in the schools organized by La Salle : —

" There shall always be two or three scholars kneeling, one from each class, who will tell their beads one after another."

" Care will everywhere be taken that the scholars hear the holy mass every day."

" A half hour each day shall be devoted to the cate-chism."

291. METHOD OF TEACHING. — The Institute of the Brethren has often been criticised for the mechanical character of its instruction. The Frère Philip, in the edition of the *Conduct* published in 1870, implicitly acknowledges the justice of this criticism when he writes : " Elementary instruction has assumed a particular character in these last days, *of which we must take account.* Proposing for its chief end to train the judgment of the pupil, it gives less importance than heretofore to the culture of the memory ; it makes especial use of methods which call into activity the intelligence, and lead the child to reflect, to take account of facts, to withdraw from the domain of words to enter into that of ideas." Do not these wise cautions unmistakably betray the existence of an evil tradition which should be corrected, but which tends to hold its ground? He who has read the *Conduct* is not left in doubt that the general character of the pedagogy of the Christian Schools, at the first, was a mechanical and routine exercise of the memory, and the absence of life.

292. CHRISTIAN POLITENESS. — Under the title of *Rules of Decorum and Christian Civility*, La Salle had composed a reading book, intended for pupils already somewhat advanced, and printed in Gothic characters.[1] It was not only a manual of politeness, but was, the *Conduct* claims, a treatise on ethics, "containing all the duties of children, both towards God and towards their parents." But we would examine the work in vain for the justification of this remark. In it are discussed only the puerile details of outward behavior and of worldly bearing. It would, however, be in bad taste to criticise at this day a book of another age, whose artlessness makes us smile. La Salle's purpose was certainly praiseworthy, though attempting a little too much. It is said in the *Preface* that "there is not a single one of our actions which ought not to be regulated by motives purely Christian." Hence an infinite number of minute prescriptions upon the simplest acts of daily life.[2]

But here are a few specimens of this pretended elementary ethics : —

"It is not proper to talk when one has retired, the bed being made for rest."

" One should try to make no noise and not to snore while asleep ; nor should one often turn from side to side in bed as if he were restless and did not know on which side to lie."

" It is not becoming, when one is in company, to take off one's shoes."

---

[1] We have before us the sixth edition of this work: Rouen, 1729. La Salle had written it towards the year 1703.

[2] See, for example, the following chapters: upon the nose and the manner of using the handkerchief and of sneezing (chap. vii.); upon the back, the shoulders, the arms, and the elbow (chap. viii.); on the manner in which one ought to behave with respect to the bones, the sauce, and the fruit (chap. vi., of the second part); on the manner of behaving while walking in the streets, on journeys, in carriages, and on horseback (chap. x.).

"It is impolite to play with a stick or a cane, and to use it to strike the ground or pebbles, etc., etc."

How many mistakes in politeness we should make every day of our lives if the rules of La Salle were infallible!

293. CORPORAL CHASTISEMENTS. — The Brethren, within two centuries, have singularly ameliorated their system of correction. "*Imperative circumstances,*" said the Frère Philip in 1870, "no longer permit us to tolerate corporal punishment in our schools." Already, in 1811, there was talk of suppressing entirely, or at least modifying, the use of these punishments. The instruments of torture were perfected. "We reduce the heavy ferule, the inconvenience of which has been only too often felt, to a simple piece of leather, about a foot long and an inch wide, and slit in two at one end; still we hope that by divine help and by the mildness of our very dear and dearly beloved colleagues, they will make use of it only in cases of unavoidable necessity, and only to give a stroke with it on the hand, without the permission ever to make any other use of it."

But at first, and in the original *Conduct*,[1] corporal punishment is freely permitted and regulated with exactness. La Salle distinguished five sorts of corrections, — reprimand, penances, the fernle, the rod, expulsion from school.

294. REPRIMANDS. — Silence, we have seen, is the fundamental rule of La Salle's schools : "There must be as little speaking as possible. Consequently, corrections by word of mouth are very rarely to be employed." It even seems, adds the *Conduct*, that "it is much better not to use them at all"!

A curious system of discipline, verily, where it is as good

---

[1] See the edition of 1720, from page 140 to page 180.

as forbidden to resort to admonitions, to severe reprimands, to an appeal through speech to the reason and the feelings of the child; where, consequently, there is no place for the moral authority of the teacher, but where there is at once invoked the *ultima ratio* of constraint and violence, of the ferule and the rod!

295. PENANCES. — La Salle recommends penances as well as corporal corrections. By this term he means punishments like the following: maintaining a kneeling posture in the school; learning a few pages of the catechism by heart; "holding his book before his eyes for the space of half an hour without looking off;" keeping motionless, with clasped hands and downcast eyes, etc.

296. THE FERULE. — We have not to discuss in this place the use of material means of correction. The Brethren themselves have repudiated them. Only it is provoking that they bow to what they call "imperative circumstances," and not to considerations based on principles. But it is interesting, were it only from an historical point of view, to recall the minute prescriptions of the founder of the Order.

The *Conduct* first describes the fernle, "an instrument formed of two pieces of leather sewed together; it shall be from ten to twelve inches long, including the handle; the palm shall be oval, and two inches in diameter; the palm shall be lined on the inside so as not to be wholly flat, but rounded to fit the hand." Nothing is overlooked, we observe; the form of the ferule is officially defined. But what shocks us still more is the nature of the faults that provoke the application of the ferule: "1. for not having attended to the lesson, or for having played; 2. for being tardy at school; 3. for not having obeyed the first signal." It is true that La Salle, always preoccupied with writing, orders the ferule to be applied only to the left hand; the right hand shall always be spared. The child, moreover, is not to cry while he receives the ferule; if he does, he is to be punished and corrected anew.

297. THE ROD. — In the penal code of La Salle, the categories of faults worthy of punishment are sharply defined. The rod shall be employed for the following faults: 1. refusal to obey; 2. when the pupil has formed the habit of not giving heed to the lesson; 3. when he has made blots upon his paper instead of writing; 4. when he has had a fight with his comrades; 5. when he has neglected his prayers in church; 6. when he has been wanting in "modesty" at mass or during the catechism; 7. when he has been absent from school, from mass, or from the catechism.

Even supposing that the principle of the rod is admissible, we must still condemn the wrong use which La Salle makes of it, for faults manifestly out of proportion to such a chastisement.

I very well know that the author of the *Conduct* requires that corrections shall be rare; but could he be obeyed, when he put into the hands of his teachers scarcely any other means of discipline?

But to comprehend to what extent La Salle forgot what is due to the dignity of the child, and considered him as a machine, without any regard to the delicacy of his feelings, with no respect for his person, we must read to the end the strange prescriptions of this manual of the rod. The precautions that La Salle exacts make still more evident the impropriety of such punishments: —

" When the teacher would punish a scholar with the rod, he will make the ordinary sign to summon the attention of the school; next he will indicate by means of the *signal* the decree which the pupil has violated, and then show him the place where correction is ordinarily administered ; and he will at once go there, and will prepare to receive the punishment, standing in such a way as not to be seen indecently by any one. This practice of having the scholar prepare himself for receiving the correction, without any need on the part of the teacher of putting his hand upon him, shall be very exactly observed.

" While the scholar is preparing himself to receive the correction, the teacher shall be making an inward preparation to give it in a spirit of love, and in a clear view of God. Then he will go from his desk with dignity and gravity.

" And when he shall have reached the place where the scholar is " (it is stated, moreover, that this place should be in one of the most remote and most obscure parts of the school, where the nakedness of the victim cannot be seen), " he will speak a few words to him to prepare him to receive the correction with humility, submission, and a purpose of amendment ; then he will strike three blows as is usual ; to go beyond five blows, there would be needed a special order of the director.

" He shall be careful not to put his hand on the scholar. If the scholar is not ready, he shall return to his desk without saying a word ; and when he returns, he shall give him the most severe punishment allowed without special permission, that is, five blows.

" When a teacher shall have thus been obliged to compel a scholar to receive correction, he shall attempt in some way a little time afterwards to make him see and acknowledge his fault, and shall make him come to himself, and give him a strong and sincere resolution never to allow himself again to fall into such a revolt."

The moment is perhaps not well chosen to preach a sermon and to violate the rule which forbids the Brethren the use of the reprimand.

" After the scholar has been corrected, he will modestly kneel in the middle of the room before the teacher, with arms crossed, to thank him for having corrected him, and will then turn towards the crucifix to thank God for it, and to promise Him at the same time not again to commit the fault for which he had just been corrected. This he will do without speaking aloud; after which the teacher will give him the sign to go to his place."

Is it possible to have a higher misconception of human nature, to trifle more ingeniously with the pride of the child, and with his most legitimate feelings, and to mingle, in the most repulsive manner, indiscreet and infamous practices with the exhibition of religious sentiments?

" It is absurd," says Kant, " to require the children whom we punish to thank us, to kiss our hands, etc. This is to try to make servile creatures of them."

To justify La Salle, some quotations from his works have been invoked.

" For the love of God, do not use blows of the hand. Be very careful never to give children a blow."

But it is necessary to know the exact thought of the author of the *Conduct*, and this explains the following passage : —

" No corrections should be employed save those which are in use in the schools ; and so scholars should never be struck with the hand or the foot."

In other words, the teacher should never strike except with the authorized instruments, and according to the official regulations.

298. MUTUAL ESPIONAGE. — We may say without exaggeration that the *Conduct* recommends mutual espionage : —

" The inspector of schools shall be careful to appoint one of the most prudent scholars to observe those who make a noise while they assemble, and this scholar shall then report to the teacher what has occurred, without allowing the others to know of it."

299. REWARDS. — While La Salle devotes more than forty pages to corrections, the chapter on rewards comprises two small pages.

Rewards shall be given " from time to time." They shall be of three kinds : rewards for piety, for ability, and for diligence. They shall consist of books, pictures, plaster casts, crucifix and virgin, chaplets, engraved texts, etc.

300. CONCLUSION. — We have said enough to give an exact idea of the Institute of the Christian Brethren in its primitive form. Its faults were certainly grave, and we cannot approve the general spirit of those establishments for education where pupils are forbidden " to joke while they are at meals " ; to give anything whatsoever to one another ; where children are to enter the school-room so deliberately and quietly that the noise of their footsteps is not heard ; where teachers are forbidden " to be familiar " with the pupils, " to allow themselves to descend to anything common, as it would be to laugh . . ." But whatever the distance which separates those gloomy schools from our modern ideal, — from the pleasant, active, animated school, such as we conceive it to-day, — there is none the less obligation to do justice to La Salle, to pardon him for the practices which were those of his time, and to admire him for the good qualities that were peculiarly his own. The criticism that is

truly fruitful, is that which is especially directed to the good, without caviling at the had.[1]

[301. ANALYTICAL SUMMARY. — 1. This study exhibits the zeal of the Catholic Church in the education of the children of the poor. The motive was not the spirit of domination, as in the case of the Jesuits, but a sincere desire to engage in a humane work.

2. A proof of the multiplication of schools, and so of the diffusion of the new educational spirit, is the wretched quality of those who were allowed to teach. There must be schools even if they are poor ones.

3. The need of competent teachers led to the establishment of the *Teachers' Seminary*, the parent of the modern normal school. The two elements in this professional instruction seem to have been a knowledge of the subjects to be taught and of methods of organization and discipline.

4. The severe discipline and enforced silence of La Salle's schools permit the inference that the school of the period was the scene of lawlessness and disorder. The reaction went to an extreme; but considering the times, this excess was a virtue.

5. The scarcity of teachers and the abundance of pupils led to the expedient of mutual and simultaneous instruction. While this method is absolutely bad, it was relatively good.

6. To the benevolent and inventive spirit of La Salle is due the organization of industrial schools.]

---

[1] The influence of the teaching congregations in general, and of this one in particular, on public education as administered by the State, is very strikingly exhibited by Meunier in his *Lutte du Principe Clérical et du Principe Laique dans l'Enseignement* (Paris: 1861). There is also interesting information concerning La Salle. See particularly the introductory *Letter* and Chaps. I. and II. (P.)

CHAPTER XIII.

ROUSSEAU AND THE ÉMILE.

THE PEDAGOGY OF THE EIGHTEENTH CENTURY; THE PRECURSORS OF
ROUSSEAU; THE ABBÉ DE SAINT PIERRE; OTHER INSPIRERS OF
ROUSSEAU; PUBLICATION OF THE ÉMILE (1762); ROUSSEAU AS A
TEACHER; GENERAL PRINCIPLES OF THE ÉMILE; ITS ROMANTIC
AND UTOPIAN CHARACTER; DIVISION OF THE WORK; THE FIRST TWO
BOOKS; EDUCATION OF THE BODY AND OF THE SENSES; LET NATURE
ACT; THE MOTHER TO NURSE HER OWN CHILDREN; NEGATIVE EDU-
CATION; THE CHILD'S RIGHT TO HAPPINESS; THE THIRD BOOK OF
THE ÉMILE; CHOICE IN THE THINGS TO BE TAUGHT; THE ABBÉ
DE SAINT PIERRE AND ROUSSEAU; ÉMILE AT FIFTEEN; EDUCATION OF
THE SENSIBILITIES; THE FOURTH BOOK OF THE ÉMILE; GENESIS
OF THE AFFECTIONS; MORAL EDUCATION; RELIGIOUS EDUCATION;
THE PROFESSION OF FAITH OF THE SAVOYARD VICAR; SOPHIE
AND THE EDUCATION OF WOMEN; GENERAL CONCLUSION; INFLU-
ENCE OF ROUSSEAU; ANALYTICAL SUMMARY.

302. THE PEDAGOGY OF THE EIGHTEENTH CENTURY. —
The most striking of the general characteristics of French
pedagogy in the eighteenth century, is that in it the lay spirit
comes into mortal collision with the ecclesiastical spirit.
What a contrast between the clerical preceptors of the seventeenth century and the philosophical educators of the eighteenth! The Jesuits, all-powerful under Louis XIV., are
to be decried, condemned, and finally expelled in 1762.
The first place in the theory and in the practice of education
will belong to laymen. Rousseau is to write the *Émile*.
D'Alembert and Diderot will be the educational advisers of
the Empress of Russia. The parliamentarians, **La Chalotais**

and Rolland, will attempt to substitute for the action of the
Jesuits the action of the State, or, at least, one of the powers
of the State. Finally, with the Revolution, the lay spirit
will succeed in triumphing.

Again, the pedagogy of the eighteenth century is distinguished by its critical and reformatory tendencies. The
century of Louis XIV. is, in general, a century of content;
the century of Voltaire, a century of discontent.

Besides, the philosophical spirit, which associates the
theory of education with the laws of the human spirit, which
is not content to modify routine by a few ameliorations of
detail, which establishes general principles and aspires to an
ideal perfection, — the philosophical spirit, with its excel-
lencies and with its defects, — will come to the light in the
Émile, and in some other writings of the same period.

Finally, and this last characteristic is but the consequence
of the others, education tends to become national, and at the
same time humane. Preparation for life replaces preparation
for death. During the whole of the eighteenth century, a
conception is in process of elaboration which the men of the
Revolution will exhibit in its true light, — that of an education, public and national, which makes citizens, which works
for country and for real life.

303. PRECURSORS OF ROUSSEAU. — The greatest educational
event of the eighteenth century, before the expulsion of the
Jesuits and the events of the French Revolution, is the publication of the *Émile*. Rousseau is undeniably the first in
rank among the founders of French pedagogy, and his influence will be felt abroad, especially in Germany. But whatever may be the originality of the author of the *Émile*, his
system is not a stroke of genius for which no preparation
had been made. He had his precursors, and he profited by
their works. A Benedictine, who might have spent his

strength to better advantage, has written a book on the
Plagiarisms of J. J. Rousseau.[1]

We do not propose to treat Rousseau as a plagiarist, for he
surely has inspiration of his own, and his own boldness in
invention ; but however much of an innovator he may be, he
was inspired by Montaigne, by Locke, and without speaking
of those great masters whom he often imitated, he had his
immediate predecessors, whose ideas on certain points are in
conformity with his own.

304. THE ABBÉ DE SAINT PIERRE (1658–1743). — Among
the precursors of Rousseau, a place among the first must be
assigned to the Abbé de Saint Pierre, a dreamy, fantastic
spirit, fitted more to excite curiosity than to deserve admiration, whom Rousseau himself called "a man of great projects and petty views." His projects in fact were great,
at least in number. Between "a *project* to make sermons
more useful, and a *project* to make roads more passable,"
there came, in his incoherent and varied work, several projects for perfecting education in general, and the education
of girls in particular.

The dominant idea of the Abbé de Saint Pierre is his
anxiety in behalf of moral education. In proportion as we
advance towards the era of liberty, we shall notice a growing interest in the development of the moral virtues.

The Abbé de Saint Pierre requires of man four essential
qualities : justice, benevolence, the discernment of virtue or
judgment, and, lastly, instruction, which holds but the lowest
rank. Virtue is of more worth than the knowledge of Latin.

"It cannot be said that a great knowledge of Latin is not
an excellent attainment ; but in order to acquire this knowl-

---

1 Dom Joseph Cajet, *Les Plagiats de J. J. R. de Genève sur l'éducation,*
1768.

edge, it is necessary to give to it an amount of time that would be incomparably better employed in acquiring great skill in the observation of prudence. Those who direct education make a very great mistake in employing tenfold too much time in making us scholarly in the Latin tongue, and in employing tenfold too little of it in giving us a confirmed use of prudence."[1]

But what are the means proposed by the Abbé de Saint Pierre? All that he has devised for organizing the teaching of the social virtues is reduced to the requirement of reading \ edifying narratives, of playing moral pieces, and of accustoming young people to do meritorious acts in the daily intercourse of the school. When the lessons have been recited and the written exercises corrected, the teacher will say to the pupil: " Do for me an act of prudence, or of justice, or of benevolence." This is easier to say than to do. College life scarcely furnishes occasion for the application of the social virtues.

But the Abbé de Saint Pierre should be credited with his good intentions. He is the first in France to give his thought to this matter of professional instruction. The mechanic arts, the positive sciences, the apprenticeship to trades, — these things he places above the study of languages. Around his college, and even in his college, there are to be mills, printing offices, agricultural implements, garden tools, etc.

Was it not also an idea at once new and wise, to establish a *continuous department* of public instruction, a sort of permanent council, charged with the reformation of methods and with establishing, as far as possible, uniformity in all the colleges of the kingdom?

Finally, we shall commend the Abbé de Saint Pierre for having persistently urged the necessity of the education of

---

[1] *Œuvres diverses*, Tome I. p. 12.

women. From Fénelon to the Abbé de Saint Pierre, from
1680 to 1730, great progress was made in this question. We
seem already to hear Condorcet when we read the following
passage : —

"The purpose should be to instruct girls in the elements
of all the sciences and of all the arts which can enter into
ordinary conversation, and even in several things which relate to the different employments of men, such as the history
of their country, geography, police regulations, and the principal civil laws, *to the end that they can listen with pleasure to
what men shall say to them*, ask relevant questions, and easily
keep up a conversation with their husbands on the daily
occurrences in their occupations."

For the purpose of sooner attaining his end, the Abbé de
Saint Pierre, anticipating the centuries, demanded for women
national establishments, colleges of secondary instruction.
He did not hesitate to cloister young girls in boarding-schools,
and in boarding-schools without vacations ; and he entreated
the State to organize public courses for those who, he said,
" constitute one-half of the families in society."

305. OTHER INSPIRERS OF ROUSSEAU. — With the eighteenth century there begins for modern thought, in education
as in everything else, an era of international relations, of
mutual imitation, of the action and reaction of people on
people. The Frenchman of the seventeenth century had almost absolutely ignored Comenius. Rousseau knows Locke,
and also the Hollander Crousaz,[1] whom, by the way. he treats
rather shabbily, speaking of him as " the pedant Crousaz."

Crousaz, however, had some good ideas. He criticised
the old methods, which make " of the knowledge of Latin

---

[1] *De l'éducation des enfants*, la Haye, 1722; *Pensées libres sur les instructions publiques des bas collèges*, Amsterdam, 1727.

and Greek the principal part of education "; and he preached scientific instruction and moral education.

In the *Spectacle of Nature*, which was so popular in its day, the Abbé Pluche also demanded that the study of the dead languages should be abridged[1]: —

"Experience with the pitiable Latinity which reigns in the colleges of Germany, Flanders, Holland, and in all places where the habit of always speaking Latin is current, suffices to make us renounce this custom which prevents a young man from speaking his own tongue correctly."

The Abbé Pluche demanded that the time saved from Latin be devoted to the living languages. On the other hand, he insisted on early education, and on this point he was the complement to his master, Rollin, who, he said, wrote rather "for the *perfection* of studies than for their beginning."

Still other writers were able to suggest to Rousseau some of the ideas which he developed in the *Émile*. Before him, La Condamine declared that the *Fables* of La Fontaine are above the capacity of children.[2] Before him, Bonneval, much interested in physical education, violently criticised the use of long clothes, and claimed for children an education of the senses. He demanded, besides, that in early instruction, the effort of the teacher should be limited to the keeping of evil impressions from the childish imagination, and that instruction in the truths of religion should be held in abeyance.

We shall discover in the *Émile* all these ideas in outline revived and developed with the power and with the brilliancy of genius, sometimes transformed into boisterous paradoxes, but sometimes, also, transformed into solid and lasting truths.

---

[1] *Spectacle de la nature*, Paris, 1732, Vol. VI. *Entretien sur l'éducation.*
[2] *Lettre critique sur l'éducation*, Paris, 1751.

306. Publication of the Émile (1762).—Rousseau has made striking statements of nearly all the problems of education, and he has sometimes resolved them with wisdom, and always with originality.

Appearing in 1762, at the moment when the Parliament was excluding the Jesuits from France, the *Émile* came at the right moment in that grand overthrow of routine and tradition to disclose new hopes to humanity, and to announce the advent of philosophic reason in the art of educating men. But Rousseau, in writing his book, did not think of the Jesuits, of whom he scarcely speaks ; he wrote, not for the man of the present, but for the future of humanity ; he composed a book endowed with endless vitality, half. romance, half essay, the grandest monument of human thought on the subject of education.   The *Émile*, in fact, is not a work of ephemeral polemics, nor simply a practical manual of pedagogy, but is a general system of education, a treatise on psychology and moral training, a profound analysis of human nature.

307. Was Rousseau prepared to become a Teacher?—Before entering upon the study of the *Émile*, it is well to inquire how the author had been prepared by his character and by his mode of life to become a teacher.   The history of French literature offers nothing more extraordinary than the life of Jean Jacques Rousseau.   Everything is strange in the destiny of that unfortunate great man.   Rousseau committed great faults, especially in his youth ; but at other moments of his life he is almost a sage, a hero of private virtues and civic courage.   He traversed all adventures and all trades.   Workman, servant, charlatan, preceptor, all in turn ; he lodged in garrets at a son, and experienced days when he complained that bread was too dear.   Through all

these miseries and these humiliations a soul was in process of formation made up, above all else, of sensibility and imagination.

Rousseau's sensibility was extreme. The child who, unjustly treated, experienced one of those violent fits of passion which he has so well described in his *Confessions*, and who writhed a whole night in his bed, crying " *Carnifex*, *carnifex!* " was surely not an ordinary child. " I had no idea of things, but all varieties of feeling were already known to me. I had conceived nothing; I had felt everything." Even a mediocre representation of *Alzire* made him beside himself, and he refused witnessing the play of tragedies for fear of becoming ill.

The sentiment of nature early inspired him with a passion which was not to be quenched. His philosophic optimism and his faith in providence were never forgotten. Other pure and generous emotions filled his soul. The study of Plutarch had inspired him with a taste for republican virtues and with an enthusiasm for liberty. Falsehood caused him a veritable horror. He had the feeling of equity in a high degree. Later, to the hatred of injustice there was joined in his heart an implacable resentment against the oppressors of the people. He had doubtless received the first germ of this hate when, making the journey afoot from Paris to Lyons, he entered the cabin of a poor peasant, and there found, as in a picture, the affecting summary of the miseries of the people.

At the same time he was an insatiable reader. He nourished himself on the poets, historians, and philosophers of antiquity, and he studied the mathematics and astronomy. As some one has said, " That life of reading and toil, interrupted by so many romantic incidents and adventurous undertakings, had vivified his imagination as a regular course of study in the College of Plessis could not possibly have done."

It is in this way that his literary genius was formed, and, in due order, his genius for pedagogy. We need not seek in the life of Rousseau any direct preparation for the composition of the *Émile*. It is true that for a time he had been preceptor, in 1739, in the family of Mably, but he soon resigned duties in which he was not successful. A little essay which he composed in 1740 [1] does not yet give proof of any great originality. On the other hand, if he loved to observe children, he observed, alas, only the children of others. There is nothing sadder than that page of the *Confessions* in which he relates how he often placed himself at the window to observe the dismission of school, in order to listen to the conversations of children as a furtive and unseen observer !

The *Émile* is thus less the result of a patient induction and of a real experience than a work of inspiration or a brilliant improvisation of genius.

308. GENERAL PRINCIPLES OF THE ÉMILE. — A certain number of general principles run through the entire work, and give it a systematic form and a positive character.

The first of these is the idea of the innocence and of the perfect goodness of the child. The *Émile* opens with this solemn declaration : —

" Everything is good as it comes from the hands of the Author of nature ; everything degenerates in the hands of man." And in another place, " Let us assume as an incontestable maxim that the first movements of nature are always right ; there is no original perversity in the human heart."

Without doubt Rousseau was right in opposing the pessi-

---

[1] *Projet pour l'éducation de M. de Ste-Marie.*

mism of those who see in the child a being thoroughly wicked and degraded before birth ; he is deceived in turn when he affirms that there is no germ of evil in human nature.

Society is wicked and corrupt, he says, and it is from society that all the evil comes ; it is from its pernicious influence that the soul of the child must be preserved ! But, we reply, how did society itself happen to be spoiled and vitiated? It is nothing but a collection of men ; and if the individuals are innocent, how can the aggregate of individuals be wicked and perverse? But let the contradictions of Rousseau pass ; the important thing to note is that from his optimism are derived the essential characteristics of the education which he devises for Émile. This education will be at once natural and negative : —

"Émile," says Gréard, " is a child of nature, brought up by nature, according to the rules of nature, for the satisfaction of the needs of nature. This sophism is not merely inscribed at random on the frontispiece of the book, but is its very soul ; and it is by reason of this sophistry that, separated from the body of reflections and maxims that give it so powerful an interest, Rousseau's plan of education is but a dangerous chimera."

Everything that society has established, Rousseau condemns in a lump as fictitious and artificial. Conventional usages he despises ; and he places Émile at the school of nature, and brings him up almost like a savage.

On the other hand, the education of Émile is negative, at least till his twelfth year ; that is, Rousseau lets nature have her way till then. For those who think nature evil, education ought to be a work of compression and of repression. But nature is good ; and so education consists simply in letting her have free course. To guard the child from the shock of opinions, to form betimes a defence about his soul, to assure against every exterior influence the free development of his faculties — such is the end that he proposes to himself.

Another general principle of the *Émile*, another truth which Rousseau's spirit of paradox quickly transforms into error, is the idea of the distinction of ages : —

" Each age, each state of life, has its proper perfection, and a sort of maturity which is its own. We have often heard of a man grown ; but let us think of a child grown. That sight will be newer to us, and perhaps not less agreeable."

" We do not know infancy. With the false ideas we have, the further we go, the more we are astray. The most learned give their attention to that which it is important for men to know without considering what children are in a condition to comprehend. They always look for the man in the child, without thinking of what he was before he became a man."

" Everything is right so far, and from these observations there proceeds a progressive education, exactly conforming in its successive requirements to the progress of the faculties. But Rousseau does not stop in his course, and he goes beyond progressive education to recommend an education in fragments, so to speak, which isolates the faculties in order to develop them one after another, which establishes an absolute line of demarkation between the different ages, and which ends in distinguishing three stages of progress in the soul. Rousseau's error on this point is in forgetting that the education of the child ought to prepare for the education of the young man. Instead of considering the different ages as the several rings of one and the same chain, he separates them sharply from one another. He does not admit that marvellous unity of the human soul, which seems so strong in man only because God has, so to speak, woven its bands into the child and there fastened them." (Gréard).

309. ROMANTIC CHARACTER OF THE ÉMILE. — A final observation is necessary before entering into an analysis of the *Émile ;* it is that in this, as in his other works, Rousseau is not averse to affecting singularities, and with deliberation and effrontery to break with received opinions. Doubtless we should not go so far as to say with certain critics that the *Émile* is rather the feat of a wit than the serious expression of a grave and serious thought; but what it is impossible not to grant is that which Rousseau himself admits in his preface : " One will believe that he is reading, not so much a book on education as the reveries of a visionary." Émile, in fact, is an imaginary being whom Rousseau places in strange conditions. He does not give him parents, but has him brought up by a preceptor in the country, far from all society. Émile is a character in a romance rather than a real man.

310. DIVISION OF THE WORK. — Without doubt, there are in the *Émile* long passages and digressions that make the reading of it more agreeable and its analysis more difficult. But, notwithstanding all this, the author confines himself to a methodical plan, at least to a chronological order. The different ages of Émile serve as a principle for the division of the work. The first two books treat especially of the infant and of the earliest period of life up to the age of twelve. The only question here discussed is the education of the body and the exercise of the senses. The third book corresponds to the period of intellectual education, from the twelfth to the fifteenth year. In the fourth book, Rousseau studies moral education, from the fifteenth to the twentieth year.

Finally, the fifth book, in which the romantic spirit is still rampant, is devoted to the education of woman.

311. THE FIRST TWO BOOKS OF THE ÉMILE. — It would be useless to search-this first part of the *Émile* for precepts rela-

tive to the education of the mind and the heart. Rousseau
has purposely eliminated from the first twelve years of the
child's life everything which concerns instruction and moral
discipline. At the age of twelve, Émile will know how to
run, jump, and judge of distances; but he will be perfectly
ignorant. The idea would be that he has studied nothing at
all, and "that he has not learned to distinguish his right
hand from his left."

The exclusive characteristic of Émile's education, during
this first period, is, then, the preoccupation with physical
development and with the training of the senses.

Out of many errors, we shall see displayed some admirable
flashes of good sense, and grand truths inspired by the principle of nature.

312. LET NATURE HAVE HER WAY. — What does nature
demand? She demands that the child have liberty of movement, and that nothing interfere with the nascent activities
of his limbs. What do we do, on the contrary? We put
him in swaddling clothes; we imprison him. He is deformed
by his over-tight garments, — the first chains that are imposed
on a being who is destined to have so many others to bear!
On this subject, the bad humor of Rousseau does not tire.
He is prodigal in outbreaks of spirit, often witty, and sometimes ridiculous.

"It seems," he says, "as though we fear that the child
may appear to be alive." "Man is born, lives, and dies, in a
state of slavery; at his birth he is stitched into swaddling-
clothes; at his death he is nailed in his coffin; and as long
as he preserves the human form he is held captive by our
institutions."

We shall not dwell on these extravagances of language
which transforms a coffin and a child's long-clothes into *insti-*

tutions. The protests of Rousseau have contributed towards a reformation of usages ; but, even on this point, with his great principle that everything must be referred to nature, because whatever nature does she does well, the author of *Émile* is on the point of going astray. No more for the body than for the mind is nature sufficient in herself ; she must have help and watchful assistance. Strong supports are needed to prevent too active movements and dangerous strains of the body ; just as, later on, there will be needed a vigorous moral authority to moderate and curb the passions of the soul.

313. THE MOTHER TO NURSE HER OWN CHILDREN. — But there is another point where it has become trite to praise Rousseau, and where his teaching should be accepted without reserve. This is when he strongly protests against the use of hired nurses, and when he eloquently summons mothers to the duties of nursing their own children. Where there is no mother, there is no child, says Rousseau, and he adds, where there is no mother, there is no family ! "Would you recall each one to his first duties? Begin with the mothers. You will be astonished at the changes you will produce!" It would be to fall into platitudes to set forth, after Rousseau, and after so many others, the reasons which recommend nursing by the mother. We merely observe that Rousseau insists on this, especially on moral grounds. It is not merely the health of the child ; it is the virtue and the morality of the family ; it is the dignity of the home, that he wishes to defend and preserve. And, in fact, how many other duties are provided for and made easier by the performance of a primal duty.

314. HARDENING OF THE BODY. — So far, the lessons of nature have instructed Rousseau. He is still right when he

wishes Émile to grow hardy, to become inured to privations, to become accustomed at an early hour to pain, and to learn how to suffer; but from being a stoic, Rousseau soon becomes a cynic. Contempt for pain gives place to a contempt for proprieties. Émile shall be a barefoot, like Diogenes. Locke gives his pupil thin shoes ; Rousseau, surpassing him, completely abolishes shoes. He would also like to suppress all the inventions of civilization. Thus Émile, accustomed to walk in the dark, will do without candles. "I would rather have Émile with eyes at the ends of his fingers than in the shop of a candle-maker." All this tempts us to laugh ; but here are graver errors. Rousseau objects to vaccination, and proscribes medicine. Émile is forehanded. He is in duty bound to be well. A physician will be summoned only when he is in danger of death. Again, Rousseau forbids the washing of the new-born child in wine, because wine is a fermented liquor, and nature produces nothing that is fermented. And so there must be no playthings made by the hand of man. A twig of a tree or a poppy-head will suffice. Rousseau, as we see, by reason of his wish to make of his pupil a man of nature, brings him into singular likeness with the wild man, and assimilates him almost to the brute.

315. NEGATIVE EDUCATION. — It is evident that the first period of life is that in which the use of negative education is both the least dangerous and the most acceptable. Ordinarily, Émile's preceptor will be but the inactive witness, the passive spectator of the work done by nature. Had Rousseau gone to the full length of his system, he ought to have abolished the preceptor himself, in order to allow the child to make his way all alone. But if the preceptor is tolerated, it is not to act directly on Émile, it is not to per-

form the duties of a professor, in teaching him what it is important for a child to know ; but it is simply to put him in the way of the discoveries which he ought to make for himself in the wide domain of nature, and to arrange and to combine, artificially and laboriously, those complicated scenes which are intended to replace the lessons of ordinary education. Such, for example, is the scene of the juggler, where Émile is to acquire at the same time notions on physics and on ethics. Such, again, is the conversation with the gardener, Robert, who reveals to him the idea of property. The preceptor is no longer a teacher, but a mechanic. The true educator is nature, but nature prepared and skillfully adjusted to serve the ends that we propose to attain. Rousseau admits only the teaching of things : —

" Do not give your pupil any kind of verbal lesson ; he should receive none save from experience." " The most important, the most useful rule in all education, is not to gain time, but to lose it."

The preceptor will interfere at most only by a few timid and guarded words, to aid the child in interpreting the lessons of nature. " State questions within his comprehension, and leave him to resolve them for himself. Let him not know anything because you have told it to him, but because he has comprehended it for himself."

" For the body as for the mind, the child must be left to himself."

" Let him run, and frolic, and fall a hundred times a day. So much the better ; for he will learn from this the sooner to help himself up. The welfare of liberty atones for many bruises."

In his horror for what he calls " the teaching and pedantic mania," Rousseau goes so far as to proscribe an education in habits : —

" The only habit that a child should be allowed to form is to contract no habit."

316. The Child's Right to Happiness. — Rousseau did not tire of demanding that we should respect the infancy that is in the child, and take into account his tastes and his aptitudes. With what eloquence he claims for him the right of being happy !

"Love childhood. Encourage its sports, its pleasures, and its instinct for happiness. Who of you has not sometimes regretted that period when a laugh was always on the lips, and the soul always in peace? Why will you deny those little innocents the enjoyment of that brief period which is so soon to escape them, and of that precious good which they cannot abuse? Why will you fill with bitterness and sorrow those first years so quickly passing which will no more return to them than they can return to you? Fathers, do you know the moment when death awaits your children? Do not lay up for yourselves regrets by depriving them of the few moments that nature gives them. As soon as they can feel the pleasure of existence, try to have them enjoy it, and act in such a way that at whatever hour God summons them they may not die without having tasted the sweetness of living."

317. Proscription of Intellectual Exercises. — Rousseau rejects from the education of Émile all the intellectual exercises ordinarily employed. He proscribes history on the pretext that Émile cannot comprehend the relations of events. He takes as an example the disgust of a child who had been told the anecdote of Alexander and his physician : —

" I found that he had an unusual admiration for the courage, so much lauded, of Alexander. But do you know in what he saw that courage? Simply in the fact that he swallowed a drink that had a bad taste."

And from this Rousseau concludes that the child's intelligence is not sufficiently open to comprehend history, and that he ought not to learn it. The paradox is evident. Because Émile is sometimes exposed to the danger of falling into errors of judgment, must he be denied the opportunity of judging? Similarly, Rousseau does not permit the study of the languages. Up to the age of twelve, Émile shall know but one language, because, till then, incapable of judging and comprehending, he cannot make the comparison between other languages and his own. Later, from twelve to fifteen, Rousseau will find still other reasons for excluding the study of the ancient languages. And it is not only history and the languages; it is literature in general from which Émile is excluded by Rousseau. No book shall be put into his hands, not even the *Fables* of La Fontaine. It is well known with what resolution Rousseau criticises *The Crow and the Fox*.

318. EDUCATION OF THE SENSES. — The grand preoccupation of Rousseau is the exercise and development of the senses of his pupil. The whole theory of object lessons, and even all the exaggerations of what is now called the intuitive method, are contained in germ in the *Émile:* —

" The first faculties which are formed and perfected in us are the senses. These, then, are the first which should be cultivated; but these are the very ones that we forget or that we neglect the most."

Rousseau does not consider the senses as wholly formed by nature; but he makes a special search for the means of forming them and of perfecting them through education.

" To call into exercise the senses, is, so to speak, to learn to feel; for we can neither touch, nor see, nor hear, except as we have been taught."

Only, Rousseau is wrong in sacrificing everything to this

education of the senses. He sharply criticises this favorite maxim of Locke, " We must reason with children." Rousseau retards the education of the judgment and the reason, and declares that " he would as soon require that a child be five feet high as that he reason at the age of eight."

319. THE THIRD BOOK OF THE ÉMILE. — From the twelfth to the fifteenth year is the length of time that Rousseau has devoted to study and to intellectual development proper. It is necessary that the robust animal, " the roe-buck," as he calls Émile, after a negative and temporizing education of twelve years, become in three years an enlightened intelligence. As the period is short, Rousseau disposes of the time for instruction with a miser's hand. Moreover, Émile is very poorly prepared for the rapid studies which are to be imposed on him. Not having acquired in his earlier years the habit of thinking, having lived a purely physical existence, he will have great difficulty in bringing to life, within a few months, his intellectual faculties.

But without dwelling on the unfavorable conditions of Émile's intellectual education, let us see in what it will consist.

320. CHOICE IN THE THINGS TO BE TAUGHT. — The principle which guides Rousseau in the choice of Émile's studies is no other than the principle of utility : —

" There is a choice in the things which ought to be taught as well as in the time fit for learning them. Of the knowledges within our reach, some are false, others are useless, and still others serve to nourish the pride of him who has them. Only the small number of those which really contribute to our good are worthy the care of a wise man, and consequently of a child whom we wish to render such. It is not a question of knowing what is, but only what is useful."

321. ROUSSEAU AND THE ABBÉ DE SAINT PIERRE. — Among\
educators, some wish to teach everything, while others demand a choice, and would retain only what is necessary.
The Abbé de Saint Pierre follows the first tendency. He
would have the scholar learn everything at college ; a little
medicine towards the seventh or eighth year, and in the
other classes, arithmetic and blazonry, jurisprudence, German, Italian, dancing, declamation, politics, ethics, astronomy, anatomy, chemistry, without counting drawing and the
violin, and twenty other things besides.   Rousseau is wiser.
He is dismayed at such an accumulation, at such an obstrue-
tion of studies, and so yields too much to the opposite tendency, and restricts beyond measure the list of necessary
studies.

322. ÉMILE'S STUDIES. — These, in fact, are the studies to
which Émile is limited : first, the physical sciences, and, at
the head of the list, astronomy, then geography, geography
taught without maps and by means of travel : —

"You are looking for globes, spheres, maps.   What
machines ! Why all these representations? Why not begin
by showing him the object itself?"

Here, as in other places, Rousseau prefers what would be
best, but what is impossible, to that which is worth less, but
which alone is practicable.

But Rousseau does not wish that his pupil, like the pupil of
Rabelais, become an " abyss of knowledge."   ·

" When I see a man, enamored of knowledge, allow himself to yield to its charms. and run from one kind to another
without knowing where to stop, I think I see a child on the
sea-shore collecting shells, beginning by loading himself with
them ; then, tempted by those he still sees, throwing them
aside, picking them up, until, weighed down by their number,

and no longer knowing which to choose, he ends by rejecting everything, and returns empty-handed."

No account is made of grammar and the ancient languages in the plan of Émile's studies. Graver still, history is proscribed. This rejection of historical studies, moreover, is systematically done. Rousseau has placed Émile in the country, and has made him an orphan, the better to isolate him ; to teach him history would be to throw him back into society that he abominates.

323. No Books save Robinson Crusoe. — One of the consequences of an education that is natural and negative is the suppression of books. Always going to extremes, Rousseau is not content to criticise the abuse of books. He determines that up to his fifth year Émile shall not know what a book is : —

" I hate books," he exclaims ; " they teach us merely to speak of things that we do not know."

Besides the fact that this raving is rather ridiculous in the case of a man who is a writer by profession, it is evident that Rousseau is roving at random when he condemns the use of books in instruction.

One book, however, one single book, has found favor in his sight. *Robinson Crusoe* will constitute by itself for a long time the whole of Émile's library. We understand without difficulty Rousseau's kindly feeling for a work which, under the form of a romance, is, like the *Émile*, a treatise on natural education. Émile and Robinson strongly resemble each other, since they are self-sufficient and dispense with society.

324. Excellent Precepts on Method. — At least in the general method which he commends, Rousseau makes amends for the errors in his plan of study : —

" Do not treat the child to discourses which he cannot understand. No descriptions, no eloquence, no figures of speech. Be content to present to him appropriate objects. Let us transform our sensations into ideas. But let us not jump at once from sensible objects to intellectual objects. Let us always proceed slowly from one sensible notion to another. In general, let us never substitute the sign for the thing, except when it is impossible for us to show the thing."

" I have no love whatever for explanations and talk. Things! things! I shall never tire of saying that we ascribe too much importance to words. With our babbling education we make only babblers."

But the whole would bear quoting. Almost all of Rousseau's recommendations, in the way of method, contain an element of truth, and need only to be modified in order to become excellent.

325. EXCLUSIVE MOTIVES OF ACTION. — A great question in the education of children is to know to what motive we shall address ourselves. Here again, Rousseau is exclusive and absolute. Up to the age of twelve, Émile will have been guided by necessity ; he will have been made dependent on things, not on men. It is through the possible and the impossible that he will have been conducted, by treating him. not as a sensible and intelligent being, but as a force of nature against which other forces are made to act. Not till the age of twelve must this system be changed. Émile has now acquired some judgment ; and it is upon an intellectual motive that one ought now to count in regulating his conduct. This motive is utility. The feeling of emulation cannot be employed in a solitary education. Finally, at the age of fifteen, it will be possible to appeal to the heart, to

feeling, and to recommend to the young man the acts we set before him, no longer as necessary or useful, but as noble, good, and generous. The error of Rousseau is in cutting up the life of man to his twentieth year into three sharply defined parts, into three moments, each subordinated to a single governing principle. The truth is that at every age an appeal must be made to all the motives that act on our will, that at every age, necessity, interest, sentiment, and finally, the idea of duty, an idea too often overlooked by Rousseau, as all else that is derived from reason, — all these motives can effectively intervene, in different degrees, in the education of man.

326. Émile learns a Trade. — At the age of fifteen, Émile will know nothing of history, nothing of humanity, nothing of art and literature, nothing of God; but he will know a trade, a manual trade. By this means, he will be sheltered from need in advance, in case a revolution should strip him of his fortune.

"We are approaching," says Rousseau, with an astonishing perspicacity, "a century of revolutions. Who can give you assurance of what will then become of you? I hold it to be impossible for the great monarchies of Europe to last much longer. They have all had their day of glory, and every State that dazzles is in its decline."

We have previously noticed, in studying analogous ideas in the case of Locke, for what other reasons Rousseau made of Émile an apprentice to a cabinet-maker or a carpenter.

327. Émile at the Age of Fifteen. — Rousseau takes comfort in the contemplation of his work, and he pauses from time to time in his analyses and deductions, to trace the portrait of his pupil. This is how he represents him at the age of fifteen : —

"Émile has but little knowledge, but that which he has is really his own; he knows nothing by halves. In the small number of things that he knows, and knows well, the most important is that there are many things which he does not know, but which he can some day learn; that there are many more things which other men know, but which he will never know; and that there is an infinity of other things which no man will ever know. He has a universal mind, not through actual knowledge, but through the ability to acquire it. He has a mind that is open, intelligent, prepared for everything, and, as Montaigne says, if not instructed, at least capable of being instructed. It is sufficient for me that he knows how to find the *of what good is it?* with reference to all that he does, and the *why?* of all that he believes. Once more, my object is not at all to give him knowledge, but to teach him how to acquire it as he may need it, to make him estimate it at its exact worth, and to make him love truth above everything else. With this method, progress is slow; but there are no false steps, and no danger of being obliged to retrace one's course."

All this is well; but it is necessary to add that even Émile has faults, great faults. To mention but one of them, but one which dominates all the others, he sees things only from the point of view of utility, and he would not hesitate, for example, " to give the Academy of Sciences for the smallest bit of pastry."

328. EDUCATION OF THE SENSIBILITIES. — It is true that Rousseau finally decides to make of Émile an affectionate and reasonable being. " We have formed," he says, " his body, his senses, his judgment; it remains to give him a heart." Rousseau, who proceeds like a magician, by wave of wand and clever tricks, flatters himself that within a day's

' time Émile is going to become the most affectionate, the most moral, and the most religious of men.

329. THE FOURTH BOOK OF THE ÉMILE. — The development of the affectionate sentiments, the culture of the moral sentiment, and that of the religious sentiment, such is the triple subject of the fourth book, — vast and exalted questions that lend themselves to eloquence in such a way that the fourth book of the *Émile* is perhaps the most brilliant of the whole work.

330. GENESIS OF THE AFFECTIONATE SENTIMENTS. — Here Rousseau is wholly in the land of chimeras. Émile, who lives in isolation, who has neither family, friends, nor companions, is necessarily condemned to selfishness, and everything Rousseau can do to warm his heart will be useless. Do we wish to develop the feelings of tenderness and affection? Let us begin by placing the child under family or social influences which alone can furnish his affections the occasion for development. For fifteen years Rousseau leaves the heart of Émile unoccupied. What an illusion to think he will be able to fill it all at once! When we suppress the mother in the education of a child, all the means that we can invent to excite in his soul emotions of gentleness and affection are but palliatives. Rousseau made the mistake of thinking that a child can be taught to love as he is taught to read and write, and that lessons could be given to Émile in feeling just as lessons are given to him in geometry.

331. MORAL EDUCATION. — Rousseau is more worthy of being followed when he demands that the moral notions of right and wrong have their first source in the feelings of sympathy and social benevolence, on the supposition that according to his system he can inspire Émile with such feelings.

" We enter, finally, the domain of morals," he says. " If this were the place for it, I would show how from the first emotions of the heart arise the first utterances of the con-science, and how, from the first feelings of love and hate arise the first notions of good and evil. I would make it appear that *justice* and *goodness* are not merely abstract terms, conceived by the understanding, but real affections of the soul enlightened by the reason."

Yes ; let the child be made to make his way gradually towards a severe morality, sanctioned by the reason, in having him pass through the gentle emotions of the heart. Nothing can be better. But this is to be done on one condi-tion : this is, that we shall not stop on the way, and that the vague inspirations of the sensibilities shall be succeeded by the exact prescriptions of the reason. Now Rousseau, as we know, was never willing to admit that virtue was anything else than an affair of the heart. His ethics is wholly an ethics of sentiment.

332. RELIGIOUS EDUCATION. — We know the reasons which determined Rousseau to delay till the sixteenth or eighteenth year the revelation of religion. It is that the child, with his sensitive imagination, is necessarily an idolater. If we speak to him of God, he can form but a superstitious idea of him. " Now," says Rousseau, pithily, " when the imagina-tion has once seen God, it is very rare that the understanding conceives him." In other terms, once plunged in supersti-tion, the mind of the child can never extricate itself from it. We must then wait, in the interest of religion itself, till the child have sufficient maturity of reason and sufficient power of thought to seize in its truth, divested of every veil of sense, the idea of God, whose existence is announced to him for the first time.

It is difficult to justify Rousseau. First, is it not to be feared that the child, if he has reached his eighteenth year in ignorance of God, may find it wholly natural to be ignorant of him still, and that he reason and dispute at random with his teacher, and that he doubt instead of believe? And if he allows himself to be convinced, is it not at least evident that the religious idea, tardily inculcated, will have no profound hold on his mind? On the other hand, will the child, with his instinctive curiosity, wait till his eighteenth year to inquire the cause of the universe? Will he not form the notion of a God in his own way?

" One might have read, a few years ago," says Villemain, " the account, or rather the psychological confession, of a writer (Sentenis), a German philosopher, whom his father had submitted to the experiment advised by the author of *Émile*. Left alone by the loss of a tenderly loved wife, this father, a learned and thoughtful man, had taken his infant son to a retired place in the country ; and not allowing him communication with any one, he had cultivated the child's intelligence through the sight of the natural objects placed near him, and by the study of the languages, almost without books, and in carefully concealing from him all idea of God. The child had reached his tenth year without having either read or heard that great name. But then his mind found what had been denied it. The sun which he saw rise each morning seemed the all-powerful benefactor of whom he felt the need. He soon formed the habit of going at dawn to the garden to pay homage to that god that he had made for himself. His father surprised him one day, and showed him his error by teaching him that all the fixed stars are so many suns distributed in space. But such was then the disappointment and the grief of the child deprived of his worship,

ROUSSEAU AND THE ÉMILE.   305

that the father, overcome, acknowledged to him that there
was a God, the Creator of the heavens and the earth." [1]

333. THE SAVOYARD VICAR'S PROFESSION OF FAITH. —
Rousseau has at least attempted to retrieve, by stately language and an impassioned demonstration of the existence of
God, the delay which he has spontaneously imposed on his
pupil.

The *Savoyard Vicar's Profession of Faith* is an eloquent
catechism on natural religion, and the honest expression of a
sincere and profound deism. The religion of nature is evidently the only one which, in Rousseau's system, can be
taught, and ought to be taught, to the child, since the child is
exactly the pupil of nature. If Émile wishes to go beyond
this, if he needs a positive religion, this shall be for himself
to choose.

334. SOPHIE AND THE EDUCATION OF WOMEN.—The weak-
est part of the *Émile* is that which treats of the education of
woman. This is not merely because Rousseau, with his
decided leaning towards the romantic, leads Émile and his
companion into odd and extraordinary adventures, but it is
especially because he misconceives the proper dignity of
woman. Sophie, the perfect woman, has been educated only
to complete the happiness of Émile. Her education is wholly
relative to her destiny as a wife.

"The whole education of women should be relative to men ;
to please them, to be useful to them, to make themselves
honored and loved by them, to educate the young, to care for
the older, to advise them, to console them, to make life agreeable and sweet to them, — these are the duties of women in
every age."

---

[1] Report of Villemain on the Work of the Père Girard (1844).

" Sophie," says Gréard, " has but virtues of the second order, virtues of conjugal education." It has been said that marriage is a second birth for man, that he rises or falls according to the choice which he makes. For woman, according to the theory of Rousseau, it is the true advent into life. According to the expressive formula of Michelet, who, in a sentence, has given a marvellous summary of the doctrine, but in attaching to it a sense which poetizes it, " the husband creates the wife." Sophie, up to the day of her marriage, did not exist. She had learned nothing and read nothing " except a Barême and a Télémaque which have chanced to fall into her hands." She has been definitely admonished, " that were men sensible, every lettered girl will remain a girl." It is Émile alone who is to instruct her, and he will instruct her and mould her into his own ideal, and in conformity to his individual interest.

While it was only in his youth that he received the first principles of the religious feeling, Sophie must be penetrated with it from infancy, in order that she may early form the habit of submission. He commands and she obeys, the first duty of the wife being meekness. If, during her youth, she has freely attended banquets, amusements, balls, the theatre, it is not so much to be initiated into the vain pleasures of the world, under the tutelage of a vigilant mother, as to belong, once married, more fully to her home and to her husband. She is nothing except as she is by his side, or as dependent on him, or as acting through him. Strange and brutal paradox, which Rousseau, it is true, corrects and repairs in detail, at every moment by the most happy and charming inconsistencies."

Sophie, briefly, is an incomplete person whom Rousseau is not careful enough to educate for herself.

In her subordinate and inferior position, the cares of the

household occupy the largest place. She cuts and makes her own dresses : —

" What Sophie knows best, and what was taught her with most care, is the work of her sex. There is no needle-work which she does not know how to make."

It is not forbidden her, but is even recommended that she introduce a certain coquetry into her employments : —

" The work she loves the best is lace-making, because there is no other that gives her a more agreeable attitude, and in which the fingers are used with more grace and deftness."

She carries daintiness a little too far : —

" She does not love cooking ; its details have some disgust for her. She would sooner let the whole dinner go into the fire than to soil her cuffs."

Truly this is fine housewifery ! We feel that we have here to do with a character in a romance who has no need to dine. Sophie would not have been well received at Saint Cyr, where Madame de Maintenon so severely scolded the girls who were too fastidious, " fearing smoke, dust, and disagreeable odors, even to making complaints and grimaces on their account as though all were lost."

335. GENERAL CONCLUSION. — In order to form a just estimate of the *Émile*, it is necessary to put aside the impressions left by the reading of the last pages. We must consider as a whole, and without taking details into account, that work, which, notwithstanding all, is very admirable and profound. It is injured by analysis. To esteem the *Émile* at its real worth, it must be read entire. In reading it, in fact, we are warmed by contact with the passion which Rousseau puts into whatever he writes. We pardon his errors and chimeras by reason of the grand sentiments and the grand truths which we meet at every step. We must also take into account the

time when Rousseau lived, and the conditions under which he
wrote. We have not a doubt that had it been written thirty
years later, in the dawn of the Revolution, for a people who
were free, or who desired to be free, the *Émile* would have
been wholly different from what it is. Had he been working
for a republican society, or for a society that wished to become
such, Rousseau would not have thrown himself, out of
hatred for the reality, into the absurdities of an over-spe-
cialized and exceptional education. We can judge of what
he would have done as legislator of public instruction in the
time of the Revolution, by what he wrote in his *Considerations
on the Government of Poland : —*

" National education belongs only to people who are
free. . . . It is education which is to give to men the national
mould, and so to direct their opinions and their tastes that
they will become patriots by inclination, by passion, and by
necessity " (we would only add, by duty). " A child, in
opening his eyes, ought to see his country and nothing but
his country. Every true republican, along with his mother's
milk, will imbibe love of country, that is, of law and liberty.
This love constitutes his whole existence. He sees but his
country, he lives but for her. So soon as he is alone, he is
nothing ; so soon as there is no more of country, he is no
more. . . . While learning to read, I would have a child of
Poland read what relates to his country ; at the age of ten, I
would have him know all its productions ; at twelve, all its
provinces, all its roads, all its cities ; at fifteen, the whole of
its history ; and at sixteen, all its laws ; and there should not
be in all Poland a notable deed or an illustrious man, of which
his memory and his heart were not full."

336. INFLUENCE OF THE ÉMILE. — That which proves
better than any commentary can the high standing of the
Émile, is the success which it has obtained, the influence

which it has exerted, both in France and abroad, and the durable renown attested by so many works designed, either to contradict it, to correct it, or to approve it and to disseminate its doctrines. During the twenty-five years that followed the publication of the *Émile*, there appeared in the French language twice as many books on education as during the first sixty years of the century. Rousseau, besides all that he said personally which was just and new, had the merit of stimulating minds and of preparing through his impulsion the rich educational harvest of this last one hundred years.

To be convinced of this, it suffices to read this judgment of Kant : —

" The first impression which a reader who does not read for vanity or for killing time derives from the writings of Rousseau, is that this writer unites to an admirable penetration of genius a noble inspiration and a soul full of sensibility, such as has never been met with in any other writer, in any other time, or in any other country. The impression which immediately follows this, is that of astonishment caused by the extraordinary and paradoxical thoughts which he develops. . . . I ought to read and re-read Rousseau, till the beauty of his style no more affects me. It is only then that I can adjust my reason to judge of him."

[337. ANALYTICAL SUMMARY. — 1. The study of the *Émile* exhibits, in a very striking manner, the contrast between the respective agencies of art and nature in the work of education, and also the power of sentiment as a motor to ideas.

2. What Monsieur Compayré has happily called Rousseau's " misuse of the principle of nature" marks a recoil against the artificial and fictitious state of society and opinion in France in the eighteenth century. In politics, in religion, and in philosophy, there was the domination of authority, and

but a small margin was left for the exercise of freedom, versatility, and individual initiative; while education was administered rather as a process of manufacture, than of regulated growth.

3. The conception that the child, by his very constitution, is predetermined, like plants and animals, to a progressive development quite independent of artificial aid, easily degenerates into the hypothesis that the typical education is a process of spontaneous growth.

4. The error in this hypothesis is that of exaggeration or of disproportion. Education is neither a work of nature alone, nor of art alone, but is a natural process, supplemented, controlled, and perfected by human art. What education would become when abandoned wholly to "nature" may be seen in the state of a perfected fruit which has been allowed to revert to its primitive or natural condition.

5. Man is distinguished from all other creatures by the fact that he is not the victim of his environment, but is endowed with the power to control his environment, almost to re-create it, and so to rise superior to it. This ability gives rise to human art, which is a coördinate factor with nature in the work of education.

6. This convenient fiction of "Nature," conceived as an infallible and incomparable guide in education, has introduced countless errors into educational theory; and Miss E. R. Sill is amply justified in saying that "probably nine-tenths of the popular sophistries on the subject of education, would be cleared away by clarifying the word Nature."[1]

7. In spite of its paradoxes, its exaggerations, its overwrought sentiment, and florid declamation, the *Émile*, in its general spirit, is a work of incomparable power and of perennial value.]

---

[1] *Atlantic Monthly*, February, 1883, p. 178.

CHAPTER XIV.

THE PHILOSOPHERS OF THE EIGHTEENTH CENTURY.— CONDILLAC, DIDEROT, HELVETIUS, AND KANT.

THE PHILOSOPHERS OF THE EIGHTEENTH CENTURY; CONDILLAC (1715–1780); ABUSE OF THE PHILOSOPHIC SPIRIT; MUST WE REASON WITH CHILDREN? PRELIMINARY LESSONS; THE ART OF THINK-ING; OTHER PARTS OF THE COURSE OF STUDY; PERSONAL REFLECTION; EXCESSES OF DEVOTION CRITICISED; DIDEROT (1713–1784); HIS PEDAGOGICAL WORKS; HIS QUALITIES AS AN EDUCA-TOR; NECESSITY OF INSTRUCTION; IDEA OF A SYSTEM OF PUBLIC INSTRUCTION; CRITICISM OF FRENCH COLLEGES; PROPOSED RE-FORMS; PREFERENCE FOR THE SCIENCES; INCOMPLETE VIEWS ON THE PROVINCE OF LETTERS; OPINION OF MARMONTEL; OTHER NOVELTIES OF DIDEROT'S PLAN; HELVETIUS (1715–1771); PARADOXES OF THE TREATISE ON MAN; REFUTATION OF HELVETIUS BY DIDEROT; INSTRUCTION SECULARIZED; THE ENCYCLOPÆDISTS; KANT (1724–1804); HIGH CONCEPTION OF EDUCATION; PSYCHOLOGICAL OP-TIMISM; RESPECT FOR THE LIBERTY OF THE CHILD; CULTURE OF THE FACULTIES; STORIES INTERDICTED; DIFFERENT KINDS OF PUNISHMENT; RELIGIOUS EDUCATION; ANALYTICAL SUMMARY.

---

338. THE PHILOSOPHERS OF THE EIGHTEENTH CENTURY.— If there has been considerable progress made in education in the eighteenth century, it is due, in great part, to the efforts of the philosophers of that age. It is no longer alone the men who are actually engaged in the schools that are pre-occupied with education; but nearly all the illustrious thinkers of the eighteenth century have discussed these great questions with more or less thoroughness. The subject is far from being exhausted by the study of Rousseau. Besides the educational current set in movement by the *Émile*, the other philosophers of that period, in their isolated and inde-

pendent march, left original routes which it remains to follow. From out their errors and conceptions of systems there
emerge some new outlooks and some definite truths.

339. CONDILLAC (1715-1780). — An acute and ingenious
psychologist, a competitor and rival of Locke in philosophy,
Condillac is far from having the same authority in matters
pertaining to education ; but still there is profit to be derived
from the reading of his *Course of Study*, which includes not
less than thirteen volumes. This important work is a collection of the lessons which he had composed for the education
of the infant Ferdinand, the grandson of Louis XV., and
heir of the dukedom of Parma, whose preceptor he became
in 1757.

340. ABUSE OF THE PHILOSOPHIC SPIRIT. — It is certainly
a matter of congratulation that the philosophical spirit is
entering more and more largely into the theories of education, and there would be only words of commendation for
Condillac had he restricted himself to this excellent declaration, that pedagogy is nothing if it is not a deduction from
psychology. But he does not stop there, but with an indiscretion that is to be regretted, he arbitrarily transports into
education certain philosophical principles which it is not
proper to apply to the art of educating men, whatever may
be their theoretical truth ; thus Condillac, having established
the natural order of the development of the sciences and the
arts in the history of humanity, presumes to impose the same
law of progress upon the child.

" The method which I have followed does not resemble the
usual manner of teaching ; but it is the very way in which
men were led to create the arts and the sciences." [1]

---

[1] *Discours préliminaire sur la grammaire*, in the *Œuvres complètes* of
Condillac, Tome VI. p. 264.

In other terms, the child must do over again, on his own account, "that which the race has done." He must be compelled to follow, step by step, in its long gropings, the slow progress made by the race.[1]

There is, doubtless, an element of truth in the error of Condillac. The sciences and the arts began with the observation of particulars, and thence slowly rose to general principles ; and to-day no one thinks of denying the necessity of proceeding in the same manner in education, so far as this is possible. It is well at the first to present facts to the child, and to lead him step by step, from observation to observation, to the law which governs them and includes them ; but there is a wide distance between the discreet use of the inductive and experimental method, and the exaggerations of Condillac. No one should seriously think of absolutely suppressing the synthetic method of exposition, which, taking advantage of the work accomplished through the centuries, teaches at the outset the truths that have been already acquired. It would be absurd to compel the child painfully to recommence the toil of the race.[2]

---

[1] This is also the main principle in Mr. Spencer's educational philosophy. "The education of the child must accord both in mode and arrangement with the education of mankind as considered historically ; or, in other words, the genesis of knowledge in the individual must follow the same course as the genesis of knowledge in the race." — *Education*, p. 122. (P.)

[2] The general law of human progress is *inheritance supplemented by individual acquisition*. Using the symbols i (inheritance) and a (acquisition), the progress of the race from its origin upwards, through successive generations, may be exhibited by this series: i ; $i + a$; $i (2 a) + a$; $i (3 a) + a$; $i (4 a) + a$. If the factor of inheritance could be eliminated, as Condillac and Spencer recommend, the series would take this form: a' ; a'' ; a''' ; a^{iv} ; a^{v} : the successive increments in acquisition being due to successive increments in power gained through heredity. But, happily, the law of inheritance cannot be abrogated, and so philosophers write books in order to save succeeding generations from the fate of Sisyphus. (P.)

THE HISTORY OF PEDAGOGY.

Graver still, Condillac, led astray by his love for philosophizing, presumes to initiate the child, from the very beginning of his studies, into psychological analysis.

" The first thing to be done is to make the child acquainted
with the faculties of his soul, and to make him feel the need
of making use of them."

In other terms, the analysis of the soul shall be the first
object proposed to the reflection of the child. It is not
proposed to make him attentive, but to teach him what
attention is.

How can one seriously think of making of the child a little
psychologist, and of choosing as the first element of his education the very science that is the most difficult of all, the
one which can be but the coronation of his studies?

341. MUST WE REASON WITH CHILDREN?—Rousseau had
sharply criticised the famous maxim of Locke: "We must
reason with children." Condillac tries to restore it to credit,
and for this purpose he invokes the pretended demonstra-
tions of a superficial and inexact psychology.

" It has been proved," he says, "that the faculty of
reasoning begins as soon as the senses commence to develop ; and we have the early use of our senses only because
we early began to reason." Strange assertions, which are
disproved by the most elementary observation of the facts in
the case. Condillac here allows himself to be imposed upon
by his sensational psychology, the tendency of which is to
efface the peculiar character of the different intellectual
faculties, to derive them all from the senses, and, consequently, to suppress the distance which separates a simple
sensation from the subtile, reflective, and abstract process
which is called reasoning. It cannot be admitted for a
single instant that the faculties of the understanding are, as
he says, "the same in the child as in the mature man."

There is, doubtless, in the child a beginning of reasoning, a sort of instinctive logic ; but this infantile reasoning can be applied only to familiar objects, such as are sensible and concrete. It were absurd to employ it on general and abstract ideas.

342. PRELIMINARY LESSONS.—We shall quote, without comment, the first subjects of instruction which, under the title of *Leçons préliminaires*, Condillac proposes to his pupil: 1. the nature of ideas ; 2. the operations of the soul ; 3. the habits ; 4. the difference between the soul and the body ; 5. the knowledge of God.

How are we to conceive that Condillac had the pretension to place these high philosophical speculations within the reach of a child of seven years who has not yet studied the grammar of his native language ! How much better some fables or historical narratives would answer his purpose !

But Condillac does not stop there. When his pupil has a systematic knowledge of the operations of the soul, when he has comprehended the genesis of ideas ; in a word, when, towards the age of eight or ten, he is as proficient in philosophy as his master, and almost as capable of writing the *Treatise on Sensations*, what do you think he is invited to study ? Something which very much resembles the philosophy of history : —

" After having made him reflect on his own infancy, I thought that the infancy of the world would be the most interesting subject for him, and the easiest to study."

343. THE ART OF THINKING. — It is only when he judges that the mind of his pupil is sufficiently prepared by psychological analysis and by general reflections on the progress of humanity, that Condillac decides to have him enter upon the ordinary course of study. Here the spirit of system dis-

appears, and gives place to more judicious and more practical ideas. Thus Condillac thinks that "the study of grammar would be more wearisome than useful if it come too early." Would that he had applied this principle to psychology! Before studying grammar, then, Condillac's pupil reads the poets, — the French poets, of course, — and preferably the dramatic authors, Racine especially, whom he reads for the twelfth time. The real knowledge of the language precedes the abstract study of the rules. Condillac himself composed a grammar entitled the *Art of Speaking*. In this he imitates the authors of Port Royal, "who," he says, "were the first to write elementary books on an intelligent plan." After the *Art of Speaking* he calls the attention of his pupil to three other treatises in succession, — the *Art of Writing*, or rhetoric, the *Art of Reasoning*, or logic, and the *Art of Thinking*. We shall not attempt an analysis of these works, which have gone out of date, notwithstanding the value of certain portions of them. The general characteristic of these treatises on intellectual education is that the author is pre-occupied with the relations of ideas more than with the exterior elegancies of style, with the development of thought more than with the beauties of language : —

"Especially must the intelligence be nourished, even as the body is nourished. We must present to it knowledge, which is the wholesome aliment of spirit, opinions and errors being aliment that is poisonous. It is also necessary that the intelligence be active, for the thought remains imbecile as long as, passive rather than active, it moves at random."

344. OTHER PARTS OF THE COURSE OF STUDY. — It seems that Condillac is in pursuit of but one single purpose, — to make of his pupil a thinking being. The study of Latin is postponed till the time when the intelligence, being completely formed, will find in the study of that language

only the difficulty of learning words. Condillac has but little taste for the study of the ancient languages. He relegates the study of Latin to the second place, and omits Greek entirely. But he accords a great importance to historical studies.

"After having learned to think, the Prince made the study of history his principal object for six years."

Twelve volumes of the *Course of Study* have transmitted to us Condillac's lessons in history. In this he does not take delight, as Rollin does, in long narrations ; but he analyzes, multiplies his reflections, and abridges facts ; he philosophizes more than he recites the facts of history.

345. PERSONAL REFLECTION. — What we have said of Condillac's *Course of Study* suffices to justify the judgment expressed of his pedagogy by one of his disciples, Gérando, when he wrote : " He who had so thoroughly studied the manner in which ideas are formed in the human mind, had but little skill in calling them into being in the intelligence of his pupil."

But we would judge our author unjustly if, after the criticisms we have made of him, we were not to accord him the praise he deserves, especially for having comprehended, as he has done, the value of personal reflection, and the superiority of judgment over memory. A few quotations will rehabilitate the pedagogy of Condillac in the minds of our readers.

Above all else there must be an exercise in personal reflection : —

" I grant that the education which cultivates only the memory may make prodigies, and that it has done so ; but these prodigies last only during the time of infancy. . . . He who knows only by heart, knows nothing. . . . He who has not learned to reflect has not been instructed, or, what is still worse, has been poorly instructed."

" True knowledge is in the reflection, which has acquired it, much more than in the memory, which holds it in keeping; and the things which we are capable of recovering are better known than those of which we have a recollection. It does not suffice, then, to give a child knowledge. It is necessary that he instruct himself by seeking knowledge on his own account, and the essential point is to guide him properly. If he is led in an orderly way, he will acquire exact ideas, and will seize their succession and relation. Then, able to call them up for review, he will be able to compare them with others that are more remote, and to make a final choice of those which he wishes to study. Reflection can always recover the things it has known, because it knows how it originally found them; but the memory does not so recover the things it has learned, because it does not know how it learns."

This is why Condillac places far above the education we receive, the education that we give ourselves : —

"Henceforth, Sir, it remains for you alone to instruct yourself. Perhaps you imagine you have finished; but it is I who have finished. You are to begin anew l "

346. EXCESSIVE DEVOTION CRITICISED. — What beautiful lessons Condillac also addresses to his pupil to induce him to enfranchise himself from ecclesiastical tutelage ! Written by an abbot, the eloquent page we are about to read proves how the lay spirit tended to pronounce itself in the eighteenth century.

"You cannot be too pious, Sir; but if your piety is not enlightened, you will so far forget your duties as to be engrossed in the little things of devotion. Because prayer is necessary, you will think you ought always to be praying, not considering that true devotion consists first of all in fulfilling the duties of your station in life : it will not be your fault that you do not live in your heart as in a cloister. Hypocrites will swarm around you, the monks will issue from their cells. The priests will abandon the service of the altar in order to be edified with the sight of your holy works. Blind prince! you will not perceive how their conduct is in contradiction with their language. You will not even observe that the men who praise you for always being at the foot of the altar, themselves forget that it is their own duty to be there. You will unconsciously take their place and leave to them your own. You will be continually at prayer, and you will believe that you assure your salvation. They will cease to pray, and you will believe that they assure their salvation. Strange contradiction, which turns aside ministers from the Church to give bad ministers to the State." [1]

347. DIDEROT (1713–1784). — To him who knows nothing of Diderot save his works of imagination, often so liceutious, it will doubtless be a surprise to see the name of this fantastic writer inscribed in the catalogue of educators. But this astonishment will disappear if we will take the trouble to recollect with what versatility this mighty spirit could vary the subject of his reflections, and pass from the gay to the solemn, and especially with what ardor, in conjunction with D'Alembert, he was the principal founder of the *Encyclopédie*, and the indefatigable contributor to it.

348. HIS PEDAGOGICAL WORKS. — But there is no room for doubt. Diderot has written at least two treatises that belong to the history of education: first, about 1773, *The Systematic Refutation of the Book of Helvetius on Man*, an incisive and eloquent criticism of the paradoxes and errors of Helvetius; and, in the second place, about 1776, a com-

---

[1] *Cours d'études*, Tome X. Introduction.

plete scheme of education, composed at the request of Catherine II., under the title, *Plan of a University*.[1]

349. HIS MERITS AS AN EDUCATOR. — Doubtless Diderot
did not have sufficient gravity of character or sufficiently
definite ideas to be a perfect educator ; but, by way of compensation, the natural and acquired qualities of his mind
made him worthy of the confidence placed in him by Catherine II. in entrusting him with the organization, at least in
theory, of the instruction of the Russian people.   First of
all, he had the merit of being a universal thinker, "sufficiently versed in all the sciences to know their value, and
not sufficiently profound in any one to give it a preference
inspired by predilection."   Engaged in the scientific movement, of which the *Encyclopédie* was the centre, he at the
same time cherished an enthusiastic passion for letters.   He
worshipped Shakespeare and modern poetry, but he was not
less enamored of classical antiquity, and for several years,
he says, "he thought it as much a religious duty to read a
song of Homer as a good priest would to recite his breviary."

350. NECESSITY OF INSTRUCTION. — Diderot, and this is
to his praise, is distinguished from the most of his contemporaries, and especially from Rousseau, by his ardent faith
in the moral efficacy of instruction : —

"Far from corrupting," he exclaims, "instruction sweet-
ens character, throws light on duty, makes vice less gross,
and either chokes it or conceals it. . . . I dare assert that
purity of morals has followed the progress of dress, from the
skin of animals to fabrics of silk."

Hence he decides on the necessity of instruction for all : —

"From the prime minister to the lowest peasant, it is good
for every one to know how to read, write, and count."

<hr>

[1] See *Œuvres complètes* of Diderot. Edited by Tourneux, 1876-77.
Tomes II. and III.

And he proposes to all people the example of Germany, with her strongly organized system of primary instruction. He demands schools open to all children, " schools of reading, writing, arithmetic, and religion," in which will be studied both a moral and a political catechism. Attendance on these schools shall be obligatory, and to make compulsion possible, Diderot demands gratuity. He goes even farther, and would have the child fed at school, and with his books would have him find bread.

351. THE CONCEPTION OF PUBLIC INSTRUCTION. — Like all who sincerely desire a strong organization of instruction, Diderot assigns the direction of it to the State. His ideal of a Russian university bears a strong resemblance to the French University of 1808. He would have at its head a politician, a statesman, to whom should be submitted all the affairs of public instruction. He even went so far as to entrust to this general master of the university the duty of presiding over the examinations, of appointing the presidents of colleges, of excluding bad pupils, and of deposing professors and tutors.

352. CRITICISM OF FRENCH COLLEGES. — Secondary instruction, what was then called the *Faculty of Arts*, is the principal object of Diderot's reflections. He criticises the traditional system with extreme severity, and his charge, thought sometimes unjust, deserves to be quoted : —

" It is in the Faculty of Arts that there are still taught to-day, under the name of belles-lettres, two dead languages which are of use only to a small number of citizens ; it is there that they are studied for six or seven years without being learned ; under the name of rhetoric, the art of speaking is taught before the art of thinking, and that of speaking elegantly before having ideas ; under the name of logic, the head is filled with the subtilties of Aristotle, and of his very

sublime and very useless theory of the syllogism, and there
is spread over a hundred obscure pages what might have been
clearly stated in four; under the name of ethics, I do not
know what is said, but I know that there is not a word said
either of the qualities of mind or heart; under the name of
metaphysics, there are discussed theses as trifling as they are
knotty, the first elements of scepticism and bigotry, and the
germ of the unfortunate gift of replying to everything; under
the name of physics, there is endless dispute about the elements of matter and the system of the world; but not a word
on natural history, not a word on real chemistry, very little
on the movement and fall of bodies; very few experiments,
less still of anatomy, and nothing of geography." [1]

353. Proposed Reforms. — After such a spirited criticism,
it was Diderot's duty to propose earnest and radical reforms;
but all of those which he suggests are not equally com-
mendable.

Let us first note the idea revived in our day by Auguste
Comte and the school of positivists, of a connection and a
subordination of the sciences, classified in a certain order,
according as they presuppose the science which has preceded,
or as they facilitate the study of the science which follows,
and also according to the measure of their utility.[2] It is
according to this last principle in particular, that Diderot
distributes the work of the school, after having called attention to the fact that the order of the sciences, as determined
by the needs of the school, is not their logical order: —

" The natural connection of one science with the others
designates for it a place, and the principle of utility, more
or less general, determines for it another place."

---

[1] *Œuvres*, Tome III. p. 459.
[2] For Comte's classification of the sciences, see Spencer's *Illustrations
of Universal Progress*, Chap. III. (P.)

But Diderot forgets that we must take into account, not alone the principle of utility in the distribution of studies, but that the essential thing of all others is to adapt the order of studies to the progress of the child in age and aptitudes.

354. PREFERENCES FOR THE SCIENCES. — Although equally enamored of letters and the sciences, Diderot did not know how to hold a just balance between a literary and a scientific education. Anticipating Condorcet and Auguste Comte, he displaces the centre of instruction, and gives a preponderance to the sciences. Of the eight classes comprised in his Faculty of Arts, the first five are devoted to the mathematics, to mechanics, to astronomy, to physics, and to chemistry. Grammar and the ancient languages are relegated to the last three years, which nearly correspond to what are called in our colleges the " second " and " rhetoric." [1]

The charge that must be brought against Diderot in this place, is not merely that he puts an unreasonable restriction on literary studies, but also that he makes a bad distribution of scientific studies in placing the mathematics before physics. It is useless for him to assert that " it is easier to learn geometry than to learn to read." He does not convince us of this. It is a grave error to begin by keeping the child's attention on numerical abstractions, by leaving his senses unemployed, by postponing so long the study of natural history and experimental physics, those sciences expressly adapted to children, because, as Diderot himself expresses it, " they involve a continuous exercise of sight, smell, taste, and memory."

To excuse Diderot's error, it does not suffice to state that his pupil does not enter the Faculty of Arts till his twelfth year. Till that period, he will learn only reading, writing, /

---

[1] See note, p. 131.

and orthography. There is ground for thinking that these first years will be rather poorly employed; but besides this, it is evident that even at the age of twelve the mind is not sufficiently mature to be plunged into the cold deductions of mathematics.

355. INCOMPLETE VIEWS AS TO THE SCOPE OF LITERARY STUDIES. — Diderot's attitude with respect to classical studies is a matter of surprise. On the one hand, he postpones their study till the pupil's nineteenth and twentieth year. On the other, with what enthusiasm this eloquent scholar speaks of the ancients, particularly of Homer!

" Homer is the master to whom I am indebted for whatever merit I have, if indeed I have any at all. It is difficult to attain to excellence in taste without a knowledge of the Greek and Latin languages. I early drew my intellectual nourishment from Homer, Virgil, Horace, Terence, Anacreon, Plato, and Euripides on the one hand, and from Moses and the Prophets on the other."

How are we to explain this contradiction of an inconsistent and ungrateful humanist who extols the humanities to the skies, and at the same time puts such restrictions on the teaching of them as almost to annihilate them? The reason for this is, that, in his opinion, the belles-lettres are useful only for the training of orators and poets, but are not serviceable in the general development of the mind. Consequently, being fancy studies, so to speak, they are fit only for a small minority of pupils, and have no right to the first place in a common education, destined for men in general. Diderot is not able to discern what, in pedagogy, is their true title to nobility, — that they are an admirable instrument of intellectual gymnastics, and the surest and also the most convenient means of acquiring those qualities of justness, of precision, and of clearness, which are needed by all conditions of men, and are applicable to all the special employments of life.[1]

356. OPINION OF MARMONTEL. — Diderot seems to reduce the office of letters to a study of words, and to an exercise of memory. He might have learned a lesson from one of his contemporaries, Marmontel, whose intellect, though less brilliant, was sometimes more just, an advantage which the intelligence gains from early discipline in the study of the languages : —

"The choice and use of words, in translating from one language to another, and even then some degree of elegance in the construction of sentences, began to interest me ; and this work, which did not proceed without the analysis of ideas, fortified my memory. I perceived that it was the idea attached to the word which made it take root, and reflection soon made me feel that the study of the languages was also the study of the art of distinguishing shades of thought, of decomposing it, of forming its texture, and of catching with precision its spirit and its relations ; and that along with words, an equal number of new ideas were introduced and developed in the

[1] This thought will bear extension as in the following quotation : "The reasoning that I oppose starts from the low and false assumption that instruction serves only for the practical use that is made of it; for example, that he who, by his social position, does not make use of his intellectual culture, has no need of that culture. Literature, from this point of view, is useful only to the man of letters, science only to the scientist, good manners and fine bearing only to men of the world. The poor man should be ignorant, for education and knowledge are useless to him. Blasphemy, Gentlemen! The culture of the mind and the culture of the soul are duties for every man. They are not simple ornaments; they are things as sacred as religion" (Renan, *Famille et État*, p. 3). This is a sufficient answer to Mr. Spencer's assumption (*Education*, p. 84), that the studies that are best for guidance are at the same time the best for discipline. See also Dugald Stewart (*Elements*, p. 12). (P.)

heads of the young,[1] and that in this way the early classes were a course in elementary philosophy, much more rich, more extended, and of greater real utility than we think, when we complain that in our colleges nothing is learned but Latin."[2]

357. OTHER NOVELTIES IN DIDEROT'S PLAN. — Without entering into the details of the very elaborate organization of Diderot's *Russian University*, we shall call attention to some other novelties of his system : —

1. The division of the classes into several series of parallel courses : first, the series of scientific and literary courses ; then, the series of lectures devoted to religion, to ethics, and to history ; and finally, courses in drawing, music, etc.

2. The whimsical idea of teaching history in an inverted order, so to speak, in beginning with the most recent events, and little by little going back to antiquity.

3. His extreme estimate of the art of reading : " Let a teacher of reading be associated with a professor of drawing ;

---

[1] This thought throws light on a dictum of current pedagogy, " First, the idea, then the term." It shows that very often, in actual experience, the sequence is from term to idea. The relation between term and idea is the same in kind as that between sentence and thought. Must we then say, " First the thought, then the sentence "? Or, " First the thought, then the chapter or the book "?

The disciplinary value of translation is also well stated. It may be doubted whether the schools furnish a better "intellectual gymnastic." Three high intellectual attainments are involved in a real translation: 1. The separation of the thought from the original form of words; 2. The seizing or comprehension of the thought as a mental possession; and 3. The embodying of the thought in a new form. A strictly analogous process, of almost equal value in its place, is that variety of reading in which the pupil is required to express the thought of the paragraph *in his own language*. This exercise involves the three processes above stated, and may be called " the translation of thought from one form into another, in the same language." (P.)

[2] Marmontel, *Mémoires d'un père pour servir à l'instruction de ses enfants*, Tome I. p. 19.

there are so few men, even the most enlightened, who know
how to read well, a gift always so agreeable, and often so
necessary."

4. A special regard for the study of art and for æsthetic
education, which could not be a matter of indifference to the
great art critic who wrote the *Salons*.

5. A reform in the system of ushers.[1] Diderot would
have for supervising assistants in colleges, educated men,
capable on occasion of supplying the places of the professors themselves. To attach them to their duties, he requires
that some dignity be given to their modest and useful functions, and that the usher be a sort of supernumerary, or
" professor in reversion," who aspires to the chair of the professor, whose place he supplies from time to time, and which
he may finally attain.

358. HELVETIUS (1715–1771). — In undertaking the study
of the thoughts of Helvetius on education, and the rapid
analysis of his *Treatise on Man*, we shall not take leave of
Diderot, for the work of Helvetius has had the good or the
bad fortune of being commented on and criticised by his
illustrious contemporary. Thanks to the *Systematic Refutation of the Book of Helvetius on Man*, which forms a charming
accompaniment of pungent or vigorous reflections to a dull
and languid book, the reading of the monotonous treatise of
Helvetius becomes easy and almost agreeable.

359. THE TREATISE ON MAN. — Under this title, a little
long, *De l'homme, de ses facultés intellectuelles et de son éducation*, Helvetius has composed a large work which he had in
contemplation for fifteen years, and which did not appear
till after his death, in 1772. As a matter of fact, education
does not directly occupy the author's attention except in the

---

[1] *Maître d'étude :* "He who in a lycée, college, or boarding-school, has
oversight of pupils during study hours and recreations." — LITTRÉ.

first and the last chapters (sections I. and X.). With this exception, the whole book is devoted to long developments of the favorite maxims of his philosophy : as the intellectual equality of all men, and the reduction of all the passions to the pursuit of pleasure ; or to platitudes, such as the influence of laws on the happiness of people, and the evils which result from ignorance.

360. POTENCY OF EDUCATION. — When he does not fall into platitudes, Helvetius goes off into paradoxes that are presumptuous and systematic. His habitual characteristic is pedantry in what is false. According to him, for example, education is all-powerful ; it is the sole cause of the difference between minds. The mind of the child is but an empty capacity, something indeterminate, without predisposition. The impressions of the senses are the only elements of the intelligence ; so that the acquisitions of the five senses are the only thing that is of moment; " the senses are all that there is of man." It is not possible to push sensationalism further than this.

The impressions of the senses are, then, the basis of human nature, and as these impressions vary with circumstances, Helvetius arrives at this conclusion, that chance is the great master in the formation of mind and character. Consequently, he undertakes to produce at will men of genius, or, at least, men of talent. For this purpose, it suffices to ascertain, by repeated observations, the means which chance employs for making great men. These means once discovered, it remains only to set them at work artificially and to combine them, in order to produce the same effects.   •

" Genius is a product of chance. Rousseau, like a countless number of illustrious men, may be regarded as one of the masterpieces of chance."

361. HELVETIUS REFUTED BY DIDEROT. — It is easy to
reply to extravagant statements of this sort. Had Helvetius consulted teachers and parents, had he observed himself,
had he simply reflected on his two daughters, so unequally
endowed though identically educated, he would doubtless
have felt constrained to acknowledge the limitations of
education ; he would have comprehended that it cannot give
imagination to minds of sluggish temperament, nor enthusiasm and sensibility to inert souls, and that the most marvel-
lonsly helpful circumstances will not make of a Helvetius a
Montesquieu or a Voltaire.

But if it is easy to refute Helvetius, it is impossible to
criticise him with more brilliancy and eloquence than Diderot
has done. With what perfection of reason he restores to
nature, to innate and irresistible inclinations, the influence
which Helvetius denies to them in the formation of character !

" The accidents of Helvetius," he says, " are like the
spark which sets on fire a cask of wine, and which is extin-
guished in a bucket of water."

" For thousands of centuries the dew of heaven has fallen
on the rocks without making them fertile. The sown fields
await it in order to become productive, but it is not the dew
that scatters the seed. Accidents themselves no more produce anything, than the pick of the laborer who delves
in the mines of Golconda produces the diamond that it
brings to the surface."

Doubtless education has a more radical effect than that
which is attributed to it by La Bruyère when he said that
" it touches only the surface of the soul." But if it can do
much, it cannot do all. It perfects if it is good ; it deadens
and it perverts if it is bad ; but it can never be a substitute
for lacking aptitude, and can never replace nature.

362. SECULARIZED INSTRUCTION. — In other parts of his system Helvetius is in accord with Diderot. Like him, he believes the necessary condition of progress in education is that it be made secular and entrusted to the civil power. The vices of education come from the opposition of the two powers, spiritual and temporal, that assume to direct it. Between the Church and the State there is an opposition of interests and views. The State would have the nation become brave, industrious, and enlightened. The Church demands a blind submission and unlimited credulity. Hence there is contradiction in pedagogical precepts, diversity in the means that are employed, and, consequently, an education that is hesitating, that is pulled in opposite directions, that does not know definitely where it is going, that misses its way, that gropes and wastes time.

But the conclusion of Helvetius is not as we might expect, — the separation of Church and State in the matter of instruction and education, such as recent laws have established in France. No; Helvetius would have the State absorb the Church, and have religious power and civil power lodged in the same hands and both belong to those who control the government, — a vexatious confusion that would end in the oppression of consciences.

Helvetius, whatever may be thought of him, does not deserve to claim our attention for any length of time, and we cannot seriously consider as an authority in pedagogy a writer who, in intellectual as in moral education, reduces everything to a single principle, the development and the satisfaction of physical sensibility.[1]

---

[1] It is a matter of surprise that in a German *Pedagogical Library* the very first French work published is the *Traité de l'Homme* of Helvetius. This is giving the place of honor to what is perhaps of the most ordinary value in French pedagogical literature.

363. THE ENCYCLOPÆDISTS. — The vast collection which, under the name *Encyclopédie*, sums up the science and the philosophy of the eighteenth century, touches educational questions only in passing. Properly speaking, the *Encyclopédie* contains no system of pedagogy. The principal fragment is the article *Éducation*, written by the grammarian and Latinist Dumarsais.

But this piece of work is little worthy of its author, and little worthy in particular of the *Encyclopédie*. It contains scarcely anything but vague and trite generalities, and belongs to the category of those articles for padding which caused Voltaire to say : "You accept articles worthy of the Journal of Trévoux." We shall notice, however, in this article, the importance accorded to the study of physics, and to the practice of the arts, even the most common, and the marked purpose to " subordinate " knowledges and studies, or to distribute them in a logical, or rather psychological, order ; for example, to cause the concrete always to precede the abstract. But, after having lost himself in considerations of but little interest on the development of ideas and sentiments in the human soul, the author, who is decidedly far below his task, concludes by recommending to young people " the reading of newspapers."

The other pedagogical articles of the *Encyclopédie* are equally deficient in striking novelties. If the great work of D'Alembert and Diderot has contributed something to the progress of education, it is less through the insufficient efforts which it has directly attempted in this direction, than through the general influence which it has exercised on the French mind in extolling the sciences in their theoretical study as well as in their practical applications, in diffusing technical knowledge, in glorifying the industrial arts, and in thus preparing for the coming of a scientific and positive education in place of an education exclusively literary and of pure form.

364. Kant (1724–1804). — We know the considerable influence which, for a century, Kant has exercised on the development of philosophy. Since Descartes, no thinker had to the same degree excited an interest in the great problems of philosophy, nor more vigorously obliged the human reason to render an account of itself. It is then a piece of good fortune for the science of education that a philosopher of this order has taken up the discussion of pedagogical questions, and has thrown upon them the light of his penetrating criticism. The admiration which he felt for Rousseau, his attentive and impassioned reading of the *Émile*, his own reflections on the monastic education which he had received at the Collegium Fredericianum, a sort of small seminary conducted by the Pietists, the experience which he had had as a preceptor in several families that entrusted him with their children, and finally, above all else, his profound studies on human nature and his exalted moral philosophy, had given him a capital preparation for treating educational questions. Professor at the University of Königsberg, he several times resumes the discussion of pedagogical subjects with a marked predilection for them, and the notes of his lectures, collected by one of his colleagues, formed the little *Treatise on Pedagogy* which we are about to analyze.[1]

365. High Conception of Education. — In the opinion of Kant, the art of educating men, with that of governing them, is the most difficult and the most important of all. It is by education alone that humanity can be perfected and regenerated : —

[1] See the French translation of this tract at the end of the Volume, published by Monsieur Barni, under the title, *Éléments métaphysiques de la doctrine de la vertu.* Paris, 1855. The work of Kant appeared in German in 1803.

"'It is pleasant to think that human nature will always be better and better developed by education, and that at last there will thus be given it the form which best befits it. "To know how far the omnipotence of education can go, it would be necessary that a being of a superior order should undertake the bringing up of men." But in order that it may attain this exalted end, education must be set free from routine and traditional methods. It must bring up children, not in view of their success in the present state of human society, but➔ in view of a better state, possible in the future, and according to an ideal conception of humanity and of its complete destination." *Kant.*

366. PSYCHOLOGICAL OPTIMISM. — Kant comes near accepting the opinion of Rousseau on the original innocence of man and the perfect goodness of his natural inclinations : —

" It is said in medicine that the physician is but the servant of nature. This is true of the moralist. Ward off the bad influences from without, and nature can be trusted to find for herself the best way."[1]

Thus Kant does not tire of exalting the service which Rousseau had rendered pedagogy, in recalling educators to the confidence and respect that are due to calumniated human nature. Let us add, however, that the German philosopher is not content to repeat Rousseau. He corrects him in affirming that man, at his birth, is neither good nor evil, because he is not naturally a moral being. He does not become such till he raises his reason to the conception of duty and law. In other terms, in the infant everything is in germ. The infant is a being in preparation. The future alone, the development which he will receive from his education, will make him good or bad. At the beginning, he has but inde-

---

[1] Extract from Kant's *Fragments posthumes.*

terminate dispositions, and evil will come, not from a definite
inclination of nature, but solely from the fact that we will
not have known how to direct it, — from the fact, according
to Kant's own expression, that we will not have " subjected
nature to rules."

367. RESPECT FOR THE LIBERTY OF THE CHILD. — The
psychological optimism of Kant inspires him, as it does
Rousseau, with the idea of a negative education, respectful
of the liberty of the child : —

" In general, it must be noted that the earliest education
should be negative ; that is to say, nothing should be added
to the precautions taken by nature, and that the effort should
be limited to the preservation of her work. . . . It is well to
employ at first but few helps, and to leave children to learn
for themselves. Much of the weakness of man is due, not
to the fact that nothing is taught him, but to the fact that
false impressions are communicated to him."

Without going so far as to say with Rousseau that all
dependence with respect to men is contrary to order, Kant
took great care to respect the liberty of the pupil. He complains of parents who are always talking about " breaking
the wills of their sons." He maintains, not without reason,
that it is not necessary to offer much resistance to children,
if we have not begun by yielding too readily to their caprices,
and by always responding to their cries. Nothing is more
harmful to them than a discipline which is provoking and
degrading. But, in his zeal for human liberty, the theorist
of the autonomy of wills goes a little too far. He fears, for
example, the tyranny of habits. He requires that they be
prevented from being formed, and that children be accustomed to nothing. He might as well demand the suppression
of all education, since education should be but the acquisition
of a body of good habits.

368. STORIES INTERDICTED. — In the education of the intellectual faculties or talents, which he calls the *physical culture* of the soul, as distinguished from *moral culture*, which is the education of the will, Kant also approaches Rousseau. He proscribes romances and stories. " Children have an extremely active imagination which has no need of being developed by stories." It may be said in reply, that fables and fictions, at the same time that they develop the imagination, also direct it and adorn it with their own proper grace, and may even lend it moral support. Rousseau, notwithstanding the ardor of his criticisms on the *Fables* of La Fontaine, himself admitted the moral value of the apologue.

369. CULTURE OF THE FACULTIES. — That which distinguishes Kant as an educator is that he is pre-occupied with the culture of the faculties much more than with the acquisition of knowledge. He passes in review the different intellectual forces, and his reflections on each of them might be collected as the elements of an excellent system of educational psychology. He will criticise, for example, the abuse of memory : —

" Men who have nothing but memory," he says, " are but living lexicons, and, as it were, the pack-horses of Parnassus."

For the culture of the understanding, Kant proposes " at first to train it passively to some degree," by requiring of the child examples which illustrate a rule, or, on the contrary, the rule which applies to particular examples.

For the exercise of the reason, he recommends the Socratic method, and, in general, for the development of all the faculties of the mind, he thinks that the best way of proceeding is to cause the pupil to be active : —

" The best way to comprehend is to do. What we learn the most thoroughly is what we learn to some extent by ourselves."

370. DIFFERENT KINDS OF PUNISHMENTS. — Kant has made a subtile analysis of the different qualities with which punishment may be invested. He distinguishes from *physical punishment*, *moral punishment*, which is the better. It consists in humiliating the pupil, in greeting him coolly, "in encouraging the disposition of the child to be honored and loved, that auxiliary of morality." Physical punishments ought to be employed with precaution, "to the end that they may not entail servile dispositions."

Another distinction is that of *natural* punishments and *artificial* punishments. The first are preferable to the second, because they are the very consequences of the faults which have been committed; "indigestion, for example, which a child brings on himself when he eats too much." Another advantage of natural punishment, Kant justly remarks, "is that man submits to it all his life."[1]

Finally, Kant divides punishments into *negative* and *positive*. The first are to be used for minor faults, and the others are to be reserved for the punishment of conduct that is absolutely bad.

Moreover, whatever punishment may be applied, Kant advises the teacher to avoid the appearance of feeling malice towards the pupil : —

"The punishments we inflict while exhibiting signs of anger have a wrong tendency."

371. RELIGIOUS EDUCATION. — At first view, we might be tempted to think that Kant has adopted the conclusions of Rousseau, and that, like him, he refuses to take an early

---

[1] Monsieur Compayré seems to give his sanction to the "Discipline of Consequences." I think that Mr. Fitch has correctly stated its limitations (*Lectures.* p. 117). Kant doubtless borrowed the idea from Rousseau, who employs it in the government of his imaginary pupil. (See Miss Worthington's translation of the *Émile*, p. 66.) This doctrine is the basis of Mr. Spencer's chapter on *Moral Education.* (P.)

occasion to inculcate in the child's mind the notion of a Supreme Being : —

" Religious ideas always suppose some system of theology. Now, how are we to teach theology to the young, who, far from knowing the world, do not yet know themselves? How shall the young who do not yet know what duty is, be in a condition to comprehend an immediate duty towards God?"

To speak of religion to a young man, it would then be logical to wait till he is in a condition to form a clear and fixed conception of the nature of God. But it is impossible to do this, says Kant, because the young man lives in a society where he hears the name of the Divinity spoken at each moment, and where he takes part in continual observances of piety. It is better, then, to teach him at an early hour true religious notions, for fear that he may borrow from other men notions that are superstitious and false. In reality, Kant dissents from Rousseau only because, re-establishing the conditions of real life, he restores Émile to society, no longer keeping him in a fancied state of isolation. What a broad and noble way, moreover, of conceiving religious education! The best way of making clear to the mind of children the idea of God, is, according to Kant, to seek an analogy in the idea of a human father. It is necessary, moreover, that the conception of duty precede the conception of God ; that morality precede, and that theology follow. Without morality, religion is but superstition ; without morality, the pretended religious man is but a courtier, a suitor for divine favor.

372. MORAL CATECHISM. — Those who know to what a height Kant could raise the theory of morality, will not be surprised at the importance which he ascribes to the teaching of morals.

" Our schools," he says, " are almost entirely lacking in

one thing which, however, would be very useful for training
children in probity, — I mean a catechism on duty. It should
contain, in a popular form, cases concerning the conduct to
be observed in ordinary life, and which would always naturally
raise this question : Is this right or not?"

He had begun to write a book of this kind under the title
Moral Catechism;[1] and he would have desired that an hour
a day of school time be given to its study, "in order to
teach pupils to know and to learn by heart their duty to men,
— that power of God on the earth." The child, he says
again, would there learn to substitute the fear of his own
conscience for that of men and divine punishment, inward
dignity for the opinion of others, the intrinsic value of
actions for the apparent value of words, and, finally, a serene
and cheerful piety for a sad and gloomy devotion.

[373. ANALYTICAL SUMMARY. — 1. This study exhibits the
influence of philosophical systems on education. New conceptions of human destiny, new theories with respect to the
composition of human nature, or a new hypothesis concerning
man's place in nature, determine corresponding changes in
educational theory.

2. Perhaps the broadest generalization yet reached in
educational theory is the assumption made by Condillac,
that the education of each individual should be a repetition
of civilization *in petto*. With Mr. Spencer this hypothesis
becomes a law.

3. In theory, the secularization of education has begun.
The Church is to lose one of its historical prerogatives, and
the modern State is to become an educator.

---

[1] Helvetius, but poorly qualified for teaching moral questions, had had
the idea of a *Catéchisme de probité*. Saint Lambert published, in 1798, a
Catéchisme universel.

4. Helvetius typifies what may be called the *plastic theory* in education, or the conception that the teacher, if wise enough, may ignore all differences in natural endowment. This makes man the victim of his environment. The truth evidently is that man is the only creature which can bend circumstances to his will; and he has such an endowment of power in this direction that he can virtually recreate his environment and thus rise superior to it. And farther than this, there are innate differences in endowment that will persist in spite of all that education can do.

5. The culture value of literary studies is justly exhibited in the quotation from Marmontel, and in particular the disciplinary value of translation.

6. Education for training, discipline, or culture, as distinguished from an education whose chief aim is to impart knowledge, receives definite recognition from Kant.]

CHAPTER XV.

THE ORIGIN OF LAY AND NATIONAL INSTRUCTION. — LA CHALOTAIS AND ROLLAND.

JESUITS AND PARLIAMENTARIANS; EXPULSION OF THE JESUITS (1764); GENERAL COMPLAINTS AGAINST THE EDUCATION OF THE JESUITS; EFFORTS MADE TO REPLACE THEM; LA CHALOTAIS (1701-1785); HIS ESSAY ON NATIONAL EDUCATION (1763); SECULARIZATION OF EDUCATION; PRACTICAL END OF INSTRUCTION; NEW SPIRIT IN EDUCATION; INTUITIVE AND NATURAL INSTRUCTION; STUDIES OF THE EARLIEST PERIOD; CRITICISM OF NEGATIVE EDUCATION; HISTORY AVENGED OF THE DISDAIN OF ROUSSEAU; GEOGRAPHY; NATURAL HISTORY; PHYSICAL RECREATIONS; MATHEMATICAL RECREATIONS; STUDIES OF THE SECOND PERIOD; THE LIVING LANGUAGES; OTHER STUDIES; THE QUESTION OF BOOKS; ARISTO-CRATIC PREJUDICES; INSTRUCTION WITHIN THE REACH OF ALL; NORMAL SCHOOLS; SPIRIT OF CENTRALIZATION; TURGOT (1727-1781); ANALYTICAL SUMMARY.

374. JESUITS AND PARLIAMENTARIANS. — Of the educators of the eighteenth century of whom we have been speaking up to the present time, no one has been called to exercise an immediate and direct action on the destinies of public education; no one of them had the power to apply the doctrines which were so dear to him to college education; so that, so far, we have studied the theory and not the practice of education in the eighteenth century.

On the contrary, the members of the French Parliaments, after having solicited and obtained from the king the expulsion of the Jesuits, made memorable efforts, from 1762 up to the eve of the Revolution, to supply the places of the teachers whom they had driven away, to correct the faults of the ancient education, and to give effect to the idea, cherished by the most of the great spirits of that time, of a national education adapted to the needs of civil society. They were the practical organizers of instruction ; they prepared the foundation of the French University of the nineteenth century; they resumed, not without lustre, the struggle too often interrupted, which the Jansenists had sustained against the Jesuits.

375. EXPULSION OF THE JESUITS (1764). — The causes of the expulsion of the Jesuits were doubtless complex, and, above all else, political. In attacking the Company of Jesus, the Parliaments desired especially to defend the interests of the State, compromised by a powerful society which tended to dominate all Christian nations. But reasons of an educational character had also some influence on the condemnation pronounced against the Jesuits by all the Parliaments of France. From all quarters, in the reports which were drawn up by the municipal or royal officers of all the cities where the Jesuits had colleges, complaint is made of the scholastic methods and usages of the Company. Reforms were demanded which they were incapable of realizing.

And it is not in France alone that the faults in the education of the Jesuits were vigorously announced. In the edict of 1759, by which the king of Portugal expelled the Jesuits from his kingdom, it was said: " The study of the humanities has declined in the kingdom, and the Jesuits are evidently the cause of the decadence into which the Greek and Latin tongues have fallen." Some years later, in 1768, the king of Portugal congratulated himself on having banished " the moral corruption, the superstition the .fanaticism, and the ignorance, which had been introduced by the Society of Jesus."

376. GENERAL COMPLAINTS AGAINST THE EDUCATION OF THE
JESUITS. — Even in the middle of the eighteenth century the
Jesuits were still addicted to their old routine, and even their
faults were aggravated with the times.

At Auxerre, complaint is made that pupils study in their
schools only a few Latin authors, and that they leave them
without ever receiving into their hands a single French
author.

At Moulins, a request is made that at least one hour a
week be devoted to the history of France, which proves that
the Society of Jesus, always enslaved to its immobile formalism, did not grant even this little concession to the teaching
of history.

At Orleans, the necessity of teaching children the French
language is insisted on.

At Montbrison, the wish is expressed that pupils be taught
a smattering of geography, especially of their own country.

At Auxerre, it is proved that in the teaching of philosophy the time is employed " in copying and learning note-
books filled with vain distinctions and frivolous questions."

At Montbrison, the request is made " that the rules of
reasoning be explained in French, and that there be a disuse
of debates which train only disputants and not philosophers."

It would be interesting to pursue this study, and to collect
from these reports of 1762, — real memorials of a scholastic
revolution, — all the complaints of public opinion against the
Jesuits.   Even in religion, the Company of Jesus is charged
with substituting for the sacred texts, books of devotion composed by the Fathers.   At Poitiers, a demand is made in
favor of the Old and the New Testaments, the study of
which was wholly neglected.   From time to time the Jesuits
were accused of continually mixing religious questions with
classical studies and of catechising at every turn.   " The

masters of the fifth and sixth forms in the College of Auxerre dogmatize in the themes which they dictate to the children." Finally, the Company of Jesus maintained in the schools the teaching of moral casuistry; it encouraged bigotry and superstition; it relaxed nothing from the severity of its discipline, and provoked violent recriminations among some of its former pupils who had preserved a painful recollection of corrections received in its colleges.[1]

377. EFFORTS MADE TO DISPLACE THE JESUITS. — The Parliaments, then, did nothing more, so to speak, than register the verdict of public opinion everywhere excited against the Jesuits. But while they heartily joined in the general reprobation, they undertook to determine the laws of the new education. "It is of little use to destroy," they said, "if we do not intend to build. The public good and the honor of the nation require that we should establish a civil education which shall prepare each new generation for filling with success the different employments of the State." It is not just to say with Michel Bréal, that "once delivered from the Jesuits, the University installed itself in their establishments and continued their instruction." Earnest attempts were made to reform programmes and methods. La Chalotais, Guyton de Morveau, Rolland, and still others attempted by their writings, and, when they could, by their acts, to establish a system of education which, while inspired by Rollin and the Jansenists, attempted to do still better.

378. LA CHALOTAIS (1701-1785). — Of all the parliamentarians who distinguished themselves in the campaign undertaken towards the middle of the eighteenth century against the pedagogy of the Jesuits, the most celebrated, and the

---

[1] See the pamphlet published in 1764 entitled: *Mémoires historiques sur l'orbilianisme et les correcteurs des Jésuites.*

most worthy of being such, is undoubtedly the solicitor-general of the Parliament of Bretagne, René de la Chalotais. A man of courage and character, he was arrested and imprisoned in the citadel of Saint Malo for having upheld the franchise of the province of Bretagne; and it was in his prison, in 1765, that he drew up for his defence an eloquent and impassioned memorial, of which Voltaire said, "Woe to every sensitive soul that does not feel the quivering of a fever in reading it!"

379. HIS ESSAY ON NATIONAL EDUCATION. — The *Essai* of La Chalotais appeared in 1763, one year after the *Émile*. Coming after the ambitious theories of a philosopher who, scorning polemics and the dissensions of his time, had written only for humanity and the future, this was a modest and opportune work, the effort of a practical man who attempted to respond to the aspirations and the needs of his time. Translated into several languages, the *Essai d'éducation nationale* obtained the enthusiastic approval of Diderot, and also of Voltaire, who said, "It is a terrible book against the Jesuits, all the more so because it is written with moderation." Grimm carried his admiration so far as to write, "It would be difficult to present in a hundred and fifty pages more reflections that are wise, profound, useful, and truly worthy of a magistrate, of a philosopher, of a statesman." Too completely forgotten to-day, this little composition of La Chalotais deserves to be republished. Notwithstanding some prejudices that mar it, it is already wholly penetrated with the spirit of the Revolution.

380. SECULARIZATION OF EDUCATION. — As a matter of fact, the whole pedagogy of the eighteenth century is dominated by the idea of the necessary secularization of instruction. Thorough-going Gallicans like La Chalotais or Rolland, dauntless free-thinkers like Diderot or Helvetius, all believe

and assert that public instruction is a civil affair, a "government undertaking," as Voltaire expressed it. All wish to substitute lay teachers for religious teachers, and to open civil schools upon the ruins of monastic schools.

"Who will be persuaded," says Rolland in his report of 1708, "that fathers who feel an emotion that an ecclesiastic never should have known, will be less capable than he of educating children?"

La Chalotais also demands these citizen teachers. He objects to those instructors who, from interest as well as from principle, give the preference in their affections to the supernatural world over one's native land.

"I do not presume to exclude ecclesiastics," he said, "but I protest against the exclusion of laymen. I dare claim for the nation an education which depends only on the State, because it belongs essentially to the State; because every State has an inalienable and indefeasible right to instruct its members; because, finally, the children of the State ought to be educated by the members of the State.' This does not mean that La Chalotais is irreligious; but he desires a national religion which does not subordinate the interests of the country to a foreign power. What he wants especially is, that the Church, reserving to herself the teaching of divine truth, abandon to the State the teaching of morals, and the control of purely human studies. He is of the same opinion as his friend Duclos, who said: —

"It is certain that in the education which was given at Sparta, the prime purpose was to train Spartans. It is thus that in every State the purpose should be to enkindle the spirit of citizenship; and, in our case, to train Frenchmen, and in order to make Frenchmen, to labor to make men of them."[1]

---

[1] Duclos, *Considérations sur les mœurs de ce siècle.* Ch. II. *Sur l'éduca-tion et les préjugés.*

381. PRACTICAL PURPOSE OF INSTRUCTION. — The particular charge brought by La Chalotais against the education of his time, against that of the University as well as against that of the Jesuits, is, that it does not prepare children for real life, for life in the State. "A stranger who should visit our colleges might conclude that in France we think only of peopling the seminaries, the cloisters, and the Latin colonies." How are we to imagine that the study of a dead language, and a monastic discipline, are the appointed means for training soldiers, magistrates, and heads of families?

" The greatest vice of education, and perhaps the most inevitable, while it shall be entrusted to persons who have renounced the world, is the absolute lack of instruction on the moral and political virtues. Our education does not affect our habits, like that of the ancients. After having endured all the fatigues and irksomeness of the college, the young find themselves in the need of learning in what consist the duties common to all men. They have learned no principle for judging actions, evils, opinions, customs. They have everything to learn on matters that are so important.. They are inspired with a devotion which is but an imitation of religion, and with practices which take the place of virtue, and are but the shadow of it."

382. INTUITIVE AND NATURAL INSTRUCTION. — A pupil of the sensational school, a disciple of Locke and of Condillac, La Chalotais is too much inclined to misconceive, in the development of the individual, the play of natural activities and innate dispositions. But, by way of compensation, his predilection for sensationalism leads him to excellent thoughts on the necessity of beginning with sensible objects before . advancing to intellectual studies, and first of all to secure an education of the senses.

" I wish nothing to be taught children except facts which

are attested by the eyes, at the age of seven as at the age of thirty.

" The principles for instructing children should be those by which nature herself instructs them. Nature is the best of teachers.

" Every method which begins with abstract ideas is not made for children.

" Let children see many objects; let there be a variety of such, and let them be shown under many aspects and on various occasions. The memory and the imagination of children cannot be overcharged with useful facts and ideas of which they can make use in the course of their lives."

Such are the principles according to which La Chalotais organizes his plan of studies.

383. THE NEW SPIRIT IN EDUCATION. — The purpose, then, is to replace that monastic and ultramontane education (this is the term employed by La Chalotais), and also that narrow education, and that repulsive and austere discipline, " which seems made only to abase the spirit"; that sterile and insipid teaching, " the most usual effect of which is to make study hated for life"; those scholastic studies where young men " contract the habit of disputing and caviling"; and those ascetic regulations " which set neatness and health at defiance." The purpose is to initiate children into our most common and most ordinary affairs, into what forms the conduct of life and the basis of civil society.

" Most young men know neither the world which they inhabit, the earth which nourishes them, the men who supply their needs, the animals which serve them, nor the workmen and citizens whom they employ. They have not even any desire for this kind of knowledge. No advantage is taken of their natural curiosity for the purpose of increasing it.

learn all that up to this time they had been permitted to be ignorant of.

384. STUDIES OF THE FIRST PERIOD. — Education, according to La Chalotais, should be divided into two periods : the first from five to ten, the second from ten to seventeen.

During the first period, we have to do with children who have no experience because they have seen nothing, who have no power of attention because they are incapable of any sustained effort, and no judgment because they have not yet any general ideas ; but who, by way of compensation, have senses, memory, and some power of reflection. It is necessary, then, to make a careful choice of the subjects of study which shall be proposed to these tender intelligences ; and La Chalotais decides in favor of history, geography, natural history, physical and mathematical *recreations.*

" The exercises proposed for the first period," he says, " are as follows : learning to read, write, and draw ; dancing and music, which ought to enter into the education of persons above the commonalty ; historical narratives and the lives of illustrious men of every country, of every age, and of every profession ; geography, mathematical and physical recreations ; the fables of La Fontaine, which, whatever may be said of them, ought not to be removed from the hands of children, but all of which they should be made to learn by heart ; and besides this, walks, excursions, merriment, and recreations ; I do not propose even the studies except as amusements."

385. CRITICISM OF NEGATIVE EDUCATION. — La Chalotais is often right as against Rousseau. For example, he has abundantly refuted the utopia of a negative education in

which nature is allowed to have her way, and which considers the toil of the centuries as of no account. It is good sense
itself which speaks in reflections like these : —
" If man is not taught what is good, he will necessarily
become preoccupied with what is bad. The mind and the
heart cannot remain unoccupied. . . . On the pretext of
affording children an experience which is their own, they are
deprived of the assistance of others' experience."

386. HISTORY AVENGED OF THE DISDAIN OF ROUSSEAU. —
The sophisms of Rousseau on history are brilliantly refuted.
History is within the comprehension of the youngest. The
child who can understand Tom Thumb and Blue Beard, can
understand the history of Romulus and of Clovis. Moreover, it is to the history of the most recent times that
La Chalotais attaches the greatest importance, and in this
respect he goes beyond his master Rollin : —
" I would have composed for the use of the child histories
of every nation, of every century, and particularly of the
later centuries, which should be written with greater detail,
and which should be read before those of the more remote
centuries. I would have written the lives of illustrious men
of all classes, conditions, and professions, of celebrated
heroes, scholars, women, and children."

387. GEOGRAPHY. — La Chalotais does not separate the
study of geography from that of history, and he requires
that, without entering into dry and tedious details, the pupil
be made to travel pleasantly through different countries, and
that stress be put " on what is of chief importance and interest in each country, such as the most striking facts, the
native land of great men, celebrated battles, and whatever
is most notable, either as to manners and customs, to
natural productions, or to arts and commerce."

388. NATURAL HISTORY. — Another study especially
adapted to children, says La Chalotais with reason, is
natural history: " The principal thing is first to show the
different objects just as they appear to the eyes. A representation of them, with a precise and exact description, is
sufficient."

" Too great detail must be avoided, and the objects chosen
must be such as are most directly related to us, which are
the most necessary and the most useful."

" Preference shall be given to domestic animals over those
that are wild, and to native animals over those of other
countries. In the case of plants, preference shall be given
to those that serve for food and for use in medicine."

As far as possible, the object itself should be shown, so
that the idea shall be the more exact and vivid, and the
impression the more durable.

389. RECREATIONS IN PHYSICS. — La Chalotais explains
that he means by this phrase observations, experiments, and
the simplest facts of nature. Children should early be made
acquainted with thermometers, barometers, with the microscope, etc.

390. RECREATIONS IN MATHEMATICS. — All this is excellent,
and La Chalotais enters resolutely into the domain of modern
methods. What is more debatable is the idea of putting
geometry and mathematics into the programme of children's
studies, under this erroneous pretext, that " geometry presents nothing but the sensible and the palpable." Let us
grant, however, that it is easier to conceive " clear ideas of
bodies, lines, and angles that strike the eyes, than abstract
ideas of verbs, declensions, and conjugations, of an accusa-
tive, an ablative, a subjunctive, an infinitive, or of the
omitted *that*."

391. STUDIES OF THE SECOND PERIOD. — La Chalotais postpones the study of the classical languages till the second
period, the tenth year.   The course of study for this second
period will comprise: 1. French and Latin literature, or the
humanities ; 2. a continuation of history, geography, mathematics, and natural history ; 3. criticism, logic, and metaphysics ; 4. the art of invention ; 5. ethics.

La Chalotais complains that his contemporaries neglect
French literature, as though we had not admirable models in
our national language.   Out of one hundred pupils there are
not five who will find it useful to write in Latin ; while there
is not one of them who will have occasion to speak or write
in Greek, and to construct Latin verses.   All, on the contrary, ought to know their native language.   Consequently,
our author suggests the idea of devoting the morning session
to French, and that of the afternoon to Latin, so that the
pupils who have no need of the ancient languages may pursue only the courses in French.

392. THE LIVING LANGUAGES. — La Chalotais thinks the
knowledge of two living languages to be necessary, " the /
English for science, and the German for war."   German
literature had not yet produced its masterpieces, and it is
seen that at this period the utility of German appears especially with reference to military affairs.   However it may be,
let us be grateful to him for having appreciated, as he has
done, the living languages.   " It is wrong," he says, " to
treat them nearly as we treat our contemporaries, with a sort
of indifference.   Without the Greek and Latin languages
there is no real and solid erudition ; and there is no complete
erudition without the others."

393. OTHER STUDIES. — How many judicious or just reflections we have still to gather from the *Essay on National Educa-*

tion, as upon the teaching of the ancient languages, which **La** Chalotais, however, is wrong in restricting to too small a number of years ; upon the necessity of presenting to pupils as subjects for composition, not puerile amplifications, or dissertations on facts or matters of which they are ignorant, but things which they know, which have happened to them, " their occupations, their amusements, or their troubles"; upon logic or criticism, the study of which should not be deferred till the end of the course, as is still done in our day ; upon philosophy, which is, he says, " the characteristic of the eighteenth century, as that of the sixteenth was erudition, and that of the seventeenth was talent!" La Chalotais reserves the place of honor to ethics, " which is the most important of all the sciences, and which is, as much as any other, susceptible of demonstration."

394. THE QUESTION OF BOOKS. — In tracing his programme of studies, so new in many particulars, La Chalotais took into account the difficulties that would be encountered in assuring, and, so to speak, in improvising, the execution of it, at a time when there existed neither competent teachers nor properly constructed books. Teachers especially, he said, are difficult to train. But, while waiting for the re-cruiting of the teaching force, La Chalotais puts great dependence on elementary books, which might, he thought, be composed within two years, if the king would encourage the publication of them, and if the Academies would put them up for competition.

" These books would be the best instruction which the masters could give, and would take the place of every other method. Whatever course we may take, we cannot dispense with new books. These books, once made, would make trained teachers unnecessary, and there would then be no longer any occasion for discussion as to their qualities, whether they should be priests, or married, or single. All would be good, provided they were religious, moral, and knew how to read; they would soon train themselves while training their pupils."

There is much exaggeration in these words. The book, as we know, cannot supply the place of teachers. But the language of La Chalotais was adapted to circumstances as they existed. He spoke in this way, because, in his impatience to reach his end, he would try to remedy the educational poverty of his time, and supply the lack of good teachers by provisional expedients, by means which he found within his reach.

395. ARISTOCRATIC PREJUDICES. — That which we would expunge from the book of La Chalotais is his opinion on primary instruction. Blinded by some unexplained distrust of the people, and dominated by aristocratic tendencies, he complains of the extension of instruction. He demands that the knowledge of the poor do not extend beyond their pursuits. He bitterly criticises the thirst for knowledge which is beginning to pervade the lower classes of the nation.

" Even the people can study. Laborers and artisans send their children to the colleges of the smaller cities. . . . When these children have accomplished a summary course of study which has taught them only to disdain the occupation of their father, they rush into the cloisters and become ecclesiastics; or they exercise judicial functions, and often become subjects harmful to society. The Brethren of the Christian Doctrine (*sic*), who are called *ignorantins*, have just appeared to complete the general ruin ; they teach people to read and write who ought to learn only to draw, and to handle the plane and the file, but have no disposition to do it. They are the rivals or the successors of the Jesuits."

A singular force of prejudice was necessary to conceive that the Brethren of the Christian Schools were instructing the people too highly.

Let it be said, however, towards exonerating La Chalotais, that he perhaps does not so much attack the instruction in itself, as the bad way in which it is given. What he censures is instruction that is badly conceived, that which takes people from their own class. In some other passages of his book we see that he would be disposed to disseminate the new education among the ranks of the people.

("It is the State, it is the larger part of the nation, that must be kept principally in view in education; for twenty millions of men ought to be held in greater consideration than one million) and the *peasantry, who are not yet a class* in France, as they are in Sweden, *ought not to be neglected in a system of instruction.* Education is equally solicitous that letters should be cultivated, and that the fields should be plowed; that all the sciences and the useful arts should be perfected; that justice should be administered and that religion should be taught; that there should be instructed and competent generals, magistrates, and ecclesiastics, and skillful artists and citizens, all in fit proportion. It is for the government to make each citizen so pleased with his condition that he may not be forced to withdraw from it."

Let us quote one sentence more, which is almost the formula that to-day is so dear to the friends of instruction: —

"We do not fear to assert, in general, that in the condition in which Europe now is, the people that are the most enlightened will always have the advantage over those who are the less so."

396. GENERAL CONCLUSION. — Notwithstanding the faults which mar it, the work of La Chalotais is none the less one of the most remarkable essays of the earlier French pedagogy. "La Chalotais," says Gréard, "belongs to the school of

Rousseau ; but on more than one point he departs from the plan traced by the master. He escapes from the allurements of the paradox. Relatively he has the spirit of moderation. He is a classic without prejudices, an innovator without temerity."

His book is pre-eminently a book of polemics, written with the ardor of one who is engaged in a fight, and overflowing with a generous passion. What noble words are the following : —

" Let the young man learn what bread a ploughman, a day laborer, or an artisan eats. He will see in the sequel how they are deprived of the bread which they earn with so much difficulty, and how one portion of men live at the expense of the other."

In these lines, which breathe a sentiment of profound pity for the disinherited of this world, we already hear, as it were, the signal cry announcing the social reclamations of the French Revolution.

379.   ROLLAND (1734–1794). — La Chalotais, after having criticised the old methods, proposed new ones ; Rolland attempted to put them in practice. La Chalotais is a polemic and a theorist ; Rolland is an administrator. President of the Parliament of Paris, he presented to his colleagues, in 1768, a Report which is a real system of education.[1] But above all, he gave his personal attention to the administration of the College Louis-le-Grand. An ardent and impassioned adversary of the Jesuits, he used every means to put public instruction in a condition to do without them. " Noble and wise spirit, patient and courageous reason, who, for twenty years, even during exile and after the dissolution of his society, did not abandon for a single moment the work he

---

[1] See the *Recueil* of the works of President Rolland, printed in 1783, by order of the executive committee of the College Louis-le-Grand.

had undertaken, but brought it, almost perfected, to the
very confines of the Revolution ; a heart divested of every
ambition, who, chosen by popular wish, and by the cabinet
of the king, as director of public instruction, obstinately
entrenched himself in the peace of his studious retreat." This
is the judgment of a member of the University, in the nineteenth century, Dubois, director of the Normal School.

No doubt Rolland is not an original educator. "It is in
Rollin's *Traité des études*," he says, "that every teacher will
find the true rules for education." Besides, he borrowed
ideas from La Chalotais, and also from the *Mémoires* which
the University of Paris drew up in 1763 and 1764 at the
request of Parliament; so that the interest in his work is
less, perhaps, in its personal views than in the indications
it furnishes relative to the situation of the University and
its tendency towards self-reformation.

398. INSTRUCTION WITHIN THE REACH OF ALL. — At least
on one point Rolland is superior to La Chalotais; he takes a
bold stand for the necessity of primary instruction, and for
the progress and diffusion of human knowledge.

"Education cannot be too widely diffused, to the end that
there may be no class of citizens who may not be brought to
participate in its benefits. It is expedient that *each citizen
receive the education* which is adapted to his needs." [1]

It is true that Rolland joins in the wish expressed by the
University, which demanded a reduction in the number of
colleges. But only colleges for the higher studies were in
question, and Rolland thought less of restricting instruction
than of proportioning and adapting it to the needs of the
different classes of society.

"*Each one ought to have the opportunity to receive the
education* which is adapted to his needs. . . . Now each

---

[1] *Recueil*, etc., p. 25.

soil," adds Rolland, " is not susceptible of the same culture and the same product. Each mind does not demand the same degree of culture. All men have neither the same needs nor the same talents ; and it is in proportion to these talents and these needs that public education ought to be regulated."

• Rolland shared the prejudices of La Chalotais against "the new Order founded by La Salle " ; but none the less on this account did he demand instruction for all.

" The knowledge of reading and writing, which is the key to all the other sciences, ought to be universally diffused. Without this the teachings of the clergy are useless, for the memory is rarely faithful enough ; and reading alone can impress in a durable manner what it is important never to forget." Would it be granted by every one to-day, affected by prejudices that are ever re-appearing, that " the laborer who has received some sort of instruction is but the more diligent and the more skillful by reason of it "?

399. THE NORMAL SCHOOL. — We shall not dwell upon the methods and schemes of study proposed by Rolland. Save very urgent recommendations relative to the study of the national history and of the French language, we shall find nothing very new in them. What deserve to be pointed out, by way of compensation, are the important innovations which he wished to introduce into the general organization of public instruction.

First there was the idea of a higher normal school, of a seminary for professors. The University had already expressed the wish that such an establishment should be founded. To be convinced how much this pedagogical seminary, conceived as far back as 1763, resembled our actual Normal School, it suffices to note the following details. The establishment was to be governed by professors drawn from the different faculties, according to the different subjects of instruction. The young men received on competitive examination were to be divided into three classes, corresponding to the three grades of admission. Within the establishment they were to take part in a series of discussions, after a given time to submit to the tests for graduation, and finally to be placed in the colleges. Is it not true that there was no important addition to be made to this scheme? Rolland also required that pedagogics have a place among the studies of these future professors, and that definite and systematic instruction be given in this art, so important to the teachers of youth.

Rolland does not stop even there. He provides for inspectors, or *visitors*, who are to examine all the colleges each year. Finally, he subjects all scholastic establishments to one single authority, to a council of the government, to which he applies the rather odd title, the "Bureau of Correspondence."

400. SPIRIT OF CENTRALIZATION. — Whatever opinion may be formed of absolute centralization, which, in our century, has become the law of public instruction, and has caused the disappearance of provincial franchises, it is certain that the parliamentarians of the eighteenth century were the first to conceive it and desire it, if not to realize it. Paris, in Rolland's plan, becomes the centre of public instruction. The universities distributed through the provinces are co-ordinated and made dependent on that of Paris.

"Is it not desirable," said Rolland, "that the good taste which everything concurs to produce in the capital, be diffused to the very extremities of the kingdom; that every Frenchman participate in the treasures of knowledge which are there accumulating from day to day; that the young men who have the same country, who are destined to serve the same prince and to fulfill the same functions, receive the same lessons and be imbued with the same maxims ; that one part of France be not under the clouds of ignorance while letters shed the purest light in another ; in a word, that the time come when a young man educated in a province cannot be distinguished from one who has been trained in the capital?" And he adds that " the only means for attaining an end so desirable is to make Paris the centre of public instruction."

Besides the gain that will thus accrue to instruction, Rolland sees this other advantage, that, through uniformity in instruction, there will be secured a uniformity in manners and in laws. By means of a uniform education, " the young men of all the provinces will divest themselves of all their prejudices of birth ; they will form the same ideas of virtue and justice ; they will demand uniform laws, which would have offended their fathers."

By this means, finally, there will be developed a national spirit, a national character, and a national jurisprudence, " the only means of recreating love of country." Is it not true that the great magistrates of the close of the eighteenth century deserve also to be counted among the founders of French unity?

401. TURGOT (1727–1781). — In his *Mémoires* to the king (1775), Turgot set forth analogous ideas, and also demanded the formation of a council of public instruction. He made an eloquent plea for the establishment of a civil and national education which should be extended to the country at large.

" Your kingdom, Sir, is of this world. Without opposing any obstacle to the instructions whose object is higher, and which already have their rules and their expounders, I think I can propose to you nothing of more advantage to your people than to cause to be given to all your subjects an instruction which shows them the obligations they owe to society and to your power which protects them, the duties which those obligations impose on them, and the interest which they have in fulfilling those duties for the public good and their own. This moral and social instruction requires books expressly prepared, by competition, and with great care, and a schoolmaster in each parish to teach them to children, along with the art of writing, reading, counting, measuring, and the principles of mechanics."

" The study of the duty of citizenship ought to be the foundation of all the other studies."

" There are methods and establishments for training geometricians, physicists, and painters, but there are none for training citizens."

In a word, La Chalotais, Rolland, Turgot, and some of their contemporaries, were real precursors of the French Revolution in the matter of education. At the date of 1762 the scholastic revolution began, at least so far as secondary instruction is concerned. The Parliaments of that period conceived the plan of the University of the nineteenth century, and prepared for the work of Napoleon I. But they left to the men of the Revolution the honor of being the first to organize primary instruction.

[402. ANALYTICAL SUMMARY. — 1. This study exhibits the evils brought upon a country by an education controlled and administered by a dominant Church for the attainment of its own ends ; and also the efforts of a nation to save itself from imminent disaster by making the State the great public educator.

2. The right of the State to self-preservation is the vindication of its right to control and direct public education. The State thus becomes the patron of the public school ;

the product it requires is good citizenship; and for the sake of securing this product the State endows the school, wholly or in part.

3. The situation in France, as described in this study, is an aggravated case of what may occur whenever education is administered by a class having special interests and ambitions; and under some form there must be the intervention of the State as a means of protecting its own interests.

4. When education is administered in the main by the literary class, there is some danger that the instruction may not be that which is best adapted to the needs of other classes.]

CHAPTER XVI.

THE FRENCH REVOLUTION. — MIRABEAU, TALLEYRAND, CONDORCET.

CONTRADICTORY JUDGMENTS ON THE WORK OF THE FRENCH REVOLU-
TION; GENERAL CHARACTER OF THAT WORK; THE STATE OF PRI-
MARY INSTRUCTION; WHAT WAS TAUGHT IN THE SCHOOLS; DISCIPLINE;
THE SITUATION OF TEACHERS; THE RECRUITMENT OF TEACHERS;
WHAT THE SCHOOL ITSELF WAS; THE PECULIAR WORK OF THE
REVOLUTION; THE CAHIERS OF 1789; MIRABEAU (1749–1791) AND
HIS TRAVAIL SUR L'INSTRUCTION PUBLIQUE; DANGERS OF
IGNORANCE; LIBERTY OF TEACHING; THE CONSTITUENT ASSEMBLY
AND THE RAPPORT OF TALLEYRAND; TALLEYRAND (1758–1838);
POLITICAL PRINCIPLES OF UNIVERSAL INSTRUCTION; FOUR GRADES
OF INSTRUCTION; POLITICAL CATECHISM; INDEPENDENT MORALITY;
THE LEGISLATIVE ASSEMBLY AND THE RAPPORT OF CONDORCET;
CONDORCET (1743–1794); GENERAL CONSIDERATIONS ON EDUCATION;
INSTRUCTION AND MORALITY; INSTRUCTION AND PROGRESS; LIBER-
ALITY OF CONDORCET; FIVE GRADES OF INSTRUCTION; PURPOSE
AND PROGRAMME OF PRIMARY INSTRUCTION; IDEA OF COURSES
FOR ADULTS; THE EDUCATION OF WOMEN; PREJUDICES; FINAL
JUDGMENT; ANALYTICAL SUMMARY.

---

404. CONTRADICTORY JUDGMENTS ON THE WORK OF THE
REVOLUTION. — An historian of education in France, Théry,
opens his chapter on the Revolution with these contemptuous
words, "One does not study a void, one does not analyze a
negation."[1] A more recent historian of public instruction
during the Revolution, Albert Duruy, arriving at the work
of Condorcet, certainly the most important undertaking of

---

[1] Théry, *Histoire de l'éducation en France*, Paris, 1861, Tome II. p. 188.

the pedagogy of the Revolution, does not hesitate to record this absolute and summary judgment: " We are now no longer in the real and in the possible ; we are travelling in the land of chimeras ; we are soaring in space at heights which admit of only ideal attainment."[1]

How easy it is to say this ! To believe these facile judges, one who would estimate the efforts of the Revolution in the matter of public instruction would have to choose between a nothing and a chimera. The men of the Revolution have done nothing, say some ; they are dreamers and idealists, say others.

These assertions do not bear examination. For every impartial observer it is certain that the Revolution opened a new era in education, and the proof of this is to be found in the very documents that our opponents so triflingly condemn, and the practical spirit of which they misconceive.

405. GENERAL CHARACTER OF THAT WORK. — It is not that the men of the Revolution were educators in the strict sense of the term. The science of education is not indebted to them for new methods. They have not completed the work of Locke, of Rousseau, and of La Chalotais ; but they were the first to attempt a legislative organization of a vast system of public instruction. It is just to place them in the front rank of the men who might be called " the politicians of education." Doubtless they lacked time for applying their ideas, but they had at least the merit of having conceived these ideas, and of having embodied them in legislative acts. The principles which we proclaim to-day, they formulated. The solutions which we attempt to put in practice after a century of waiting, were decreed by them. The reader who will follow the long series of reports and

---

[1] Albert Duruy, L'instruction publique et la Révolution, p. 80.

decrees which constitutes the pedagogical work of the Revolution will have witnessed the genesis of popular instruction in France.

406. THE STATE OF PRIMARY INSTRUCTION. — In order
to form a proper appreciation of the merits of the men of
the Revolution, it is first necessary to consider in what a
deplorable state they found primary instruction. What a
contrast between that which they hoped to do and the actual
situation in 1789! I very well know that fancy sketches
have been drawn of the old régime. A very showy enumeration has been made of the number of colleges; but we
have not been told how many of these colleges had no professors, and how many had no pupils. And so of the
schools; they are found everywhere, but it remains to be
shown what was taught in them, and whether anything was
taught in them.[1]

Party writers who are bound to gainsay the work of the
French Revolution in the matter of education, generally put
under contribution, to serve their political prejudices, the old
communal archives. They cite imaginary statistics which
prove, for example, that in the diocese of Rouen, in 1718,
there were 855 schools for boys, and 306 schools for girls,
for a territory of 1159 parishes.

It is first necessary to verify these statistics, whose accuracy has not been demonstrated, and whose figures were
evidently obtained only by counting a school wherever the
rector of the parish gave lessons in reading and in the catechism to three or four children.

But there are other replies to make to the traducers of the
Revolution who tax their ingenuity to prove that instruction
was flourishing under the old régime, and that the Revolution

---

[1] J. Simon, *Dieu, patrie, et liberté*, p. 11.

destroyed more than it created. With this assumed effio-
rescence of schools of which we hear, it is necessary to
contrast the results as shown by authentic statistics of the
number of illiterates. In 1790 there was 53 per cent of men
and 73 per cent of women who could not sign their names
to their marriage contracts.

Besides, we must inquire what was taught in these pretended schools, how many children attended them, and what
was the material and moral condition of the teachers who
directed them.

407. WHAT WAS TAUGHT IN THE SCHOOLS. — Instruction
was reduced to the catechism, to reading and writing. On
this point there can be no dispute. The official programme of the Brethren of the Christian Schools did not go
beyond this. The ordinance of Louis XIV., dated in 1698,
has been pompously quoted.

" We would have appointed," it is there said, "as far as
it shall be possible, masters and mistresses in all the parishes where there are none, to instruct all children, and *in
particular those whose parents have made profession of the
pretended reformed religion*, in the catechism and the prayers
which are necessary ; to take them to mass on every work
day ; and also to teach reading and writing *to those who will
need this knowledge*."

But does not this very text support those who maintain
that the Monarchy and the Church have never encouraged
primary instruction except as required by the necessities of
the struggle against heresy, and that primary instruction
under the old régime was scarcely more than an instrument
of religious domination?

Most often the school was simply a place to which parents
sent their children for temporary care. Writing was not
always taught in it. A school-mistress of Haute-Marne

was forbidden to teach writing " for fear her pupils might employ their knowledge in writing love-letters."

408. DISCIPLINE. — Corporal punishments were more than ever the order of the day. The bishop of Montpellier, at the end of the seventeenth century, forbids, it is true, beating with sticks, kicks, and raps on the head ; but he authorizes the ferule and the rod, on the condition that the patient be not completely exposed.

409. CONDITION OF THE TEACHERS. — That which is graver still is that the teachers themselves (I speak of lay teachers, who, it is true, were not numerous) lived in a wretched condition, without material independence and without moral dignity. In general, there were no fixed salaries. Wages varied from 40 to 200 francs, arbitrarily fixed by the vestry-board or by the community, in return for a great number of services the most various and the least exalted. The school-masters were far less teachers than sextons, choristers, beadles, bell-ringers, clock-makers, and even grave-diggers. " Attendance at marriages and at burials was counted at the rate of 15 sols and dinner for marriages, and 20 sols for burials." And Albert Duruy concludes that in this there were *substantial advantages* to the school-masters ; [1] — advantages dearly bought in every case, and repudiated by those who were interested in them. " The more services we render the community," said the teachers of Bourgogne in their complaints in 1789, " the more we are degraded."[2] The school-masters were scarcely more than the domestics of the *curé*.

---

[1] Albert Duruy, *op. cit.*, p. 16.

[2] *Doléances* presented to the States-General by the teachers of the smaller cities, hamlets, and villages of Bourgogne.

In order to live, they were not only obliged to accept these church services, but they also became shoemakers, tailors, innkeepers, millers, etc. The teacher of the commune of Angles, in the High Alps, was a "barbers' surgeon."

Thus there was no assured salary, and consequently no moral consideration. " In the communes, teachers were regarded as strangers and not as citizens ; like tramps and vagrants, they were not admitted to the assemblies of the commune."

410. THE RECRUITMENT OF TEACHERS. — Nowhere were there normal schools for the training of teachers. The schools were entrusted to the first comer. The bishop granted his approbation, or permission to teach, after an examination of the most summary kind. The duties of teaching were the means of subsistence which were accepted without call and without serious preparation. In Provence, school-masters attended kinds of " teachers' fairs " for the purpose of being hired. In the Alps, teachers were numerous, but only in winter. They tarried in the plain and in the valleys only during the inclement season. They returned home for the labors of the summer.

Consequently, most of the schools existed only in name. " The schools," we are told,[1] " were in vacation for four or five months." For a half of the year, the school-masters were free to follow another trade, or, rather, to devote themselves more completely to their ordinary trade, which their school duties did not always interrupt.

411. WHAT THE SCHOOL ITSELF WAS. — School-houses were most frequently merely wretched huts, wooden cots, and narrow ground-floors, badly lighted, which served at the same

---

[1] A. Duruy, *op. cit.*, p. 10.

time as a domicile for the school-master and his family, and
as a class-room for pupils. Benches and tables were things
rarely seen, and pupils wrote while standing.

In a word, the state of primary instruction, when the
States-General opened in 1789, was as follows: schools
few in number and poorly attended; few lay teachers, trained
no one knows how, without thorough instruction, and, as
they themselves said, "degraded" by their inferior position;
few or no elementary books; gratuity only partial; finally,
a general indifference for elementary instruction, which philosophers like Voltaire, and Rousseau, and Parliamentarians
like La Chalotais, themselves lightly esteemed.

412. THE PROPER WORK OF THE REVOLUTION. — I do not
say that the Revolution accomplished all that there was to be
attempted in order to bring instruction up to the needs of the
new society; but it purposed to do this. Every time a liberal ministry has decided to work for the promotion of instruction, it has revived its plans; and it is these same plans
that by a vigorous effort public authority has attempted to
realize in recent times.

413. THE REPORTS OF 1789. — Already, in the reports of
1789, public opinion vigorously pronounced itself in favor of
educational reforms. "The *cahiers* of 1789, even those
of the clergy and the nobility, demand the reorganization of
public instruction on a comprehensive plan. The *cahiers*
of the clergy of Rodez and of Saumur demand 'that there
may be formed a plan of *national education* for the young';
those of Lyons, that education be restricted ' to a teaching
body whose members may not be removable except for negligence, misconduct, or incapacity; that it may no longer be
conducted according to arbitrary principles, and that all public instructors be obliged to conform to a uniform plan

adopted by the States-General.' The *cahiers* of the nobility of Lyons insist that ' a national character' be impressed on the education of both sexes. Those of Paris demand ' that public education be perfected, and extended to all classes of citizens.' Those of Blois, ' that there be established a council composed of the most enlightened scholars of the capital and of the provinces and of the citizens of the different orders, to form a plan of national education, for the use of all the classes of society, and to edit elementary treatises.' " [1]

414. MIRABEAU (1749-1791). — From the first days of the Revolution, pedagogical literature abounds, and gives evidence of the ever-growing interest which public opinion attaches to educational questions. The Oratorians, of whom La Chalotais said, " that they were free from the prejudices of the school and of the cloister, and that they were citizens," present to the National Assembly a series of scholastic plans. On its part, the Assembly sets itself at work ; Talleyrand prepares his great report, and Mirabeau embodies his own reflections in four eloquent discourses.

Mirabeau's discourses, published after his death through the good offices of his friend Cabanis, had the following titles : 1. *Draft of a Law for the Organization of the Teaching Body; 2. Public and Military Festivals; 3. Organization of a National Lycée; 4. The Education of the Heir Presumptive of the Crown.*

415. THE DANGERS OF IGNORANCE. — With what brilliancy the illustrious orator made appear the advantages and the necessity of instruction !

" Those who desire that the peasant may not know how to *read or write*, have doubtless made a patrimony of his

---

[1] See the *Dictionnaire de Pédagogie*, Article FRANCE.

ignorance, and their motives are not difficult to appreciate; but they do not know that when they have made a wild beast of a man, they expose themselves to the momentary danger of seeing him transformed into a savage beast. Without intelligence there is no morality. But on whom, then, is it important to bestow intelligence, if it is not upon the rich? Is not the safeguard of their enjoyments the morality of the people? Through the influence of the laws, through that of a wise administration, through the efforts to which each one should be inspired by the hope of ameliorating the condition of his fellows, exert yourselves, public and private citizens, to diffuse in all quarters the noble fruits of knowledge. Believe that in dissipating one single error, in propagating one single wholesome truth, you will do something for the happiness of the human race; and whoever you are, do not have the least doubt that it is only by this means that you can assure your own happiness."

But through some inexplicable spirit of timidity, Mirabeau did not draw from these principles the consequences that they permit. He does not admit that the State can impose the obligation to attend school.

" Society," he says, " has not the right to prescribe instruction as a duty. . . . Public authority has not the right, with respect to the members of the social body, to go beyond the limits of watchfulness against injustice and of protection against violence. . . ." " Society," he adds, " can exact of each one only the sacrifices necessary for the maintenance of the liberty and the safety of all."

Mirabeau forgets that the obligation to send children to school is exactly one of those necessary sacrifices which the State has the right to impose on parents.

Hostile to obligation, Mirabeau feels no greater partisanship for gratuity: —

"Gratuitous education," he said, "is paid for by everybody, while its fruits are immediately gathered by only a small number of individuals."

410. LIBERTY OF TEACHING. — Like so many other generous spirits, Mirabeau cherished the dream of the most complete liberty of teaching.[1]

"Your single purpose," he said to the members, "is to give to man the use of all his faculties, to make him enjoy all his

---

[1] What is meant by "liberty of teaching" will be better understood from the following quotations from the *Dictionnaire de Pédagogie*, Première Partie, p. 1575 *et seq.:* —

"Liberty of teaching, in a country which has proclaimed obligatory instruction, is the equal right of all to give that instruction, or the prohibition of every monopoly which would put that instruction into the hands either of privileged individuals, or of corporations, or even of the State, to the exclusion of every other teaching body."

"Under the old régime, the education of the masses was committed to the hands of the Church; the colleges, directed by a body of men who were all ecclesiastics, gave 'a vain pretence of an education, where the memory alone was exercised, and where the reason was insulted in the forms of reasoning.'"

"The purpose of the men of the Revolution was, then, above all else, to emancipate science, and to guarantee the right of free inquiry; and while rescuing instruction from the tyranny of the Church, to assure to citizens in general the opportunity to acquire the knowledge that is essential to man. On the one hand, they would take precautions against the abuse of power by a government which had always shown itself hostile to free thought . . . ; on the other, in opposition to the old doctrine which condemned the people to ignorance, they proclaimed the duty of the State to create a system of *public instruction*, common to all citizens."

"It is at this point of view that we must place ourselves in order to gain a correct notion of the plans that were submitted to the Constituent Convention and the Legislative Assembly. What Talleyrand and Condorcet desired was, first, to organize, under the form of a public service, a system of national education in which all might participate; and in the second place, to take precautions against the Church and the royal authority, and so prevent despotic power from attempting to prevent the development of new truths and the teaching of theories which it judged contrary to its policy and interests. For them, liberty of teaching is the demand of philosophic liberty against ecclesiastical and secular authority." (P.)

rights, to develop the corporate life out of all the individual
lives freely developed, and the will of the whole out of all
personal wills."

417. DISTRIBUTION OF STUDIES. — In Mirabeau's plan,
public and national instruction depends, not on the executive
power, but on " the magistrates who truly represent the people, that is to say, who are elected and often renewed by the
people," — in other terms, the officers of departments or districts. Establishments for instruction ought not to form a
consolidated body.

Let us observe, finally, that by the side of the primary
schools Mirabeau established a college of literature for each
department, and at Paris, a single National Lycée, "designed
to secure to a select number of French youth the means of
finishing their education." In this he established a chair of
method, which, he said, ought to be the basis of instruction.

In conclusion, the work of Mirabeau is but a very imperfect sketch, and a sort of graduated transition between the
old and the new régime.

· We do not yet find in it the grand ideas which are to
impassion men, and it is the *Rapport* of Talleyrand which
constitutes the real introduction to the educational work of
the Revolution.

418. THE CONSTITUENT ASSEMBLY AND TALLEYRAND. —
The constitution of Sept. 4, 1791, announced the following
provision : —

" There shall be created and organized a system of public
instruction, common to all citizens, and gratuitous with respect to those branches of instruction which are indispensable
for all men."

It was to put in force the decree of the Constitution that
Talleyrand drew up his *Rapport* and presented it to the

Assembly at the sessions of September 10 and 11. The entire bill contained not less than 208 articles. Having reached the term of its troubled existence, the Assembly did not find the time to discuss it, and, while regretting "not having established the bases of the regeneration of education," it referred the examination of Talleyrand's work to the Legislative Assembly.

The Legislative Assembly showed but little anxiety to accept the legacy of its predecessor. Another report, that of Condorcet, was prepared, so that the bill of Talleyrand never had the honor of a parliamentary discussion.

419. TALLEYRAND (1758–1838). — The ex-bishop of Autun, having become a revolutionist of 1789, before being the chamberlain of Napoleon I. and the minister of Louis XVIII., scarcely deserves by his character the esteem of history; he too often gave a striking example of political versatility. But at least, by his supple and acute intelligence, and by the abundance of his ideas, he has always risen to the height of the various tasks that he has undertaken, and his *Rapport* is a remarkable work.

420. GENERAL PRINCIPLES. — As Montesquieu has said, "the laws of education ought to be relative to the principles of government." It is by this truth that Talleyrand is inspired in the long considerations that serve as a preamble to his bill.

What was to be done in the presence of a constitution which, limiting the powers of the king, called the entire people to participate in political life? That constitution would have remained sterile, would have been but a dead letter, if a suitable education had not come to vivify it by causing it to pass, so to speak, into the blood of the nation. In what did the new régime consist? You have separated, said

Talleyrand to the members, you have separated the will of the whole, or the power of making the laws, from the executive power, which you have reserved to the king. But that general will must be upright, and, in order to be upright, it must be enlightened and instructed. After having given power to the people, you ought to teach them wisdom. Of what use would it be to enfranchise brutal and unconscious forces, to turn them over to their own keeping? Instruction is the necessary counterpoise of liberty. The law, which is henceforth the work of the people, ought not to be at the mercy of the tumultuous opinions of an ignorant multitude.

421. EDUCATION AS RELATED TO LIBERTY AND EQUALITY. — Talleyrand is pleased with his thought, and, considering in turn the two fundamental ideas of the Revolution, the idea of equality and the idea of liberty, he shows, not without some length of analysis, that instruction is necessary, on the one hand, to create free individuals, by giving to them a conscience and a reason, and on the other, to draw men together by diminishing the inequality of intelligences.

422. RULES FOR PUBLIC INSTRUCTION. — Instruction is due to all. There must be schools in the villages as in the cities. Instruction ought to be given by all; there ought to be no privilege in instruction. Finally, instruction ought to extend to all subjects; everything shall be taught which can . be taught : —

" In a well organized society, though no one can attain to universal knowledge, it should nevertheless be possible to learn everything."

423. POLITICAL EDUCATION. — At the basis of every educational system there is always a dominant and essential thought. In the Middle Age — and the Middle Age is continued in the schools of the Jesuits — it is the idea of salva-

tion, it is the preparation of the soul for the future life. In the seventeenth century it is the conception of a perfect justness of spirit joined to uprightness of heart; such was the ideal of the solitaries of Port Royal. In 1792 politics became the almost exclusive preoccupation of the educators of youth. Everything else — religion, accuracy of judgment, nobility of heart — is relegated to the second place: man is nothing more than a political animal, brought into the world to know, to love, and to obey the constitution.

The *Declaration of the Rights of Man* became, in the system of Talleyrand, the catechism of childhood. It is ueeessary that the future citizen learn to know, to love, to obey, and finally to perfect the constitution. We cannot help thinking that Talleyrand himself showed a marvellous aptitude for loving and obeying the constitution. Unfortunately this has not always been the case!

424. UNIVERSAL MORALITY. — One of the most beautiful pages of Talleyrand's work is certainly that in which he recommends the teaching of universal morality, and claims the autonomy of natural laws, distinct from all positive religion.

" We must learn to infuse ourselves with morality, which is the first need of all constitutions. . . . Morality must be taught as a real science, whose principles will be demonstrated to the reason of all men, and to that of all ages. It is only in this way that it will resist all trials. It has long been a matter of lamentation to see men of all nations and of all religions make it depend exclusively on that multitude of opinions which divide them. From this have resulted great evils; for abandoning morality to uncertainty, and often to absurdity, it has necessarily been compromised; it has been made versatile and unsettled. It is time to establish it upon its own bases, and to show men that if baneful

divisions separate them, they at least have in morality a
common meeting place where they all ought to take refuge
and unite for protection. It is necessary, then, to detach it
in some sort from everything else, in order to reunite it at
once to that which merits our approval and our homage.
. . . This change is simple and injures nothing; above all,
it is possible. How is it possible not to see, in fact, that
abstraction being made of every system and of every opinion,
and by considering in men only their relations with other
men, they can be taught what is good and just, made to love
it, and made to find happiness in virtuous actions and
wretchedness in those which are not so?"

425. FOUR GRADES OF INSTRUCTION. — The organization
of instruction, in Talleyrand's bill, was " to be combined
with that of the government," and to be modeled after the
division of administrative functions.   The *Rapport* established four grades of instruction. There was a school for
each *canton*, corresponding to each primary assembly. Then
came intermediate or secondary instruction, intended, if not
for all, at least for the greater number, and given in the
principal town of the district, or *arrondissement*. In the third
place, special schools, scattered over the territory of the
kingdom, in the principal towns of the departments, prepare
young men for the different professions. Finally, the select
intelligences find at Paris, in the National Institute, all that
constitutes the higher instruction.

The great novelty of this system was the creation of cantonal schools, open to peasants and to workmen, to those
whom, up to this time, improvidence or the purpose of the
great sent off to their plows or to their planes.

426. GRATUITY OF PRIMARY INSTRUCTION. — Talleyrand did
not desire compulsory education any more than Mirabeau;

but, in accordance with the constitution of 1791, he demands the gratuity of primary instruction. Society is under obligations to give elementary instruction, but not intermediate and secondary instruction, and still less, special and higher instruction. Gratuitous for the lowest grade, and in case of that elementary knowledge which constitutes for every civilized man a real moral necessity, instruction ought not to be free to young men who aspire to a liberal profession, because they have leisure, and who have leisure because they have wealth. However, Talleyrand admits exceptions in the case of talent. By the creation of national scholarships, the doors of all the schools will be opened to select intelligences whom the lowness of their condition would condemn to remain obscure and unappreciated, did not society lend to them a helping hand.

427. PROGRAMME OF PRIMARY INSTRUCTION. — Primary instruction should comprise the principles of the national language, the elementary rules of calculation and mensuration ; the elements of religion, the principles of morals, the principles of the constitution ; finally, the development of the physical, intellectual, and moral powers.

428. MEANS OF INSTRUCTION. — We shall not insist on the details of the organization of the different parts of that which Talleyrand himself called his " immense machine." Let us notice only the last part of his work, where he discusses a certain number of general questions under this arbitrary and unjustifiable title : Des moyens d'instruction. The professors, carefully chosen, shall be elected by the king. Talleyrand does not determine that they shall be irremovable, but he requires that their situation shall be surrounded by all possible guarantees. Prizes, and rewards of every kind, shall encourage the teachers of youth to re-

double their zeal and to find new methods. Talleyrand counts on dramatic representations and on national holidays to hasten the progress of instruction. Finally, let it be added that he entrusts the supreme direction of public instruction to six commissioners, chosen by the king and obliged to make an annual report.

429. THE EDUCATION OF WOMEN. — Talleyrand, in his proposal, has not wholly forgotten women, and what he has said of them is just and sensible. He discusses the question of their political rights, and, in accord with tradition and good sense, he concludes that the happiness of women, their own interests, their nature and their proper destination, ought to forbid them from entering the political arena. What is particularly fit for them is a domestic education, which, received in the family, prepares them for living there. Like Mirabeau, he wishes woman to remain a woman. Her function, said the great orator, is to perpetuate the species, to watch with solicitude over the perilous periods of early youth, and "to enchain to her feet all the energies of the husband by the irresistible power of her weakness." Without being as gallant in his expressions, Talleyrand's thought is the same. He thought it necessary, however, in order to respond to certain proprieties, that the State should establish institutions of public education destined to replace the convents.

This desire sets right whatever was unreasonable in this passage of his proposed law : —

" Girls shall not be admitted to the primary schools after the age of eight. After that age the National Assembly advises parents to entrust the education of their daughters only to themselves, and reminds them that this is their first duty."

430. THE LEGISLATIVE ASSEMBLY AND CONDORCET. — Of all the educational undertakings of the Revolution, the most remarkable is that of Condorcet. His *Rapport* presented to the Legislative Assembly, in behalf of the committee on public instruction, April 20 and 21, 1792, reprinted in 1793 by order of the Convention, did not directly have the honor of a public discussion ; but it contained principles and solutions which are found in the deliberations and legislative acts of his successors. It remained, during the whole duration of the Convention, the widely accessible source whence the legislators of that time, like Romme, Bouquier, and Lakanal, drew their inspiration.

431. CONDORCET (1743-1794). — Condorcet was admirably qualified for the task which the Legislative Assembly imposed on him, in charging him with the organization of public instruction. During the first years of the Revolution he had employed his leisure (he was not a member of the Constituent Assembly) in writing five *Mémoires* on instruction, which appeared in a periodical called the *Bibliothèque de l'homme public.* The *Rapport* which he submitted to the Assembly was a sort of résumé of his long reflections. Condorcet brought to this work, not the indiscreet imagination of an improvised educator, but the authority of a competent thinker, who, if he had no personal experience in teaching, had at least reflected much on these topics and was conscious of all their difficulties. Besides, he devoted himself to his work with the ardor of an enthusiastic nature, and with the serious convictions of a mind that had carried farther than any one else the religion of progress and zeal for the public good.

432. GENERAL CONSIDERATIONS UPON INSTRUCTION. — All the Revolutionists have sung the praises of instruction, of

which they were the passionate admirers. Condorcet is its reflective partisan. He did not love it more than the others, but he comprehended it better, and better stated why it should be loved. He first takes up the ideas of Talleyrand, and shows that without instruction, liberty and equality would be chimeras : —

" A free constitution which should not be correspondent to the universal instruction of citizens, would come to destruction after a few conflicts, and would degenerate into one of those forms of government which cannot preserve the peace among an ignorant and corrupt people."

Anarchy or despotism, such is the future of peoples who have become free before having been enlightened.

As to equality, without falling into the chimeras of an instruction which should be the same for all, and which should reduce all men to the same level, Condorcet desires to realize it so far as it is possible. He desires that the poorest and the humblest shall be sufficiently instructed to belong to himself, and not to be at the mercy of the first charlatan who comes along, and also to be able to fulfill his civil duties, to be an elector, a juror, etc.

433. INSTRUCTION AND MORALITY. — The instrument of liberty and equality, instruction, in the opinion of Condorcet, is, in addition, the real source of public morality and of human progress. If it were not correspondent to the advances in knowledge, a free and impartial constitution would be hostile rather than favorable to good morals.

" Instruction alone can give the assurance that the principle of justice which the equality of rights ordains, shall not be in contradiction with this other principle, which prescribes that only those rights shall be accorded to men which they can exercise without danger to society."

But it is moral reasons still more than political motives that make instruction the condition of virtue. Condorcet has shrewdly seen that the vices of the people come chiefly from their intellectual impotency.

" These vices come," he says, " from the need of escaping from *ennui* in moments of leisure, and in escaping from it through sensations and not through ideas."

These are notable words which should never be lost sight of by the teachers and moralists of the people.

To cause gross natures to pass from the life of the senses to the intellectual life ; to make study agreeable to the end that the higher pleasures of the spirit may struggle success- fully against the appetites for material pleasures ; to put the book in the place of the wine bottle ; to substitute the library for the saloon ; in a word, *to replace sensation by idea*, — such is the fundamental problem of popular education.

434. INSTRUCTION AND PROGRESS. — Condorcet was a fanatic on the subject of progress. Up to the last moment of his life he dreamed of progress, its conditions, and its laws. Now the most potent means of hastening progress is to instruct men ; and here is the final reason why instruction is so dear to him.

These are grand words : —

"If the indefinite improvement of our species is, as I be- lieve, a general law of nature, man ought no longer to regard himself as a being limited to a transitory and isolated exis- tence, destined to vanish after an alternative of happiness or of misery for himself, and of good and evil for those whom chance has placed near him ; but he becomes an active part of the grand whole, and a fellow-laborer in a work that is eternal. In an existence of a moment, and upon a point in space, he can, by his works, compass all places, relate himself to all the centuries, and continue to act long centuries after his memory has disappeared from the earth." And further on : "For a long time I have considered these views as dreams which were to be realized only in an indefinite future, and for a world where I should not exist. A happy event has suddenly opened an immense career to the hopes of the human race ; a single instant has put a century of distance between the man of to-day and him of to-morrow."

435. THE LIBERALITY OF CONDORCET. — Wrongly credited with a despotic and absolute habit of mind, Condorcet is, on the contrary, full of scruples and penetrated with respect as regards the liberty of individual opinions. In fact, he carefully distinguishes instruction from education. Instruction has to do with positive and certain knowledge, the truths of fact and of calculation; education, with political and religious beliefs. Now, if the State is the natural dispenser of instruction, it ought, on the contrary, in the matter of education, to forbear, and to declare itself incompetent. In other words, the State ought not to abuse its power by imposing by force on its citizens such or such a religious *Credo*, such or such a political dogma.

"Public authority cannot establish a body of doctrine which is to be exclusively taught. No public power ought to have the authority, or even the permission, to prevent the development of new truths, or the teaching of theories contrary to its particular policy or to its momentary interests."

436. FIVE GRADES OF INSTRUCTION. — Condorcet distinguishes five grades of instruction : 1. Primary schools proper ; 2. Secondary schools, that is, such as we now call higher primary schools ; 3. *Institutes*, or colleges of secondary instruction ; 4. *Lycées*, or institutions of higher instruction ; 5. The *National Society of Sciences and Arts*, which corresponds to our Institute.

Two things are especially to be noted: first, Condorcet establishes for the first time higher primary schools, and demands one for each district, and in addition one for each town of four thousand inhabitants ; then, for primary schools proper, he takes the population as a basis for their establishment, and requires one for each four hundred inhabitants.[1]

437. PURPOSE AND PLAN OF PRIMARY INSTRUCTION. — Condorcet has admirably defined the purpose of primary instruction : —

"In the primary schools there is taught that which is necessary for each individual in order to direct his own conduct and to enjoy the plenitude of his own rights."—

The programme comprised (reading, writing, some notions on grammar, the rules of arithmetic) simple methods of measuring a field and a building with exactness ; a simple description of the productions of the country, of the processes . in agriculture and the arts ; the development of the first moral ideas and the rules for conduct derived from them ; finally, such of the principles of social order as can be put within the comprehension of children.

438. THE IDEA OF COURSES FOR ADULTS. — Condorcet was strongly impressed with the necessity of continuing the instruction of the workman and of the peasant after withdrawal from school : —

---

[1] Public instruction as now organized in France is of three grades, as follows: —

"Primary instruction, which gives the elements of knowledge, reading, writing. and arithmetic. Secondary instruction, embracing the study of the ancient languages, of rhetoric, and the first elements of the mathematical and physical sciences, and of philosophy. This is given in the lycées and colleges, as well as in the smaller seminaries. Superior instruction, designed to teach in all their completeness letters, the languages, the sciences, and philosophy. This is given in the Faculties, in the College of France, and in the larger seminaries." — LITTRÉ. (P.)

"We have observed that instruction ought not to abandon individuals the moment they leave the schools ; that it ought to embrace all ages ; that there is no period of life when it is not useful and possible to learn, and that this supplementary instruction is so much the more necessary as that of infancy has been contracted to the narrowest limits. Here is one of the principal causes of the ignorance in which the poor classes of society are to-day plunged ; they lacked not nearly so much the possibility of receiving an elementary instruction as that of preserving its advantages."

Consequently, Condorcet proposed, if not courses of instruction for adults, at least something very like them, — weekly lectures, given each Sunday by the village teachers, a kind of lay sermons.

"Each Sunday the teacher shall give a public lecture which citizens of all ages will attend. In this arrangement we have seen a means of giving to young people those necessary parts of knowledge, which, however, did not form a part of their primary education."

439. PROFESSIONAL AND TECHNICAL EDUCATION. — But Condorcet does not think his duty to the people done when he has given them intellectual emancipation. He is very anxious to give in addition to the sons of peasants or workmen the means of struggling against misery, by diffusing more and more among the masses of the people a technical knowledge of the arts and trades. He deserves to be counted among the adepts in professional instruction and in industrial education. He asks that there be placed in the schools "models of machines or of trades" ; and in all grades of instruction, he recommends with a special solicitude the teaching of the practical arts.

We fancy we are doing something new to-day when we establish school museums. "Each school," says Condorcet, "shall have a small library, and a small cabinet in which shall be placed some meteorological instruments or some specimens of natural history."

440. THE EDUCATION OF WOMEN. — Condorcet may be regarded as one of the most ardent apostles of the education of women. He wishes education to be common and equal. He is evidently wrong when he dreams of a perfect identity of instruction for the two sexes, when he forgets the particular destination of women, and the special character of their education. But we have found so many educators disposed to depreciate the abilities of woman, that we are happy to find at last one voice that exalts them, even beyond measure.

Let us recall, however, the excellent reasons which he gives in support of his thesis on the equality of education. It is necessary that women should be instructed: 1. in order that they may be able to bring up their children, of whom they are the natural instructors; 2. in order that they may be the worthy companions, the equals of their husbands, that they may feel an interest in their pursuits, share in their preoccupations, and, finally, participate in their life, such being the condition of conjugal happiness; 3. in order, further, by an analogous reason, that they may not quench, by their ignorance, that inspiration of heart and mind which previous studies have developed in their husbands, but that they may nourish this flame by conversation and reading in common; 4. finally, because this is just, — because the two sexes have an equal right to instruction.

441. RESERVATIONS TO BE MADE. — All is not equally worthy of commendation in the work of Condorcet. Some faults and some omissions mar this fine piece of political pedagogy. The faults are, first, the exaggerated idea of lib-

erty and of equality. From Condorcet's ardors for liberty there issues, in his plan for education, a grave error, — the idea of making of the teaching body a sort of State within the State, an independent authority, a fourth power, released from all exterior authority, governing itself and administering its own affairs, the State intervening only as treasurer to pay for the services which it neither regulates nor supervises. The liberal Daunou, while explaining the system of our author, has criticised it on this point.[1] "Condorcet," he said, "the enemy of corporations, has sanctioned one in his scheme of national instruction ; he established, as it were, an academic church. This is because Condorcet, the enemy of kings, would add in the balance of public powers one counter-balance more to that royal power whose monstrous existence, in a free constitution, is sufficiently attested by the alarms and fears of all the friends of liberty."

The passion for equality led Condorcet into another chimera, — that of the absolute gratuity of instruction of all grades.

Finally, in his dreams of infinite perfectibility, Condorcet allows himself to be carried so far away as to imagine for man, and to expect from instruction, results that are utterly unattainable. Instruction, according to him, ought to be so complete " as to cause the disappearance of every inequality which induces dependence."

442. PREJUDICES OF THE MATHEMATICIAN. — From another point of view, Condorcet was led astray by his predilection for the sciences. He so far forgot that he was a member of the French Academy as to obey only his tendencies, a little too exclusive, as a mathematician and a member of the Academy of Sciences. By a reaction, natural enough, against those long centuries in which an abuse was made of

---

[1] See the *Rapport* of Daunou presented to the National Convention, 27 Vendémiaire, year IV.

literary culture, Condorcet is too prompt to underrate the influence of letters in education, and to invest the sciences with the place of honor. The reasons which he invokes to justify his preference are not all conclusive.

443. OMISSIONS. — The idea of obligatory instruction is still wanting in the scheme we are examining. We shall be surprised, perhaps, that Condorcet, who has so clearly proclaimed the necessity of universal instruction, did not think to impose obligatory attendance, which is the only means of establishing it. This is because the early revolutionists, in the ardor of their enthusiasm, did not suspect the opposition to the accomplishment of their plans that was to come from the indifference of the greater number, and from the prejudices of those who, as Condorcet has eloquently said, " thought they were obeying God while betraying their country." It seemed to them that when centres of light had been made to glow over the whole surface of the country, citizens would hasten after them, impelled by a natural appetite, spontaneously thirsting for enlightenment. They were deceived. These hopes, a little artless, were destined to be disproved by facts ; and it was to triumph over the neglect of some, and the resistance of others, that the Convention, supplying one of the rare defects in Condorcet's plan, decreed, on several occasions, instruction " imperative and forced," as was then said.

On still another point, Condorcet remained inferior to his successors ; in his report there was no mention made of the organization of normal schools. In this grave and fundamental question of the education of the teaching body, Condorcet contented himself with a provisional expedient, which consisted in entrusting to the professors of the grade immediately higher the care of preparing teachers for the grade lower.

444. FINAL CONCLUSION. — But even with these reservations, the work of Condorcet deserves scarcely anything but
praise. We have commended its new and exalted conceptions. Its beautiful and exact arrangement and its masterly
style also deserve praise. Condorcet's periods are symmetrical in their fullness, and the expression is precise and vigorous. Doubtless there is some monotony and some frigidity
in that style so concise and strong. But at intervals there
are outbursts of passion. The man whom his contemporaries compared to " an enraged lamb," or to a " volcano
covered with snow," is painted to the life in his writings.
His *Rapport* is like a beautiful and finished statue of marble,
cold to the touch, but upon which the hand might feel beating in places a vein warm with life.

[445. ANALYTICAL SUMMARY. — 1. The more important
lessons to be derived from this study are the following : the
necessity of making instruction universal and of having it
administered by the State ; the need of making instruction
obligatory, and, in certain grades, gratuitous ; the value of
intellectual culture as a moral safeguard.

2. The right of the State to self-preservation carries with
it the right to ordain the establishment of schools for giving
a certain kind and degree of instruction. This constitutes
the first form of compulsion.

3. When there is not a voluntary and general attendance
on the schools ordained by the State, it may avail itself of
the supplementary right to make attendance obligatory.
This constitutes the second form of compulsion.

4. Gratuity is the logical sequence to compulsion. If the
State may require all children to partake of a certain degree
of instruction. it must make such instruction free.

5. Should instruction that is above the compulsory grade
be free? This depends on the question whether the State

needs a certain amount of the higher culture, and whether this required amount will be secured at the pupils' own expense. Monsieur Compayré decides, as against Condorcet (paragraph 441), that the higher grades of instruction should not be gratuitous. In this country the prevailing theory is that the higher education should be endowed by the State.

6. The relation of instruction to morality has never been more justly and pointedly stated than in paragraph 433. This is not only good sense but sound philosophy.]

CHAPTER XVII.

THE CONVENTION. — LEPELLETIER SAINT-FARGEAU, LAKANAL, DAUNOU.

446. THE CONVENTION. — The Constituent Assembly and the Legislative Assembly had done nothing more than to prepare reports and projected decrees, without either discussing them or bringing them to a vote. The Convention went so far as to vote, but it did not have the time to execute the resolutions, contradictory and incoherent, which it was forced to adopt, one after another, by the fluctuation of political currents.

447. SUCCESSIVE MEASURES. — Nothing definite in the way of execution issued from the enthusiastic passion which the Convention exhibited for the organization of primary instruction. First there was a triumph of modern ideas in

the bill of Lanthenas, the first article of which was adopted December 12, 1792 ; and they appeared again in the bill of Sieyès, Dannon, and Lakanal, presented June 26, 1793, and defeated after an exciting discussion. But the influence of the Girondists was succeeded by the domination of the Montagnards[1] whose dictatorial and violent spirit is indicated : 1. in the bill of Lepelletier, adopted through the support of Robespierre, August 13, 1793 ; 2. in the bill projected and presented by Romme in behalf of the commission of public instruction, October 20, 1793, and passed on the following day ; 3. and lastly in the bill of Bouquier, which, presented December 19, 1793, became the decree of December 26. The reaction which followed resulted in the legislative acts by which the Convention finished its educational work. The bill of Sieyès, Daunou, and Lakanal was reconsidered, and November 17, 1793, it was substituted for the bill of Bouquier. Finally, when the constitution of 1794 was substituted for the constitution of 1793, a new law of public instruction was passed on the report of Daunou, October 27, 1795, and it is this law which presided over the organization of schools under the Directory.

In this confusion, this chaos of bills and counter-bills, it is difficult to establish any clew that is wholly trustworthy. We shall restrict ourselves to noting the points that seem essential.[2]

Impatient to finish its business, the committee on public

---

[1] A term applied to the most pronounced revolutionists of the Convention and of the National Assembly.

[2] It is impossible, within the limits prescribed by the character and plan of this work, to enter into detail and enumerate all the decrees and counter-decrees of the Convention on the subject of public instruction. To see clearly into this chaos and this confusion, it is necessary to read the excellent article of Monsieur Guillaume in the *Dictionnaire de Pédagogie*, article CONVENTION.

instruction, which the Convention had appointed October 2, 1792, decided to put aside, for the present, the other branches of public instruction, and proposed for immediate action only the organization of primary schools, by taking, as a point of departure, the bill which Condorcet had presented to the Legislative Assembly. The report of Lanthenas and a proposed decree were within a few weeks the results of these deliberations ; but in all its parts this result is scarcely more than the reproduction of Condorcet's work, and presents nothing original. Let us note, however, the idea of associating the pupil with his teacher in the work of instruction : —

"Teachers will call to their aid the pupils whose intelligence shall have made the most rapid progress ; and they will thus be able, *very easily*, to give to four classes of pupils, in the same session, all the attention needed for their progress. At the same time, the efforts made by the most competent to teach what they know to their schoolmates, will be much more instructive to themselves than the lessons they receive from their masters."

Further, let us notice title III. of the proposed decree relative to the measures to be taken in order to make obligatory the use of the French language, and to abolish the *patois*, or particular idioms. The minimum salary of men teachers was fixed at six hundred francs. The appointment of teachers was entrusted to the heads of families, who were to elect one from a list prepared by a " commission of educated persons" appointed by the Councils-General of the communes and the Directories of departments.

448. THE BILL OF LANTHENAS. — The discussion of the bill of Lanthenas began on December 12, 1792, but only article first was carried, and the bill itself did not become a law.

On December 20, another member of the Convention, Romme, mathematician, deputy from Puy-de-Dôme, read a new report on public instruction.

449. THE BILL OF ROMME. — The bill of Lanthenas aimed at only the first grade of instruction, but the report of Romme embraced the four grades of instruction, and was but little more than a reproduction of Condorcet's work. But no legislative measure followed the reading of his bill, and up to the 30th of May, 1793, there is scarcely anything to be noted, as the educational work of the Convention, save the bill of Raband Saint-Étienne on public festivals, and the report of Arbogast on elementary books.

450. NATIONAL HOLIDAYS. — It is difficult to form an idea of the importance which the men of this period attributed to the educational influence of national holidays. At variance on so many points, they all agree in thinking that the French people could be instructed and regenerated simply by establishing popular solemnities.

" It is a kind of institution," said Robespierre, " which ought to be considered as an essential part of public education, — I mean national holidays."

Daunou also persisted in considering national holidays as the most certain and the most comprehensive means of public instruction. The decree passed at his request established seven national holidays: that of the foundation of the Republic, of young men, of husbands, of thanksgiving, of agriculture, of liberty, of old men.

451. ELEMENTARY BOOKS. — An important point in the pedagogy of the Revolution was the attention given to the composition of elementary books. On several occasions the Convention put up at competition these modest works intended to aid parents or teachers in their task. It was one

of the happiest thoughts of that period to desire that there should be placed in the hands of parents simple methods and well-arranged books which might teach them how to bring up their children. The difficulty of this kind of composition was understood, and so application was made to the most distinguished writers. Bernardin de Saint-Pierre was employed to edit the *Elements of Morality*.

December 24, 1792, Arbogast had submitted to the Convention a proposed decree in which it was said : —

" It is only the superior men in a science, or in an art, those who have sounded all its depths, and have carried it to its farthest limits, who are capable of composing such elementary treatises as are desirable."

452. DECREE OF MAY 30, 1793. — The first decree of the Convention relative to primary schools was passed May 30, 1793. But this laconic law contained nothing very new. Besides, it was forgotten in the storm which on the next day, May 31, swept away the Girondists, and gave to the Montagnards the political supremacy.

453. LAKANAL (1762–1845). — After the revolution of May 31, among the men who, in the committee on public instruction and in the assembly itself, were occupied with the educational organization of France, we must assign the first place to Lakanal and Dannon. On June 26, 1793, three days after the adoption of the new constitution, Lakanal brought to the tribune the bill which he had drawn up in conjunction with Dannon and Sieyès.

Lakanal is one of the purest and most remarkable characters of the French Revolution.[1] " Lakanal," said Marat, to whom some one had denounced him, " works too much to

---

[1] See a recent sketch, *Lakanal*, by Paul Legendre (Paris, 1882), with a Preface by Paul Bert.

have the time to conspire." Industrious and thoughtful, after having taught philosophy with the "Doctrinaires," of whom he was the pupil, he became the first, after Condorcet, of the educators of the Revolution. "His appearance," says Paul Bert, "has always particularly attracted me. It unites gentleness with force, energy with serenity. We feel that this austere citizen has never known any other passion than that of well-doing, and has neither desired nor obtained any other reward than that of having done his duty. He despises violence of language, and hates that of acts; and so we do not find him, under the Empire, a baron like Jean-Bon Saint André, a minister like Fouché, or a senator like a whole herd."

454. Daunou (1761–1840). — At an early period in his life, Dannou had taught philosophy in the colleges of the Oratorians, of whom he was a member. In 1789 he published in the *Journal Encyclopédique*, a plan of national education which was approved by the Oratory, and which he presented to the Constituent Assembly in 1790. In the Convention he took an active part in the work of the committee on public instruction, and assisted in the preparation of Lakanal's first bill. In the same year he published an *Essay on Public Instruction.* In the Council of the Five Hundred he was appointed to make a report on the organization of special schools. Under the Empire he accepted the management of the national archives. Under the Restoration he was appointed professor of history in the College of France. Finally, after 1830, we find him once more in the Chamber of Deputies, giving proof of unusual energy and vitality, and presenting in opposition to the minister of public instruction, de Montalivet, a counter-bill, the principal aim of which was to lodge with the municipal authorities the administration of schools, a power which the government wished to leave in the hands of the inspectors.

455. THE BILL OF LAKANAL, SIEYÈS, AND DAUNOU. —
These are the principal provisions of this bill : a school for
each thousand inhabitants ; separate schools for girls and
boys ; the election of teachers entrusted to a board of inspectors composed of three members, and located at the government centre of each district ; the general organization of
methods, regulations, and school régime placed in the hands
of a central commission sitting with the Corps Lègislatif,
and placed under its authority ; an education which embraces
the whole man, at once intellectual, physical, moral, and industrial ; the first lessons in reading given to boys as to girls
by a woman teacher; arithmetic, geometry, physics, and
morals included in the programme of instruction ; visits to
hospitals, prisons, and workshops ; finally, liberty granted to
private initiative to found schools.

" The law can put no veto on the right which all citizens
have to open private courses and schools, free in all grades
of instruction, and to direct them as shall seem to them
best." (Art. 61.)

This was pushing liberality rather far.

Another distinctive feature of this bill, which is not without value, is the respect shown the character and functions
of the teacher. On public occasions the schoolmaster shall
wear a medal with this inscription : *He who instructs is a
second father.* The form is rather pretentious, but the sentiment is good. Other articles do not merit the same commendation, particularly the one which established theatres in
each canton, in which men and women would take part in
music and dancing.

The bill of Lakanal, vigorously opposed by a part of the
Assembly, was not adopted. Under the leadership of Robespierre, the Convention gave preference to the dictatorial and
violent measure of Lepelletier Saint-Fargeau.

456. LEPELLETIER SAINT-FARGEAU (1760–1793). — Assassinated in 1793, Lepelletier Saint-Fargeau left among his papers an educational bill which Robespierre took up, and which he presented to the Assembly July 13, 1793, on the occasion of the debate opened on the motion of Barrère. A month later the bill was passed by the Convention, but before being carried into operation, the decree was revoked. The Assembly receded from the accomplishment of a reform in which some good intentions could not atone for measures that, on the whole, were mischievous and tyrannical.

457. HIS SCHEME OF EDUCATION. — The plan of Lepelletier scarcely deserves the admiration which Michelet gives it, who salutes in this work the "*revolution of childhood*," and who declares that it is " admirable in spirit, and in no respect chimerical." An imitation with but little originality of the institutions of Lycurgus and the reveries of Plato, the plan of Lepelletier is scarcely more than an historical curiosity.

458. LEPELLETIER AND CONDORCET. — Lepelletier accepted Condorcet's plan in all that relates to *secondary schools, institutes*, and *lycées*, that is to say, higher primary instruction, secondary instruction, and superior instruction.

" I find," he said, " in these three courses a plan which seems to me wisely conceived."

But Lepelletier follows only his own fancy in the conception of those curious boarding-schools, little barracks for childhood, in which he confined all children by force, wresting them from their parents, and placing at the expense of the State their moral training, as well as their material support.

459. OBLIGATORY ATTENDANCE IN BOARDING-SCHOOLS. — In education, Lepelletier represents the doctrine of the Jacobins. In order to make France republican, he would employ radical and absolute measures.

" Let us ordain," he says, " that all children, girls as well as boys, girls from five to eleven, and boys from five to twelve, shall be educated in common, at the expense of the State, and shall receive, for six or seven years, the same education."

In order that there may be complete equality, their food, like their instruction, shall be the same ; even more, their dress shall be identical. Does Lepelletier then desire, in his craze for equality, that girls shall be dressed like boys?

460. THE CHILD BELONGS TO THE REPUBLIC. — The idea of Lepelletier is that the child is the property of the State, a chattel of the Republic. The State must make the child in its own image.

" In our system," he says, " the entire being of the child belongs to us ; the material never leaves the mould." And he adds, " Whatever is to compose the Republic ought to be cast in the republican mould."

Lepelletier imposes on all children, girls and boys, the same studies, — reading, writing, numbers, natural morality, domestic economy. This is almost the programme of Condorcet. But he adds to it manual labor. All children shall be employed in working the soil. If the college has not at its disposal enough land to cultivate, the children shall be taken out on the roads, there to pick up stones or to scatter them. Can we imagine, without smiling, a system of education, in which our future advocates and writers are to spend six years in transporting material upon the highways?

461. ABSOLUTE GRATUITY. — The colleges in which Lepelletier sequesters and quarters all the children are to be absolutely free. Three measures were proposed for covering the expense : 1. tuition paid by parents in easy circumstances ; 2. the labor of the children ; 3. the balance needed furnished

by the State. But is there not just a little of the chimerical in counting much on the work of children of that age?

462. The Rights of the Family. — Lepelletier takes but little account of the rights of the family. However, notice must be taken of that idea which Robespierre thought " sublime," — the creation, at each college, of a council of heads of families, entrusted with the oversight of teachers and their children.

463. Saint-Just. — Saint-Just, in his *Institutions républicaines*, maintains opinions analogous to those of Lepelletier. He admits that the child belongs to his mother till the age of five ; but from the age of five till death he belongs to the Republic. Till the age of sixteen boys are fed at the expense of the State. It is true that their food is not expensive. It is composed of grapes, fruit, vegetables, milk-diet, bread, and water. Their dress is of cotton in all seasons. However, Saint-Just did not subject girls to the same régime. More liberal on this point than Lepelletier, he would have them brought up at home.

464. The Romme Law (Oct. 30, 1793). — Romme was one of the most active members of the committee on public instruction. He was the principal author of the bill which the Convention passed in October, 1793, the principal articles of which were conceived as follows —:

" Art. 1. There are primary schools distributed throughout the Republic in proportion to the population.

" Art. 2. In these schools children receive their earliest physical, moral, and intellectual education, the best adapted to develop in them republican manners, love of country, and taste for labor.

" Art. 3. They learn to speak, read, and write the French language.

" They are taught the acts of virtue which most honor free men, and particularly the acts of the French Revolution most fit to give them elevation of soul, and to make them worthy of liberty and equality.

" They acquire some notions of the geography of France.

" The knowledge of the rights and duties of the man and the citizen is brought within their comprehension through examples and their own experience.

" They are given the first notions of the natural objects that surround them, and of the natural action of the elements.

" They have practice in the use of numbers, of the compass, the level, weights and measures, the lever, the pulley, and in the measurement of time.

" They are often allowed to witness what is done in the fields and in workshops ; and they take part in these employments as far as their age permits."

But the bill of Romme was not put in operation. The Convention presently decided on a revision of the decree it had passed, and the bill of Bouquier was substituted for the bill of Romme.

465. THE BOUQUIER LAW (Dec. 19, 1793). — Bouquier was a man of letters, deputy from Dordogne, and belonged to the Jacobinic party. He spoke of his bill as follows : —

" It is a simple and natural scheme, and one easy to execute ; a plan which forever proscribes all idea of an academic body, of a scientific society, of an educational hierarchy ; a plan, finally, whose bases are the same as those of the constitution, liberty, equality, and simplicity."

The Bouquier bill was adopted December 19, and remained in force till it was superseded by the Lakanal law.

These are its principal provisions : —

" The right to teach is open to all." " Citizens, men and women, who would use the liberty to teach, shall be required to produce a certificate of citizenship and good morals, and to fulfill certain formalities." " They shall be designated as *instituteurs* and *institutrices*." They shall be placed " under the immediate supervision of the municipality, of parents, and of all the citizens." " They are forbidden to teach anything contrary to the laws and to republican morality." On the other hand, parents are required to send their children to the primary schools. Parents who do not obey this order are sentenced, for the first offence, to pay a fine equal to a fourth of their school tax. In case of a second offence, the fine is to be doubled and the children to be suspended for ten years from their rights as citizens. Finally, young people who, on leaving the primary schools, " do not busy themselves with the cultivation of the soil, shall be required to learn a trade useful to society."

Enforced school attendance, and what is an entirely different thing, the obligation of citizens to work, were thus established by the Bouquier law.

Let us add that the author of this bill, which, like so many others, was not executed, had strange notions on the sciences and on instruction.

" The speculative sciences," he says, " detach from society the individuals who cultivate them. . . . Free nations have no need of speculative scholars, whose minds are constantly travelling over desert paths."

Hence, no scientific instruction. The real schools, " the noblest, the most useful, the most simple, are the meetings of committees. The Revolution, in establishing national holidays, in creating popular associations and clubs, has placed in all quarters inexhaustible sources of instruction. Then let us not go and substitute for this organization, as

simple and sublime as the people that creates it, an artificial
organization, based on academic statutes which should no
longer infect a regenerated nation."

466. THE LAKANAL LAW (Nov. 17, 1794). — There still
remained something of the spirit of Lepelletier in the Bouquier
law, though the idea of an education in common had been
abandoned ; but the Lakanal law openly breaks with the tendencies of Robespierre and his friends.

The law which was passed November 17, 1794, upon the
report of Lakanal, reproduced in its spirit and in its principal
provisions the original bill which the influence of Robespierre
had defeated.

The following was the programme of instruction contained
in this law.

The instructor shall teach : —

" 1. Reading and writing ; 2. the declaration of the
rights of man and the constitution ; 3. elementary lessons
on republican morals ; 4. the elements of the French language both spoken and written ; 5. the rules of simple calculation and of surveying ; 6. lessons on the principal
phenomena and the most common productions of nature ;
there shall be taught a collection of heroic actions and songs
of triumph."

At the same time the bill required that the schools be
divided into two sections, one for the girls and the other for
the boys, and distributed in the proportion of one to each
thousand inhabitants. The teachers, nominated by the people
and confirmed by a jury of instruction, are to receive salaries
as follows : men, twelve hundred francs ; women, one thousand francs.

467. PEDAGOGICAL METHODS. — Lakanal had given much
thought to pedagogical methods. It is the interior of the
school, not less than its exterior organization, that preoc-

cupied his generous spirit. Like the most of his contemporaries, a partisan of Condillac's doctrine, he believed that the idea could not reach the understanding except through the mediation of the senses. Consequently, he recommended the method which consists "in first appealing to the eyes of pupils, . . . in creating the understanding through the senses, . . . in developing morals out of the sensibility, just as understanding out of sensation." This is an excellent method if we add to it a corrective, if we do not forget to excite the intelligence itself, and to make an appeal to the interior forces of the soul.

468. ELEMENTARY BOOKS. — A few other quotations will suffice to prove with what acuteness of pedagogic sense Lakanal was endowed.[1] Very much interested in the composition of works for popular instruction, he sharply distinguished the elementary book, which brings knowledge within the reach of children, from the abridgment, which does no more than condense a long work. "The abridged," he said, "is exactly opposed to the elementary." No one has better comprehended than he the difficulty of writing a treatise on morals for the use of children : —

"It requires special genius. Simplicity in form and artless grace should there be mingled with accuracy of ideas; the art of reasoning ought never to be separated from that of interesting the imagination; such a work should be conceived by a profound logician and executed by a man of feeling. There should be found in it, so to speak, the analytical mind of Condillac and the soul of Fénelon."

469. GEOGRAPHY. — Lakanal has defined with the same exactness the method to be followed in the teaching of geography. "First let there be shown," he says, "in

---

[1] See in the *Revue politique et littéraire*, for Oct. 7, 1882, an excellent article on Lakanal, by Monsieur Janet.

every school, the plan of the commune in which it is situated, and then let the children see a map of the canton of which the commune forms a part; then a map of the department, and then a map of France; after which will come the map of Europe and of other parts of the world, and lastly a map of the world.[1]

470. LETTERS AND SCIENCES. — More just than Condorcet, Lakanal did not wish scientific culture to do prejudice to literary culture : —

" For a long time we have neglected the belles-lettres, and some men who wish to be considered profound regard this study as useless. It is letters, however, which open the intelligence to the light of reason, and the heart to impressions of sentiment. They substitute morality for interest, give pupils polish, exercise their judgment, make them more sensitive and at the same time more obedient to the laws, more capable of grand virtues."

471. NECESSITY OF NORMAL SCHOOLS. — Lakanal's highest title to glory is that he has associated his name with the foundation of normal schools. The idea of establishing pedagogical seminaries was not absolutely new. A number of the friends of instruction, both in the seventeenth and in the eighteenth century,[2] had seen that it would be useless to open schools, if good teachers had not been previously

---

[1] If the consensus of philosophic opinion is trustworthy, there is no basis whatever in psychology for this sequence. On the almost uniform testimony of psychologists, the organic mental sequence is from aggregates to parts; so that if the method of presentation is to be in harmony with the organic mode of the mind's activities, the sequence should be as follows: the globe; the eastern continent; Europe; France; the department; the canton; the commune. On the mental sequence, see Hamilton's *Lectures*, Vol. I. pp. 69, 70, 368, 371, 469, 498, 500, 502, 503. (P.)

[2] Dumonstier, rector of the University of Paris in 1645, La Salle, and in the eighteenth century, the Abbé Courtalon.

trained; but the Convention has the honor of having for the first time given practical effect to this vague aspiration.

Decreed June 2, 1793, the foundation of normal schools was the object of a report by Lakanal on October 26, 1794. In a style which was inferior to his ideas, and which would have been more effective had it been simpler, Lakanal sets forth the necessity of teaching the teachers themselves before sending them to teach their pupils: —

"Are there in France, are there in Europe, are there in the whole world, two or three hundred men (and we need more than this number) competent to teach the useful arts and the necessary branches of knowledge, according to methods which make minds more acute, and truths more clear, — methods which, while teaching you to know one thing, teach you to reason upon all things? No, that number of men, however small it may appear, exists nowhere on the earth. It is necessary, then, that they be trained. In being the first to decree normal schools, you have resolved to create in advance a very large number of teachers, capable of being the executors of a plan whose purpose is the regeneration of the human understanding, in a republic of twenty-five millions of men, all of whom democracy renders equal."

The term *normal schools* (from the Latin word *norma*, a rule) was not less new than the thing. Lakanal explains that it was designed by this expression to characterize with exactness the schools which were to be the type and the standard of all the others.

472. THE NORMAL SCHOOL OF PARIS. — To accomplish his purpose, Lakanal proposed to assemble at Paris, under the direction of eminent masters, such as Lagrange, Berthollet, and Daubenton, a considerable number of young men, called from all quarters of the Republic, and designated "by their talents as by their state of citizenship." The masters

of this great normal school were to give their pupils " lessons
on the art of teaching morals, . . . and teach them to apply
to the teaching of reading and writing, of the first elements
of calculation, of practical geometry, of history and of
French grammar, the methods outlined in the elementary
courses adopted by the National Convention and published
by its orders." Once instructed " in the art of teaching
human knowledge," the pupils of the Normal School of Paris
were to go and repeat in all parts of the Republic the " grand
lectures " they had heard, and there form the nucleus of provincial normal schools. And thus, says Lakanal with exaggeration, " that fountain of enlightenment, so pure and so
abundant, since it will proceed from the foremost men of the
Republic of every class, poured out from reservoir to reservoir, will diffuse itself from place to place throughout all
France, without losing anything of its purity in its course."

October 30, 1794, the Convention adopted the proposals
of Lakanal. The Normal School opened January 20, 1795.
Its organization was defective and impracticable. First, there
were too many pupils, — four hundred young men admitted
without competitive tests, and abandoned to themselves in
Paris ; professors who were doubtless illustrious, but whose
literary talent or scientific genius did not perhaps adapt itself
sufficiently to the needs of a normal course of instruction and
of a practical pedagogy ; lectures insufficient in number,
which lasted for only four months, and which, on the testimony of Dannon, " were directed rather towards the heights
of science than towards the art of teaching." Thus the
experiment, which terminated May 6, 1795, did not fulfill
the hopes that had been formed of it : the idea of establishing provincial normal schools was not carried out. But no
matter ; a memorable example had been given, and the fruitful principle of the establishment of normal schools had made
a start in actual practice.

473. CENTRAL SCHOOLS. — The *central schools*, designed to replace the colleges of secondary instruction, were established by decree of February 25, 1795, on the report of Lakanal. Dannou modified them in the law of October 25, 1795. They continued, without great success, till the law of May 1, 1802, which suppressed them.

474. DEFECTS OF THE CENTRAL SCHOOLS. — The Central Schools of Lakanal resembled, trait for trait, the Institutes of Condorcet. And it must be confessed that here the imitation is not happy. Lakanal made the mistake of borrowing from Condorcet the plan of these poorly defined establishments, in which the instruction was on too vast a scale, and the programmes too crowded, where the pupil, it seems, was to learn to discuss *de omni re scibili*. Condorcet went so far as to introduce into his Institutes a course of lectures on midwifery! The Central Schools, in which the instruction was a defile. of studies indiscreetly presented to an overdriven auditory, do honor neither to the Convention that organized them, nor to Condorcet who had traced the first sketch of them.

475. POSITIVE AND PRACTICAL SPIRIT. — However, there was something correct in the idea which presided over the foundation of the Central Schools. We find this expressed in the *Essays on Instruction*, by the mathematician, Lacroix.[1] Lacroix calls attention to the fact that the progress of the sciences and the necessity of learning a great number of new things, impose on the educator the obligation to take some account of space ; and, if I may so speak, of clipping the wings of studies which, like Latin, had thus far been the unique and exclusive object of instruction. .

---

[1] Essais sur l'enseignement. Paris, 1805.

In the Central Schools, in fact, the classical languages held only the second place. Not only were the mathematical sciences, and those branches of knowledge from which the pupil can derive the most immediate profit, associated with the classics, but the preference was given to them. In the minds of those who organized these schools, the positive and practical idea of success in life was substituted for the speculative and disinterested idea of mental development for its own sake. In reality, these two ideas ought to complete each other, and not to exclude each other. The ideal of education consists in finding a system which welcomes both. But in the Central Schools the first point of view absorbed the second. These establishments resembled the industrial schools of our day, but with this particular defect, that there was a determination to include everything in them, and to give a place to new studies without wholly sacrificing the old. Let there be created colleges of practical and special instruction ; nothing can be better, for provision would thus be made for the needs of modern society. But let no one force literary studies and the industrial arts to live together under the same roof.

476. GREAT FOUNDATIONS OF THE CONVENTION. — In the first years of its existence, the Convention had given its attention only to primary schools. It seemed as though teaching the illiterate to read was the one need of society. In the end the Convention rose above these narrow and exclusive views, and turned its attention towards secondary instruction and towards superior instruction. It is particularly by the establishment of several special schools for superior instruction that the Convention gave proof of its versatility and intelligence. .

In quick-succession it decreed and founded the Polytechnic School, under the name of the Central School of Public Works

(March 11, 1794) ; the Normal School (October 30, 1794) ; the School of Mars (June 1, 1794) ; the Conservatory of Arts and Trades (September 29, 1794). The next year it organized the Bureau of Longitudes, and finally the National Institute. What a magnificent effort to repair the ruins which anarchy had made, or to supply the omissions which the old régime had patiently suffered ! Of these multiplied creations the greater number remain and still flourish.

477. LAW OF OCTOBER 27, 1795. — Those who ask us to see in the decree of October 27, 1795, " the capital work of the Convention in the matter of instruction, the synthesis of all its previous labors and proposals, the most serious effort of the Revolution,"[1] evidently put forward a paradox. Lakanal and his friends would certainly have disavowed a law which cancels with a few strokes of the pen the grand revolutionary principles in the matter of education, — the gratuity, the obligation, and the universality of instruction.

The destinies of public instruction are allied to the fate of constitutions. To changes of policy there correspond, by an inevitable recoil, analogous changes in the organization of instruction. Out of the slightly retrograde constitution of 1793 there issued the educational legislation of 1794, of which it could be said that " the spirit of reaction made itself painfully felt in it."

Daunou, who was the principal author of it, doubtless had high competence in questions of public instruction ; but with a secret connivance of his own temperament he yielded to the tendencies of the times. He voluntarily condescended to the timidities of a senile and worn-out Assembly, which, having become impoverished by a series of suicides, had scarcely any superior minds left within it.

[1] Albert Duruy, *op. cit.* p. 137.

478. Insufficiency of Daunou's Scheme. — Nothing could be more defective than Dannou's plan. The number of primary schools was reduced. It is no longer proposed to proportion them to the population. Dannon goes back to the cantonal schools of Talleyrand : " There shall be established in each canton of the Republic one or more primary schools." We are far from Condorcet, who required a school for each group of four hundred souls, and from Lakanal, who demanded one for each thousand inhabitants. On the other hand, teachers no longer receive a salary from the State. The State merely assures to them a place for a class-room and lodging, and also a garden ! " There shall likewise be furnished the teacher the garden which happens to lie near these premises." There is no other remuneration save the annual tuition paid by each pupil to the teacher. At the same stroke the teacher was made the hireling of his pupils, and gratuity of instruction was abolished. Only the indigent pupils, a fourth of the whole number, could be exempted by the municipal administration from the payment of school fees. Finally, the programme of studies was reduced to the humblest proportions : reading, writing, number, and the elements of republican morality.

After so many noble and generous ambitions, after so many enthusiastic declarations in favor of the absolute gratuity of primary instruction, after so many praiseworthy efforts to raise the material and moral condition of teachers, and to cause instruction to circulate to the minutest fibres of the social tissue, the Convention terminated its work in a mean conception which thinned out the schools, which impoverished the programmes, which plunged the teacher anew into a precarious state of existence, which put him anew at the mercy of his pupils, without, however, taking care to assure him of patronage, and which, for his sole compensation in case he had no pupils to instruct, guaranteed him the right to cultivate a garden, if, indeed, there should be one in the neighborhood of the school! Had the law of 1795 been in fact the educational will of the Convention, is it not true, at least, that it is after the manner of those wills extorted by undue means, where a man by his final bequests recalls his former acts, and proves himself faithless to all the aspirations of his life?

No, it is not from Dannon, but from Talleyrand, from Condorcet, and from Lakanal that we must seek the real educational thought of the Revolution. Doubtless the measure of Dannou had over all previous measures the advantages of being applied, and of not remaining a dead letter; but the glory of the early Revolutionists should not be belittled by the fact that circumstances arrested the execution of their plans, and that a century was necessary in order that society might attain the ideal which they had conceived. They were the first to proclaim the right and the duty of each citizen to be instructed and enlightened. We are ceaselessly urged to admire the past and to respect the work of our fathers. We do not in the least object to this, but the Revolution itself also forms a part of that past, and we regret that the men who so eloquently preach the worship of traditions and respect for ancestors, are precisely those who the most harshly disparage the efforts of the Revolution.

[479. ANALYTICAL SUMMARY. — 1. The educational legislation of the French Revolution, apparently so inconsiderate, so vacillating, and so fruitless, betrays the instinctive feeling of a nation in peril, that the only constitutional means of regeneration is universal instruction, intellectual and moral.

2. Out of the same instinct grew the conception that the starting-point in educational reform is the instruction and

inspiration of the teaching body. The normal school lies at the very basis of national safety and prosperity.

3. The immediate fruitlessness of the educational legislation of the Revolution, is another illustration of the general fact that no reform is operative, which in any considerable degree antedates the existing state of public opinion. Could there be a revelation of the ideal education, human society could grow into it only by slow and almost insensible degrees. While there can be rational growth only through some degree of anticipation, it is perhaps best that educators have only that prevision which is provisional.]

CHAPTER XVIII.

PESTALOZZI.

GERMAN PEDAGOGY; THE PIETISTS AND FRANCKE (1663–1727); THE PHILANTHROPISTS AND BASEDOW (1723–1790); THE PEOPLE'S SCHOOLS; PESTALOZZI (1746–1827); THE EDUCATION OF PESTALOZZI; PESTALOZZI AS AN AGRICULTURIST; HOW PESTALOZZI BECAME A TEACHER; EDUCATION OF HIS SON; THE SCHOOL AT NEUHOF (1775–1780); PESTALOZZI AS A WRITER (1780–1787); LEONARD AND GERTRUDE (1781); NEW EXPERIMENTS IN AGRICULTURE; OTHER WORKS; THE ORPHAN ASYLUM AT STANZ (1798–1799); METHODS FOLLOWED AT STANZ; THE SCHOOLS AT BURGDORF (1799–1801); HOW GERTRUDE TEACHES HER CHILDREN (1801); PESTALOZZI'S STYLE; ANALYSIS OF THE GERTRUDE; THE INSTITUTE AT BURGDORF (1801–1804); THE INSTITUTE AT YVERDUN (1805–1825); TENTATIVES OF PESTALOZZI; ESSENTIAL PRINCIPLES; EDUCATIONAL PROCESSES; SIMPLIFICATION OF METHODS; ANALYTICAL SUMMARY.

480. GERMAN PEDAGOGY. — For two centuries Germany has been the classical land of pedagogy; and to render an account of all the efforts put forth in that country in the domain of education it would be necessary to write several volumes.

From the opening of the eighteenth century, says Dittes, "a change for the better takes place. Ideas become facts. The importance of education is more and more recognized; pedagogy shakes off the ancient dust of the school and interests itself in actual life; it is no longer willing to be a collateral function of the Church, but begins to become an independent art and science. A few theologians will still render it important service, but in general they will do this outside the Church, and often in opposition to it."

While awaiting the grand and fruitful impulsion of Pestalozzi, the history of pedagogy ought to mention at least the
Pietists, "whose educational establishments contributed to
prepare the way for the new methods," and after them, the
Philanthropists, of whom Basedow is the most celebrated
representative.

481. The Pietists and Francke (1663–1727).— Francke
played nearly the same part in Germany that La Salle did in
France. He founded two establishments at Halle, the *Pædagogium* and the *Orphan Asylum*, which, in 1727, contained
more than two thousand pupils. He belonged to the sect of
Pietists, Lutherans who professed an austere morality, and,
in conformity with the principles of his denomination, he
made piety the supreme end of education.

That which distinguishes and commends Francke, is his
talent for organization. He was right in giving marked attention to the material condition of schools and to needed
supplies of apparatus. The Pædagogium was installed in 1715
in comfortable quarters, and there were annexed to it a
botanical garden, a museum of natural history, physical apparatus, a chemical and an anatomical laboratory, and a shop
for the cutting and polishing of glass.

After him his disciples, Niemeyer, Semler, and Hecker,
continued his work, and, in certain respects, reformed it.
They founded the first *real schools* of Germany. They kept
up the practical spirit, the professional pedagogy of their
master, and assured the development of those educational
establishments which still exist to-day under the name of
the *Institutions* of Francke.

482. The Philanthropists and Basedow (1723–1790).—
With Basedow, a more liberal spirit, borrowed in part from
Rousseau, gained entrance into German pedagogy. Basedow

founded at Dessau a school which received the praise of the philosopher Kant, and of the clergyman Oberlin. He designated it by a name which reflects his humanitarian intentions, the *Philanthropinum*. In the methods which he employed in it he seems always to have had before his eyes the exclamation of Rousseau: "Things, things! Too many words!" The intuitive method, or that of *teaching by sight*, was practised in the school of Dessau.

The principal work of Basedow, his *Elementary Book*, is scarcely more than the *Orbis Pictus* of Comenius reconstructed according to the principles of Rousseau. At Dessau, the pretence was made of teaching a language in six months. "Our methods," says Basedow, "make studies only one-third as long and thrice as agreeable." An abuse was made of mechanical exercises. The children, at the command of the master : *Imitamini sartorem, — Imitamini sutorem*, — all began to imitate the motions of a tailor who is sewing, or of a shoemaker who is using his awl. Graver still, Basedow made such an abuse of *object lessons* as to represent to children certain scenes within the sick-chamber, for the purpose of teaching them their duties and obligations to their mothers.[1]

483. SCHOOLS FOR THE PEOPLE. — Great efforts were made in the eighteenth century, in the Catholic, as well as in the Protestant countries of Germany, towards the development of popular instruction. Maria Theresa and Frederick II. considered public instruction as an affair of the State. Private enterprise was added to the efforts of the government. In Prussia, a nobleman, Rochow (1734–1805), founded village

---

1 Besides Basedow, there should be mentioned among the educators who have become noted in Germany under the name of Philanthropists, Salzman (1744–1811) and Campe (1746–1818).

schools; and in Austria, two ecclesiastics, Felbiger (1724–1788) and Kindermann (1740–1801), contributed by their activity in education to the reform of schools.

Nevertheless, the results were still very poor, and the public school, especially the village school, remained in a sorry condition.

" Almost everywhere," says Dittes, " there were employed as teachers, domestics, corrupt artisans, discharged soldiers, degraded students, and, in general, persons of questionable morality and education. Their pay was mean, and their authority slight. Attendance at school, generally very irregular, was almost everywhere entirely suspended in summer. Many villages had no school, and scarcely anywhere was the school attended by all the children. In many countries, most of the children, especially the girls, were wholly without instruction. The people, especially the peasantry, regarded the school as a burden. The clergy, it is true, always regarded themselves as the proprietors of the school, but on the whole they did but very little for it, and even arrested its progress. The nobility was but little favorable, in general, to intellectual culture for the people. . . . Instruction remained mechanical and the discipline rude. It is reported that a Suabian schoolmaster, who died in 1782, had inflicted during his experience in teaching 911,527 canings, 124,010 whippings, 10,235 boxes on the ear, and 1,115,800 thumps on the head. Moreover, he had made boys kneel 777 times on triangular sticks, had caused the fool's cap to be worn 5001[1] times, and the stick to be held in air 1707 times. He had used something like 3000 words of abuse. . . ."

---

[1] What a painstaking soul to be so exact in his accounts! Doubtless he had an eye to the future publication of his record as a *maitre de fouet!* This account is rather too exact to be trustworthy. (P.)

484. PESTALOZZI (1746-1827). — In Switzerland, the situation of primary instruction was scarcely better. The \ teachers were gathered up at hazard ; their pay was wretched ; in general they had no lodgings of their own, and they were obliged to hire themselves out for domestic service among the well-off inhabitants of the villages, in order to find food and lodging among them. A mean spirit of caste still dominated instruction, and the poor remained sunk in ignorance.

It was in the very midst of this wretched and unpropitious state of affairs that there appeared, towards the end of the eighteenth century, the most celebrated of modern educators, a man who, we may be sure, was not exempt from faults, whose mind had deficiencies and weaknesses, and whom we have no intention of shielding from criticism, by covering him with the praises of a superstitious admiration ; but who is pre-eminently great by reason of his unquenchable love for the people, his ardent self-sacrifice, and his pedagogic instinct. During the eighty years of his troubled life, Pestalozzi never ceased to work for children, and to devote himself to their instruction. War or the ill-will of his countrymen destroyed his schools to no purpose. Without ever despairing, he straightway rebuilt them farther away, sometimes succeeding, through the gift of ardent speech, which never deserted him, in communicating the inspiration to those about him ; gathering up in all places orphans and vagabonds, like a kidnapper of a new species ; forgetting that he was poor, when he saw an occasion to be charitable, and that he was ill, when it was necessary to teach ; and, finally, pursuing with an unconquerable energy, through hindrances and obstacles of every description, his educational apostleship. " It is death or success ! " he wrote. " My zeal to accomplish the dream of my life would have carried me through air or through fire, no matter how, to the highest peak of the Alps ! "

485. THE EDUCATION OF PESTALOZZI. — The life of Pestalozzi is intimately related to his educational work. To
comprehend the educator, it is first necessary to have become
acquainted with the man.

Born at Zurich in 1746, Pestalozzi died at Brugg in Argovia in 1827. This unfortunate great man always felt the
effects of the sentimental and unpractical education given
him by his mother, who was left a widow with three children
in 1751. He early formed the habit of feeling and of being
touched with emotion, rather than of reasoning and of reflecting. The laughing-stock of his companions, who made sport
of his awkwardness, the little scholar of Zurich accustomed
himself to live alone and to become a dreamer. Later,
towards 1760, the student of the academy distinguished himself by his political enthusiasm and his revolutionary daring.
At that early period he had conceived a profound feeling for
the miseries and the needs of the people, and he already proposed as the purpose of his life the healing of the diseases of
society. At the same time there was developed in him an
irresistible taste for a simple, frugal, and almost ascetic life.
To restrain his desires had become the essential rule of his
conduct, and, to put it in practice, he forced himself to sleep
on a plank, and to subsist on bread and vegetables. Life in
the open air had an especial attraction for him. Each year
he spent his vacations in the country at his grandfather's, who
was a minister at Hœngg. *Omne malum ex urbe* was his
favorite thought.

486. PESTALOZZI AN AGRICULTURIST (1765–1775). — Pestalozzi's call to be a teacher manifested itself at first only by
some vague aspirations, of which it would be easy to find the
trace in the short essays of his youth, and in the articles
which he contributed in his twentieth year to a students'
journal published at Zurich. After having tried his hand

unsuccessfully at theology and law, he became an agriculturist. When he established at Neuhof an agricultural enterprise, he thought less of enriching himself than of raising the material condition of the Swiss peasantry by organizing new industries. But notwithstanding his good intent, and the assistance of the devoted woman whom he had married in 1769, Anna Schultess, Pestalozzi, more enterprising than skillful, failed in his industrial establishments. In 1775 he had exhausted his resources. It is then that he formed an heroic resolution which typifies his indiscreet generosity. Poor, and scarcely more than able to support himself, he opened on his farm an asylum for poor children.

487. HOW PESTALOZZI BECAME AN EDUCATOR. — The asylum for poor children at Neuhof (1775–1780) is, so to speak, the first step in the pedagogical career of Pestalozzi. The others will be the orphan asylum at Stanz (1798–1799), the primary schools at Burgdorf (1799), the institute at Burgdorf (1801–1804), and, finally, the institute at Yverdun (1805–1825).

The first question that is raised when we study systems of education, is, how the authors of those systems became teachers.

The best, perhaps, are those who became such because of their great love for humanity, or because of their tender love for their children. Pestalozzi is of this class. It is because he has ardently dreamed from his youth of the moral amelioration of the people ; and it is also because he has followed with a tender solicitude the first steps of his little son Jacob on life's journey, that he became a great teacher.

488. THE EDUCATION OF HIS SON. — The *Father's Journal*,[1] where Pestalozzi noted from day to day the progress of

---

[1] See interesting quotations from the "*Journal d'un père*," in the excellent biography of Pestalozzi, by Roger de Guimps.

his child, shows him intent on applying the principles of
Rousseau. At the age of eleven, Jacob, like Émile, did not
yet know how to read or to write. Things before words, the
intuition of sensible objects, few exercises in judgment,
respect for the powers of the child, an equal anxiety to husband his liberty and to secure his obedience, the constant
endeavor to diffuse joy and good humor over education, —
such were the principal traits of the education which Pestalozzi gave his son, an education which was a real experiment
in pedagogy, from which the pupil perhaps suffered somewhat, but from which humanity was to derive profit. From
this period Pestalozzi conceived some of the ideas which became the principles of his method. The father had made the
educator. One of the superiorities of Pestalozzi over Rousseau is, that he loved and educated his own child.

489. THE ASYLUM AT NEUHOF. — Madame de Staël was
right in saying that "we must consider Pestalozzi's school
as limited to childhood. The education which it gives is
designed only for the common people." And, in fact, the
first and the last establishments of Pestalozzi were schools
for small children. In the last years of his life, when he
was obliged to leave the institute of Yverdun, he returned
to Neuhof, and there had constructed a school for poor
children.

The school at Neuhof was to be above all else, in Pestalozzi's thought, an experiment in moral and material regen-
cration through labor, through order, and through instruction.
Many exercises in language, singing, reading of the Bible, —
such were the intellectual occupations. But the greater part
of the time was devoted to agricultural labor, to the cultivation of madder.

Notwithstanding his admirable devotion, Pestalozzi did not
long succeed in his philanthropic plans. He had to contend

against the prejudices of parents, and the ingratitude of the
children. Very often the little beggars whom he had gathered up waited only till they had received from him new
clothing, and then ran away and resumed their vagabond
life. Besides, he lacked resources. He became poor, and
fell more and more into debt. His friends, who had aided
him on the start, warned him that he would die in a hospital
or in a mad-house.

"For thirty years," he says himself, "my life was a desperate struggle against the most frightful poverty. . . . More
than a thousand times I was obliged to go without dinner,
and at noon, when even the poorest were seated around a
table, I devoured a morsel of bread upon the highway . . . ;
and all this that I might minister to the needs of the poor,
by the realization of my principles."

490. PESTALOZZI A WRITER. — After the check to his undertaking at Neuhof, Pestalozzi renounced for some time all
practical activity, and it was by his writings that he manifested, from 1780 to 1787, his zeal in education.

In 1780 appeared the *Evening Hours of a Recluse*, a series
of aphorisms on the rise of a people through education. In
this, Pestalozzi sharply criticised the artificial method of the
school, and insisted on the necessity of developing the soul
through *what is within*, — through interior culture : —

"The school everywhere puts the order of words before
the order of free nature."

"The home is the basis of the education of humanity."

"Man, it is within yourself, it is in the inner sense of your
power, that resides nature's instrument for your development."

491. LEONARD AND GERTRUDE. — In 1781 Pestalozzi
published the first volume of *Leonard and Gertrude*. He

had written it within the blank spaces of an old account book. This book, the most celebrated perhaps of all Pestalozzi's writings, is a sort of popular romance in which the author brings upon the stage a family of working-people. Gertrude here represents the ideas of Pestalozzi on the education of children. The three other volumes (1783, 1785, 1787) relate the regeneration of a village through the concerted action of legislation, administration, religion, and the school, and especially the school, " which is the centre whence everything should proceed."

Leonard and Gertrude is the only one of Pestalozzi's works which Diesterweg[1] recommends to practical teachers.

" It was my first word," says Pestalozzi, " to the heart of the poor and of the abandoned of the land."

In making Gertrude the principal character of his romance, Pestalozzi wished to emphasize one of his fundamental ideas, which was to place the instruction and the education of the people in the hands of mothers.

492. NEW EXPERIMENTS IN AGRICULTURE. — From 1787 to 1797 Pestalozzi returned to farming. It is from this period that date his relations with Fellenberg, the celebrated founder of *Agricultural Institutes*, and with the philosopher Fichte, who showed him the agreement of his ideas with the doctrine of Kant. His name began to become celebrated, and, in 1792, the Legislative Assembly proclaimed him a French citizen, in company with Washington and Klopstock.

During these years of farm labor, Pestalozzi had meditated different works which appeared in 1797.

493. OTHER WORKS OF PESTALOZZI. — Educational thought pervades all the literary works of Pestalozzi. Thus his *Fables*, short compositions in prose, all have a moral and

---

[1] See Chap. XIX.

educational tendency. Also, in his *Researches on the Course of Nature in the Development of the Human Race*, he sought to justify the preponderant office which he accorded to nature in the education of man. But Pestalozzi was not successful in philosophical dissertations.

" This book," he says himself, " is to me only another proof of my lack of ability ; it is simply a diversion of my imaginative faculty, a work relatively weak. . . . No one,' he adds, " understands me, and it has been hinted that the whole work has been taken for nonsense."

This judgment is severe, but it is only just. Pestalozzi had an intuition of truth, but he was incapable of giving a theoretical demonstration of it. His thought all aglow, and his language all imagery, did not submit to the concise and methodical exposition of abstract truths.

494. THE ORPHAN ASYLUM AT STANZ (1798–1799). — Up to 1798 Pestalozzi had scarcely found the occasion to put in practice his principles and his dreams. The Helvetic Revolution, which he hailed with enthusiasm as the signal of a social regeneration for his country, finally gave him the means of making a trial of his theories, which, by a strange destiny, had been applied by other hands before having been applied by his own.

The Helvetic government, whose sentiments were in harmony with the democratic sentiments of Pestalozzi, offered him the direction of a normal school. But he declined, in order that he might remain a teacher. He was about to take charge of a school, the plan of which he had organized, when events called him to direct an orphan asylum at Stanz.

495. METHODS FOLLOWED AT STANZ. — From six to eight o'clock in the morning, and from four to eight in the afternoon, Pestalozzi heard the lessons of his pupils. The rest

of the time was devoted to manual labor. Even during the lesson, the child at Stanz "drew, wrote, and worked." To establish order in a school which contained eighty pupils, Pestalozzi had the idea of resorting to rhythm; " and it was found," he says, " that the rhythmical pronunciation increased the impression produced by the lesson." Having to do with pupils absolutely ignorant, he kept them for a long time on the elements; he practised them on the first elements till they had mastered them. He simplified the methods, and sought in each branch of instruction a point of departure adapted to the nascent faculties of the child. The mode of teaching was simultaneous. All the pupils repeated in a high tone of voice the words of the teacher; but the instruction was also mutual: —

"Children instructed children; they themselves tried the experiment; all I did was to suggest it. Here again I obeyed necessity. Not having a single assistant, I had the idea of putting one of the most advanced pupils between two others who were less advanced."

Reading was combined with writing. Natural history and geography were taught to children under the form of conversational lessons.

But what engrossed Pestalozzi above all else was to develop the moral sentiments and the interior forces of the conscience. He wished to make himself loved by his pupils, to awaken among them, in their daily association, sentiments of fraternal affection, to excite the conception of each virtue before formulating its precept, and to give the children moral lessons through the influence of nature which surrounded them and through the activity which was imposed on them.

Pestalozzi's chimera, in the organization at Stanz, was to transport into the school the conditions of domestic life, — the desire to be a father to a hundred children.

" I was convinced that my heart would change the condi- \
tion of my children just as promptly as the sun of spring \
would reanimate the earth benumbed by the winter."

" It was necessary that my children should observe, from
dawn to evening, at every moment of the day, upon my brow
and on my lips, that my affections were fixed on them, that
their happiness was my happiness, and that their pleasures
were my pleasures."

" I was everything to my children. I was alone with them
from morning till night. . . . Their hands were in my hands.
Their eyes were fixed on my eyes."

496. RESULTS ACCOMPLISHED. — Without plan, without
apparent order ; merely by the action and incessant communication of his ardent soul with children ignorant and
perverted by misery ; reduced to his own resources in a
house where he was himself " steward, accountant, footman,
and almost servant all in one," Pestalozzi obtained surprising results.

" I saw at Stanz," he says, " the power of the human
faculties. . . . My pupils developed rapidly ; it was another
race. . . . The children very soon felt that there existed in
them forces which they did not know, and in particular they
acquired a general sentiment of order and beauty. They
were self-conscious, and the impression of weariness which
habitually reigns in schools vanished like a shadow from my
class-room. They willed, they had power, they persevered,
they succeeded, and they were happy. They were not
scholars who were learning, but children who felt unknown
forces awakening within them, and who understood where
these forces could and would lead them, and this feeling
gave elevation to their mind and heart."

" It is out of the folly of Stanz," says Roger de Guimps,

" that has come the primary school of the nineteenth century."

While the pupils prospered, the master fell sick of overwork. When the events of the war closed the orphan asylum, it was quite time for the health of Pestalozzi. He raised blood and was at the limit of his strength.

497. THE SCHOOLS OF BURGDORF (1799–1802). — As soon as he had recovered his health, Pestalozzi resumed the course of his experiments. Not without difficulty he succeeded in having entrusted to him a small class in a primary school of Burgdorf. He passed for an ignoramus. "It was whispered that I could neither write, nor compute, nor even read decently." Pestalozzi does not defend himself against the charge, but acknowledges his incapacity, and even asserts that it is to his advantage.

" My incapacity in these respects was certainly an indispensable condition for my discovery of the simplest method of teaching."

What troubled him most in the school at Burgdorf " was that it was subjected to rules." " Never in my life had I borne such a burden. I was discouraged. I cringed under the routine yoke of the school."

Nevertheless, Pestalozzi succeeded admirably in his little school. Then more advanced pupils were given him, but here his success was less. He always proceeded without a plan, and he gave himself great trouble in obtaining results that he might have attained much more easily with a little more system. Blunders, irregularities, and whimsicalities were ever compromising the action of his good will. To be convinced of this, it suffices to read the books which he published at this period, and in particular the most celebrated, of which we shall proceed to give a brief analysis.

but the ... of c.427 L

498. How Gertrude teaches her Children. — It is under this title that in 1801 Pestalozzi published an exposition of his doctrine.[1] "It is the most important and the most profound of all his pedagogical writings," says one of his biographers. We shall not dispute this; but this book also proves how the mind of Pestalozzi was inferior to his heart, how the writer was of less worth than the teacher. Composed under the form of letters addressed to Gessner, the work of Pestalozzi is too often a tissue of declamations, of rambling thoughts, and of personal grievances. It is the work of a brain that is in a state of ferment, and of a heart that is overflowing. The thought is painfully disentangled from out a thousand repetitions. Why need we be astonished at this literary incompetence of Pestalozzi when he himself makes the following confession: "For thirty years I had not read a single book; I could not longer read them."

499. Pestalozzi's Style. — The style of Pestalozzi is the very man himself: desultory, obscure, confused, but with sudden flashes and brilliant illuminations in which the warmth of his heart is exhibited. There are also too many comparisons; the imagery overwhelms the idea. Within a few pages he will compare himself, in succession, "to a sailor, who, having lost his harpoon, would try to catch a whale with a hook," to depict the disproportion between his resources and his purpose; then to a straw, which even a cat would not lay hold of, to tell how he was despised; to an owl, to express his isolation; to a reed, to indicate his feebleness; to a mouse which fears a cat, to characterize his timidity.

[1] A second edition appeared in the lifetime of the author, in 1820, with some important modifications. The French translation published in 1882 by Dr. Darin was made from the first edition.

500. ANALYSIS OF THE GERTRUDE. — It is not easy to
analyze one of Pestalozzi's books. To begin with, *How
Gertrude teaches her Children* is a very bad title, for Gertrude
is not once mentioned in it. This proper name became for
Pestalozzi an allegorical term by which he personifies himself.

The first three letters are rather autobiographical memoirs
than an exposition of doctrine. Pestalozzi here relates his
first experiments, and makes us acquainted with his assistants at Burgdorf, — Krüsi, Tobler, and Buss. In the letters
which follow, the author attempts to set forth the general
principles of his method. The seventh treats of language;
the eighth, of the intuition of forms, of writing, and of
drawing; the ninth, of the intuition of numbers and of computation; the tenth and twelfth, of intuition in general.
For Pestalozzi, intuition was, as we know, direct and experimental perception, either in the domain of sense, or in
the interior regions of the consciousness. Finally, the last
letters are devoted to moral and religious development.

Without designing to follow, in all its ramblings and in all
its digressions, the mobile thought of Pestalozzi, we shall
gather up some of the general ideas which abound in this
overcharged and badly composed work.

501. METHODS SIMPLIFIED. — The purpose of Pestalozzi
was indeed, in one sense, as he was told by one of his
friends, to *mechanize* instruction. He wished, in fact, to
simplify and determine methods to such a degree that they
might be employed by the most ordinary teacher, and by the
most ignorant father and mother. In a word, he hoped to
organize a pedagogical machine so well set up that it could
in a manner run alone.

" I believe," he says, " that we must not dream of making
progress in the instruction of the people as long as we have

not found the forms of instruction which make of the
teacher, at least so far as the completion of the elementary
studies is concerned, the simple mechanical instrument of a
method which owes its results to the nature of its processes,
and not to the ability of the one who uses it. I assert that
a school-book has no value, save as it can be employed by a
master without instruction as well as by one who has been
taught."

This was sheer exaggeration, and was putting too little
value on the personal effort and merit of teachers. On this
score, it would be useless to found normal schools. Pestalozzi, moreover, has given in his own person a striking
contradiction to this singular theory ; for he owed his success
in teaching much more to the influence of his living speech,
and to the ardent communication of the passion by which his
heart was animated, than to the methodical processes which
he never succeeded in combining in an efficient manner.

502. THE SOCRATIC METHOD. — Pestalozzi recommends
the Socratic method, and he indicates with exactness some of
the conditions necessary for the employment of that method.
He first observes that it requires on the part of the teacher
uncommon ability.

" A superficial and uncultivated intelligence," he says,
" does not sound the depths whence a Socrates made spring
up intelligence and truth."

Besides, the Socratic method can be employed only with
pupils who already have some instruction. It is absolutely
impracticable with children who lack both the point of departure, that is, preliminary notions, and the means of
expressing these notions, that is, a knowledge of language.
And as it is always necessary that Pestalozzi's thought
should wind up with a figure of speech, he adds : —

" In order that the goshawk and the eagle may plunder eggs from other birds, it is first necessary that the latter should deposit eggs in their nests."

503. WORD, FORM, AND NUMBER. — A favorite idea of Pestalozzi, which remained at Yverdun, as at Burgdorf, the principle of his exercises in teaching, is that all elementary knowledge can and should be related to three principles, — *word*, *form*, and *number*. To the *word* he attached language, to *form*, writing and drawing, and to *number*, computation.

" This was," he says, " like a ray of light in my researches, like a *Deus ex machina!* " Nothing justifies such enthusiasm. It would be very easy to show that Pestalozzi's classification, besides that it offers no practical interest, is not justifiable from the theoretical point of view, first because one of the elements of his trilogy, the *word*, or language, comprises the other two ; and then because a large part of knowledge, for example, all physical qualities, does not permit the distinction of which he was superstitiously fond.

504. INTUITIVE EXERCISES. — What is of more value is the importance which Pestalozzi ascribes to intuition. An incident worthy of note is that it is not Pestalozzi himself, but one of the children of his school, who first had the idea of the direct observation of the objects which serve as the text for the lesson. One day as, according to his custom, he was giving his pupils a long description of what they observed in a drawing where a window was represented, he noticed that one of his little auditors, instead of looking at the picture, was attentively studying the real window of the school-room.

From that moment Pestalozzi put aside all his drawings, and took the objects themselves for subjects of observation.

" The child," he said, " wishes nothing to intervene be- |
tween nature and himself."

Ramsauer, a pupil at Burgdorf, has described, not without some inaccuracy perhaps, the intuitive exercises which
Pestalozzi offered to his pupils : —

" The exercises in language were the best we had, especially those which had reference to the wainscoting of the
school-room. He spent whole hours before that wainscoting, very old and torn, busy in examining the holes and
rents, with respect to number, form, position, and color, and
in formulating our observations in sentences more or less developed. Then Pestalozzi would ask us, Boys, what do you
see? (He never mentioned the girls.)

Pupil : I see a hole in the wainscoting.

Pestalozzi : Very well ; repeat after me —:
I see a hole in the wainscoting.
I see a large hole in the wainscoting.
Through the hole I see the wall, etc., etc."

505. THE BOOK FOR MOTHERS. — In 1803 Pestalozzi published a work on elementary instruction, which remained un-
finished, entitled *The Book for Mothers.* This was another
Orbis Pictus without pictures. Pestalozzi's intention was to
introduce the child to a knowledge of the objects of nature
or of art which fall under his observation. In this he tarried too long over the description of the organs of the body
and of their functions. A French critic, Dussault, said,
with reference to this : —

" Pestalozzi gives himself much trouble to teach children
that their nose is in the middle of their face." In his anxiety
to be simple and elementary, Pestalozzi often succeeds in
reality in making instruction puerile. On the other hand,
.the Père Girard complains that the exercises in language

which compose *The Book for Mothers*, " really very well arranged, are also very dry and monotonous."

506. A Swiss Teacher in 1793. — To form a just estimate of the efforts of Pestalozzi and his assistants, we must take into account the wretched state of instruction at the period when they attempted to reform the methods of teaching. Krüsi, Pestalozzi's first assistant, one of those who were perhaps the nearest his heart, has himself related how he became a teacher. He was eighteen, and till then his only employment had been that of a peddler for his father. One day, as he was going about his business with a heavy load of merchandise on his shoulders, he meets on the road a revenue officer of the State, and they enter into conversation. " Do you know," said the officer, " that the teacher of Gais is about to leave his school? Would you not like to succeed him? — It is not a question of what I would like; a schoolmaster should have knowledge, in which I am absolutely lacking. — What a school-master can and should know with us, you might easily learn at your age." — Krüsi reflected, went to work, and copied more than a hundred times a specimen of writing which he had procured; and be declares that this was his only preparation. He registered for examination. The day for the trial arrived.

" There were but two competitors of us," he says. " The principal test consisted in writing the Lord's Prayer, and to this I gave my closest attention. I had observed that in German, use was made of capital letters; but I did not know the rule for their use, and took them for ornaments. So I distributed mine in a symmetrical manner, so that some were found even in the middle of words. In fact. neither of us knew anything.

" When the examination had been estimated, I was summoued, and Captain Schœpfer informed me that the examiners had found us both deficient; that my competitor read the better, but that I excelled him in writing; . . . that, besides, my apartment, being larger than that of the other candidate, was better fitted for holding a school, and, finally, that I was elected to the vacant place."

Is it not well to be indulgent to teachers whom we meet on the highway, who scarcely know how to write, and whom a captain commissions?

507. THE INSTITUTE AT BURGDORF (1802). — When Pestalozzi published the *Gertrude* and *The Book for Mothers*, he was not simply a school-master at Burgdorf; he had taken charge of an institute, that is, of a boarding-school of higher primary instruction. There also he applied the natural method, "which makes the child proceed from his own intuitions, and leads him by degrees, and through his own efforts, to abstract ideas." The institute succeeded. The pupils of Burgdorf were distinguished especially by their skill in drawing and in mental arithmetic. Visitors were struck with their air of cheerfulness. Singing and gymnastics were held in honor, and also exercises on natural history, learned in the open field, and during walks. Mildness and liberty characterized the internal management. "It is not a school that you have here," said a visitor, "but a family!"

508. JOURNEY TO PARIS. — It was at this period that Pestalozzi made a journey to Paris, as a member of the *consulta* called by Bonaparte to decide the fate of Switzerland. He hoped to take advantage of his stay in France to disseminate his pedagogical ideas. But Bonaparte refused to see him, saying that he had something else to do besides discussing questions of *a b* c. Monge, the founder of the Polytechnic School, was more cordial, and kindly listened to the explana-

tions of the Swiss pedagogue. But he concluded by saying, " It is too much for us ! " More disdainful still, Talleyrand had said, " It is too much for the people ! "

On the other hand, at the same period, the philosopher Maine de Biran, then sub-prefect at Bergerac, called a disciple of Pestalozzi, Barraud, to found schools in the department of Dordogne, and he encouraged with all his influence the application of the Pestalozzian method.

509. THE INSTITUTE AT YVERDUN (1805–1825). — In 1803 Pestalozzi was obliged to leave the castle of Burgdorf. The Swiss government gave him in exchange the convent of München-Buchsee. Pestalozzi transferred his institute to this place, but only for a little time. In 1805 he established himself at Yverdun, at the foot of Lake Neufchâtel, in French Switzerland ; and here, with the aid of several of his colleagues, he developed his methods anew, with brilliant success at first, but afterwards through all sorts of vicissitudes, difficulties, and miseries.

The institute at Yverdun was rather a school of secondary instruction, devoted to the middle classes, than a primary school proper. Pupils poured in from all sides. The character of the studies, however, was poorly defined, and Pestalozzi found himself somewhat out of his element in his new institution, since he excelled only in elementary methods and in the education of little children.

510. SUCCESS OF THE INSTITUTE. — Numerous visitors betook themselves to Yverdun, some through simple love of strolling. The institute of Yverdun made a part, so to speak, of the curiosities of Switzerland. People visited Pestalozzi as they went to see a lake or a glacier. As soon as notice was given of the arrival of a distinguished personage, Pestalozzi summoned one of his best masters, Ramsauer or Schmid.

" Take your best pupils," he said, " and show the Prince what we are doing. He has numerous serfs, and when he is convinced, he will have them instructed."

These frequent exhibitions entailed a great loss of time. Disorder reigned in the instruction. The young masters whom Pestalozzi had attached to his fortunes were overwhelmed with work, and could not give sufficient attention to the preparation of their lessons. Pestalozzi was growing old, and did not succeed in completing his methods.

511. THE TENTATIVES OF PESTALOZZI. — The teaching of Pestalozzi was in reality but a long groping, an experiment ceaselessly renewed. Do not require of him articulate ideas, and methods definitely established. Always on the alert, and always in quest of something better, his admirable pedagogic instinct never came to full satisfaction. His merit was that he was always on the search for truth. His theories almost always followed, rather than preceded, his experiments. A man of intuition rather than of reasoning, he acknowledges that he went forward without considering what he was doing. He had the merit of making many innovations, but he was wrong in taking counsel of no one but himself, and of his personal feelings. " We ought to read nothing," he said ; " we ought to discover everything." Pestalozzi never knew how to profit by the experience of others.

He never arrived at complete precision in the establishment of his methods. He complained of not being understood, and he was not in fact. One of his pupils at Yverdun, Vulliemin, thus expresses himself : —

" That which was called, not without pretense, the *method* of Pestalozzi was an enigma for us. It was for our teachers themselves. Each of them interpreted the doctrine of the master in his own way ; but we were still far from the time

when these divergencies engendered discord; when our
principal teachers, after each had given out that he alone
had comprehended Pestalozzi, ended by asserting that Pestalozzi himself was not understood; that he had not been
understood except by Schmid, said Schmid, and by Niederer,
said Niederer."

512. METHODS AT YVERDUN. — The writer whom we have
just quoted gives us valuable information on the methods
which were in use at Yverdun : —

" Instruction was addressed to the intelligence rather than
to the memory. (Attempt, said Pestalozzi to his colleagues,
to *develop* the child, and not to *train* him as one trains a
dog.)

" Language was taught us by the aid of intuition; we
learned to see correctly, and through this very process to
form for ourselves a correct idea of the relations of things.
What we had conceived clearly we had no difficulty in
expressing clearly."

" The first elements of geography were taught us on the
spot. . . . Then we reproduced in relief with clay the valley
of which we had just made a study."

" We were made to invent geometry by having marked
out for us the end to reach, and by being put on the route.
The same course was followed in arithmetic; our computa-
tions were made in the head and *viva voce*, without the aid
of paper."

513. DECADENCE OF THE INSTITUTE. — Yverdun enjoyed
an extraordinary notoriety for some years. But little by
little the faults of the method became apparent. Internal
discords and the misunderstanding of Pestalozzi's colleagues, of Niederer, " the philosopher of the method," and
of Schmid, the mathematician, hastened the decadence of

an establishment in which order and discipline had never reigned. Pestalozzi was content with being the spur of the institute. He became more and more unfit for practical affairs. He allowed all liberty to his assistants, and also to his pupils. At Yverdun the pupils addressed their teachers in familiar style. The touching fiction of paternity transported into the school, which was successful with Pestalozzi in his first experience in teaching, and with a small number of pupils, was no longer practicable at Yverdun, with a mass of pupils of every age and of every disposition.

514. JUDGMENT OF PÈRE GIRARD. — In 1809 the Père Girard[1] was commissioned by the Swiss government to inspect the institute. The result was not favorable, though Girard acknowledges that he conceived the idea of his own method from studying at first hand that of Pestalozzi.

The principal criticism of Girard bears on the abuse of mathematics, which, under the influence of Schmid, became in fact more and more the principal occupation of teachers and pupils.

"I made the remark," he says, "to my old friend Pestalozzi, that the mathematics exercised an unjustifiable sway in his establishment, and that I feared the results of this on the education that was given. Whereupon he replied to me with spirit, as was his manner: 'This is because I wish my children to believe nothing which cannot be demonstrated as clearly to them as that two and two make four.' My reply was in the same strain: 'In that case, if I had thirty sons, I would not entrust one of them to you, for it would be impossible for you to demonstrate to him, as you can that two and two make four, that I am his father, and that I have a right to his obedience.'"

---

[1] See the following chapter.

It is evident that Pestalozzi was deviating from his own inclinations. The general character of his pedagogy is in fact to avoid abstraction, and in all things to aim at concrete and living intuition. Even in religion, he deliberately excluded dogmatic teaching, precise and literal form, and sought only to awaken in the soul a religious sentiment, sincere and profound. The Père Girard had remarked to him that the religious instruction of his pupils was vague and indeterminate, and that their aspirations lacked the doctrinal form. " The form," replied Pestalozzi, " I am still looking for it ! "

515. THE LAST YEARS OF PESTALOZZI. — Disheartened by the decadence of his institute, Pestalozzi left Yverdun in 1824, and sought a retreat at Neuhof, on the farm where he had tried his first experiments in popular education. It is here that he wrote his last two works, — *The Swan's Song* and *My Destinies.* January 25, 1827, he was taken to Brugg to consult a physician. He died there February 17 ; and two days after he was buried at Birr. It is there that the Canton of Argovia erected a monument to him in 1846, with the following inscription : —

" Here lies Henry Pestalozzi, born at Zurich, January 12, 1746, died at Brugg, February 17, 1827, savior of the poor at Neuhof, preacher of the people in *Leonard and Gertrude,* father of orphans at Stanz, founder of the new people's school at Burgdorf and at München-Buchsee, educator of humanity at Yverdun, man, Christian, citizen : everything for others, nothing for himself. Blessed be his name."

516. ESSENTIAL PRINCIPLES. — Pestalozzi never took the trouble to formulate the essential principles of his pedagogy. Incapable of all labor in abstract reflection, he borrowed from his friends, on every possible occasion, the logical

exposition of his own methods. In his first letter to Gessner, he is only too happy to reproduce the observations of the philanthropist Fischer, who distinguished five essential principles in his system: —

1. To give the mind an intensive culture, and not simply extensive: to form the mind, and not to content one's self with furnishing it;

2. To connect all instruction with the study of language;

3. To furnish the mind for all its operations with fundamental data, mother ideas;

4. To simplify the mechanism of instruction and study;

5. To popularize science.

On several points, indeed, Pestalozzi calls in question the translation which Fischer has given of his thought; but, notwithstanding these reservations, powerless to find a more exact formula, he accepts as a finality this interpretation of his doctrine.

Later, another witness of the life of Pestalozzi, Morf, also condensed into a few maxims the pedagogy of the great teacher: —

1. Intuition is the basis of instruction;

2. Language ought to be associated with intuition;

3. The time to learn is not that of judging and of criticising;

4. In each branch, instruction ought to begin with the simplest elements, and to progress by degrees while following the development of the child, that is to say, through a series of steps psychologically connected;

5. We should dwell long enough on each part of the instruction for the pupil to gain a complete mastery of it;

6. Instruction ought to follow the order of natural development, and not that of synthetic exposition;

7. The individuality of the child is sacred;

8. The principal end of elementary instruction is not to cause the child to acquire knowledge and talents, but to develop and increase the forces of his intelligence ;

9. To wisdom there must be joined power ; to theoretical knowledge, practical skill ;

10. The relations between master and pupil ought to be based on love ;

11. Instruction proper ought to be made subordinate to the higher purpose of education.

Each one of these aphorisms would need a long commentary. It is sufficient, however, to study them in the aggregate, in order to form an almost exact idea of that truly humane pedagogy which reposes on psychological principles.

Krüsi could say of his master: " With respect to the ordinary knowledge and practices of the school, Pestalozzi was far below a good village *magister;* but he possessed something infinitely superior to that which can be given by a course of instruction, whatever it may be. He knew·that which remains concealed from a great number of teachers, — the human spirit and the laws of its development and culture, the human heart and the means of vivifying it and ennobling it."

517. PEDAGOGICAL PROCESSES. — The pedagogy of Pestalozzi is no less valid in its processes than in its principles. Without presuming to enumerate everything, we will indicate succinctly some of the scholastic practices which he employed and recommended : —

The child should know how to speak before learning to read.

For reading, use should be made of movable letters glued on pasteboard. Before writing, the pupil should draw. The first exercises in writing should be upon slates.

In the study of language, the evolution of nature should \ be followed, first studying nouns, then qualificatives, and finally propositions.

The elements of computation shall be taught by the aid of material objects taken as units, or at least by means of strokes / drawn on a board. Oral computation shall be the most employed.

The pupil ought, in order to form an accurate and exact idea of numbers, to conceive them always as a collection of strokes or of concrete things, and not as abstract figures. A small table divided into squares in which points are represented, serves to teach addition, subtraction, multiplication, and division.

There was neither book nor copy-book in the schools of) Burgdorf.

The children had nothing to learn by heart. They had to repeat all at once and in accord the instructions of the master. Each lesson lasted but an hour, and was followed by a short interval devoted to recreation.

Manual labor, making paper boxes, working in the garden, gymnastics, were associated with mental labor. The last hour of each day was devoted to optional labor. The pupils said, " We are working for ourselves."

A few hours a week were devoted to military exercises.

Surely everything is not to be commended in the processes which we have just indicated. It is not necessary, for example, that the child conceive, when he computes, the content of numbers, and Pestalozzi sometimes makes an abuse of sense intuition. He introduces analysis, and an analysis too subtile and too minute, into studies where nature alone does her work. " My method," he said, " is but a refinement of the processes of nature." He refines too much.

518. PESTALOZZI AND ROUSSEAU. — Pestalozzi has often acknowledged what he owed to Rousseau. "My chimerical and unpractical spirit was taken," he said, "with that chimerical and impracticable book. . . . The system of liberty ideally established by Rousseau, excited in me an infinite longing for a wider and more bounteous sphere of activity."

The great superiority of Pestalozzi over Rousseau is that he worked for the people, — that he applied to a great number of children the principles which Rousseau embodied only in an individual and privileged education. Émile, after all, is an aristocrat. He is rich, and of good ancestry; and is endowed with all the gifts of nature and fortune. Real pupils do not offer, in general, to the action of teachers, material as docile and complaisant. Pestalozzi had to do only with children of the common people, who have everything to learn at school, because they have found at home, with busy or careless parents, neither encouragement nor example, — because their early years have been only a long intellectual slumber. For these benumbed natures, many exercises are necessary which would properly be regarded as useless if it were a question of instructing children of another condition. Before condemning, before ridiculing, the trifling practices of Pestalozzi, and of teachers of the same school, we should consider the use to which these processes were applied. The real organizer of the education of childhood and of the people, Pestalozzi has a right to the plaudits of all those who are interested in the future of the masses of the people.

519. CONCLUSION. — We should not flatter ourselves that merely by means of an analysis of Pestalozzi's methods, we can comprehend the service of a man who excelled in the warmth of his charity, in his ardor of devotion and of propagandism, and in I know not what that makes a grand per-

sonality, more than by the clearness and the exactness of his theories. It is somewhat with Pestalozzi as with those great actors who carry with them to their tomb a part of the secret of their art.

He was especially great in heart and in love. To read some of his writings, we would sometimes be tempted to say that his intellect was far inferior to the expectation excited by his name ; but what a splendid revenge he takes in the domain of sentiment !

He passionately loved the people. He knew their sufferings, and nothing turned him from his anxiety to cure them. In the presence of a beautiful landscape, he thought less of the charming scene that was displayed before his eyes than of the poor people who, under those splendors of nature, led a life of misery.

That which assures him an immortal glory is the high purpose that he set before himself, — his ardor to regenerate humanity through instruction. Of what consequence is it that the results obtained were so disproportionate to his efforts, and that he could say, " The contrast between what I would and what I could is so great that it cannot be expressed"? Even the French Revolution did not succeed in the matter of instruction, in making its works commensurate with its aspirations.

The love and the admiration of all the friends of instruction are forever secured to Pestalozzi. He was the most suggestive, the most stimulating, of modern educators. If it was not given him to act sufficiently on French pedagogy, he was in Germany the great inspirer of reform in popular education. While he was despised by Bonaparte, he obtained, in 1802, from the philosopher Fichte, this fine compliment, " It is from the institute of Pestalozzi that I expect the regeneration of the German nation."

[520. ANALYTICAL SUMMARY. — 1. *Inveniam viam aut faciam*. To know the end is to find the way ; and to be possessed of an impulse to reach an end is to make a way. There are thus two categories of educational reformers. Some see a goal by the light of reason and reflection, and then lay out a logical route to it which they may or may not traverse, but which some one will ultimately traverse. Others are dominated by an intense feeling, and grope their uncertain way towards a goal whose outline and position are only dimly discerned through the mists of emotion. With some, the motive is intellectual, with others, it is emotional ; and in their higher manifestations these endowments are mutually exclusive.

2. Pestalozzi belongs pre-eminently to the emotional reformers. He felt intensely, but he saw vaguely. His impulses were the highest and the noblest that can animate the human soul, but at every stage in his career his success was compromised by his inability to see things in their normal relations and proportions. Conscious of his inability to frame a rational defence of his system, he was glad to borrow philosophic insight from abroad ; but he could not live with colleagues who would test the logic of his methods.

3. Tested by the simplest rules of order, symmetry, and economy, the schools organized by Pestalozzi were failures ; but tested by the exalted humanity, the heroic devotion, and self-sacrifice of their founder, and by the new life which, through his example, was henceforth to animate the teaching profession, his schools were successful beyond all precedent. Judged by modern standards, Pestalozzi was a poor teacher, but an unsurpassed educator.

4. The conception which the humanitarian warmth of Pestalozzi's nature converted into a motive, was that true edution is a growth, the outward evolution of an inward life.

The conception itself was as old as David and Socrates, but it had ceased to have the power of a living truth.

5. The history of human thought shows that there has ever been a tendency to separate form from content, or letter from spirit, and as constant a predilection for form or letter, as distinguished from content or spirit; and the essential work of reform has consisted in reanimation. This illustrates and defines Pestalozzi's mission as an educator. The story of his devotion and suffering is the most pathetic in the history of education, and it should be unnecessary to repeat the lesson that was taught at such cost.]

CHAPTER XIX.

THE SUCCESSORS OF PESTALOZZI. — FRŒBEL AND PÈRE GIRARD.

---

521. THE PEDAGOGY OF THE NINETEENTH CENTURY
Pestalozzi really belongs to our century by the close of
career, and especially by the posthumous glory of his ne
With Frœbel and the Père Girard, we enter comple
upon the nineteenth century; both, in different degrees
with characteristics of their own, continue the worl
Pestalozzi.

522. Frœbel (1782–1852). — It may be said of Frœbel as of Pestalozzi, that in France at least, he is more praised than known, more celebrated than studied. We have been tardy in speaking of him, — it is scarcely twenty years since ; but it seems that our admiration has sought to atone for the slowness of its manifestation by its vivacity and its ardor. The name of the founder of *Kindergartens* has become almost popular, while his writings have remained almost unknown.

An impartial and thorough study of Frœbel's work will abate rather than encourage this excessive infatuation and this somewhat artificial enthusiasm. Assuredly, Frœbel had grand qualities as a teacher ; but he lacked a profound classical culture and also the sense of proportion. Like most of the Germans of this century, he has ventured on the conceptions of a nebulous philosophy, and following the steps of Hegel, he has too often deserted the route of observation and experiment, to strike out into metaphysical divagations. Frœbel's imagination magnifies and distorts everything. He cannot see objects as they are, but lends them a symbolical meaning, and wanders off into transcendental and obscure considerations. But his practical work is worth more than his writings, and he cannot be denied the glory of having been a bold and happy innovator in the field of early education.

523. The Youth of Frœbel. — Frœbel was born in Thuringia in 1782. He lost his mother almost at birth, and was educated by his father and his uncle, both village pastors. We recollect that by a contrary destiny, Pestalozzi was brought up by his mother. From his earliest years he manifested remarkable traits of character, and also mental tendencies which were a little singular. He was dreamy and wholly penetrated with a profound religious sentiment.

Thus, the day when he believed that he was assured by peremptory reasoning that he was not doomed to eternal flames, was an event in his life. Ardently enamored of nature, he considers her as the true inspirer of humanity. This had also been the conception of Rousseau and of Pestalozzi, but it exhibits itself with much more power in the case of Frœbel.

It is difficult to comprehend the exaggeration of his thought when he says that nature, attentively observed, appears to us as the symbol of the highest aspirations of human life.

" Entire nature, even the world of crystals and stones, teaches us to recognize good and evil, but nowhere in a more living, tranquil, clear, and evident way than in the world of plants and flowers."

Morality, thus understood, is a little vague. We do not deny that the calm life of the fields contributes to surround us with a pure atmosphere, and to beget within us wholesome and elevated aspirations; but one must have a singularly sentimental temperament to believe that nature can give us " the clearest and the most obvious " lessons in morals.

524. DIFFERENT OCCUPATIONS. — The first part of Frœbel's life gives evidence of a certain unsteadiness of mind. Inconstant in his tastes, he cannot settle on a fixed mode of life. Improvident and poor, like Pestalozzi, he is in turn forester, intendant, architect, preceptor; he feels his way up to the day when his vocation as a teacher is suddenly revealed to him. Moreover, he studies everything, — law, mineralogy, agriculture, mathematics.

525. VOCATION TO TEACH. — It was in 1805, at Frankfort, that Frœbel began to teach. He was then twenty-three. The teacher Gruner offered him a position as instructor in

the model school which he directed; Frœbel accepted, but he was of that number who do nothing artlessly.

"An accidental circumstance determined my decision. I received news that my certificates were lost [certificates that he had sent to an architect to secure a position with him]. I then concluded that Providence had intended, by this incident, to take from me the possibility of a return backward."

At the end of a few days he wrote to his brother Christopher : —

"It is astonishing how my duties please me. From the first lesson it seemed to me that I had never done anything else, and that I was born for that very thing. I could no longer make it seem to me that I had previously thought of following any occupation but this, and yet I confess that the idea of becoming a teacher had never occurred to me."

526. FRŒBEL AND PESTALOZZI. — At the school in Frankfort, Frœbel, still a novice in the art of teaching, attempted scarcely more than scrupulously to apply the Pestalozzian methods.

And upon many points Frœbel remained to the end a faithful disciple of Pestalozzi. Intuition is the fundamental principle of his method, and we might say that his effort in pedagogy consists chiefly in organizing into a system the sense intuitions which Pestalozzi proposed to the child somewhat at random and without plan.

Frœbel had had direct relations with Pestalozzi. In 1808 he went to Yverdun with three of his pupils, and there spent two years, taking part in the work of the institute, and becoming acquainted with the methods of the master. He declares that it was a " decisive " epoch in his life.

But let us note, in passing, the difference in character between Pestalozzi and Frœbel. While Pestalozzi is ever ready to accuse himself with a touching humility, Frœbel regards himself as almost infallible. He never attributes failure to his own insufficiency, but lays the blame on destiny or on the ill-will of others. Pestalozzi is ever forgetting himself, and he is so neglectful as to be uncouth in his attire. " He never knew how to dress," say his biographers ; " his distraction made him forget sometimes his cravat, and at others his garters." Frœbel, on the contrary, affected an elegant and theatrical bearing. He studied effect. At certain periods, as we are told, he wore Hessian boots and a Tyrolese cap with high plumes.

527. THE TREATISE ON SPHERICITY (1811). — It was about 1811 that the peculiar originality of Frœbel manifested itself, and this was done, it must be confessed, in an unfortunate way, by the publication of his *Treatise on Sphericity*.

Pestalozzi somewhere wrote : " If my life is entitled to any credit, it is that of having placed the square at the basis of an intuitive instruction which has never yet been given to a people."[1] This language coming from Pestalozzi is certainly calculated to surprise us ; but at least Pestalozzi meant square in the proper sense of the term, as a geometrical figure, or as a form for drawing. When Frœbel speaks to us of the sphere, and makes of it the basis of education, it is a wholly different thing.

In reading the *Treatise on Sphericity*, we are sometimes tempted to inquire whether we have to do with a well-balanced mind, or whether an exuberant imagination has not caused the author to lose the consciousness of reality.

According to Frœbel, the sphere is the ideal form : —

" The sphere seems like the prototype or the unity of all bodies and of all forms. Not an angle, not a line, not a

---

[1] *Comment Gertrude instruit ses enfants,* translated by Darin, p. 204.

plane, not a surface, is shown in it, and yet it has all points and all surfaces."

Let this pass; but besides this, the sphere has mysterious relations with spiritual things; it teaches the perfection of the moral life.

"To labor conscientiously at the development of the spherical nature of a being, is to effect the education of a being."

An incident borrowed from the life of Frœbel will complete the picture. He enlisted as a volunteer in 1812, and made the campaigns of 1812–1813, with Langethal and Middendorf, who were afterward to be his colleagues. After the war, he returned to Berlin, passing through the whole of Germany. During the whole journey, he says, "I was seeking something, but without reaching a definite idea of what I was in quest of, and nothing could satisfy me. Wholly engrossed in this thought, I entered one day into a very beautiful garden, ornamented with plants the most various. I admired them, and yet none of them brought relief to my inmost feeling.

"Passing them in review, at a glance, in my soul, I suddenly discovered that among them there was no lily. . . . Then I knew what was lacking in that garden, and what I was looking for. How could my inmost feeling have manifested itself to me in a more beautiful way? You seek, I said to myself, tranquil peace of heart, harmony of life, and purity of soul, in the image of the lily, that peaceful flower, simple and pure. The garden, with all its varied flowers, but without the blossoms of the lily, was for me like life agitated and variegated, but without harmony and without unity."

528. NEW STUDIES. — Frœbel returned to Berlin in 1814, and there obtained an assistant's place in the mineralogical

museum. He there studied at leisure the geometrical forms
of crystals, and reflected anew on their symbolical meaning.
Perhaps he derived from these studies the idea of the first
gifts which he afterwards introduced into his *Kindergartens*.
It was not till two years afterwards that he formed the definite resolution to devote himself to the education of youth
(1816). He first established himself at Griesheim, and then
at Keilhau (a league's distance from Rudolstadt), where,
with five pupils, all his nephews, he opened a school which
he called by a pompous title, and one hardly justifiable at
the beginning, the *General German Institute of Education*.
He succeeded in associating with himself Langethal and
Middendorf. The establishment was administered at first on
a very modest scale, as the resources were slender ; but it
prospered little by little, and in 1826 it numbered more than
fifty pupils.

529. INSTITUTE AT KEILHAU. — The principles of Pestalozzi
were applied at Keilhau. Langethal and Middendorf
passed their apprenticeship in the Pestalozzian method under
the direction of Frœbel. The three professors met in the
common hall, and there were frequently heard as echoes
from their discussion the words : *intuition, personal initiative, proceeding from the known to the unknown.* " They are
learning the system," said the children who heard them.

At Keilhau, physical, intellectual, and moral education
marched abreast. The master was to attempt to penetrate
the individuality of each child, to the end that he might thence
provoke the free development of that individuality. The
government was austere and the fare frugal. The system
of physical hardening was carried to an extreme. The
pupils, winter and summer, wore a blouse and cotton trou-
sers. A considerable time was devoted to religious excr-

cises. Frœbel always remained attached to the Lutheran Church, though his orthodoxy might have seemed open to suspicion, and he always thought that education ought to be essentially religious.

" All education that is not founded on religion is sterile." And be adds, " All education that is not founded on the Christian religion is defective and incomplete." [1]

530. THE EDUCATION OF MAN. — It was at Keilhau in 1826, that Frœbel published his principal work, *The Education of Man*.[2]

At that date, the idea of *Kindergartens* had not yet taken form in his mind ; and *The Education of Man* was not so much the exposition of the practical applications of Frœbel's method, as a nebulous and tumid development of his metaphysical principles. It is a book little read, and, let it be confessed, partly illegible ! We have ventured to speak of the nonsense written by Pestalozzi. What shall be said of the mystical dreams of Frœbel? The pedagogy of the Germans, like their philosophy, has for a century often lost its way in strange theories which absolutely surpass the comprehension of the French mind. From a mass of vague and pretentious speculations on universal nature, there are culled with difficulty some ideas which are well founded. However, let us try to gather up the obscure idea of Frœbel, made still more obscure by the exterior form of the work. In the first edition Frœbel had omitted to introduce into the text any division into chapters and paragraphs. The reading of this uninterrupted text could not fail to be laborious ; even with the somewhat artificial divisions which were subse-

---

[1] See the *Aphorisms* published by Frœbel in 1821.
[2] See the French translation by Madame de Crombrugghe, Paris, 1881. Also, the English translation by Josephine Jarvis, New York, 1885.

quently introduced, *The Education of Man* remains difficult to read and to analyze.

531. ANALYSIS OF THE WORK. — The introduction is the most interesting part of the work. We might reduce the somewhat confused ideas which it contains to three essential points, to three general ideas, of philosophy, of psychology, and of pedagogy.

The idea of general philosophy is this : " Everything comes solely from God. In God is the unique principle of all things."

It is a vague pantheism which consists in believing that all the objects of nature are the direct manifestations of the divine activity.

" The end, the destiny of each thing, is to publish abroad its being, the activity of God which operates in it, and the manner in which this activity is combined with the thing." From these premises Frœbel is logically brought to this psychological statement, that everything is good in man, for it is God who acts in him. He pushes his optimism so far as to say : —

" From his earliest age the child yields himself to justice and right with a surprising tact, for we rarely see him avoiding them voluntarily."

The pedagogical conclusion is easy to guess : Education shall be essentially a work of liberty and of spontaneity. It ought to be indulgent, flexible, supple, and restricted to protecting and overseeing.

" The vocation of man, considered as a reasonable intelligence, is to let his nature act in manifesting the action of God, who operates in him ; to publish God outwardly, to acquire the knowledge of his real destiny, and to accomplish it in all *liberty* and *spontaneity*."

These last two words are repeated *ad nauseam*. Frœhel goes so far as to say that there can be no general form of education to impose or even to recommend, because account must be taken of the nature of each child, and the free development of his individuality provoked by inviting him to action and to personal exertion. The choice in the manifestation of the exterior form of education ought to be left to the intelligence of the educator, and there ought to be almost as many ways of educating men as there are individuals, with their own natures aspiring to a personal development.

532. LOVE FOR CHILDREN. — Frœbel, and this is perhaps his best quality, loves children tenderly. He speaks of them with touching accents, but he does not fail to mingle with his affection for them his habitual symbolism. The child is not for him simply the little real being that he has under his eyes. He sees him through mystic veils, so to speak, and, as it were, crowned with an aureole : —

" Let the child always appear to us as a living pledge of the presence, of the goodness, and of the love of God."

533. UNITY OF EDUCATION. — Frœbel is always bitterly complaining of the fragmentary and scrappy character of the ordinary education. His dream was to introduce unity into it. In this respect he separates himself squarely from Rousseau. The different stages of life form an uninterrupted chain. " Let life be considered as being but one in all its phases, as forming one complete whole."

534. DIFFERENT STAGES IN THE DEVELOPMENT OF MAN. — Frœbel, in *The Education of Man*, considers in succession the different periods of life. The first three chapters treat of the *first stages of development* in man, — the nurseling, the child, the young boy. We here find pages full of charm,

upon the education of the child by the mother, and upon the progress of the faculties; but pretentious considerations and whimsical interpretations too often come to spoil the psychology of Frœbel.

"The child," he says, "scarcely knows whether he loves the flowers for themselves, for the delight which they give him, . . . or for the vague intuition which they give him of the Creator."

Farther on he speaks of introducing the child to colors, and from this exercise he at once draws moral conclusions: the child loves colors because he comes by means of them "to the knowledge of an interior unity."

535. THE NATURALISM OF FRŒBEL. — The elements of education according to Frœbel are, with religion, the artistic studies, mathematics, language, and, above all, nature. "Teachers should scarcely let a week pass without taking to the country a part of their pupils. They shall not drive them before them like a flock of sheep. . . . They shall walk with them as a father among his children, or a brother among his brothers, in making them observe and admire the varied richness which nature displays to their eyes at each season of the year."

536. NEW EXPERIMENTS IN TEACHING. — The institute of Keilhau did not long prosper. In 1829 it was necessary to close it for lack of pupils. Frœbel lacked the practical qualities of an administrator. In 1831 he tried in vain to open a new school at Wartensee in Switzerland. The attacks of the clerical party obliged him to abandon his project. After several other attempts he was elected director of an orphan asylum at Burgdorf; and it was there that he resolved to devote his pedagogical efforts to the education of early childhood.

The little village of Burgdorf had the honor, within a period of thirty-five years, of offering an asylum to Pestalozzi and to Frœbel, and of being the scene of their experiments in pedagogy.

537. THE KINDERGARTENS. — The master conception of Frœbel, the creation of the *Kindergarten*, was only slowly developed in his mind. It was only in 1840 that he invented the term. Of course, given the imagination of Frœbel, and his tendency to symbolism, *children's garden* ought to be taken in its allegorical sense. The child is a plant, the school a garden, and Frœbel calls teachers "gardeners of children."[1]

But before giving a name to his school for early childhood, Frœbel had long cherished the idea of it. In 1835, at Burgdorf, he attempted to realize it; in 1837, at Blankenburg, near Rudolstadt, he founded his first infant school.

538. ORIGIN OF THE KINDERGARTEN. — Without wishing to belittle the originality of Frœbel's creation, it is right to say that it was suggested to him in part by Comenius. The philosopher Krause had pointed out to him the importance of the writings of the Slavic educator. He studied them, and the *Kindergarten* certainly has some relations of parenthood with the *schola materni gremii*. There is, however, one essential difference between the idea of Comenius and that of Frœbel, — the first confided to the mother the cares which the second relegates to the teachers of the children's gardens.

It is said that it was from seeing a child playing at ball that Frœbel conceived the first idea of his system. We know

---

[1] Consequently it is wrong to take Frœbel's expression in the sense that he wished to establish by the side of each school a garden, a lawn planted with trees and adorned with flower-beds. See Gréard, *L'instruction primaire à Paris*, 1877, p. 73.

what importance he attached to the spherical form and to play. The first principle of his *Kindergarten* was then that the child ought to play, and to play at ball.

But Frœbel enveloped the simplest ideas in prolix and whimsical theories. If he recommends the ball, it is not for positive reasons, nor because it is an inoffensive play, very appropriate to the need of movement which characterizes the child. It is because the ball is the symbol of unity. The cube, which was to succeed the ball, represents diversity in unity. It is also because the word *ball* is a symbolic word, formed from letters borrowed from the German words *Bild von all, picture of the whole.*

Frœbel came to attribute an occult meaning to the different letters of words. He thought he found in the figures of the year 1836, the date of his first conception of the *Kindergarten,* the proof that that year was to open to humanity a new era, and he expressed his views in an essay entitled: *The Year 1836 requires a Renovation of Life.* In this we read such things as these: "The word marriage (German *Ehe*) represents by its two vowels e–e, *life;* these two vowels are united by the consonant *h*, thus symbolizing a double life which the spirit unites; again, the two halves thus united are similar and equal each to each: e–*h*–e." And farther on: "What does the word *German* (*Deutsch*) signify? It is derived from the word *deuten* (signifying to manifest), which designates the act by which self-conscious thought is clearly manifested outwardly. . . . To be a German is then to raise one's self as an individual and as a whole, by a clear manifestation of one's self, to a clear consciousness of self."

539. THE GIFTS OF FRŒBEL. — Under the graceful name of gifts, Frœbel presents to the child a certain number of objects which are to serve as material for his exercises.

The five gifts are contained in a box from which they are taken in succession, as the children are in a condition to receive them. In the original plan of Frœbel, these gifts were: 1. the ball; 2. the sphere and the cube; 3. the cube divided into eight equal parts; 4. the cube divided into eight rectangular parallelopipeds, in the form of building-bricks, which the child will use as material for little constructions; 5. the cube divided in each of its dimensions, that is, cut into twenty-seven equal cubes; three of them are subdivided into two prisms, and three others into four prisms, by means of an oblique section, single or double.[1] And to these gifts Frœbel added other objects, such as thin strips of wood and little sticks for constructing figures; and bits of paper for braiding, folding, dotting, etc.

The conception of Frœbel does not rest, as one might think, on the adaptation of the objects which he chooses in succession, to the faculties of the child. It is not this at all which interests him. The order which he has adopted is derived from another principle. According to him, the form of bodies has an intimate relation with the general laws of the universe. There is, consequently, a methodical gradation to be observed, according to the intrinsic character of the objects themselves, for the purpose of initiating the child into the laws of the divine thought symbolized in the sphere, in the cube, in the cylinder, etc. Frœbel was greatly irritated at those of his scholars who misunderstood the philosophical import of his " gifts," and who saw in them only plays. " If my material for instruction possesses some utility," he said, " it does not owe it to its exterior appearance, which has nothing striking and offers no novelty. It owes it sim-

---

[1] The disciples of Frœbel have modified in different manners his system of gifts. See, for example, the *Jardin d'enfants*, by Goldammer, French translation by Louis Fournier, 1877.

ply to the way in which I use it, that is, to my method
and to the philosophical law on which it is founded. The
justification of my system of education is entirely in this law;
according as this law is rejected or admitted, the system falls
or continues· with it. All the rest is but material without any
value of its own."

It is this " material," however, which for Frœbel had no
value, that his admirers have above all preserved of his
method, without longer caring for the allegorical sense which
he attached to it.

540. APPEAL TO THE INSTINCTS OF THE CHILD. — That
which makes, notwithstanding so much that is whimsical, the
lasting merit of Frœbel's work, that which justifies in part
the admiration which it has excited, is that he organized the
salle d'asile, the infant school, and that he realized for it
that which Pestalozzi had attempted for the elementary
school. He knew how to make an appeal to the instincts of
the youngest child, to combine a system of exercises for the
training of the hand, for the education of the senses, to
satisfy the need of movement and activity which develops
itself from the first day of life, and, finally, to make of the
child a creator, a little artist always at work.

For the old education, which he calls " a hot-house education," and in which the instruction, premature through language, smothers in their germs the native powers of the
child, in order to excite his memory and his judgment by
artificial means, — for this education he substitutes a free and
cheerful education which cultivates the faculties of the child
by love, and which makes a just estimate of his instincts.
Books are suppressed, and lessons also. The child freely
expands in play.

541. THE IMPORTANCE OF PLAY. — With Frœbel, play became an essential element of education. This ingenious

teacher knew how to make of it an art, an instrument for the development of the infant faculties.

"The plays of the child," he said, "are, as it were, the germ of the whole life which is to follow, for the whole man develops and manifests itself in it; in it he reveals his noblest aptitudes and the deepest elements of his being. The whole life of man has its source in that epoch of existence, and whether that life is serene or sad, tranquil or agitated, fruitful or sterile, whether it brings peace or war, that depends on the care, more or less judicious, given to the beginnings of existence."

542. PRINCIPAL NEEDS OF THE CHILD. — Gréard, in a remarkable study on the method of Frœbel, reduces the aspirations of the child to three essential instincts : —

1. The taste for observation : —

"All the senses of the child are on the alert; all the objects which his sight or his hand encounters attract him, interest him, delight him.".

2. The need of activity, the taste for construction : —

"It is not enough that we show him objects; it is necessary that he touch them, that he handle them, that he appropriate them to himself. . . . He takes delight in constructing ; he is naturally geometrician and artist."

3. Finally, the sentiment of personality : —

"He wishes to have his own place, his own occupation, his own teacher."

Now Frœbel's method has precisely for its object the satisfaction of these different instincts.

"To place the child before a common table." says Gréard, "but with his own chair and a place that belongs to him, so that he feels that he is the owner of his little domain ; to excite at the very beginning his good will by the promise of

an interesting game ; to develop in succession under his
very eyes the marvels of the five gifts : to teach him in the
first place, from concrete objects exposed to his sight, balls
of colored worsted and geometrical solids, to distinguish
color, form, material, the different parts of a body, so as to
accustom him to *see*, that is, to seize the aspects, the figures,
the resemblances, the differences, the relations of things ;
then to place the objects in his hands, and to teach him to
make with the balls of colored worsted combinations of colors agreeable to the eye, to arrange, with matches united
by balls of cork, squares, angles, triangles of all sorts, to
set up little cubes in the form of crosses, pyramids, etc. ; —
then, either by means of strips of colored paper placed in
different directions, interlaced into one another, braided as a
weaver would make a fabric, or with the crayon, to drill him
in reproducing, in creating, designs representing all the
geometrical forms, so that to the habit of observation is
gradually joined that of invention ; finally, while his hand
is busy in concert with his intelligence, and while his need of
activity is satisfied, to take advantage of this awakened and
satisfied attention to fix in his mind by appropriate questions
some notions of the properties and uses of forms, by relating
them to some great principle of general order, simple and
fruitful, to mingle the practical lesson with moral observations, drawn in particular from the incidents of the school
— this, in its natural progress and its normal development, is
the method of Frœbel."

543. DEFECTS IN FRŒBEL'S METHOD. — There is ground
for thinking, notwithstanding all, that Frœbel's method is a
little complicated, a little artificial, and that it sometimes
proceeds in opposition to the natural disposition of children.
Their soul, he said, cannot in the first period of its develop-

ment, recognize itself, apprehend itself, save in the perception of the simplest forms of the exterior world, presented in
a concrete manner. Now nature of herself does not offer
these elementary forms ; it is necessary to know how to extract them from the infinite diversity of things. And Froebel found these simple forms in the sphere, the cube, and the
cylinder.

But these forms, we reply, are but abstractions ; it does
not suffice to say that the cube and the sphere are material
and palpable, — they are none the less the product of abstract thought on this account ; nature does not present these
simple geometrical forms ; everything in them is complex.
Now the nascent thought is employed at first on real things,
on the living and irregular forms of animals and vegetables ;
then in this case, the mind proceeds naturally from the complex to the simple, from the concrete to the abstract. It
seems, on the contrary, that Froebel begins with the abstract
in order to arrive at the concrete.

In the school of Froebel other defects have been developed.
An abuse has been made of the exercises in imitation and
invention. The child has been made to produce marvels of
construction which take too much of his time and demand of
him too much effort. It has been forgotten that these employments should be preparatory exercises, — means, and
not the end of education.

544. THE LAST ESTABLISHMENTS OF FROEBEL. — Towards
1840, the ideas of Froebel began to become popular. His
methods attracted attention. Then he wished to transform
his school at Blankenburg into a model establishment. He
addressed an appeal to the German nation in favor of his
work, but it was only slightly successful. Obliged in 1844
to close his institute, through lack of resources, he then

travelled through Germany in order to make known his methods. He did not derive from his journey the profit that he expected from it, and, discouraged, he returned once more to Keilhau, where he opened a course in method, or a normal course, for the use of young women who were preparing themselves for the education of infants. This association with women, in which Frœbel lived till his death, exercised a profound influence on the development of his system. A much greater share of attention was given to the practical exercises, and the mathematics was put in the background.

In 1850 he obtained through the intervention of the Baroness von Marenholtz, one of his most ardent admirers, the lease of the Castle of Marienthal, and to this he transferred his establishment. A long period of activity seemed opening before him. He personally directed the games of the children, and trained the teachers; but he died suddenly in 1852.

545. FRŒBEL AND DIESTERWEG. — However, before his death, Frœbel was able to witness the growing success of his work. Each day he received eminent adhesions; for example, that of Diesterweg.[1] It was through the mediation of the Baroness von Marenholtz that Frœbel and Diesterweg, the celebrated director of the normal school of Berlin, became acquainted. Diesterweg was a strong and practical spirit, who contributed much to the development of instruction in Prussia. At first he had a contempt for Frœbel, whom he treated as a charlatan; but on his first conversation with him he changed his opinion. He was taken to the schoolroom in which Frœbel was teaching; but wholly intent on

---

[1] See on Diesterweg the article by Pécaut, in the *Dictionnaire de Pédagogie*.

his work, Frœbel did not observe the presence of the visitor. Diesterweg was impressed by seeing this old man devoting himself entirely to his little pupils, and his prejudices disappeared. To a certain extent he became the propagator of Frœbel's ideas. He agreed with him on his general conception of the needs of the child, and of the province of woman as the earliest educator.

546. SUCCESS OF FRŒBEL'S WORK.—Frœbel had other imitators. Like Pestalozzi, he inspired a large number of minds by his writings, and through the zeal of Madame von Marenholtz, and of some other disciples, his practical work prospered. The *Kindergartens* have been multiplied in many places, and particularly in Austria.

547. THE PÈRE GIRARD (1765-1850). — The Père Girard is the most eminent educator of modern Switzerland. Less celebrated than Pestalozzi and Frœbel, he yet has this advantage over them, of having been better prepared for his profession as an educator. After having finished a thorough and complete course of classical study, he for a long time taught the same subjects in the same school. He acquired experience and wrote his treatises only in an advanced age, at a time when he was in complete possession of his ideas. He was in fact seventy-nine years old when he published his book *On the Systematic Teaching of the Mother Tongue*. It is a work of mature thought, and sums up a whole lifetime of labor. Less addicted to system than Frœbel and Pestalozzi, the Père Girard still carries mere system too far, and makes a misuse of the principle which consisted in making of all the parts of instruction the elements of moral education.

548. LIFE OF THE PÈRE GIRARD. — Girard was born in Friburg in 1765. His pedagogic instinct manifested itself

at an early hour. While still very young he aided his mother in instructing his fourteen brothers and sisters. Like Frœbel, he was passionately fond of religious questions. One day as he had heard his preceptor say that there was no salvation outside of the Roman Church, he sought his mother in tears, and asked her if the Protestant tradesman who brought her fruit each day would be damned. His mother reassured him, and he always remained faithful to what he called "the theology of his mother," — a tolerant and broad theology which brought on him the hatred of the Jesuits.

At the age of sixteen he entered the order of the Gray Friars, and completed his novitiate at Lucerne. He then taught in several convents, in particular at Wurtzburg, where he remained four years (1785–1788). He returned to Friburg in 1789, and for ten years he devoted himself almost exclusively to his ecclesiastical functions.

But his vocation as an educator was even then indicated by some things that he had written.

In 1798, under the influence of the ideas of Kant, whose philosophical doctrine he had ardently studied, he published a *Scheme of Education for all Helvetia*, addressed to the Swiss minister Stapfer, who was also the patron of Pestalozzi.

It was only in 1804, that Girard devoted himself entirely to teaching, the very year in which Frœbel began his work. He was appointed to direct the primary school at Friburg, which had just been entrusted to the Gray Friars. Girard received the title of " prefect of studies," and for nineteen years, from 1805 to 1823, he exercised his functions as a teacher in that school. Very small in the beginning, the school had a remarkable growth. There was added to it even a school for girls. At first Girard had Gray Friars for colleagues ; but he soon replaced them with lay teachers, who obeyed him better and devoted themselves more entirely to their task. The teacher of drawing was a Protestant.

549. SUCCESS OF THE SCHOOL AT FRIBURG. — A disciple and an admirer of Girard, the pastor Naville, has related in his work on *Public Education* [1] the brilliant results obtained by Girard in his school at Friburg.

" He had trained a body of youth the like of which perhaps no city in the world could furnish. It was not without a profound emotion that the friends of humanity contemplated a spectacle so new and so touching. That ignorant and boorish class, full of prejudices, which everywhere abounds, was no longer met with at Friburg. . . . The young there developed graces of an amiable deportment which were never marred by anything disagreeable in tone, speech, or manner. If, seeing children approaching you covered with rags, you approached them thinking that you were about to encounter little ruffians, you were wholly surprised to have them reply to you with politeness, with judgment, and with that accent which bespeaks genteel manners and a careful education. . . . You will find the explanation in the school, when you observe the groups where these same children exercise by turns, as in playing, their judgment and their conscience. Three or four hours a day employed in this work gave the young that intelligence, those sentiments, and those manners which delighted you."

550. THE LAST YEARS OF THE PÈRE GIRARD. — Notwithstanding the success of his instruction, the Père Girard was obliged to abandon the charge of his school in 1823. His loss of position was the result of the intrigues of the Jes-

---

[1] *De l'éducation publique.* Paris, 1833, p. 158. Naville (1784–1846) founded in 1817, at Vernier, near Geneva, an institute where he applied with success the educative method of the Père Girard.

uits, whose college had been re-established in 1818.   He left
Friburg amid universal regrets, and retired to Lucerne, where
he taught philosophy till 1834.   At that date he returned to
his native city and lived a life of seclusion.   It was then
that he wrote his pedagogical works.   But through his disciples, and particularly through the pastor Naville, the methods
of the Père Girard were known before he had published anything.

551. TEACHING OF THE MOTHER TONGUE. — Let us now
examine the general spirit of the pedagogy of Girard.   It is
in the theoretical work which he published in 1844, and
which was crowned by the French Academy in the same year,
that we must look for the principles of his method.   It consisted in " choosing a study which may be considered as one
essential part of the instruction common to all the classes of
society, and which nevertheless is fit for calling into exercise
all the intellectual powers."   This study was the mother
tongue, which Girard employed for the moral and religious
development of children.

Villemain, in his report on the books of Girard, has clearly defined the purpose of the common school as conceived by
the educator of Friburg : —

" Where the period of instruction is necessarily short and
its object limited, a wise choice of method is the thing of
first importance, for upon this choice will depend the education itself.   If that method is purely technical, if its exclusive object is reading, writing, and the rules of grammar and
computation, the child of the common people will be poorly
instructed and will not be educated at all.   A difficult task
burdens his memory without developing his soul.   A new
process is placed at his disposal, one workshop more is open
to him, so to speak ; but the trace left by that instruction

will not be deep, will sometimes even be lost through lack of application and exercise, and will not have acted on the moral nature, too often absorbed eventually by a monotonous devotion to duty or the excessive fatigue of bodily labor. The only, the real people's school, is then that in which all the elements of study serve for the culture of the soul, and in which the child grows better by the things which he learns and by the manner in which he learns them."

552. ANALYSIS OF THIS WORK. — The book of Girard is divided into four parts. The first contains *general considerations* on the manner in which the mother teaches her children to speak, upon the purpose of a course of instruction on the mother tongue, and on the elements which should compose it.

The second part is entitled: *The Systematic Teaching of the Mother Tongue considered solely as the Expression of Thought.* It is language considered in itself; but Girard desires that the word should always be united to the thought. It is not necessary that the teaching of grammar should be reduced to verbal instruction; it should also serve to develop the thought of pupils.

In the third part, the *Systematic Teaching of the Mother Tongue considered as the Means of Intellectual Culture*, Girard considers everything which can contribute to the development of the faculties.

In the fourth part, the *Systematic Teaching of Language employed for the Culture of the Heart*, Girard shows how the teaching of language may assist in moral education.

A fifth part, *Use of the Course in the Mother Tongue*, is, so to speak, the material part of the book, and, as it were, the outline of the great practical work of Girard, the *Educative* [1] *Course in the Mother Tongue.*

---

[1] I am aware that this term is not found in the latest Webster, but I see no other way of expressing the force of the word *éducatif*, which seems to signify the disciplinary, or rather the culture, value of a study. (P.)

553. The Grammarian, the Logician, the Educator. — Iu other terms, Girard places himself in succession at four different points of view in the teaching of language : —

" Four persons," he says, " ought to concur in construct- ing the course in the mother tongue : the grammarian, the logician, the educator, and, finally, the man of letters."

The task of the grammarian is to furnish the material of the language and its proper forms.

The logician will teach us what must be done in order to cultivate the intelligence of the young.

The educator will ever be inspired by this grand truth :- ".. Man acts as he loves, and he loves as he thinks." He will try to grave in the souls of children all the beautiful and grand truths which can awaken and nourish pure and noble affections.

Finally, the man of letters has also his part in the course in language, in the sense that pupils, besides being required from the beginning of their studies to invent propositions and sentences, will have a little later to compose narratives, letters, dialogues, etc.

554. The Grammar of Ideas. — Elementary instruction should have for its purpose the development of the mind and the judgment. It is no longer a question of cultivating the memory alone and of causing words to be learned. The Père Girard would have grammar made an exercise in thinking.

" The grammars in use," he says, " are intended simply to teach correctness in speaking and writing. By their aid we are able finally to avoid a certain number of faults in style and orthography. . . . This instruction becomes a pure affair of memory, and the child becomes accustomed to pronounce sounds to which he attaches no meaning. The child needs a *grammar of ideas*. . . . Our *grammars of words* are the plague of education." In other terms, grammar should be made above all else an exercise in thinking, and, as it were, "the logic of childhood."

555. DISCREET USE OF RULES. — The Père Girard does not proscribe rules. The teaching of language cannot do without them; "but there is," he says, "a proper manner of presenting them to children, and a just medium to hold."

In the teaching of grammar we must follow the course which the grammarians themselves have followed in order to construct their science: "The rules were established on facts. It is then to facts that they must be referred in instruction, in order that by this means children may be taught to do intelligently what they have hitherto done through blind imitation. . . . Few rules, many exercises. Rules are always abstract, dry, and for this very reason poorly adapted to please children, even when they can comprehend them. We ought, then, in general, to make a very sparing use of them."

So the Père Girard particularly recommends practical exercises, oral instruction, the continual use of the blackboard, the active and animated co-operation of all the members of the class, rapid interrogation, the Socratic method, the abuse of which, however, he criticises.[1]

556. MORAL ARITHMETIC.[2] — The Père Girard, like almost all the men who have conceived an original idea, has fallen

---

[1] See Chap. III. of Book III. paragraph 1st. *Just medium between two extremes.*

[2] Here is an example from Père Girard's arithmetic: —

"A father had the habit of going every evening to the dram-shop, and often left his family at home without bread. During the five years that he led this life, he spent, the first year, 197 francs, the second, 204 francs, into the love of systematizing. He believed that not only language, but all the branches of study might contribute to moral education.

"He conceived," says Naville, "that by means of a selection of problems adapted to the development of the social affections in the family, the commune, and the State, one might give to arithmetic such a wholesome direction that it might be made to contribute, not only to making the child prudent and economical, but even more to extend his views beyond the narrow circle of selfishness, and to cultivate in him beneficent dispositions."[1]

557. MORAL GEOGRAPHY. — It is in the same spirit that he claimed to find in the study of geography a means of contributing to the development of the moral nature.

"According to my honest conviction, every elementary work for children ought to be a means of education. If it is limited to giving knowledge, if it is limited to developing the faculties of the pupil, I can approve the order and the life which the author has known how to put into his work; but I am not satisfied with it. I am even offended to find only a teacher of language, of natural history, of geography, etc., when I expected something much greater, — an instructor of the young, training the mind in order to train the heart. . . . Geography lends itself as marvellously to this sublime purpose, although in a sphere a little narrower."[2]

558. EDUCATIVE COURSE IN THE MOTHER TONGUE. — Girard is not content to state his doctrine in his book *On the*

---

the third, 212 francs, and the fourth, 129 francs. How many francs would this unfortunate father have saved if he had not had a taste for drink?" (P.)

[1] Naville, *De l'Éducation publique*, p. 411.

[2] *Explication du plan de Fribourg en Suisse*, 1817.

Systematic Teaching of the Mother Tongue ; but in the four volumes of his *Educative Course* (1844–1846) he has applied his method. Full of new and radical views, original in the arrangement of material as in its system of exposition, revolutionary even in its grammatical terminology, this book is a mine from which we may borrow without stint, only we shall not advise wholesale adoption : there is matter to take and to leave.[1]

559. ANALYSIS OF THIS WORK. — The title indicates the general character of the work. In his *Cours éducatif*, Girard does not separate education from instruction. The purpose is to develop the moral and religious sentiments of the child, no less than to teach him his native language.

The first lessons in grammar ought to be lessons in things. The child is made to name the objects which he knows, — persons, animals, things, — and through these he is made to acquire notions of nouns, common and proper, of gender and number. He is then induced to find for himself the physical, intellectual, and moral qualities of objects, and by this means is made familiar with qualifying adjectives. Care is taken, moreover, while causing each quality to be named, as farther on while causing each judgment to be expressed, to ask the child, " Is this right? Is this wrong?"

The agreement of adjective with noun is learned by practice. The child is drilled in applying adjectives to the nouns which he has found, and *vice versa.*

Once in possession of the essential elements of the proposition, the child begins the study of the proposition itself, and finally the study of the verb. Girard makes it a principle always to have the conjugations made by means of propo-

---

[1] See the interesting articles of Lafargue in the *Bulletin pédagogique de l'enseignement secondaire,* 1882.

sitious.   At first, however, he employs in simple propositions only the indicative, the infinitive, the imperative, and the participle ; he postpones till later the study of the conditional and the subjunctive.   It is to be noted, in addition, that he brings forward simultaneously the simple tenses of all the conjugations.

The order followed by Girard is wholly different from that of the ordinary grammars.   This is how he explains it : —

" In their first part, the grammars set out in a row the nine sorts of words, and thus give in rapid succession their definitions, distinctions, and variable forms, which introduces a legion of terms wholly unknown to the child.   The second part of these grammars takes up these words again in the same order, so as, in an uninteresting way, to regulate their use in construction, — a tedious and arid system, which affords the child no interest."

Elsewhere, speaking of his own work, he writes : —

" My work differs essentially from the grammars which are put in the hands of children.   When we write on language for adults, we may adhere to definitions, distinctions, rules, and exceptions, and formulate statements regarding their proper use ; but he who writes for children ought to have the education of the mind and heart in view, and regulate on that basis the course and form of instruction.   The course ought to be rigorously progressive, and the pupils ought, from beginning to end, to assist themselves in constructing a grammar of their own."

" So, instead of making generalizations on the noun, adjective. verb, etc., and of connecting with these parts of speech all that relates to them, we must apply ourselves to the substance of language, passing step by step from the simple to the complex, and teaching children to think, in order to teach them to comprehend and to speak the language of man. The little details cannot appear till later, and as occasion requires. From this there necessarily results a displacement of grammatical material which has been industriously collected and arranged. Hence, also, a great parsimony in definitions and abstract distinctions which repel children."

560. EDUCATIONAL INFLUENCE OF THE PÈRE GIRARD. — The influence of the Père Girard was not extended simply to Switzerland. It has radiated abroad. His ideas have been disseminated in Italy, propagated by the Abbé Lambruschini and by Enrico Mayer. A journal even has been founded to serve as the organ of the "Girardists" of the Peninsula. In France, Michel, in the *Journal de l'éducation pratique*, and Rapet in different works,[1] have commended to public attention the methods of the Swiss educator. Finally, it may be remarked that the principles very recently set forth by the *Conseil supérieure de l'instruction publique* (1880), on the teaching of French in the elementary classes of the lycées, are in great part the echo of the pedagogical doctrine of the Père Girard.

[561. ANALYTICAL SUMMARY. — 1. In this study we have the third exposition, in historical order, — Rousseau, Pestalozzi, Frœbel, — of the doctrine of nature as applied to education. This doctrine may be summarized as follows : —

The existing order of things is conceived as an animated organism, and is personified under the term Nature. All living things, such as plants, animals, and men, are products of the creative power that is immanent in nature, and each is predetermined to an upward development in the line of

---

[1] Monsieurs Rapet and Michel were associated in the publication of the *Cours éducatif de la langue maternelle.*

growth. This growth is an unfolding from within outward, and each individual thing, as a child, has reached the term of its development when it has grown into the type of its kind. In the case of the human species, this growth is best when it is *natural*, and it is natural to the degree in which it takes place without the deliberate intervention of art. This process of development is Nature's work, and its synonym is education. Education is best when it is most *natural*, that is, when it suffers least from human interference. The question of the relative parts to be played by Nature and by Art in education has given rise to two schools of educators.

2. In Frœbel's application of this doctrine, the original conception is obscured by three circumstances : 1. his deism ; 2. his mysticism or symbolism ; 3. his dependence on artificial agents, his "gifts," and his belief in the potency of abstractions.

3. The *Kindergarten* has introduced many ameliorations into primary instruction, and its tendency is to make child-life happy through self-activity. Its shortcomings are that it undervalues the acquisition of second-hand knowledge, obscures the distinction between work and play, and indisposes, and perhaps unfits, the pupil to contend with real difficulties.[1]

4. The effect of this new movement in primary instruction upon educational science has been wholesome. It has induced a closer study of child nature, has enlisted the sympathies

---

[1] "Man owes his growth, his energy, chiefly to that striving of the will, that conflict with difficulty, which we call effort. Easy, pleasant work does not make robust minds, does not give men a consciousness of their powers, does not train them to endurance, to perseverance, to steady force of will, that force without which all other acquisitions avail nothing." Dr. Channing.

and affections in support of elementary instruction, and has profoundly modified the conception of the primary school.

. 5. Whether the *Kindergarten* is to be maintained apart, as an institution *sui generis*, or whether it is to lose its identity by the absorption of its spirit into the primary school, is a question for the future. Probably the latter result will follow.

6. The misuse of a good thought is seen in the attempt of the Père Girard to give a distinct moral value to every school exercise. It is the verdict of experience that the moral value of science is greatest when it is taught simply as science, and that the direct teaching of ethics should be conducted on an independent basis.]

CHAPTER XX.

WOMEN AS EDUCATORS.

562. WOMEN AS EDUCATORS. — One of the characteristic
features of the pedagogy of the nineteenth century is the
constant progress in the education of women. Woman will
be better instructed, and at the same time she will play a
more important part in instruction. Primary schools for girls
did not exist, so to speak, in France, at the commencement
of this century. Fourcroy, who reported the bill of May 1,
1802, declared that "the law makes no mention of girls."
But through the efforts of the monarchy of July, and still

more of the liberal laws of the second and of the third Republic, the primary instruction of girls will become more and more general. Secondary public instruction will be created for women by the law of December 20, 1880, and the equality of the two sexes, in respect of education, will tend more and more to become a reality, through the influence of governmental action as well as that of private initiative.

But not less remarkable is the important part which women, by their abstract reflections or by their practical efforts, have taken in the progress of pedagogy. In the history of education, the nineteenth century will be noted for the great number of its women who were educators, some who were real philosophers and distinguished writers, and others, zealous and enthusiastic teachers.

563. MADAME DE GENLIS (1746–1830). — While she does not belong to the nineteenth century by her pedagogical writings, Madame de Genlis has certain rights to a foremost place in the list of the educational women of our time. She had in the highest degree the pedagogic vocation ; only, that vocation became a mania and was squandered on everything. Madame de Genlis wished to know everything in order that she might teach everything. " She was more than a woman author," says Sainte-Beuve, wittily ; " she was a woman *teacher;* she was born with the sign on her forehead."

Young girls of their own accord play *mamma* with their dolls. From the age of seven, Madame de Genlis played *teacher.*

" I had a taste for teaching children, and I became schoolmistress in a curious way. . . . Little boys from the village came under the window of my parents' country-seat to play. I amused myself in watching them, and I soon took it into my head to give them lessons."

Twenty years later, the village teacher became the governess of the daughters of the Duchesse de Chartres, and the *governor* of the sons of the Duke de Chartres (Philippe-Égalité).

564. PEDAGOGICAL WORKS. — The principal work of Madame de Genlis, *Letters on Education* (1782), treats of the education of princes and also of " that of young persons and of men." In giving it that other title, *Adèle and Théodore*, the author indicated her intention of rivaling Rousseau, and of educating a man and a woman more perfect than Émile and Sophie.

Although she had a profoundly aristocratic nature, Madame de Genlis, after the revolution of 1789, seemed for an instant to follow the liberal current which was sweeping minds along. It was then that she published the *Counsels on the Education of the Dauphin*, and some parts of her educational journal, entitled *Lessons of a Governess*. She never ceased to preach love of the people to sovereigns, and in justice this must be said to her credit, that she did not write merely for courtly people. She protests, and with spirit, " that she is the first author who has concerned herself with the education of the people. This glory," she adds, " is dear to my heart." In support of these assertions, Madame de Genlis cites the fourth volume of her *Théâtre d'éducation*, which is, she says, " solely intended for the children of tradesmen and artisans ; domestics and peasants will there see a detailed account of their obligations and their duties."

565. ENCYCLOPÆDIC EDUCATION. — It has been said with reason that Madame de Genlis was the personification of encyclopædic instruction.[1]

---

[1] Gréard, *Mémoire sur l'enseignement secondaire des filles*, p. 78.

" Her programme of instruction had no limits. She favors Latin, without, however, thinking the knowledge of it indispensable. She gives a large place to the living languages. At Saint Leu, her pupils garden in German, dine in English, and sup in Italian. At the same time she invents gymnastic apparatus, — pulleys, baskets, wooden beds, lead shoes. Nothing takes her at unawares, her over-facile pen stops at nothing ; she is universal. A plan for a rural school for children in the country is wanted, and she furnishes it."

566. IMITATION OF ROUSSEAU. — Madame de Genlis never ceased to criticise Rousseau, and yet, in her educational romances, the inspiration of Rousseau is everywhere present. How can we fail to recognize a pupil of Rousseau in the father of Adèle and Théodore, who leaves Paris in order to devote himself entirely to the education of his children, to make himself " their governor and their friend, and finally, to screen the infancy of his son and daughter from the examples of vice "? And the methods manufactured by Rousseau, the unforeseen lessons, the indirect means employed to instruct without having the appearance of doing so, — Madame de Genlis desires no others. Nothing is more amusing than the description of the country-seat of the Baron d'Almane, the father of Adèle and Théodore. It is no longer a country-seat ; it is a school-house. The walls are no longer walls ; they are charts of history and maps of geography.

" When we would have our children study history according to a chronological order, we start from my bed-chamber, which represents sacred history ; from there we enter my gallery, where we find ancient history ; we reach the parlor, which contains Roman history, and we end with the gallery of Monsieur d'Almane (it is the Baroness who speaks), where is found the history of France."

In her pedagogic fairyland, Madame de Genlis does not wish the child to meet a single object which may not be transformed into an instrument of instruction. Adèle and Théodore cannot take a hand-screen without finding a geography lesson represented on it, and drawn out at full length. Here are pictures worked in tapestry; they are historical scenes; on the back of them care has been taken to write an explanation of what they represent. At least, those five or six movable partitions which are displayed in the apartment on cold days have no instructive purposes? You are mistaken. There is painted and written on them the history of England, of Spain, of Germany, and that of the Moors and the Turks. Even in the dining-room, mythology encumbers the panels of the room, and " it usually forms the subjcet of conversation during the dinner." In that castle, bewitched, so to speak, by the elf of history, there is not a glance that is lost, not a minute without its lesson, not a corner where one may waste his time in dreaming. History pursues you like a ghost, like a nightmare, along the corridors, on the stairs, even on the carpet on which you tread, and on the chairs upon which you sit. The true way to disgust a child forever with historical studies is to condemn him to live for eight days in this house-school of Madame de Genlis.

567. Miss Edgeworth (1767–1849). — It is with the Scotch philosophy and the psychological theories of Reid and Dugald Stewart, that were inspired in different degrees two distinguished women, who honored English pedagogy at the beginning of this century, — Miss Edgeworth and Miss Hamilton.

In her book on *Practical Education*, published in 1798,[1]

---

[1] French translation by Pictet, 1801.

Miss Edgeworth does not lose herself in theoretical dissertations. Her book is a collection of facts, observations, and
precepts. The first chapter treats of toys, and the author
justifies this beginning by saying that in education there is
nothing trivial and minute. It is first by conversations, and
then by the use of the inventive, analytical, and intuitive
method, that Miss Edgeworth proposes to train her pupils ;
and her reflections on intellectual education deserve to be
considered. In moral education she agrees with Locke, and
seems to place great reliance on the sentiment of honor, and
on the love of reputation. In every case she absolutely
ignores the religious feeling. The characteristic of her system is that it makes " a total abstraction of religious ideas."

568. MISS HAMILTON (1758-1816). — Miss Hamilton is
at once more philosophical and more Christian than Miss
Edgeworth. It is from the psychologist Hartley that she
borrows her essential principle, which consists in making of
the association of ideas the basis of education. Hartley saw
in this the sovereign law of intellectual development. But,
on the other hand, she declares " that she follows no other
guide than the precepts of the Gospel."

The principal work of Miss Hamilton, her *Letters on the
Elementary Principles of Education* (1801),[1] has a more
theoretical character than the book of Miss Edgeworth.
With her it is above all else a question of principles, which,
she says, are more necessary than rules. We find but few
reflections on teaching proper. She borrows the very words
of Dugald Stewart to define the object of education : —

" The most essential objects of education are the following : *first*, to cultivate all the various principles of our nature,
both speculative and active, in such a manner as to bring

---

[1] French translation by Chéron, 2 vols., Paris, 1804.

them to the greatest perfection of which they are susceptible; and *secondly*, by watching over the impressions and
associations which the mind receives in early life, to secure
it against the influence of prevailing errors; and, as far
as possible, to engage its prepossessions on the side of
truth." [1]

To cultivate the intellectual and moral faculties, Miss
Hamilton places her chief dependence, as we have said, on
the principle of the association of ideas. We must break up,
or, rather, prevent from being formed, all false associations,
that is, all inaccurate judgments. Order once re-established
among ideas, the will will be upright, and the conduct well
regulated. In other terms, this was to subordinate, perhaps
too completely, the development of the moral faculties to the
culture of the intellectual faculties.

" It is evident," says Miss Hamilton, " that all our desires
are in accord with ideas of pleasure, and all our aversions
with ideas of pain."

The educator will then try to associate the idea of pleasure
with what is good and useful for the child and for the man.

Let us also note, in passing, the solicitude of Miss Hamilton for the education of the people : —

" From most of the writers on education it would appear
that it is only to people of rank and fortune that education
is a matter of any importance. . . . My plan has for its
object the cultivation of the faculties that are common to the
whole human race." [2]

On this point her thought was the same as that of Miss
Edgeworth, whose father, in 1799, in the Irish Parliament,
had caused the adoption of the first law on primary instruction.

---

[1] Stewart, *Elements*, p. 11.
[2] *Letters*, Vol. I. p. 11.

569. MADAME CAMPAN (1752–1822). — Twenty-five years' experience, either at the court of Louis XV., or in the school at Saint-Germain, which she founded under the Revolution, or finally in the institution at Écouen, the direction of which was entrusted to her by Napoleon I., in 1807, — such are the claims which at once assure to Madame Campan some authority on pedagogical questions.[1] Let us add that good sense, a methodical and prudent mind, — in a word, qualities which were reasonable rather than brilliant, — directed that long personal experience.

" First I saw," she said, " then I reflected, and finally I wrote."

570. EULOGY ON HOME EDUCATION. — From a teacher, from the directress of a school, we would expect prejudices in favor of public education in boarding-schools. That which secures our ready confidence, is that Madame Campan, on the contrary, appreciates better than any one else the advantages of maternal education : —

" To create mothers," she said, " this is the whole education of women." Nothing seems to her superior to a mother governess " who does not keep late hours, who rises betimes," who, finally, devotes herself resolutely to the important duty with which she is charged.

" There is no boarding-school, however well it may be conducted, there is no convent, however pious its government may be, which can give an education comparable to that which a young girl receives from a mother who is educated, and who finds her sweetest occupation and her true glory in the education of her daughter."

Madame Campan, moreover, reminds mothers who would

---

[1] See the two volumes published in 1824 by Barrière, on the *Éducation, par Madame Campan,* followed by the *Conseils aux jeunes filles.*

be the teachers of their own daughters, of all the obligations
which are involved in such a charge. Too often the mother
who jealously keeps her daughter near her, is not capable of
educating her. In this case there is only the appearance of
home education, and as Madame Campan wittily says, "this
is no longer *maternal education;* it is but *education at
home.*"

571. PROGRESS IN INSTRUCTION. — Fénelon was Madame
Campan's favorite author. On the other hand, there was
some resemblance between the rules of the school at Écouen
and those of Saint Cyr. The spirit of the seventeenth century lives again in the educational institutions of the nineteenth, and Madame Campan continues the work of Madame
de Maintenon.

However, there is progress in more than one respect, and
the instruction is more solid and more complete.

"The purpose of education," wrote Madame Campan to
the Emperor, " ought to be directed: 1. towards the domestic virtues ; 2. towards instruction, to such a degree of perfection in the knowledge of language, computation, history,
writing, and geography, that all pupils shall be assured of
the happiness of being able to instruct their own daughters."

Madame Campan desired, moreover, to extend her work.
She demanded of the Emperor the creation of several public
establishments " for educating the daughters of certain classes
of the servants of the State." She desired that the government should take under its supervision private institutions,
and contemplated for women as for men a sort of university
" which might replace the convents and the colleges." But
Napoleon was not the man to enter into these schemes. The
schools of " women-logicians " were scarcely to his taste,
and the teaching congregations, which he restored to their
privileges, the better served his purpose.

572. INTEREST IN POPULAR EDUCATION. — One might believe that Madame Campan, who had begun by being the teacher of the three daughters of Louis XV., and who associated with scarcely any save the wealthy or the titled, had never had the taste or the leisure to think of popular instruction. It is nothing of the sort, as is proved by her *Counsels to Young Girls, a work intended for Elementary Schools.*

" There is no ground for fearing that the daughters of the rich will ever be in want of books to instruct them or of governesses to direct them. It is not at all so with the children who belong to the less fortunate classes. . . .˙ I have seen with my own eyes how incomplete and neglected is the education of the daughters of country people. . . . It is for them that I have penned this little work."

The work itself has not perhaps the tone that could be desired, nor all the simplicity that the author would have wished to give it; but we must thank Madame Campan for her intentions, and we count among her highest claims to the esteem of posterity the effort which she made in her old age to become, at least in her writings, a simple school-mistress and a village teacher.

573. MADAME DE RÉMUSAT (1780–1821). — Madame de Rémusat has written only for women of the world. Herself a woman of the world, lady of the palace of the Empress Josephine, she had no personal experience in the way of teaching. She had nothing to do with the practice of education save in supervising the studies of her two sons, one of whom became a philosopher and an illustrious statesman, Charles de Rémusat. The noble book of Madame de Rémusat, her *Essay on the Education of Women*, does not commend itself by reason of its detailed precepts and scholastic methods, but by its lofty reflections and general principles.[1]

---

[1] The work of Madame de Rémusat was published in 1824, after the author's death, under the direction of Charles de Rémusat.

574. SKETCH OF FEMININE PSYCHOLOGY. — Let us first notice different passages in which the author sketches by a few touches the psychology of woman, and determines her sphere in life : —

" Woman is the companion of man upon the earth, but yet she exists on her own account; she is *inferior*, but not *subordinate*."

The expression here betrays Madame de Rémusat, and it would be more accurate to say that woman is not inferior to man, that she is his equal, but that in existing civil and social conditions she necessarily remains subordinate to him.

But with what perfect justness the amiable writer characterizes the peculiar qualities of woman !

" We lack continuity and depth when we would apply ourselves to general questions. Endowed with a quick intelligence, we hear promptly, we even divine and see just as well as men ; but too easily moved to remain impartial, too mobile to be profound, perceiving is easier for us than observing. Prolonged attention wearies us ; we are, in short, more mild than patient. More sensitive and more devoted than men, women are ignorant of that sort of selfishness which an independent being exhibits outwardly as a consciousness of his own power. To obtain from them any activity whatever, it is almost always necessary to *interest them in the happiness of another*. Their very faults are the outgrowths of their condition. The same cause will excite in man emotions of pride, and in woman only those of vanity."

575. THE SERIOUS IN EDUCATION. — Madame de Rémusat. still more than Madame Campan, belongs to the modern school. She desires for woman an education serious and grave.

" I see no reason for treating women less seriously than

men, for misrepresenting truth to them under the form of a prejudice, duty under the appearance of a superstition, in order that they may accept both the duty and the truth." She does not in the least incline to the opinion of the over-courteous moralist Joubert, who, with more gallantry than real respect for women, said : " Nothing too earthly or too material ought to employ young ladies ; only delicate material should busy their hands. . . . They resemble the imagination, and like it they should touch only the surface of things." [1]

Madame de Rémusat enters into the spirit of her time, and her admiration for the age of Louis XIV. does not make her forget what she owes to the new society, transformed by great political reforms.

" We are drawing near the time when every Frenchman shall be a citizen. In her turn, the destiny of woman is comprised in these two terms : *wife and mother of a citizen.* There is much morality, and a very severe and touching morality, in the idea which ought to be attached to that word *citizen.* After religion, I do not know a more powerful motive than the patriotic spirit for directing the young towards the good."

It is no longer a question, then, of training the woman and the man for themselves, for their individual destiny. They must be educated for the public good, for their duties in society. Madame de Rémusat is not one of those timid and frightened women who feel a homesickness for the past, whom the present terrifies. Liberal and courageous, she manfully accepts the new régime ; she proclaims its advantages, and, if she writes like a woman of the seventeenth century, almost with the perfection of Madame de Sévigné, her chosen model, she at least thinks like a daughter of the Revolution.

---

[1] Joubert, *Pensées.*

576. PHILOSOPHICAL SPIRIT. — That which is not less remarkable is the philosophical character of her reflections. She believes in liberty and in conscience. It is conscience which she purposes to substitute, as a moral rule, " for despotic and superficial caprices." It is no longer by the imperative term, *you must*, but by the obligatory term, *you ought*, that the mother should lead and govern her daughter.

" On every occasion let these words, *I ought*, re-appear in the conversation of the mother."

This is saying that the child ought to be treated as a free being. The end, and at the same time the most efficient means, of education, is the wise employment of liberty. While keeping the oversight of the child, he must be left to take care of himself, and on many occasions to follow the course that he will. By this means his will will be developed, and his character strengthened ; and this is an essential point according to Madame de Rémusat.

" If under Louis XIV.," she says, " the education of woman's mind was grave and often substantial, that of her character remained imperfect."

577. MADAME GUIZOT (1773–1827). — Madame Guizot first became known under her maiden name, Pauline de Meulan. In the closing years of the eighteenth century she had written several romances, and had contributed to the review of Suard, the *Publiciste*. In 1812 she married Guizot, the future author of the law of 1833, who had just founded the *Annals of Education*.[1] From this period, all her ideas and all her writings were directed almost exclusively

1 The *Annales de l'éducation* appeared from 1811 to 1814. It is an interesting collection to consult. In it Guizot published among other pedagogical works, his studies on the ideas of Rabelais and Montaigne, afterwards reprinted in the volume, *Études Morales*.

towards ethics and education. She published in succession, *Children* (1812), *Raoul and Victor* (1821), and, finally, her masterpiece, the *Family Letters on Education* (1826).

578. THE LETTERS ON EDUCATION. — To give at once an idea of the merit of this book,[1] we shall quote the opinion of Sainte-Beuve : —

"The work of Madame Guizot will survive the *Émile*, marking in this line the progress of the sound, temperate, and refined reason of our times, over the venturesome genius of Rousseau, just as in politics the *Démocratie* of De Tocqueville is an advance over the *Contrat Social*. Essential to meditate upon, as advice, in all education which would prepare strong men for the difficulties of our modern society, this book also contains, in the way of exposition, the noblest moral pages, the most sincere and the most convincing, which, with a few pages from Jouffroy, have been suggested to the philosophy of our age by the doctrines of a spiritualistic rationalism."

579. PSYCHOLOGICAL OPTIMISM. — The philosophical spirit is not lacking in the *Letters on Education*. The whole of Letter XII. is a plea in behalf of the relative innocence of the child. That which is bad in the disorderly inclination, says the author, is not the inclination, but the disorder : —

"The inclinations of a sentient being are in themselves what they ought to be. It has been said that a man could not be virtuous if he did not conquer his inclinations ; hence, his inclinations are evil. This is an error. No more could the tree produce good fruit, if, in pruning it, the disorderly flow of the sap were not arrested. Does this prove that the sap is harmful to the tree?"

---

[1] *Éducation domestique ou Lettres de famille sur l'éducation.* 2 vols. Paris, 1826.

It follows from these principles that discipline ought not to be severe.

" Do you not think it strange," exclaims Madame Guizot, " that for centuries education has been, so to speak, a systematic hostility against human nature ; that to correct and to punish have been synonymous ; and that we have heard only of dispositions to break, and natures to overcome, just as though it were a question of taking away from children the nature which God has given them in order to give them another such as teachers would have it? "

580. NATURE OF THE CHILD. — That which gives a great value to the work of Madame Guizot is, that besides the general considerations and the philosophical reflections, we there find a great number of circumstantial experiences and detailed observations which are admissible in a sound treatise on pedagogy. Like the psychology of the child, pedagogy itself, at least in its first chapters, ought to be conceived and written near a cradle. Madame Guizot forcibly indicates the importance of the first years, where the future destiny of the child is determined : " In those imperfect organs, in that incomplete intelligence, are contained, from the first moment of existence, the germs of that which is ever more to proceed from them either for better or for worse. The man will never have, in the whole course of his life, an impulse which does not belong to that nature, all the features of which are already foreshadowed in the infant. The infant will never receive a keen and durable impression, however slight, an impress of whatever kind, whose effects are not to influence the life of the man."

At the same time that she sees in the infant the rough draft of the man, Madame Guizot recognizes with a remarkable delicacy of psychologic sense, that which distinguishes, that which characterizes, the irreflective and inconsiderate nature of the child. What is more just than this observation? "We often deceive ourselves in attributing to the conduct of children, because it is analogous to our own, motives similar to those which guide ourselves."

What better observation than the example which Madame Guizot cites in support of this statement!

"Louise, by a sudden impulse, drops her toys, throws herself upon my neck, and cannot cease kissing me. It seems that all my mother's heart could not sufficiently respond to the warmth of her caresses; but by the same playful impulse she leaves me to kiss her doll or the arm of the chair which she meets on her way."

581. PHILOSOPHIC RATIONALISM. — Madame Guizot pushes rationalism much farther than Madame de Rémusat, and still farther than Madame Necker de Saussure. She is first a philosopher, then a Christian. She more nearly approaches Rousseau. She would first form in the minds of children the universal idea of God before initiating them into the particular dogmas of positive religions. She bases morals on the idea of duty, which is " the only basis of a complete education."

" I would place," she says, "each act of the child under the protection of an idea or of a moral sentiment."

Recalling the distinction made by Dupont de Nemours between *paternal commands* and *military commands*, the first addressing themselves to the reason, the others to be observed without protest and with a passive obedience, she does not conceal her preference for the use of the first, because she would form in the woman, as in the man, a spirit of reason and of liberty. She absolutely proscribes personal interest, and hence declares that " rewards have always seemed to her contrary to the true principle of education."

Let us say, lastly, without being able to enter into detail, that the book of Madame Guizot deserves to be read with care. There will be found in it a great number of excellent reflections on instruction which ought to be substantial rather than extensive; upon the reading of romances, and upon the theatre, which she does not forbid; upon easy methods, which she condemns; and, finally, on almost all pedagogical questions.[1]

582. MADAME NECKER DE SAUSSURE (1765–1841). — There are in the history of education privileged moments, periods that are particularly and happily fruitful. It is thus that within the space of a few years there appeared in succession the books of Madame de Rémusat, of Madame Guizot, and, the most important of all, the *Progressive Education* of Madame Necker de Saussure.[2]

A native of Geneva, like Rousseau, Madame Necker de Saussure has endowed French literature with an educational masterpiece, which for elevation of view and nobleness of inspiration, can take rank by the side of the *Émile*. Though she may sometimes be too logical and too austere, and while in general she is lacking in good humor, and while she looks upon life only through a veil of sadness, Madame Necker is an incomparable guide in educational affairs. She brings to the subject remarkable qualities of perspicacity and penetration, and a spirit of marked gravity. She takes a serious view of life, and applies herself to training the noblest qualities of the human soul. Profoundly religious, she unites a "philosophical boldness to the submission of faith." She is, in some measure, a Christian Rousseau.

---

[1] See in the *Revue pédagogique*, 1883, No. 6, an interesting study on Madame Guizot, by Bernard Perez.

[2] *L'Éducation progressive ou Étude du cours de la nature humaine.* 3 vols. 1836–1838.

583. MADAME NECKER DE SAUSSURE AND MADAME DE STAËL. — The first work of Madame Necker, *Notice of the Character and the Writings of Madame de Staël*, already gives proof of her interest in education. The author of the *Progressive Education* here studies with care the ideas of her heroine on education and instruction. It is plain that she has profited by some of the solid reflections in the noble book on *Germany*, and particularly by this opinion on the gradual and progressive method of Rousseau and of Pestalozzi : —

"Rousseau calls children into activity by degrees. He would have them do for themselves all that their little powers permit them to do. He does not in the least force their intelligence ; he does not make them reach the result without passing over the route. He wishes the faculties to be developed before the sciences are taught."

"What wearies children is to make them jump over intermediate parts, to make them advance without their really knowing what they think they have learned. With Pestalozzi there is no trace of these difficulties. With him, children take delight in their studies, because even in infancy, they taste the pleasure of grown men, namely, comprehending and completing that on which they have been engaged."

Moreover, Madame Necker must have recognized her own spirit, her preference for a severe and painstaking education, in this passage where Madame de Staël vigorously protested against amusing and easy methods of instruction : —

"The education that takes place through amusement dissipates thought; labor of some sort is one of the great aids of nature ; the mind of the child ought to accustom itself to the labor of study, just as our soul to suffering. . . . You will teach a multitude of things to your child by means of pictures and cards, but you will not teach him how to learn."

584. Progressive Education and Rousseau. — It is undeniable that Madame Necker owes much to Rousseau; but she is far from always agreeing with him.

For Rousseau, man is good; for her, man is bad. The first duty of the teacher should be to reform him, to raise him from his fall; the purpose of life is not happiness, as an immoral doctrine maintains, but it is improvement; the basis of education ought to be religion.

Even when she is inspired by Rousseau, Madame Necker is not long in separating from him. Thus we may believe that she borrows from him the fundamental idea of her book, the idea of a successive development of the faculties, to which should correspond a parallel movement in educational methods. Like the author of the *Émile*, she follows the awakening of the senses in the infant. She considers the infant as a being *sui generis* " who lives only on sensations and desires." She sees in the infant a distinct period of life, an age whose education has its own special rules. But at that point the resemblances stop; for Madame Necker de Saussure hastens to add that, from the fifth year, the child is in possession of all his intellectual faculties. He is no longer simply a sentient being, a robust animal like Émile; but he is a complete being, soul and body. Consequently, education should take account of his double nature. Moral education ought not to be separated from physical education, and cannot begin too soon.

" It is a great error to believe that nature proceeds in the systematic order imagined by Rousseau. With her, we nowhere discern a commencement; we do not surprise her at creating, and it always seems that she is developing."

So, in education, we must know how to appeal, at the same time and as soon as possible, to the different motives, instinctive or reflective, selfish or affectionate, which sway the will.

Often, in practice, the two thinkers approach each other, and, even in her protestations against her countryman, Madame Necker de Saussure preserves something of Rousseau's spirit. Thus, she does not desire the negative education which leaves everything to nature. The teacher ought not to *allow* the child to do (*laisser faire*), but *cause* him to do (*faire faire*). But, at the same time, she demands that the will be strengthened, so that education may find in it a point of support; that the character be hardened; that some degree of independence be accorded to the child; "that in permissible cases he be allowed to come to his own decision; and that half-orders, half-obligations, tacit entreaties, and insinuations, be avoided." Is not this retaining all that is just and practical in Rousseau's theory, namely, the necessity of associating the special and spontaneous powers of the child with the work of education? Madame de Saussure adopts a just medium between the active education which makes a misuse of the master's instruction, and the passive education which makes a misuse of the pupil's liberty. She would willingly have accepted this precept of Frœbel, " Let teachers not lose sight of this truth : it is necessary that always and at the same time they give and take, that they precede and follow, that they act and let act."

585. ORIGINALITY OF MADAME NECKER. — Though she had reflected much on the writings of her predecessors, it is nevertheless to her personal experience and to her original investigations that Madame Necker owes the best of her thought. She had herself followed the advice which she gives to mothers, of " observing their children, and of keeping a journal, in which a record should be made of each step of progress, and in which all the vicissitudes of physical and moral health should be noted." It is a rich psychological fund, and at the

same time a perpetual aspiration after the ideal, which makes
the strength and the beauty of the *Progressive Education*.
With what penetrating insight Madame Necker has pointed
out the difficulty and also the charm of the study of children !

" It were so delightful to fix the fugitive image of childhood, to prolong indefinitely the happiness of contemplating
their features, and to be sure of ever finding again those dear
creatures whom, alas, we are always losing as children, even
when we still have the happiness of keeping them ! "

" We must love children in order to know them, and we
divine them less by the intelligence than by the heart."

Thanks to the pronounced taste for the study of child
nature, the most just psychological observations are ever
mingled, in the *Progressive Education*, with the precepts of
education, and it has been truly said that " this book is
almost a journal of domestic education which takes the proportions of a theory."

586. DIVISION OF THE PROGRESSIVE EDUCATION. — The
Progressive Education appeared in 1836 and 1838 in three
volumes. The first three books treat of the history of the
soul in infancy ; the fourth examines the general principles
of teaching, independently of the age of the pupil ; the fifth
studies the child of from five to seven years of age ; the sixth
takes us to the tenth year ; the seventh shows " the distinctive marks of the character and the intellectual development
of boys, during the years which immediately precede ado-
lescence." Finally, the last four books form a complete
whole, and treat of the education of women during the whole
course of life.

587. DEVELOPMENT OF THE FACULTIES. — We cannot attempt in this place to analyze a work so rich in ideas as the
work of Madame Necker. Let us limit ourselves to indicating

the essential points in her system of education. First, it is the preoccupation of training the will, a faculty which is too much neglected by teachers, but which, nevertheless, is the endowment which dominates life. Madame Necker treats this subject in a masterly way in a chapter to which she prefixes these words as a superscription : —

" Obedience to law constrains the will without enfeebling it, while obedience to man injures it or enervates it.

" It is, above all, to place the interior education of the soul above superficial and formal instruction.

" To instruct a child is to construct him within ; it is to make him become a man."

588. CULTURE OF THE IMAGINATION. — Whatever importance she attaches to the active powers, Madame Necker does not neglect the contemplative faculties. The imagination, next to the will, is the faculty of the soul which has most often engrossed her attention.   -

" She has made it appear," says a distinguished writer, " that this irresistible power, when we believe it to have been conquered, takes the most diverse forms ; that it disguises its power and arouses with a secret fire the most miserable passions. If you refuse it space and liberty, it slinks away in the depths of selfishness, and under vulgar features it becomes avarice, cowardice, and vanity."

" So it is necessary to see with what tender anxiety Madame Necker watches its first movements in the soul of the child ; with what intelligent care she seeks to make of it from entrance upon life, the companion of truth ; how she surrounds it with everything which can establish it within the circle of the good. The studies which extend our intellectual horizon, the spectacle of nature in her marvelous diversities, the emotions of the arts, — nothing seems to her superfluous or dangerous for directing the imagination in the way that is good. She fears to see it escape, through the lack of pleasures that are intense enough, in the direction of other routes."[1]

In other terms, it is not proposed to repress the imagination, still less to destroy it; but merely to guide it gently, to associate it with reason and virtue, to awaken it to a taste for the good, and to an admiration for nature.

" Show him a beautiful sunset, in order that nothing which can enchant him may pass unnoticed."

589. THE EDUCATION OF WOMEN. — In her special studies on the education of women, Madame Necker, who in other parts of her work sometimes makes an improper use of vague declarations of principles, without entering sufficiently into the details of practical processes, has had the double. merit of assigning to the destiny of women an elevated ideal, and of determining with precision the means of attaining it. She complains that we too often adhere to Rousseau's programme, that of an education which relates exclusively to the conjugal duties of the woman. She recommends that the marriage of young girls be delayed, so that they may have time to become " enlightened spirits and intelligent creatures "; so that they may acquire, not " an assortment of all petty knowledges," but a solid instruction, which prepares them for the duties of society and of maternity, which make of them the first teachers of their children, which, in a word, starts them on the way towards that personal perfection which they will never completely attain except by the efforts of their whole life.[2]

---

[1] Preface to the fifth edition of the *Progressive Education*. Paris. Garnier.

[2] We must include in the educational school of Madame Necker de Saussure one of her countrymen, the celebrated Vinet (1799-1847), who, in his excellent book, *L'Éducation, la famille et la société* (Paris, 1855), has vigorously discussed certain educational questions.

590. MADAME PAPE-CARPENTIER (1815–1878). — With Madame Pape-Carpentier, we leave the region of . theories to enter the domain of facts ; we have to do with a practical teacher. In 1846, after several trials at teaching at La Flèche, her native city, and at Mans, she published her *Counsels on the Management of Infant Schools*. In 1847 she founded at Paris a *Mothers' Normal School*, which the next year, under the ministry of Carnot, became a public establishment, and which,. in 1852, under the ministry of Fortoul, took the distinctive title *Practical Courses on Infant Schools*. It is there that during twenty-seven years Madame Pape-Carpentier applied her methods and trained a large number of pupils, more than fifteen hundred, who have propagated in France and abroad her teaching and her ideas. In 1847 she was removed from the management of her normal school through intrigues ; but her loss of position was not of long duration. A little later she was appointed inspector-general of infant schools.

591. GENERAL CHARACTER OF HER WORKS. — Madame Pape-Carpentier may be considered as a pupil of Pestalozzi and of Frœbel. She was specially occupied with elementary education, and carried into her work a spirit of great simplicity. We must not demand of her ambitious generalities nor views on abstract metaphysics ; but she excels in practical wisdom, and speaks the language of childhood to perfection.

592. PRINCIPAL WORKS OF MADAME PAPE-CARPENTIER. — Among the important works of Madame Pape-Carpentier we shall recommend the following in particular : —

1. *Advice on the Management of Infant Schools* (1845). In her preface the author excuses herself for undertaking " a subject of such gravity." But she goes on to say that " no instruction has yet been given the teacher on the educa-

tion of the poor child," and she asks the privilege of speaking in the name of her personal experience. This book, often reprinted, has become *Enseignement pratique dans les salles d'asile.*[1]

2. *Narratives and Lessons on Objects* (1858). This is a collection of little stories, "simple as childhood," which were tested before children before being written, and in which Madame Pape-Carpentier attempts to teach them things which are good: "I mean," she says, "things really, seriously good."

3. *Pedagogical Discussions held at the Sorbonne* (1867). During the Universal Exposition of 1867, Monsieur Duruy had assembled at Paris a certain number of teachers before whom pedagogical discussions were held. Madame Pape-Carpentier took upon herself the special task of explaining to them how the methods of the infant school might be introduced into the primary school.

4. *Reading and Work for Children and Mothers* (1873). Here Madame Pape-Carpentier is especially intent on popularizing the methods of Frœbel; she suggests ingenious exercises which can be applied to children to give them skill in the use of their fingers, and to inspire them with a taste for order and symmetry.

5. *Complete Course of Education* (1874). This book, which would have been the general statement of the pedagogical principles of the author, was left incomplete. Only three volumes have appeared. A few quotations will make known their spirit.

"To co-operate with nature in her work, to extend it, to correct her when she goes wrong, — such is the task of the educator. In all grades of education, nature must be respected.

---

[1] See the sixth edition, Paris, Hachette, 1877.

" The child should live in the midst of fresh and soothing impressions ; the objects which surround him in the school should be graceful and cheerful.

" Socrates has admirably said, ' The duty of education is to give the idea birth rather than to communicate it.' "

6. *Note on the Education of the Senses, and some Pedagogical Appliances* (1878). Madame Pape-Carpentier is very much interested in the education of the senses, because, she says, "every child born into the world is a workman in prospect, a future apprentice to an occupation still unknown." It is then necessary to perfect at an early hour the natural tools he will need in order to fulfill his task. The education of the senses will have its place some day or other in the official programmes, and, for this sense-training, instruments are just as necessary as books are for the culture of the intellect.

593. LESSONS ON OBJECTS. — " The object-lesson is the new continent on which Madame Pape-Carpentier has planted her standard." She herself wrote a number of works which contain models of object-lessons ; she has stated the theory of them, notably in her discussions of 1867. It is even permissible to think that she has made a wrong use of them. With her, the object-lesson becomes a universal process which she applies to all subjects, to chemistry, to physics, to grammar, to geography, and to ethics.

However it may be, this is the course to follow according to her : it is necessary to conform to the order in which the perceptions of the intelligence succeed each other. The child's attention is first struck by color. Then he will distinguish the form of the object, and would know its use, its material, and mode of production. It is according to this natural development of the child's curiosity that the object-lesson should proceed.

504 THE HISTORY OF PEDAGOGY.

Moreover, it can be given with reference to everything. Madame Pape-Carpentier admits what she calls "occasional lessons"; but she also thinks that object-lessons can be given according to a plan, a fixed programme.

Madame Pape-Carpentier deserves, then, to be heard as an experienced adviser in whatever relates to elementary instruction; but that which we must admire in her still more than her professional skill and her pedagogical knowledge, is an elevated conception of the teacher's work, and a lofty inspiration coming from her devotion to children and her love for them.

"To educate children properly," she said, "ought to be for the teacher only the second part of his undertaking; the first, and the most difficult, is to perfect himself."

"What we are able to do for children is measured by the love we bear them."

594. OTHER WOMEN WHO WERE EDUCATORS. — If the education of women has received an important development in our day, it is due, then, in great part to the women who have shown what they were worth and what they could do, either as teachers or as educators. And yet the history whose principal features we have just traced remains very incomplete. By the side of the celebrated women whose works we have studied, we should mention Mademoiselle Sanvan, who, in 1811, founded at Chaillot an educational establishment which she did not leave till about 1830, to take the intellectual and moral direction of the girls' schools of Paris;[1] Madame de Maisonneuve, author of an *Essay on the Instruction of Women*,[2] in which she sums up the results of a long

---

[1] See the work entitled *Madamoiselle Sauvan, première inspectrice des écoles de Paris, sa vie, son œuvre*, par E. Gossot. Paris, 1880.

[2] *Essai sur l'instruction des femmes.* Tours, 1841.

experience acquired in the management of a private boarding-school. But men have also contributed by their theoretical objections, or by their practical efforts, to the progress of the education of women. It would be of interest, for example, to study the courses in secondary instruction of Lourmand (1834), and the *Courses in Maternal Education*, of Lévi Alvarès (1820). "Monsieur Lévi," says Gréard, "makes the mother tongue and history the basis of instruction. He himself sums up his methods in this formula of progressive education : Facts, comparison of facts, moral or philosophical consequence of facts ; that is, seeing, comparing, judging. This is the very order of nature." Let us mention also the work of Aimé Martin, *The Education of Mothers*,[1] which for several years enjoyed an extraordinary reputation that it would be rather difficult to justify.

595. DUPANLOUP AND THE EDUCATION OF WOMEN. — A bishop of the nineteenth century, Dupanloup, has assumed to rival Fénelon in the delicate question of the education of women. Different works, and in particular the one which he esteemed most, his *Letters on the Education of Girls*, published after his death in 1879, give proof of the interest which he took in these questions. These letters are for the most part real letters which were addressed to women of the time. Notwithstanding the variety and the freedom of the epistolary form, the work may be divided into three parts : 1. the principles of education ; 2. the education of young women ; 3. free and personal study in the world. Dupanloup should be thanked for having summoned woman to a true intellectual culture, and for not consenting to have her faculties remain "smothered and useless." Through the revela-

---

[1] The first edition is dated 1834. The ninth was published in 1873.

tions of the confessional and the spiritual direction of a great number of women, Dupanloup knew exactly what a void an incomplete education of the mind and heart leaves in the soul. He is indeed willing to acknowledge that piety is not enough, and with a certain breadth of spirit which drew upon him the censure of the ultramontane press, he recommends the serious studies to women. His counsels, however, are addressed only to women of the middle classes, to those who, he says, " occupy the third story of houses in Paris." His book is rather a reminiscence of the seventeenth century, of its manners and its habits of thinking, than a living work of to-day, adapted to the needs of modern society.

[596. ANALYTICAL SUMMARY. — 1. The formal discussion of woman's education by women marks an important epoch in the history of education. Had the education of men been wholly, or even chiefly, discussed by women, it cannot be doubted that it would have been more or less partial and imperfect.

2. The formal discussion of infant education by women is scarcely less important ; for nothing less than maternal instinct and affection can divine the nature and the needs of the child.

3. This study calls attention to the need of making the education of women serious instead of ornamental. Plato based his recommendation of the equal education of men and women on equality of civil functions. In modern thought it is the conception of equal rights and· of equal abilities that tends to prescribe the same course of intellectual training for both sexes.

4. The educational work of the two Englishwomen, Miss Edgeworth and Miss Hamilton, can be studied with great prof-

it.   The first excels in practical wisdom, and the second in philosophic insight.

5. The *Progressive Education* of Madame Necker is a classic which fairly ranks with the *Émile* of Rousseau, and the *Education* of Herbert Spencer.]

CHAPTER XXI.

THE THEORY AND PRACTICE OF EDUCATION IN THE NINETEENTH CENTURY.

THE PEDAGOGY OF THE NINETEENTH CENTURY; VOTES OF THE COUN-
CILS-GENERAL (1801); FOURCROY AND THE LAW OF 1802; FOUNDA-
TION OF THE UNIVERSITY (1806); ORGANIZATION OF THE IMPERIAL
UNIVERSITY; INTENTIONS OF THE DYNASTY; PRIMARY INSTRUC-
TION NEGLECTED; ORIGIN OF MUTUAL INSTRUCTION; BELL AND
LANCASTER; SUCCESS OF MUTUAL INSTRUCTION IN FRANCE; MORAL
ADVANTAGES; ECONOMICAL ADVANTAGES; ORGANIZATION OF
SCHOOLS ON THE MUTUAL SYSTEM; VICES OF THIS SYSTEM; STATE
OF PRIMARY INSTRUCTION; GUIZOT AND THE LAW OF 1833; HIGHER
PRIMARY SCHOOLS; CIRCULAR OF GUIZOT; PROGRESS IN POPULAR
INSTRUCTION; PROGRAMMES OF PRIMARY INSTRUCTION; THE
THEORISTS OF EDUCATION; JACOTOT (1770-1840); THE PARADOXES
OF JACOTOT; ALL IS IN ALL; THE SAINT-SIMONIANS AND THE
PHALANSTERIANS; FOURIER (1772-1837); AUGUSTE COMTE (1798-1857)
AND THE POSITIVISTS; DUPANLOUP (1802-1878); ANALYSIS OF THE
TREATISE ON EDUCATION; ERRORS AND PREJUDICES; THE SPIRIT-
UALISTIC SCHOOL AND THE UNIVERSITY MEN; ANALYTICAL SUM-
MARY.

597. THE PEDAGOGY OF THE NINETEENTH CENTURY. — An
effort more and more marked to organize education in accordance with the data of psychology and on a scientific basis,
and to co-ordinate pedagogical methods in accordance with a
rational plan; a manifest tendency to take ·the control of
education from the hands of the Church in order to restore it
to the State and to lay society; a larger part accorded the
family in the management of children; a faith more and more

sanguine in the efficacy of instruction, and an ever-growing purpose to have every member of the human family partici- pate in its benefits, — such are some of the characteristics of the pedagogy of the nineteenth century. Education tends more and more to become a social problem; it is to be an affair of universal interest. It is no longer to be merely a question of regulating select studies for the use of a few who are the favorites of birth and fortune; but science must be placed within the reach of all, and through the simplification of methods and the universal distribution of knowledge, it must be adapted to the democratic spirit of the new society.

We have no intention to follow in this place, in all its details, and in the diversity of its currents, this educational movement of a century which has not yet said its last word; but we must limit ourselves to calling attention to the points which seem to us essential.

598. LAWS OF THE COUNCILS-GENERAL OF 1801. — Not- withstanding the efforts of the Revolution, public instruction in France, during the first part of the nineteenth century, was far from being flourishing. There was urgent need of introducing reforms. The Councils-General were summoned in 1801 to give their advice on the organization of studies. That which is very noticeable in the State papers of the Councils-General of 1801, is that the departmental assem- blies agree in demanding the establishment of a National University. The Councils-General complain that the pro- fessors, being no longer united by the ties of solidarity, as were the members of the religious teaching congregations of the old régime, march at random, without unity, without concerted direction. They solicit, then, a uniform organi- zation of instruction. They even conceive the idea of an official instruction administered exclusively by the State.

599. Fourcroy[1] and the Law of 1802. — We have not the space to dwell long on the bill of Fourcroy, which became the law of 1802, although this measure, it has been said, was amended twenty-three times before being submitted to the Corps Législatif and to the Tribunate.

Fourcroy did not sufficiently recognize the rights of the State. Doubtless he did not go so far as to assert, with Adam Smith, that education should be abandoned entirely to private enterprise; but he thinks that the task of organizing the primary schools must be left to the communes. In his opinion, that which prevented the success of these schools was the attempt to impose too great a uniformity on them. He demands that the teachers be chosen by the mayors, or by the municipal councillors, who alone are cognizant of the local interests. The primary school is the need of all. Then let it be the affair of all. Fourcroy was mistaken. Primary instruction became a reality in France only on the day when the State vigorously put its hand on it.

On certain points, however, the law of 1802 prepared the way for the approaching creation of Napoleon ; for example, in giving to the First Consul the appointment of the professors of the colleges, and in placing the primary schools under the supervision of the prefects.

600. Foundation of the University (1806). — The law of May 11, 1806, completed by the decrees of March 17, 1808, and of 1811, established the University, that is, a teaching corporation, unique and entirely dependent on the State : —

" There shall be constituted a body charged exclusively

---

[1] Fourcroy (1755-1809), a celebrated chemist, was director-general of public instruction in 1801. He prepared, in the following years, the decrees relative to the establishment of the University.

with instruction and public education throughout the whole extent of the Empire."

Instruction thus became a function of the State, on the same basis as the administration of justice or the organization of the army.

At the same time that it lost all autonomy, all independence, the University gained the formidable privilege of being alone charged with the national instruction.

"No one can open a school or teach publicly, without being a member of the Imperial University and without having been graduated from one of its Faculties." "No school can be established outside of the University, and without the authorization of its head."

We know what protestations were excited, even on the start, by the establishment of this University monopoly. "It was not enough to enchain parents; it was still necessary to dispose of the children. Mothers have been seen hastening from the extremities of the Empire, coming to reclaim, in an agony of tears, the sons whom the government had carried off from them." Thus spoke Chateaubriand, before lavishing his adulations on the restorer of altars, and he added, with an extravagance of imagination which recoils on itself, "Children were placed in schools where they were taught at the sound of the drum, irreligion, debauchery, and contempt for the domestic virtues!" Joseph de Maistre was more just: "Fontanes,"[1] he said, "has large views and excellent intentions. The plan of his University is grand and comprehensive. It is a noble body. The soul will come to it when it can. Celibacy, subordination, devotion of the whole life without religious motive, are required. Will they be obtained?"[2]

---

[1] Fontanes (1757-1821), first Grand Master of the University.
[2] *Mémoire politique* of Joseph de Maistre, Paris, 1858, p. 30.

601. ORGANIZATION OF THE IMPERIAL UNIVERSITY. — The Imperial University comprised, like the present University, Colleges, Lycées, and Faculties. The Colleges furnished secondary instruction, like the Lycées, but less complete. There were a Faculty of Letters and a Faculty of Sciences for each academic centre; but these Faculties were very poorly equipped, with their endowment of from five to ten thousand francs at most, and with their few professors. The professors of the neighboring Lycée (professors of rhetoric and mathematics) formed a part of the establishment, and each Faculty included at most but two or three other chairs.

Latin and mathematics formed the basis of the instruction in the Lycées. The Revolution had not come in vain, since that which it had vigorously demanded was now realized; the sciences and the classical languages were put on a footing of equality.

602. DYNASTIC PREPOSSESSIONS. — That which absorbed the attention of the founder of the Imperial University was less the schemes of study than the general principles on which the rising generations were to be nourished. In this respect the thought of the Emperor is not obscure. He does not dissemble it. God and the Emperor are the two words which must be graven into the depths of the soul.

"All the schools of the Imperial University will make as the basis of their instruction : 1. the precepts of the Catholic religion ; 2. fidelity to the Emperor, to the imperial monarchy, the depository of the happiness of the people, and to the Napoleonic dynasty, the *conservator of the unity of France*, and of all the ideas proclaimed by the Constitution."

"Napoleon," as Guizot says, "attempted to convert into an instrument of despotism an institution which tended to be only a centre of light."

603. PRIMARY INSTRUCTION NEGLECTED. — Primary instruction never occupied the attention of Napoleon I. The decree of 1805 contented itself with promising measures intended to assure the recruitment of teachers, especially the creation of one or more normal classes within the colleges and lycées. Moreover, the Grand Master was to encourage and to license the Brethren of the Christian Schools, while supervising their establishments. Finally, the right to establish schools was left to families or to religious corporations, the budget of the Empire containing no item of appropriation for the cause of popular instruction.

The Restoration was scarcely more generous towards the instruction of the people. By the ordinance of February 29, 1815, it granted *fifty thousand francs* as encouragement to the primary schools. Was this derisive liberality any better than complete silence and neglect? A more important measure was the establishment of cantonal committees charged with the supervision of primary schools. These committees were placed, sometimes under the direction of the rector, and at others under the authority of the bishop, at the pleasure of the vicissitudes of politics. Certificates of qualification were delivered to the members of the authorized congregations, on the simple presentation of their letters of permission. We can imagine what a body of teachers could be assured by such a mode of recruitment.

In anticipation of the monarchy of July, which in its liberal dispositions was to appear more regardful of popular education, private initiative signalized itself under the Restoration by the foundation of the *Society for Elementary Instruction*, and also by the encouragement it gave to the first attempts at mutual instruction.

604. ORIGIN OF MUTUAL INSTRUCTION. — Two Englishmen, Bell and Lancaster, have claimed the honor of having in-

vented mutual instruction. The fact is, neither of them invented it; they simply gave it currency. It is in France, if not in India, that we must look for the real origin of mutual instruction. We have seen that Madame de Maintenon, Rollin, La Salle, and Pestalozzi, practised it, and to a certain extent gave it currency. In the eighteenth century Herbault had employed it in the hospital of La Pitié (1747), the Chevalier Paulet at Vincennes (1774), and, finally, the Abbé Gaultier,[1] also a Frenchman, had introduced the use of it into London, in 1792, some years before Bell brought it from India.

605. BELL (1753–1832) AND LANCASTER (1778–1838). — Bell and Lancaster are none the less the first authorized propagators of the mutual method, or, as the English say, of the *monitorial system*. Bell had used it at Madras, in imitation of the Hindoo teachers, and in 1798 he introduced it into England. But at the same period, a young English teacher, Lancaster, applied the same methods with success, and, so far as it appears, through a suggestion absolutely personal and original. Lancaster was a Quaker, and Bell a Churchman, so that public opinion in England was divided between the two rivals. The truth is that they had applied at the same time a system which was known before their day, and which must naturally have been suggested to all teachers who have too large a number of children to instruct, as a result of the inadequacy of their resources and the lack of a teaching force sufficiently large.

606. SUCCESS OF MUTUAL INSTRUCTION IN FRANCE. — Mutual instruction, which was maintained in certain schools of

---

1 The Abbé Gaultier (1746–1818), author of a large number of works on elementary instruction, and almost a reformer in his way. He employed *teaching by sight*, and recommended varied exercises, such as games where he introduced *counters*, tickets, interrogations in the form of *lotteries*.

Paris till 1867, for a long time enjoyed an extraordinary credit in France. Under the Restoration, its success was so great that it became the fashion, and even a craze. Patronized by the most eminent men of that day, by Royer-Collard, by Laisné, by the Duke Decazes, by the Duke Pasquier, mutual instruction became the flag of the liberal party in the matter of instruction. Political passions became involved in it. The new system came into competition with the traditional instruction of the Brethren of the Christian Schools, and was fought and denounced as immoral by all the partisans of routine. " Mutual instruction was charged with destroying the foundation of social order by delegating to children a power which ought to belong only to men. . . . Men held for or against simultaneous instruction, its rival, as if it were a question of an article of the Charter." [1]

607. MORAL ADVANTAGES. — The friends of mutual instruction, in order to justify their enthusiasm, made the most of moral reasons. What can be more touching, they said, than to see children communicating to one another the little that they know? What an excellent lesson of charity and of mutual aid! The Gospel has said, *Love one another.* Was it not giving to the divine precept a happy translation to add, *Instruct one another!* An attempt was made, moreover, to introduce mutuality into discipline and into the repression of school faults. The school, on certain solemn occasions, was converted into a court for trying criminals. " All this was done very seriously, and it was also very seriously felt that these practices, passing from a class of children to a class of adults, would contribute to introduce into society the habits of a true and useful fraternity."

---

[1] See Gréard, *L'enseignement primaire à Paris de* 1867 *à* 1877. A memoir published in 1877, pp. 75–90. See also an interesting study full of personal recollections of E. Deschamps, *L'enseignement mutual.* Toulouse, 1883.

608. Economical Advantages. — To tell the truth, mutual instruction was above all else " a useful expedient,"
according to Rollin's expression. At a period when teachers
were scarce, when the budget of public instruction did uot
exist, it was natural that an economic system which dispensed
with teachers, and which reduced to almost nothing the cost
of instruction, should be hailed with enthusiasm. Let us add
that there was also an economy in books, since " there was
need of only one book, which pupils never used; and which
would thus last for several years."

Jomard calculated that there were 3,000,000 children to
instruct, and that, according to the ordinary system, this
would require the expenditure of more than 45,000,000
francs.[1]

Now, according to the calculations of the Comte de Laborde,[2] 1000 pupils being able to be educated by one single
teacher, by the system of mutual instruction, more easily
than 30 could have been by the old system, a sum of 10,000
francs granted annually by the State would suffice to educate
in twelve years the entire generation of poor children.[3]

609. Organization of Schools on the Mutual Plan. —
Bell defined mutual instruction as " the method by means
of which a whole school may instruct itself, under the supervision of one single master."

Here is the picture of a mutual school, as described by
Gréard : —

" That was a striking spectacle at the first glance, — those

---

[1] Jomard (1777-1862), member of the Society for Elementary Instruction, author of *Tableaux des écoles élémentaires*.

[2] The Comte de Laborde (1771-1842), author of a *plan d'éducation pour
les enfants*.

[3] Among the other propagators of mutual instruction, mention should be
made of the Abbé Gaultier, Larochefoucauld-Liancourt, De Lasteyrie, etc.

long and vast structures which contained a whole school, such as the older generations of our teachers recollect still to have seen at the Halle aux Draps. In the middle of the room, throughout its entire length, were rows of tables having from five to twenty places each, having at one end, at the right, the desk of the monitor, and the board having models of writing, itself surmounted by a standard or telegraph which served to secure, by means of directions easy to read, regularity of movements; at the side of the room, and all along the walls, there were rows of semi-circles, about which were arranged groups of children; on the walls, on a line with the eye, there was a blackboard on which were performed the exercises in computation, and from which were suspended the charts for reading and grammar; right at his side, within reach of his hand, was the stick with which the teacher was provided for conducting the lesson; finally, at the lower part of the room, on a wide and high platform, accessible by steps and surrounded by a balustrade, was the chair of the master, who, employing in succession, according to fixed rules, voice, *bâton*, or whistle, surveyed the tables and groups, distributing commendation or reproof, and directing, in a word, like a captain on the deck of his vessel, the whole machinery of instruction."

In respect of systematic movements and exterior order, nothing is more charming than the appearance of a school conducted on the mutual plan. It remains to inquire what were the educational results of the system, and whether the fashion which brought it into favor was justified by real advantages.

610. VICES OF MUTUAL INSTRUCTION. — The monitor was the mainspring of the mutual method. But what was the monitor? A child, more intelligent, doubtless, than his com-

rades, but too little instructed to be equal to his task. The mutual school did not open till ten o'clock. From eight to ten there was a class for the monitors. There they learned in haste what they were, for the rest of the day, to teach to the other children. The purpose of the master being to form good instruments as quickly as possible, they were fitted up for their trade by the most expeditious methods.

" What sort of teachers could such a preparation produce? To teach is to learn twice, it has been truly said ; but on the condition of having reflected on that which has been learned and upon that which is to be taught. To convey light into the intelligence of another, it is first necessary to have produced the light within one's self, a thing which supposes the enlightened, penetrating, and persevering action of a mind relatively mature and trained. From the class where they have just been sitting as pupils, the monitors — masters improvised as by the wave of a wand, — passed to the classes of children whom they were to indoctrinate " (Gréard).

The instruction, consequently, became purely mechanical. The monitor faithfully repeated what he had been taught. Everything was reduced to mechanical processes.

Let us observe, besides, that from the moral point of view, the mutual system left much to be desired. The monitors, we are told, did not escape the intoxications of pride. Even in the family they became petty tyrants. Parents complained of their dictatorial habits and their tone of authority.

However it may be, mutual instruction has rendered undeniable services, thanks to the zeal of such teachers as Mademoiselle Sanvan and Monsieur Sarazin; but its reputation went on diminishing in proportion as the State became more and more disposed to make sacrifices, and as it was possible to multiply the services of teachers.[1]

611. THE STATE OF PRIMARY INSTRUCTION. — Under the title, *Exhibit of Primary Instruction in France*, a member of the University, P. Lorain, published in 1837 a *résumé* of the inquiry, which, by the orders of Guizot, had been made in 1833 throughout the whole extent of France, by the labors of more than 400 inspectors. Here are some of the sad results of this inquiry : all the teachers did not know how to write ; a large number employed the mechanism of the three fundamental rules without being able to give any theoretical reason for these operations. " The ignorance was general."

As under the old régime, the teacher practiced all the trades ; he was day-laborer, shoemaker, innkeeper.

" He had his wife supply his place while he went hunting in the fields."

The functions of the teacher, poorly rewarded, exposed to the risk of a very slender tuition, enjoyed no consideration.

" The teacher was often regarded in the community on the same footing as a mendicant, and between the herdsman and himself, the preference was for the herdsman."

Consequently, the situation of school-master was the most often sought after by men who were infirm, crippled, unfit for any other kind of work.

" From the teacher without arms, to the epileptic, how many infirmities to pass through ! "

612. GUIZOT AND THE LAW OF JUNE 28, 1833. — Primary instruction, so often decreed by the Revolution, was not

---

[1] Two noted attempts to extend and popularize the monitorial system are exhibited in the following works: Pillans, *The Rationale of Discipline* (Edinburgh, 1852); Bentham, *Chrestomathia* (London, 1816).

really organized in France till by the law of June 28, 1833, the honor of which is due in particular to Guizot, then minister of public instruction.[1]

Primary instruction was divided into two grades, — elementary and higher. Henceforth there was to be a school for each commune, or at least for each group of two or three communes. The State reserved the right of appointing teachers, and of determining their salary, which, it is true, in certain places, did not exceed two hundred francs. Poor children were to be received without pay.

613. HIGHER PRIMARY SCHOOLS. — One of the most praiseworthy purposes of the legislator of 1833 was the establishment of higher primary instruction.

"*Higher* primary instruction," he said, "necessarily includes, in addition to all the branches of elementary primary instruction, the elements of geometry, and its common applications, especially linear drawing and surveying, information on the physical sciences and natural history, applicable to the uses of life, singing, the elements of history and geography, and particularly of the history and geography of France. According to the needs and the resources of localities, the instruction shall receive such developments as shall be deemed proper."

A higher primary school was to be established in the chief towns of the department and in all the communes which had a population of more than six thousand souls. The law was executed in part. In 1841, one hundred and sixty-one schools were founded. But little by little, the indifference of the government, and, above all, the vanity of parents who preferred for their children worthless Latin studies to a good

---

[1] It is at the same period, in 1832, that Gérando published his *Cours normal des instituteurs*.

and thorough primary instruction, discouraged these first efforts.

The legislator of 1833 had good reason for thinking that a good vest was worth more than a poor coat. His mistake was in thinking that people would be persuaded to abandon the coat in order to take the vest.[1] The higher schools were almost everywhere annexed to the colleges of secondary instruction. To suppress their independence and their own distinctive features was to destroy them. The final blow was given them by the law of 1850, which abstained from pronouncing their name, and which condemned them by its silence.

614. CIRCULAR OF GUIZOT. — In transmitting to teachers the law of June 28, 1833, Guizot had it followed by a celebrated circular, which eloquently stated the proper office of the teacher, his duties and his rights. Here are some passages from it:

" Do not make a mistake here, Sir. While the career of primary instruction may be without renown, its duties interest the whole of society, and it is an occupation which shares the importance attached to public functions. . . . Universal primary instruction is henceforth to be one of the guarantees of order and social stability."

The circular next examines the material advantages which the new law assured to teachers, and it continues thus : —

" However, Sir, as I well know, the foresight of the law and the resources at the disposal of public authority, will never succeed in rendering the humble profession of a communal teacher as attractive as it is useful. Society could not reward him who devotes himself to this service for all that he does for it. There is no fortune to gain ; there is

---

[1] Cournot, *Des institutions d'instruction publique,* p. 315.

scarcely any reputation to acquire in the difficult duties which he performs. Destined to see his life spent in a monotonous occupation, sometimes even to encounter about him the injustice and the ingratitude of ignorance, he would often grow disheartened, and would perhaps succumb did he not draw his strength and his courage from other sources than from the prospect of an interest immediate and purely personal. It is necessary that a profound sense of the moral importance of his work sustain and animate him, and that the austere pleasure of having served men and secretly contributed to the public good, become the noble reward which his conscience alone can give. It is his glory to aim at nothing beyond his obscure and laborious condition, to spend himself in sacrifices scarcely counted by those who profit by them, and, in a word, to work for men and to look for his reward only from God."

615. PROGRESS OF POPULAR INSTRUCTION. — It would be an interesting history to relate in detail the progress of popular education in France from the law of 1833 to our day. The public bills of the Republic of 1848, the liberal propositions of Carnot and of Barthélemy Saint-Hilaire, the recoil of the law of March 15, 1850, the *statu quo* of the first years of the Second Empire, then towards the end the praiseworthy efforts and tentatives of Duruy, and, finally, under the Third Republic, the definite and triumphant organization, — all this is sufficiently known and too recent to justify us in dwelling on it here.

For successfully introducing anew into the laws the principles of gratuity, obligation, and secularization, as proclaimed by the French Revolution, not less than a century was necessary. And in particular, the better spirits allowed themselves to be convinced of the need of obligatory instruction only by slow degrees. However, in 1833, Cousin, who reported the law of Guizot to the Chamber of Peers, expressed himself as follows : —

" A law which should make of primary instruction a legal obligation seems to me to be no more above the powers of the legislator than the law on the national guard, and that which you have just made on a forced appropriation for the public good. If reasons of public utility justify the legislator in appropriating private property, why do not reasons of a much higher utility justify him in doing less, — in requiring that children receive the instruction indispensable to every human creature, to the end that he may not become dangerous to himself or to society as a whole? "

Cousin added that the commission of which he was the chairman would not have receded from measures wisely combined to make instruction obligatory, had it not been afraid of provoking difficulties, and, in this way, of postponing a law that was awaited with impatience. The evident necessity of instructing the people, the interests of society, the interests of families and individuals, — all these considerations have insensibly overcome the scruples or the illusions of a false liberality, and it is no longer necessary, to-day, to repeat the eloquent pleas of Carnot in his bill of 1848, of Duruy, and of Jules Simon.

In 1873 Guizot expressed himself as follows : —

" The liberty of conscience and that of families are facts and rights which, in this question, ought to be scrupulously respected and guaranteed; but, under the condition of this respect and of these guarantees, it may happen that the state of society and the state of minds may render legal obligation, in respect of primary instruction, legitimate, salutary, and necessary. *This is the condition of things to-day.* The movement in favor of obligatory instruction is sincere, serious, national.

Powerful examples authorize and encourage it. In Germany, in Switzerland, in Denmark, in most of the American States, primary instruction has this character, and civilization has reaped excellent fruits from it. France and its government have reason to welcome this principle."

616. PROGRAMMES OF PRIMARY INSTRUCTION. — At the same time that primary instruction made progress by its ever-growing extension, and by the participation in it of a greater number of individuals, its programmes were also extended, and it is interesting to compare in this respect the different laws which have regulated the matter of instruction in our century.

The law of 1833 said : " Elementary primary instruction necessarily comprises moral and religious instruction, reading, writing, the elements of the French language and of computation, the legal system of weights and measures."

The bill presented, June 30, 1848, by Carnot, minister of public instruction, expresses itself thus : —

" Primary instruction comprises : 1. reading, writing, the elements of the French language, the elements of computation, the metric system, the measure of distances, elementary notions of the phenomena of nature, and the principal facts of agriculture and of industry, linear drawing, singing, elementary notions on the history and geography of France ; 2. a knowledge of the duties and the rights of man and citizen, the development of the sentiments of liberty, equality, and fraternity ; 3. the elementary rules of hygiene, and useful exercises in physical development."

" The religious instruction is given by the ministers of the different communions."

According to the bill of Barthélemy Saint-Hilaire (April 10, 1849), elementary instruction for boys, necessarily comprised "moral, religious, and civic instruction, reading, writing, the elements of the French language, the elements of computation, the legal system of weights and measures, linear drawing, elementary notions of agriculture and of hygiene, singing and gymnastic exercises.

"According to the needs and resources of localities, elementary primary instruction shall receive the developments which shall be thought proper, and shall comprise, in particular, notions on the history and geography of France."

Finally,the law of March 15, 1850, is worded thus : —

"Art. 23. Primary instruction comprises moral and religious instruction, reading, writing, the elements of the French language, computation, and the legal system of weights and measures. It may comprise in addition, arithmetic applied to practical operations, the elements of history and geography, notions of the physical sciences and of natural history applicable to the ordinary purposes of life, elementary instruction on agriculture, trade, and hygiene, surveying, leveling, linear drawing, singing and gymnastics."

Progress has especially consisted, since 1850, in rendering obligatory that which was simply optional. History, for example, did not become a subject of instruction till 1867.

617. THE THEORISTS OF EDUCATION. — Along with the progress of primary instruction, the historian of the pedagogy of the nineteenth century would have also to follow the development of secondary instruction and of superior instruction. He would have to write the history of the University, reforming the methods of its lycées and its colleges, and ever enlarging in a noble spirit of liberty the studies of its faculties. But we should depart from the limits of our plan, were we to undertake this order of inquiries, and were we to enter into details which pertain to contemporary history.

That which should engage our attention is the theoretical reflections of the different thinkers who, in our century, have discussed the principles and the laws of education, of those at least who have become celebrated for their novel views.

618. JACOTOT (1770–1840). — Jacotot, who has maintained scarcely any celebrity in France except for the singularity of his paradoxes, is perhaps of all French educators of the nineteenth century the one who has received most attention abroad, particularly in Germany. "Jacotot," says Doctor Dittes, "has incited a lasting improvement in the public instruction of Germany. The reform which he introduced into the teaching of reading is important. He started with an entire sentence, which was pronounced, explained, and learned by heart by the children, and afterward analyzed into its constituent parts."[1] On the other hand, a French critic, Bernard Perez, has drawn the following portrait of Jacotot: —
"He was the best and the most lovable of men. He had the firmness, patience, honesty, and candor of superior minds, an inexhaustible goodness and a universal charity which make him close all his letters with this formula, 'I especially commend to you the poor.' This ardent philanthropy, as well as his enthusiasm and his zeal for instruction, pervades even his writings, though full of inequalities and verbal eccentricities."[2]

619. PARADOXES OF JACOTOT. — In his principal work, *Universal Instruction*,[3] Jacotot has set forth his principles, which are so many paradoxes, "All intelligences are equal"; "Every man can teach, and even teach that which he him-

---

[1] Dittes, *op. cit.* p. 272.
[2] See *Jacotot et sa méthode d'émancipation intellectuelle*, by Bernard Perez. Paris, 1883.
[3] *Enseignement universel.* Paris, 1823.

self does not know ". ; "One can instruct himself all alone"; "All is in all."

Doubtless at the basis of Jacotot's paradoxes there is an element of truth; for example, the very just idea that the best teaching is that which encourages young minds to think for themselves. Doubtless also he qualified the exaggeration of his statement when he said that the inequality of wills at once destroys the equality of intelligences. But the violent and unreasonable form which he gave to his ideas has compromised them in public opinion. That which is true and fruitful in his system has been forgotten, and we recall only the whimsical formulas in which he delighted.

620. ALL IS IN ALL. — The most famous of Jacotot's paradoxes is the formula, "All is in all." The whole of Latin is in a page of Latin; the whole of music is in a piece of music; the whole of arithmetic, in a rule of computation.

In practice, Jacotot made his pupils learn the first six books of the *Telemachus*. Upon this text, once learned, and recited twice a week, there were constructed all sorts of exercises, and these sufficed for the complete knowledge of the French language. In the same way the *Epitome Historiæ Sacræ*, put in the hands of pupils, and learned in two months, was almost the sole instrument for the study of Latin. In fact, and aside from evident exaggerations, Jacotot rightly thought that it is necessary, as he said, "to learn something well, and to connect with this all the rest."

621. THE FOLLOWERS OF SAINT SIMON AND OF FOURIER. — There is little of practical value to be gathered from the writings of the celebrated utopists, who, at the opening of this century, became known by their plans of social organization. It is the chimerical which characterizes their systems. Cabet demanded among other absurdities that all ancient books be

burned, and that no new books be written except by command of the State. Besides, he would have the school-code established by the children themselves.[1]

Victor Consedérant suppressed, not books, but discipline and authority. " The child," he said, " shall no longer be disobedient, because he shall no longer be commanded." [2]

Saint Simon, in 1816, communicated to the *Society for Elementary Instruction*, a brief essay which gave proof of his interest in education. For him and his disciples, education is " the aggregate of efforts to be employed in order to adapt each new generation to the social order to which it is called by the march of humanity." This was to mark the contrast between modern tendencies which aspire above all else to an earthly and a social end, with ancient tendencies which were subservient to supernatural ideas. Æsthetic sentiments, scientific methods, industrial activity, — such is the triple development which special and professional education should consider. But above this the Saint-Simonians place moral education, too much neglected, as they think, which should consist particularly in developing in the young the sympathetic and affectionate faculties. The Saint-Simonians placed but little dependence on science and abstract principles for assuring among men the reign of morality. Sentiment, in their view, is the true moral principle, and education, consequently, ought to be essentially the education of the heart.

622. FOURIER (1772-1837). — Fourier, like Saint Simon, had educational pretensions. There is nothing more curious than his treatise on *Natural Education*. In it there is only here and there a flash of good sense mingled with a multitude of grotesque fancies.

---

[1] Cabet, *Voyage en Icarie*. Paris, 1842.

[2] Consedérant, *Théorie d'éducation rationnelle et attrayante du dix-neuvième siècle*. Paris, 1844.

Fourier renews the utopias of Plato, and confides infants to public nurses. He is more reasonable when, in spite of his declamations on the excellence of nature, he is really willing to recognize in children a diversity of characters, and divides " the nurslings and the babies " into three classes, — " the benign, the malign, and the devilkins. " We must also commend Fourier for his efforts to encourage industrial activity. There is perhaps a valuable hint in those walks which he recommends children to take through manufactories and shops, so that at the sight of such or such a tool, their particular vocation may be suggested to them !

The instincts of the child are sacred in the eyes of Fourier, even the worst, their inclination to destroy, for example, or their contempt for the rights of property. Far from opposing them, he turns them to account and utilizes them, by employing destructive and slovenly children in occupations in accord with their tastes ; for example, in the pursuit of reptiles, and in the cleansing of sewers.

But it is useless to enter into longer details. The education of the Fourierites is neither a discipline nor a rule of life ; it is simply a system of complaisant adherence, and even of ardent provocation, to the instincts which the child inherits from nature. It is no longer a question either of directing or of training ; it is simply necessary to emancipate and to excite.

623. AUGUSTE COMTE (1798–1857) AND THE POSITIVISTS. — The positivist school, and its illustrious founder, Auguste Comte, could not omit, in their encyclopædic works, a question so important as that of education. The author of the *Course in Positive Philosophy* had even announced a special treatise on pedagogy, " a great subject," he said, " which has not yet been undertaken in a manner sufficiently systematic." [1] The promise was not kept, but from different pas-

---

[1] *Cours de philosophie positive*, second edition, 1864. Vol. VI. p. 771.

sages in the writings of Auguste Comte it is possible to re-construct, in its principal features, the education which would be derived from his system.

Comte took for his guide the natural and specific evolution of humanity.

" Individual education can be adequately estimated only according to its necessary conformity with collective evo-lution."

As positivism represents, in the view of Comte, the su-preme degree of the evolution of humanity, the new education ought to be *positive*.

" Right-minded men universally recognize the necessity of replacing our European education, a system essentially theo-logical, metaphysical, and literary, by a *positive* education, conformed to the spirit of our epoch, and adapted to the needs of modern civilization."

The teaching of science, then, shall be the basis of educa-tion ; but this teaching will bear its fruits only on one con-dition, and this is, that at last we renounce " the exclusive specialty, the too pronounced isolation, which still charac-terizes our manner of conceiving and cultivating the sciences." The precise purpose of the *Course in Positive Philosophy* was to remedy the deleterious influence of a too great specializa-tion of research, by establishing the relations and the hie-rarchy of the sciences. Comte made of mathematics the point of departure in scientific instruction. This was the very reverse of the modern tendency, which consists in begin-ning with the concrete and physical studies.

Auguste Comte, in his project for social reform, demanded universal instruction, and he bitterly complains of the indif-ference of the ruling classes for the instruction of the poor.

" Nothing is more profoundly characteristic of the exist-ing anarchy than the shameful indifference with which the

higher classes of to-day habitually regard the total absence
of popular education, the exaggerated prolongation of which,
however, threatens to exert on their approaching destiny a
frightful reaction."

Comte does not go so far, however, as to dream of an
identical education for all men, an integral education, as it
has been called. He admits degrees in instruction, " which,"
he says, " will allow varieties of extension in a system constantly similar and identical."

624. DUPANLOUP (1803–1878). — Of all the ecclesiastical
writers of our century, he who has the most ardently studied
the problems of education is certainly Bishop Dupanloup.
Important works give proof of the educational zeal of the
eloquent prelate. But they were composed with more spirit
than wisdom, and they betray the zeal of the Christian
apologist more than the inspiration of an impartial love for
the truth. Extravagances of language and exaggerations
of thought too often prevent the reader from feeling, as he
ought, the moral and religious inspiration out of which proceeded those books of ardent and profound faith, but of faith
more than of charity. Notwithstanding their length and
their vast proportions, these books are pamphlets, works of
combat. One should be on his guard against taking them
for scientific treatises. Serenity is lacking in them, and from
the very first, we feel ourselves enveloped in an atmosphere
of trouble and storm.

625. ANALYSIS OF THE TREATISE ON EDUCATION. — However, the three volumes of the *Education* will be read with
profit. The first volume treats of education in general, and
contains three books. In the first book the author determines
the character of education, which has for its purpose to *cultivate* the faculties, to *exercise* them, to *develop* them, to

strengthen them, and, finally, to *polish* them. In the following books the author studies the nature of the child, of whom he sometimes speaks with a touching tenderness ; and examines the means of education, which are " religion, instruction, discipline, and physical culture." Discipline consists in supporting, preventing, and repressing. Discipline is to education " that which the bark is to the tree which it surrounds. It is the bark which holds the sap, and forces it to ascend to the heart of the tree.'

The general title of the second volume is, *On Authority and Respect in Education.* Authority and respect, in the eyes of the author, are the two fundamental things. From this point of view, he studies what he calls the *personnel* of education ; that is, God, the parents, the teacher, the child, and the schoolmate.

The third volume, entitled *Educational Men*, treats of the qualities befitting the head master of an educational establishment, and of his different colleagues.[1]

626. ERRORS AND PREJUDICES. — Although he wrote a beautiful chapter entitled, *Of the Respect due the Dignity of the Child and the Liberty of his Nature*, Dupanloup is still more struck with the faults than with the virtues of childhood. He shudders in thinking of his thoughtlessness, of his curiosity, of his sensuality, and especially of his pride. So he distrusts commendation and rewards.

" In praising your pupils," he says to the teacher, " do you not fear to excite their pride? The pride of scholars is a terrible evil ; it begins in the ' third,' develops in the ' second,' blossoms in ' rhetoric,' and becomes established in ' philosophy.' "[2]

---

[1] The principal educational works of Dupanloup are *Éducation*, 1851, three volumes; *De la haute éducation intellectuelle*, 1855, three volumes; *Lettres sur l'éducation des filles*, 1879, one volume.

[2] See note to page 131.

To this mistrust of human nature is joined a singular pessimism with respect to the functions of the teacher. "There is found," he says, "in this service, grave troubles. Sometimes, if we are worthy of this service, if we sacrifice ourselves to it, we can find consolations in it, but pleasure, never!"

The verdict is severe and absolute, but it recoils in part on him who pronounces it. How not mistrust an educator who declares that there is no sweetness mingled with the fatigues of teaching, and who condemns the teachers of youth to a life of complete sacrifice and bitterness?

The greatest fault in the educational spirit of Dupanloup is that he does not cross the narrow limits of an education in small seminaries. Dupanloup wrote only for the middle classes. He had no interest in popular education; he does not love the lay teacher; he detests the University. Finally, he is the man who inspired the law of May 15, 1850.

627. THE SPIRITUALISTIC SCHOOL AND UNIVERSITY MEN. — The philosophers of the French spiritualistic school have not in general paid great attention to the theory of education. The most illustrious of them, Cousin (1792–1868), at the same time that he aided in organizing University instruction, carefully studied educational institutions abroad, especially in his two works, *Public Instruction in Holland* (1837), and *Public Instruction in Germany* (1840). The works of Jules Simon have the same practical character, but with a marked tendency to treat by preference the questions of primary instruction. The *School* (1864) is a manifesto in favor of gratuity and obligation.

The University men, on their part, have, in this century, acted rather than speculated. They have been intent rather on making good pupils than on composing theories. There would, however, be valuable truths to cull from the works of Cournot,[1] of Bersot,[2] and especially of Michel Bréal.[3]

[628. ANALYTICAL SUMMARY. — 1. One of the main characteristics of the educational thought of this century is doubtless the effort to deduce the rules of practice from certain first principles. The principles of instruction are to be found, for the most part, in the science of psychology, and the principles of education, in part, in social science and even in jurisprudence.

2. The purpose of Napoleon to secure the perpetuity of his dynasty through the influence of his Imperial University, is a striking proof of the belief in the potency of ideas, and of the belief in the potency of popular instruction as a means of national strength.

3. The history of mutual instruction exhibits three important facts : 1. the effect of agitation in arousing public interest in educational questions ; 2. the manner in which peculiar circumstances suggest an expedient which can be justified on no absolute grounds ; 3. the danger of converting such an expedient into a " system " for universal adoption.

4. Comenius, Pestalozzi, and Jacotot, attempted to make instruction universal by simplifying its processes to such a degree that every mother might be a teacher and every household a school.

5. In Comte we see the re-appearance of Condillac's doctrine, that the historic education of the race is the type of individual education. The same hypothesis will re-appear in Mr. Spencer's *Education*.]

---

[1] Cournot published in 1864 a remarkable book under this title : *Des institutions d'instruction publique.*

[2] See the *Essais de philosophie et de morale*, by E. Bersot, and also *Études et discours* (1879).

[3] See especially the well-known book of Bréal, *Quelques mots sur l'instruction publique en France.*

CHAPTER XXII.

THE SCIENCE OF EDUCATION. — HERBERT SPENCER AND ALEXANDER BAIN.

629. THE SCIENCE OF EDUCATION. — To-day, thanks to important works, the science of education is no longer an empty term, an object of vague aspirations for philosophers, of easy ridicule for wits. Doubtless it is far from being definitely established; but it no longer conceals its name and its pretensions; it defines its purpose and its methods; and manifests its youthful vitality in all directions.

Up to the present period, philosophers had scarcely thought of organizing pedagogy, of constructing it on a rational basis.   On the other hand, the practice of education is still less advanced than the conceptions of philosophers.   Here we the more often follow a thoughtless routine, or the vague inspirations of instinct.   The methods in use are not co-ordinated.   They present a curious mixture of old traditions and modern surcharges.   It is this lack of definiteness, of co-ordination of ideas, and the spectacle of these contradictions, which caused Richter[1] to say : "The education of the day resembles the Harlequin of the Italian comedy who comes on the stage with a bundle of papers under each arm. 'What do you carry under your right arm?' he is asked. 'Orders,' he replies.   'And under your left arm?'   'Counter-orders!'"

Quite a number of the philosophers of the nineteenth century have attempted to remedy this incoherence, and, by appealing to the scientific spirit, to regulate educational processes that have fallen into excesses of empiricism or of routine.   It is these attempts which we are summarily to recite.

630. THE GERMAN PHILOSOPHERS. — Since Kant, and by his example, the most of German philosophers have associated the theory of education with their speculations on human nature.

Fichte (1762–1814), in his *Discourse to the German Nation,* proclaimed the necessity of a national education to secure the regeneration of his country and its restoration to its former standing.   The advocate of a public and common education, because he would fight against the selfishness which family life encourages, he contributed by his eloquent

---

[1] J. P. Richter, better known under the name Jean Paul (1763–1825), the author of a spirited and scholarly book, *Levana, or the Doctrine of Education,* 1803.

appeals to restore the intellectual and moral grandeur, and consequently, the material grandeur, of Germany.

Schleiermacher (1768-1834) wrote a *Doctrine of Education*, which was not published till 1849. In this he develops, among other ideas, this proposition, that religious education does not belong to the school, but that it is the affair of the family and the Church.

Herbart (1776-1841) has composed a series of pedagogical writings which assign him a special place in the list of educational philosophers. Let us call attention, in particular, to his *General Pedagogy* (1806), and the *Outline of my Lessons on Pedagogy* (1840). That which distinguishes Herbart is his attempt to reduce to a system all the rules of pedagogy by giving them for a basis his own psychological theory. He inaugurated a new method in psychology, which does not seem, however, to have given the results that were expected from it, — the mathematical method. For him, psychology is only the mechanism of the mind, and by means of mathematical formula calculation may be applied to measure the force of ideas. The soul does not possess innate faculties ; it is developed progressively.

But it would require long efforts to enter into the secrets of Herbart's original thought. Let it suffice to say, that nurtured from an early period on the ideas of Pestalozzi, whose friend he was, he has founded a real school of pedagogy.

Beneke (1798-1854) is the author of a *Doctrine of Education and Instruction*, which is, in the opinion of Doctor Dittes, a masterpiece of psychological pedagogy. Beneke agrees with Herbart on a great number of points. His pedagogical methods have been popularized by J. G. Dressler, director of the normal school at Banzen, who died in 1860.[1]

---

[1] See *The Elements of Psychology, on the Principles of Beneke* (London, 1871).

Charles Schmidt, who died in 1864, wrote a large number of works on pedagogy, in which he is inspired by the phrenology of Gall and his fantastical hypotheses. Doubtless this inspiration is not happy, and the works of Schmidt are more valuable for their details, for their special reflections, than for their general doctrine. But from his undertaking there issues at least this truth, that the science of education should have for its basis, not only psychology, but physiology also, the science of the whole man, body and mind.

There is no country where pedagogy has received a more philosophical and a higher development than in Germany. Even the great poets, Lessing, Herder, Gœthe, and Schiller, have contributed through certain grand ideas to the construction of a science of education.

631. THE ENGLISH PHILOSOPHERS. — English philosophy, with its experimental and practical character, and with its positive and utilitarian tendencies, was naturally called to exercise a great influence on pedagogy. There are more truths to gather from the thinkers who, in different degrees, have followed Locke and Bain, and who have preserved a taste for prudent observation and careful experiments, than from the German idealists, enamored of hypothesis and systematic constructions.

Without doubt this explains the considerable success which the recent books of Herbert Spencer and Alexander Bain have obtained even in France.

632. THE BOOK OF HERBERT SPENCER. — If it were sufficient to define with exactness the end to be attained, and to discover the true method for constructing the science, Herbert Spencer's book on *Education, Intellectual, Moral, and Physical*,[1] would be a satisfactory treatise ; but it is one thing

---

[1] The first French translation appeared in 1878.

to comprehend that psychology is the only solid basis of a complete and exact pedagogy, and another thing to determine the real laws of psychology.

" Education will not be definitely systematized," says Mr. Spencer, " till the day when science shall be in possession of a rational psychology."

This day has not yet come, and Herbert Spencer, who is the first to recognize the fact, modestly presents his work only as an essay. But if it does not yet contain a perfect and fully worked out theory of education, the essay of the English philosopher is at least a vigorous effort, and a notable step towards a rational pedagogy, towards the science of education, which, as Virchow expresses it, " ought forever to proscribe the gropings of an ignorant education whose experiments are ever to be gone over anew."

633' PLAN OF THE WORK. — Every system of education supposes at the same time an ethics, — I mean a certain conception of life and of human destiny, and a psychology, — that is, a knowledge more or less exact of our faculties and of the laws which preside over their development. There are, in fact, in education, two essential questions : 1. What are the subjects of study and instruction, proper to create the qualities, the aggregate of which constitutes the type of the well-educated man? 2. By what methods shall we teach the child rapidly and well that which it is proper for him to learn? There are, in other terms, the question of end and the question of means. Ethics is necessary to resolve the first, and psychology, to illustrate the second.

● It is in accordance with this plan that Mr. Spencer has arranged the different parts of his work. The first chapter, entitled *What Knowledge is of Most Worth?* is in substance but a series of reflections on the final purpose, on the differ-

540   THE HISTORY OF PEDAGOGY.

ent forms, of human activity, and, consequently, on the relative importance, on the rank, which should be assigned to
the studies which go to compose a complete education.

In the three other chapters, *Intellectual*, *Moral*, and *Physical Education*, the author examines the methods which are
deemed the best for instructing the intelligence, perfecting
the moral character, and fortifying the body.

634. DEFINITION OF EDUCATION. — Herbert Spencer begins
with a definition of education : —

" Education," he says, " is all that we do for ourselves,
and all that others do for us, for the purpose of bringing us
nearer the perfection of our nature. . . .(The ideal of education would be to furnish man with a complete preparation
for life as a whole.\ . . Do not attempt to give an exclusive development of one order of knowledge at the expense
of the rest, however important it may be. Let us distribute
our attention over the whole, and justly proportion our efforts
to their relative value. . . . (In general, the object of education ought to be to acquire as completely as possible the
knowledge that is best adapted to develop individual and
social life under all its aspects, and to do no more than
glance at the subjects which contribute the least to this
development." [1]

This definition is wrong in being a little pretentious and
in not adapting itself to all the forms of education. It is
true, perhaps, if it is a question of the ideal to be attained in
a complete instruction, accessible to a few privileged men,
but it could not be applied to popular education. It soars
too high above human conditions and social realities.

---

[1] In this, as in several other instances, Monsieur Compayré gives a summary of the author's thought rather than an exact quotation. (P.)

635. HUMAN DESTINY. — The conception of human destiny, as Mr. Spencer outlines it in the opening of his book, has very marked utilitarian tendencies. His first complaint against the current education is that it sacrifices the useful to the agreeable ; that as matters now go, everything which pertains to mental adornment and display has precedence over the knowledge which might increase our well-being and assure our happiness. As in the history of dress, with savages for example, it is proved that the ornamental in dress precedes the useful ; so in instruction, ornamental studies are preferred to useful studies. This is especially the case with women, who have a decided preference for the qualities of pure decoration.[1]

In his rather vigorous reaction against the luxuries which in classical instruction would wrongly substitute themselves for more necessary studies, Mr. Spencer goes so far as to say : —

"Just as the Orinoco Indian paints and tattooes himself, so the child in this country learns Latin because it forms a part of the education of a gentleman."

However, we do not construe this literally. Mr. Spencer does not go so far as to suppress the disinterested studies which are as much the more necessary as they seem to be the more superfluous. He merely demands that instruction be not reduced to a training in the trivial elegancies of a dead language, or to a study of trifles in history, such as the dates of battles, and the birth and death of princes.

636. UTILITARIAN TENDENCIES. — Utility, that is, the influence on happiness, — such is the true criterion by which are

---

1 As, historically, ornament precedes dress, on Mr. Spencer's main principle, it need not be till late in life that women dress sensibly. Or ought not the genesis of dress in the individual to follow the same order as the genesis of dress in the race ? (P.)

to be estimated, admitted or excluded, and finally classified, the subjects proposed for the study of man as the elements of his education. It is understood, however, that happiness is to be considered in its widest and highest sense. Happiness does not consist in the satisfaction of such or such a privileged inclination. It consists in being all that it is possible to be, — in complete living. To prepare us for a complete life, — such is the function of education.

637. DIFFERENT CATEGORIES OF ACTIVITY. — Complete life supposes different kinds of activity, which ought to be subordinated one to another according to their importance and dignity. The following statement shows how Mr. Spencer proposes to classify these different categories of activities according to an ascending scale of progress : —

1. In the first rank is placed the activity which ministers simply to self-preservation. It would be of no consequence to be an eminent scholar, or a citizen and a patriot, or a devoted father ; or rather, all this would be impossible, if one did not first know how to assure his safety and his life.

2. Then comes the series of activities which tend *indirectly* to the same end of physical well-being, by the acquisition and production of the material goods necessary for existence, that is, industry and the different occupations.

3. In the third place, man employs his activities in the service of his family, — he has children to support and to bring up.

4. Social and political life is the fourth object of his efforts. This supposes, as a previous condition, the accomplishment of family duties, just as family life itself supposes the normal development of the individual life.

5. Finally, human existence is consummated and crowned, so to speak, in the exercise of the activities which, in a single

word, we might call æsthetic, and which, taking advantage of the leisure left from care and business, will find satisfaction in the culture of letters and the arts.

638. CRITICISM OF THIS CLASSIFICATION. — What exceptions can be taken to this exact and methodical table of the different elements of an existence complete, normal, and consequently human? Is it necessary to remark that the happiness thus understood does not differ from what we call virtue? None of the five elements distinguished by Mr. Spencer can be safely omitted. The first could not be neglected without endangering the material reality of life ; nor the last, without impairing its moral dignity. In some degree they are mutually necessary, in this sense, that the lower, or selfish activities, are the conditions which make possible the other parts of human duty ; and that the higher, or disinterested activities, become, as it were, the justification of the toil we endure in order to exist and to satisfy material necessities.

We have, however, one grave reserve to make. Mr. Spencer is wrong in putting into the last category of activities that which is the crown of the others, all that which concerns the moral development of the individual. Between the second and the third class of activities we ask to interpolate another form of activity, — that which constitutes the individual moral life, that which, in every man, even the humblest and the poorest, calls into exercise the conscience, the reason, and the will. Mr. Spencer's system is decidedly too aristocratic. It seems to reserve the moral life for men of leisure. In a democratic society, which believes in equality and which would not have this an empty term, there are efforts which must be made for the moral development of the human being in all conditions, and it would be wrong to reduce personal activity to the care of health and material well-being.

639. Effects on Education. — It is now easy to comprehend the duties of education. Conforming its efforts to nature, distributing its lessons according to the exact division of human functions, it will seek the branches of knowledge the most fit for making of the pupil, first, a sound and healthy man, then a toiler, a workman, — a man, in a word, capable of earning his livelihood ; then it will train him for the family and the State, by endowing him with all the domestic and civic virtues ; finally, it will open to him the brilliant domain of art under all its forms.

640. Science is the Basis of Education. — When we have once divided human life into a certain number of superimposed stages which education should teach us to ascend one after another, it becomes necessary to know what are the facts and the branches of knowledge which correspond to each one of these different steps. To this question Mr. Spencer replies that in all the grades of human development that which is pre-eminently necessary, that which is the basis of education, is science.

641. Science for Health and Industrial Activity. — It is in the first part of education, that which has for its object self-preservation, that science is the least useful. So far, education may be in great part negative, because nature has taken it upon herself to lead us to our destination. The child cries at the sight of a stranger, and throws himself into the arms of his mother when he feels the slightest sorrow. However, in proportion to his growth, man has more and more need of science, and he could not do without physiology and hygiene. By this means will he shun all those

little acts of imprudence, all those physical faults, which shorten life, or pave the way for infirmities in old age. By this means he will diminish the interval, which is so considerable, between the length of life as it might be and the brevity of life as it is. Evident truths, but too often unheeded!

"How many scholars," exclaims Mr. Spencer, "who would blush if caught saying Iphigénia instead of Iphigenia, show not the slightest shame in confessing that they do not know where the Eustachian tubes are, and what are the actions of the spinal cord!"

With respect to the activities which might be called lucrative, and to the kind of instruction which they require, Mr. Spencer still shows the utility of science. He knows how great a disposition there is in modern society to promote professional or industrial instruction; but he thinks, not without reason, that we do not proceed as we should in order to be completely successful in this direction. All the sciences, mathematics through its applications to the arts, mechanics through its connection with industries where machines play so great a part, physics and chemistry through the knowledge they furnish on matter and its properties, even the social sciences by reason of the relations of commerce with politics, — all the sciences, in a word, contribute to develop the skill and the prudence of the man who is employed in any trade or occupation whatever.

642. SCIENCE FOR FAMILY LIFE. — A point in which the originality of Mr. Spencer's thought is distinctly marked, and which he develops with an eloquent earnestness, is the necessity of enlightening parents, and particularly mothers, upon their obligations and duties, and of putting them in a condition to direct the education of their children by

teaching them the natural laws of body and mind: "Is it not monstrous," he says, "that the fate of a new generation should be left to the chances of unreasoning custom, impulse, fancy, — joined with the suggestions of ignorant nurses and the prejudiced counsel of grandmothers. . . . In the actual state of things the best instruction, even among the favored by fortune, is scarcely more than an instruction of celibates." We are ever saying that the vocation of woman is to bring up her children, and yet we teach her nothing of that which she ought to know in order to fulfill worthily this great task. Ignorant as she is of the laws of life and of the phenomena of the soul, knowing nothing of the nature of the moral emotions or of physical disorders, her intervention in the education of the child is often more disastrous than her absolute inaction would be.

643. SCIENCE IN ÆSTHETIC EDUCATION. — Mr. Spencer next shows that social and political activity also has need of being enlightened by science. One is a citizen only on the condition of knowing the history of his country.

That which it is more difficult to grant Mr. Spencer, is that æsthetic education, in its turn, is based on science. Is there not some exaggeration, for example, in asserting that poor musical compositions are poor because they are lacking in truth? and that they are lacking in truth "because they are lacking in science"? Does one become a man of letters and an artist as one becomes a geometrician? To cultivate with success those arts which are as the flower of civilization, is there not required, besides talent and natural gifts, a long practice, a slow initiation,. something, in a word, more delicate than the attention which suffices for being instructed in science?

644. EXAGGERATIONS AND PREJUDICES. — We believe as thoroughly as any one can in the efficiency and in the educa-

tional virtues of science, and we would willingly make it, as Mr. Spencer does, the basis of education. We must be on our guard, however, against cultivating this religion of science until it becomes a superstition. Our author is not completely exempt from this danger.

That science develops the intellectual qualities, such as judgment, memory, reasoning, we admit; that it develops them better than the study of the languages, let even this be granted! But it is impossible for us not to protest when Mr. Spencer represents science as endowed with the same efficacy for inspiring moral qualities, such as perseverance, sincerity, activity, resignation to the will of nature, piety even, and religion. Science appears to us an infallible means of animating and exciting the different energies of the soul; but will it also have the quality of disciplining them? Thanks to science, man will know that which it is proper to do, if he wishes to be a workman, a parent, or a citizen, but on this express condition, that he *wills;* and this education of the will, is it still science which shall be charged with it? We may be allowed to doubt it.

Mr. Spencer himself now seems to share this doubt, if we may trust one of his recent works.[1] " Faith in books and in nature," it is there said, " is one of the superstitions of our times." We deceive ourselves, says the author, when we establish a connection between the intelligence and the will, for conduct is determined not by knowledge but by emotion.

" He who would hope to teach geometry by giving lessons in Latin, would scarcely be more unreasonable than those who count on producing better sentiments by means of a discipline of the intellectual faculties."

---

[1] *Introduction to Social Science*, p. 390.

To tell the truth, Mr. Spencer has here fallen into another extreme, and he seems to us at one time to have granted too much, and at another too little, to the influence of instruction on morality.

645. INTELLECTUAL EDUCATION. — So far we have examined along with Mr. Spencer only the nature of the objects and of the knowledge which befit the education of man. It remains to inquire how the mind can assimilate this knowledge. Pedagogy has not only to draw up in theory a brilliant programme of necessary studies, but it also searches out the means and the methods to be employed, in order that these studies may be presented to the mind, and may have the greater chance of being thus presented with profit.

In this somewhat more practical part of his work, Mr. Spencer thinks that pedagogy should be guided by the idea of evolution; that is, of the progressive course of a being who makes himself, who creates himself little by little, and who develops in succession, according to fixed laws, powers originally enveloped in the germs that he has received from nature, or that have been transmitted to him by heredity.

646. LAWS OF INTELLECTUAL EVOLUTION. — In other terms, Mr. Spencer shows that the precepts of pedagogy cannot be definitely deduced until the laws of mental evolution have been accurately established, and he attempts to determine some of these laws.

He proves that the mind passes naturally from the simple to the complex, from the indefinite to the definite, from the concrete to the abstract, from the empirical to the rational; that the genesis of the individual is the same as the genesis of the race; that the intelligence assimilates by preference that which it discovers for itself; finally, that all culture which profits the pupil is, at the same time, an exercise which stimulates him and delights him.

From this there result these practical consequences : that it is necessary first to present to the child simple subjects of study, individual things, sensible objects, for the purpose of starting him gradually on his way towards complex truths, abstract generalities, conceptions of the reason ; that nothing can be exacted of the child's intelligence but vague and incomplete notions which the travail of the mind will gradually clarify and elaborate ; that education ought to be *in petto*, for each individual, a repetition and a copy of the general march of civilization and of the progress of humanity ; that it is necessary to count more on the personal effort of the pupil than upon the action of the teacher ; that, finally, it is necessary to find the methods which interest, and even those which amuse. Hence the educator, instead of opposing nature, instead of disconcerting her in her course and in the insensible steps of her real development, will restrict himself to following her step by step, and education will be no longer a force which obstructs, which represses, which smothers ; but, on the contrary, a force which sustains and stimulates by associating with itself the work of the spontaneous powers of the soul.

647. SELF-EDUCATION. — Mr. Spencer attaches great importance to that maxim which recommends us to encourage above all else self-education : —

"In education the process of self-development should be encouraged to the fullest extent. Children should be led to make their own investigations, and to draw their own inferences. They should be *told* as little as possible, and induced to *discover* as much as possible. Humanity has progressed solely by self-instruction ; and that to achieve the best results, each mind must progress somewhat after the same fashion, is continually proved by the marked success of self-made men. Those who have been brought up under the ordinary school-drill, and have carried away with them the idea that education is practicable only in that style, will think it hopeless to make children their own teachers. If, however, they will call to mind that the all-important knowledge of surrounding objects which a child gets in its early years is not without help, — if they will remember that the child is self-taught in the use of its mother tongue, — if they will estimate the amount of that experience of life, that out-of-school wisdom which every boy gathers for himself, — if they will mark the unusual intelligence of the uncared-for London *gamin*, as shown in all the directions in which his faculties have been tasked, — if further, they will think how many minds have struggled up unaided, not only through the mysteries of our irrationally-planned *curriculum*, but through hosts of other obstacles besides; they will find it a not unreasonable conclusion, that if the subjects be put before him in right order and right form, any pupil of ordinary capacity will surmount his successive difficulties with but little assistance."

648. MORAL EDUCATION. — Moral education, without furnishing occasion for as complete a theory as intellectual education, has, nevertheless, suggested to Mr. Spencer some important reflections.

Mr. Spencer expressly declares that he does not accept the dogma of Lord Palmerston, or what would be called in France the dogma of Rousseau, namely, that all children are born good. He would incline the rather toward the contrary opinion, which, "though untenable," he says, "seems to us less wide of the truth"! Doubtless, we must not expect too much moral goodness of children; but it may be found that Mr. Spencer exaggerates a little, and draws too dark a portrait of the child when he says, " The child resembles the savage ; his physical features, like his moral instincts, recall the savage." Taken literally, such pessimism would lead logically to an over-severe moral discipline, wholly repressive and restraining. Such, however, is not the conclusion of Mr. Spencer, who recommends a course of tolerance and mildness, a system of relative letting alone which we might almost think dictated by the optimism of Rousseau. He censures the brutal discipline of the English schools. Finally, he would have the child treated, not as an incorrigible rebel who is obedient only to force, but as a reasonable being capable of readily comprehending the reasons and the advantages of obedience, from the simple fact that he takes into account the connection of cause and effect.

.649. SYSTEM OF NATURAL PUNISHMENTS. — The true moral discipline, according to Mr. Spencer, is that which puts the child in a state of dependence on nature, who teaches him to detest his faults by reason of the natural consequences which they involve. It is necessary to renounce artificial punishments, which are almost always irritating and taken amiss, and to have recourse, as a rule, only to the privations and the inconveniencies which are the necessary consequences, and, as it were, the inevitable reactions, of the acts which have been committed.

A boy, for example, puts his room in disorder. In this case, the method of natural punishment requires that he himself shall repair the mischief ; and in this way he will soon correct himself of a turbulence from which he will be the first to suffer.

A little girl, through indolence, or through tarrying too long over her toilet, has made herself late for a walk. Let her be punished by not waiting for her, by leaving her at home.   This is the best means of curing her in the future of her indolence and coquetry.

The system which tends thus to substitute the lessons of nature for artificial penalties, certainly offers great advantages.   It subjects the child, not to the authority of a passing teacher, or of parents who will one day die, but to a law whose action neither ceases nor ever relents.   Artificial punishments often provoke the resistance of the child because he does not comprehend their meaning, and because, proceeding from the human will, they can be taxed with injustice and caprice.   Could one as easily refuse to bow before the impersonal force of nature, — a force which exactly adjusts the punishment to the fault,[1] which accepts no excuse, against which there is no appeal, and which, without threats, without anger, rigorously and silently executes the law?

650. DIFFICULTIES IN APPLICATION. — Mr. Spencer's principle is excellent, but the opportunities for applying it are far less frequent than our philosopher believes.   The child, in most cases, is too little reflective, too little reasonable, to comprehend, and especially to heed, the suggestions of personal interest.

Let us add that this principle is wholly negative, that it furnishes at most only the means of shunning evil; that even in according to it an efficacy it does not have, it would still be necessary to reproach it with narrowing moral culture by reducing it to the rather mean solicitude for simple utility; finally, that it exercises no influence on the development of the positive virtues, on the disinterested education of morality in what is noble and exalted.

---

[1] So far as experience can testify, this is a pure assumption. The most trifling injuries are often the most painful, and the most serious the most painless. (P.)

Finally, the system of natural punishments would incur the danger of often being cruel, and of causing the child an irreparable injury. Let pass the pin-cushion, the boiling water, and the candle-flame, — examples which Mr. Spencer proposes ; but what shall we say of the bar of red-hot iron which he lets the child pick up? What shall be said, above all, of the grave consequences entailed by the faults of a young man left to himself?

" Would it not be," says Gréard justly, " to condemn the child to a régime so severe as to be an injustice, to count solely on the effects of natural reactions and inevitable consequences, for the purpose of disciplining his will? The penalty which they provoke is the most often enormous as compared with the fault which has produced them, and man himself demands for his conduct other sanctions than those of a harsh reality. He desires that we judge the intention as well as the fact ; that he be commended for his efforts ; that in the first instance extreme measures be not taken against him ; that the blow fall on him if needs be, but without crushing him, and while extending to him a hand to help him up."[1]

651. RETURN TO NATURE. — However it may be, Mr. Spencer is to be commended for having shown that for moral education as for intellectual education, the method which approaches nature the nearest is also the best. The return to nature which was the characteristic of Rousseau's theories and of Pestalozzi's practice, is also the dominant trait of Mr. Spencer's pedagogy.

If we look closely into the matter, this decided purpose to follow nature implicates something besides the superficial

---

[1] See the *Esprit de discipline dans l'éducation*, a memoir of Gréard, published in the *Revue Pédagogique*, 1883, No. 11.

condemnation of methods introduced by art and human device. It supposes a fundamental belief, — the belief in the
beneficent purpose of natural instincts. To have confidence
in nature, to fall back on the spontaneous forces of the soul,
because we discern behind them or in them a higher providence or an internal foresight, is a belief generally useful and
suggestive for conducting human affairs, but particularly
necessary for directing the education of man. It is not
without some surprise that we discover this belief at the basis
of Mr. Spencer's pedagogy, as though, by a contradiction
which is not new, the evolutionist philosophy, which seems
to exclude final causes from the conception of the universe,
had been practically constrained to bow before them, and to
proclaim, at least in the matter of education, the salutary
efficacy of the theory which admits them.

Thus, in speaking of physical education, Mr. Spencer
remarks that the sensations are the natural guides, which it
would be dangerous not to follow.

" Happily, that all-important part of education which goes
to secure direct self-preservation, is in great part already
provided for. Too momentous to be left to our own blunder-
ing, Nature takes it into her own hands."

Speaking in another place of the instincts which induce
the child to move himself and to seek in physical exercise the
basis of physical well-being, he declares that to oppose these
instincts would be to go counter to the means " *divinely*
arranged" for assuring the development of the body.

652. PHYSICAL EDUCATION. — The chapter devoted by Mr.
Spencer to physical education, is such as might be expected
from a thinker who is wholly exempt from idealistic prejudices and who does not hesitate to write : —

" The history of the world shows that the well-fed races
have been the energetic and dominant races."

It is necessary first and above all to establish physical force in man, and to create within him "a robust animal." "The actual education of children is defective in several particulars : in an insufficiency of food, in an insufficiency of clothing, in an insufficiency of exercise, and in an excess of mental application."

Mr. Spencer complains that modern education has become wholly intellectual, and that it neglects the body. He reminds us that "the preservation of health is one of our duties," and that there exists a thing which might be called "physical morality."

Here, as everywhere, Mr. Spencer demands that we follow the indications of nature. He explains on physiological grounds the apparently inordinate appetite which children show for certain foods, — sugar, for example. He urgently entreats that preference shall be given to play and to free and spontaneous exercise, over gymnastics.

653. GENERAL JUDGMENT. — That which, in our opinion, attests the truth of the pedagogical laws which we have just discussed, is that they are in agreement with the general opinions of the great modern reformers in education. It is thus that Spencer's ideas are in close harmony with those which Pestalozzi had employed at Stanz. The success which he obtained there, as Mr. Spencer has remarked, depended on two things : first, on the attention which he used in determining what kind of instruction the children had need of, and next, on the pains he took to associate the new knowledge with that which they already possessed.

Mr. Spencer's essay, then, deserves the attention of educators. There is scarcely a book in which a keen scent for details comes more agreeably to animate a fund of solid arguments, and from which it is more useful to extract the

substance. However, it must not be read save with precaution. The brilliant English thinker sometimes fails in justness and measure, and his bold generalizations need to be
tested with care.

654. ALEXANDER BAIN AND EDUCATION AS A SCIENCE.—
Less brilliant than the work of Mr. Spencer, the book of
Mr. Bain, *Education as a Science*, recommends itself by
merits of studied analysis and scholarly minuteness. Others
surpass Mr. Bain in brilliancy of imagination, in originality
and in enthusiasm ; but no one equals him in richness of
details, in acuteness and abundance of observations. After
the more venturesome have taken the lead and have published the original sketch, Mr. Bain appears and writes the
methodical and complete manual. His own work resembles
that of a conscientious guard who marches in the rear of
a victorious army, and by a wise organization makes sure
the positions conquered by the march of an impetuous
commander-in-chief. His book, in other terms, is but the
studious and thorough development of Mr. Spencer's principles.

655. GENERAL IMPRESSION. — It is impossible in an analysis to bring out the merit of a book which is especially
valuable for the multiplicity of the questions which the
author discusses in it, and for the infinite variety of the
solutions which he proposes. There are landscapes which
discourage the painter, because, notwithstanding their
beauty, they are too vast, too full of details, to admit of
being crowded into a frame. We may say the same of Mr.
Bain's book. One must have studied it himself in order to
form an estimate of its value. Professors of all classes will
here find pages of well-considered counsels, and judicious
reflections upon educational methods. The nature of stud-

ies, the sequence of subjects, the gradation of difficulties, the choice of exercises, the comparison of oral instruction with text-book instruction, modes of discipline, — nothing escapes a thinker who is not a mere theorist or an amateur educator, but a professional man, a competent teacher, an experienced professor.

Indeed, no one should allow himself to be deceived by this fine phrase, *Education as a Science*, which might disconcert and turn aside whole classes of readers, such as those who, in works on education, especially desire a guide for practice. On the contrary, they will have every reason to commend a book which passes very quickly from generalities to applications, and which is above all else a manual of practical and technical pedagogy. The study of it will be profitable not merely to professors who are teaching the higher branches of literature and science, but even to the humblest instructors, and even — for Mr. Bain overlooks no detail — to teachers of reading and writing.

656. DIVISION OF THE WORK. — *Education as a Science* comprises three parts : 1. psychological data ; 2. methods ; 3. modern education.

The author first inquires in what order the faculties are developed, and what effect this order should have on the distribution of studies. This is the psychological part. Then follows a discussion of what Mr. Bain calls the logical order, that is, of the relations which exist between the studies themselves and their different parts. This is the " analytical problem " of education.[1]

These preliminaries being established, Mr. Bain enters

---

1 By the "analytical problem " of education, Mr. Bain means the determining of the education value of subjects. See *Education as a Science*, Chapter V. (P.)

upon the principal theme, — the methods of instruction. He discusses one after another the first elements of reading, object-lessons, "which, more than any other means of instruction, require to be practised with care, for without this, an admirable process might, in unskillful hands, be nothing more than a thing of seductive appearance, but without value"; then methods relating to history, geography, the sciences, and the languages.

Finally, in his third book, Mr. Bain exhibits a new plan of study, with particular reference to secondary instruction.

657. PSYCHOLOGICAL ORDER AND LOGICAL ORDER. — In his reflections on the development of the mind and upon the distribution of studies, Mr. Bain is inspired by the principles which have guided Mr. Spencer.

"Observation precedes reflection. The concrete comes before the abstract."

In education, then, the sequence should be from the simple to the complex, from the particular to the general, from the indefinite to the definite, from the empirical to the rational, from analysis to synthesis, from the outline to details ; finally, from the material to the immaterial.

Such would be the ideal order in education ; but Mr. Bain remarks that in practice all sorts of obstacles come to disturb this rigorous sequence.

658. MODERN EDUCATION. — The plan of secondary studies which Mr. Bain recommends to the reformers of teaching is the result and the résumé of all these observations.

Intellectual education, common to all young people who receive a liberal instruction, would henceforth comprise three essential parts : 1. the sciences ; 2. the humanities ; 3. rhetoric and the national literature. We see at once what is to

---

be understood by this last item; but the two others have need of some explanations.

The sciences are divided into two groups: those which are to be mastered, — arithmetic, geometry, algebra, physics, chemistry, biology, psychology; and the natural sciences, which should be studied only superficially because they would overwhelm the memory under the weight of too large a number of facts. Geography, which, one does not know why, is included in the sciences, while history is attached to the humanities, will complete the programme of scientific studies.

As to the humanities, Mr. Bain preserves scarcely more than the name while suppressing the thing; for in the curtailed and disfigured domain which he persists in calling by this name, he cuts off precisely that which has always been considered as constituting its essence, — the study of the dead languages. He excludes from it even the living languages, and that which he still decorates with the fine title of humanities, is still science, — moral science, it is true, — " history and sociology with political economy and jurisprudence."

A course in universal literature, but, be it understood, without original texts, *might* afterwards be added to this pretended teaching of the humanities.

Two or three hours a week would be devoted parallelly, during the whole course of study, which would last six years, to each of the three departments of instruction which Mr. Bain thinks equally important.

As to the real humanities, dead or living languages, they should no longer be included in education save as optional and extra studies, on the same basis as the accomplishments. And, appealing to the future, Mr. Bain even predicts that " a day will come when it will be found that this is still granting them too large a place in education."

Mr. Bain, then, gives all his preferences to scientific studies, and his book might properly be entitled, not only *Education as a Science*, but also *Science in Education*.

659. THEORETICAL ERRORS. — Mr. Bain reproaches letters with giving the mind the habit of servility. By what singular revulsion of thought can the liberal studies *par excellence* be represented as a school of intellectual servitude? It is rather to scientific instruction that we may properly return the accusation of enslaving the spirit. By their inexorable evidence and by their very exactness, do not the sciences sometimes smother the originality and the free flight of the imagination?

This defect, however, does not cut them off from a right to a place, and to a large place, in the programme of intellectual education. Let us accept with favor their alliance, let us admit them to a certain degree of fellowship, but do not let us tolerate their encroachments. In a word, the objcet of the sciences is either pure abstractions or material realities. He who studies mathematics and physics first acquires real knowledge of high value ; and, on the other hand, he strengthens his mind through the habits engendered by the rigorous methods which the sciences employ. We cheerfully grant to Mr. Bain that the sciences are at the same time admirable sources of useful truths and valuable instruments of mental discipline. By cultivating them we gain not only the positive knowledge which they teach respecting the world, but also the power, rigor, and exactness which they impose on their adepts.

660. INSUFFICIENCY OF THE SCIENCES. — But the question is to know whether the sciences, so useful and so necessary for enriching and disciplining the mind, are also the best agents for training it. The educator is not in the situation of the

farmer who has only two things to do, — to plow and sow the field which he cultivates. The work of education is vast in another direction. It has to do with developing the aptitudes or latent energies, that which the philosophy of the day hardly allows us longer to call faculties, but that which they re-establish under another name, that of the unconscious forces of the soul; it has to do, not with laboring on a soil almost entirely prepared by nature, but in great part with creating the soil itself. Now, the sciences are indeed the seed which it will be proper by and by to sow on the field, but they are not the substance which nourishes and fertilizes it.

661. SENSUALISTIC TENDENCIES. — If we go to the bottom of Mr. Bain's thought and doctrine on the mind, we shall find the secret of his ardent preference for the teaching of the sciences. His errors in practical pedagogy proceed from theoretical errors on human nature.

For him, as for Locke, there are not, properly speaking, intellectual forces independent of the facts which succeed one another in the consciousness. Consequently, there is not an education of the faculties. Memory or imagination, considered as a distinct power, as an aptitude more or less happy, is but a word. It is nothing apart from the recollections or the images which are successively graven in the mind. For Mr. Bain, as for Locke, the best education is that which places items of knowledge side by side in the mind, which accumulates facts there, but not that which seeks to enkindle in the soul a flame of intelligence.

That which also warps the theoretical views of Mr. Bain is that he accords no independence, no individual life, to the mind; and that for him, back of the facts of consciousness, there come to view, without any intermedium, the cerebral organs. Now the brain is developed of itself; it acquires fatally, with the progress of years, more weight and more volume; it passes from the age of concrete things to the age of abstractions. Hence a reduction, an inevitable contraction, of the sphere of education. There is nothing more to do than to let nature have her way, and to fill the vase which she charges herself with constructing.

662. UTILITARIAN TENDENCIES. — Finally, to conclude this indication of the general ideas which dominate and which mar the pedagogy of Mr. Bain, let us observe that a positive and practical utility, a vulgar utility, mingles too many of its inspirations with it. The criterion of utility is sometimes applied to it with an artless extravagance. Thus, in the languages, only those words should be learned which occur the most often, and in the sciences, only the parts which are of the most frequent use. Even in moral education, as it is conceived by the English philosopher, are to be found, as we might expect, these utilitarian and narrow views.

Would one believe, for example, that Mr. Bain makes the fear of the penal code the mainspring of the teaching of virtue?[1] Here, at least, we must acknowledge that science is insufficient. " To pretend, for example, that physiology can teach us moderation in the sexual appetite is to attribute to it a result which no science has yet been able to give." But must we count any more, as Mr. Bain would

---

[1] We might dwell on Mr. Bain's observations relative to punishments. Here is what Gréard says of them : " Mr. Bain, with infinite good sense and disciplinary tact, is much less concerned with applying the rule than with the conditions according to which it should be applied. On this point he enters into details full of scruples. He does not hesitate to call to his aid the knowledge of the masters of penal jurisprudence, and his recommendations, added to those of Bentham, comprise not less than thirty articles."

have us, for example, on social influences and on personal experience? In this truly experimental education in virtue, ethics would be learned just as the mother tongue is learned, by use, by the imitation of others; and moral instruction, properly so called, would be a sort of grammar which is to rectify vicious practices.

663. FINAL JUDGMENT. — But our criticisms on the general tendencies of Mr. Bain's pedagogy subtract nothing from our admiration of the sterling qualities of his *Education as a Science*. Doubtless there would also be errors of detail to notice, or some particular methods to discuss; for example, that of never doing more than one thing at a time, or the propriety of first teaching to children the history of their country. Mr. Bain forgets that mythological history and sacred history, by their legendary and fabulous character, offer a particular attraction to the childish imagination, and are better adapted than history proper to infant minds. But, aside from the portions which are debatable, how many wise observations to gather on the different processes of instruction, on the transition from the concrete to the abstract, on the discretion which must be employed in object-lessons, the use of which so easily degenerates into abuse! Even through its absolute theories, *Education as a Science* will render great services; for, to illustrate the march of thought, nothing is so valuable as opinions which are exclusive and sincere. It were even desirable, if one did not fear to experiment on human souls, *in anima sublimi*, that according to Mr. Bain's plan, the experiment should be tried of an education exclusively scientific.

664. AMERICAN EDUCATORS. CHANNING (1780–1842). — The general fault of English pedagogy is its aristocratic character. For Mr. Spencer and Mr. Bain, as for Locke, it

564   THE HISTORY OF PEDAGOGY.

is simply a question of the education of a *gentleman*. It is in America, in the writings of Channing and Horace Mann, that we must seek the elements of a theory of democratic education, and of popular instruction.[1]

Channing, a Unitarian minister, associated religious sentiment and philosophic reason, and desired that in theology itself everything should issue in the supremacy of the human judgment. The most interesting of his writings are the public lectures which he gave in Boston in 1838, and the object of which is the education one gives himself, and the elevation of the working classes. We lack the space to give an analysis of these lectures, but a few quotations will make known the general spirit of the American reformer : —

"I am not discouraged by the objection that the laborer, if encouraged to give time and strength to the elevation of his mind, will starve himself and impoverish the country, when I consider the energy, and the efficiency of Mind.

"The highest force in the universe is Mind. This created the heavens and earth. This has changed the wilderness into fruitfulness, and linked distant countries in a beneficent ministry to one another's wants. It is not to brute force, to physical strength, so much as to art, to skill, to intellectual and moral energy, that men owe their mastery over the world. It is mind which has conquered matter. To fear, then, that by calling forth a people's mind, we shall impoverish and starve them, is to be frightened at a shadow."

"It is chiefly through books that we enjoy intercourse with superior minds, and these invaluable means of communication are in the reach of all. In the best books, great men talk to us, give us their most precious thoughts, and pour their souls

---

[1] There should be added to these the works of Swiss, Italian, and French educators, particularly of Siciliani, and the original and eminently suggestive studies of Bernard Perez.

into ours. God be thanked for books. They are the voices of the distant and the dead, and make us heirs of the spiritual life of past ages. Books are the true levellers. They give to all, who will faithfully use them, the society, the spiritual presence, of the best and greatest of our race. No matter how poor I am ; no matter though the prosperous of my own time will not enter my obscure dwelling ; if the sacred writers will enter and take up their abode under my roof, if Milton will cross my threshold to sing to me of Paradise, and Shakespeare to open to me the worlds of imagination and the workings of the human heart, and Franklin to enrich me with his practical wisdom, I shall not pine for want of intellectual companionship, and I may become a cultivated man though excluded from what is called the best society in the place where I live."

665. HORACE MANN (1796–1859). — Horace Mann is not a philosopher who discusses education, but a politician who reformed and developed the education of his country. Secretary of the Massachusetts Board of Education, he opened schools, founded libraries, and pronounced a great number of discourses, the best known of which is *The Necessity of Education in a Republican Government.*

"When, then," he often said, "will men give their thought to infancy? We watch the seed which we confide to the earth, but we do not concern ourselves with the human soul till the sun of youth has set. Were it in my power, I would scatter books over all the earth as men sow wheat on the plowed fields."

Speaking to Americans, to working people, and to tradesmen, he made apparent the positive advantages of instruction : —

" If to-morrow some one were to tell you that a coal mine

had been discovered which would pay ten per cent, you would all rush to it; and yet there are men whom you let grovel in ignorance when you might realize from forty to fifty per cent on them. You are ever giving your thought to capital and to machines; but the first machine is man, and the first capital, man, and you neglect him."

But he also interested himself in the moral effects of education, especially in a democratic society, where each citizen is a sovereign : —

"The education which has already been given a people makes it necessary to give them more. By instructing them, new powers have been awakened in them, and this intellectual and moral energy must be regulated. In this case we have not to do with mechanical forces, which, once put in action, accomplish their purpose and then stop. No; these are spiritual forces endowed with a principle of life and of progress which nothing can quench."

666. CONCLUSION. — The labors of Mr. Spencer and Mr. Bain, the works of Channing and Mann, and others still, will contribute, we hope, to prepare the definite solutions demanded by our times in the matter of education. These solutions are important for the security and the greatness of our country. More than ever it is necessary that education become something else than an affair of inspiration, abandoned to caprice and hazard, but that it be a work of reflection. It is said that the future is uncertain, that events are leading French society no one knows where, and that our destinies are at the mercy of the most unforeseen storms. We do not believe this, since it is within our power that it shall be otherwise. There is a means, in fact, of assuring the future of peoples, and this is to give them an intellectual and moral education which purifies the soul and strengthens

character. Do not let us look for regeneration and progress from a sudden and miraculous transformation ; do not let us demand them even of the immediate efficiency of such or such a political institution. Everything here below is accomplished according to the laws of a slow progression, by trifling and successive modifications. Just as for the child there is no abridgment which allows us to suppress the slow steps of the insensible growth which each year brings forward, so for nations there is no other process than the action, slow but sure, of a wise and vigorous education, for causing them to pass from vice to virtue, from abasement to grandeur.

The partisans of evolution sometimes seem to announce to us the near apparition of a race superior to our own, called to supplant us, as we shall have supplanted the inferior races. One day or another we shall be liable, it seems, to meet " at the angle of a rock " the successor of the human race. We count but little on such promises, and the coming of this hypothetical race of men, suddenly evoked by a wave of the magic wand of natural selection, leaves us very incredulous.

Happily, we know another means, a much surer process, for causing to appear, not a strange race, until now unknown, but generations of more worth than our own, which are superior to it in physical force, as in qualities of mind or virtues of character. This means is to establish, through reflection and reason, an education better adapted to our destination ; an education broader and more complete, at once more severe and more liberal, since it will at the same time exact more toil and permit more scope ; in which the child will learn to count more on himself ; in which his indolence will no longer be encouraged by accustoming him inopportunely to invoke supernatural aid ; in which instruction will no longer be a formulary recited as lip-service, but an inner and profound acquisition of the soul, in which the fear of the conscience will be substituted for the other rules of conduct, and in which thought and free reflection will no longer be distrusted; finally, an education more scientific and more rational, because it will neglect nothing which can develop a human soul and bring it into likeness with its ideal. Now that education to which the future belongs, notwithstanding the obstacles which the spirit of the past will still stir up against it, — that education is not possible, its laws cannot be established, its methods cannot be practised, except on one condition; this is, that the psychology of the child be written, and well written, and that reflection draw from this psychology all the consequences which it permits.

[667. COMMENT ON MR. SPENCER'S EDUCATION. — Monsieur Compayré might have emphasized his cautions. · Read with caution, and with a purpose to weigh the truth, Mr. Spencer's *Education* is inspiring and wholesome ; but it may be doubted whether there has been written, since the *Émile*, a book on education which is so well fitted to deceive an unwary reader by its rhetoric and philosophic plausibility. The air of breadth and candor with which the writer sets out is eminently prepossessing, and the reader is almost obliged to assume that he is being led to foregone conclusions. The first chapter, in particular, is a piece of literary art, in which there is such a deft handling of· sentiment and pathos as to unfit the susceptible reader for exercising his own critical judgment.

In this place I can only indicate in the briefest manner what seem to be the fundamental errors contained in ·the book : —

1. Mr. Spencer does not distinguish between the *immedi- ate* and the *mediate* practical value of knowledges. We may admit with him that science is of inestimable value to the human race; but it does not follow by any means that every person must be versed in science. As we need not own everything that is essential to our comfort, so we need not have as a personal possession all the knowledge that we need for guidance.

2. It is a very low conception of education that would limit its function to adapting a man merely to that state in life into which he chances to be born. The Bushman, the Red Indian, and the accountant, are unfortunate illustrations of the province of education. Often the highest function of education is to lift a man out of his ancestral state.

3. That the value of a subject for guidance is the same as its value for discipline, is true under only one assumption,—that the Bushman is always to remain a Bushman, and the Red Indian always a Red Indian, as by the new philosophy of course they should. Practical teachers very well know that, as a rule, the studies that are the most valuable for practical use are the least valuable for discipline. Mr. Spencer quotes no better proof of his assumption than "the beautiful economy of Nature."

4. Mr. Spencer's proposed education is sordid in its utilitarianism. He is preoccupied with man as an instrument rather than with a human being aspiring towards the highest type of his kind. A liberal education should be preoccupied first with the training of the man, then with the training of the instrument.

5. Mr. Spencer's restatement of Condillac's and Comte's doctrine, that individual education should be a repetition of civilization *in petto*, is at best but a specious generalization. The doctrine cannot be applied to practice, in any considera-

ble degree, if we would, and should not be, if we could, for it ignores one essential factor in progress, — inheritance.

6. The part assigned to "Nature" in the work of education is so overstrained as to be unnatural and absurd. Physical science has long since discarded this myth of Nature personified. It is only in educational science that this fiction is still employed to eke out an argument.

7. The doctrine of consequences which underlies Mr. Spencer's system of moral education is applicable to but a limited number of cases, or, if applied with thoroughness, is inhuman. Not even all the fit would survive if they were not shielded from the consequences of their acts by human sympathy and oversight.]

APPENDIX.

———•◦•———

A.

THE two aims to be kept in view in the teaching of this subject are *culture* and *guidance*. The purpose should be to extend the intellectual horizon of the teacher, or, to use Plato's phrase, to make him " the spectator of all time and all existence "; and, in the second place, to furnish the teacher with a clew which will safely conduct him through the mazes of systems, methods, and doctrines. There is no other profession that has derived so little profit from capitalized experiences; and there is no profession in which culture and breadth are more necessary.

For securing the ends here proposed, it is recommended that a plan somewhat like the following be pursued in the use of this volume : —

1. If there are three recitations a week, assign one chapter for each of the first two recitations, *to be carefully and thoughtfully read*, and require each pupil to select one special topic to present and discuss when he is called upon in the recitation ; and for the *third* recitation in each week, require each pupil to select a topic from any part of the book which has thus far been studied. The purpose of this plan is to bring before the class, in sharp outline, the salient points of the subject; and, at the same time, to create a sense of the organic unity of the theme as a comprehensive

whole. When there are more than three recitations a week, only a part of a chapter need be assigned for an advance lesson.

2. When the first survey of the subject has been made in the way just suggested, a *review* may be conducted as follows : —

(1.) *Biographical.* Following a chronological order, divide the whole treatise into as many sections as there are recitations to be devoted to this purpose, and require each pupil to make a careful study of some educator, as Socrates, Montaigne, or Pestalozzi, and to present this theme when called upon in recitation. When there is opportunity, encourage pupils to amplify their themes with information derived from other sources.

(2.) *Topical.* Require each pupil to select some doctrine, system, or method, and to show, in a systematic way, its origin, progress, and termination. In this review, encourage the critical spirit, and make the recitation to consist, in part, of a free discussion of principles and doctrines. The value of this subject for *guidance* will appear in this part of the study.

(3.) *By Chapters.* Require each pupil to prepare a summary of some chapter in the book, emphasizing the more important truths that are taught in it, and showing the tendency or drift of educational thought. The *culture* value of the subject will appear in this part of the study. By this mode of treatment, the subject can be compassed, with good results, in twenty weeks.

3. Where no more than twelve or fourteen weeks can be given to this subject, it is recommended that the following chapters be selected : I., II., III., IV., V., VI., VII., X., XII., XIII., XVIII., XIX., XX., XXI., XXII.

For use in *Teachers' Meetings* held by superintendents, the following chapters are suggested: II., III., V., VI., VII., X., XIII., XVIII., XX., XXII.

For use in *Teachers' Reading Circles*, either of the above selections will serve a good purpose.

B.

A SELECT LIST OF WORKS SUPPLEMENTARY TO "COMPAYRÉ'S HISTORY OF PEDAGOGY."

1. The Cyclopædia of Education. New York.
2. Buisson. Dictionnaire de Pédagogie. Parts 1–156. Paris.
3. Lindner. Handbuch der Erziehungskunde. Wien and Leipzig.
4. K. Schmidt. Die Geschichte der Pädagogik. Cöthen.
5. G. Compayré. Historie Critique des Doctrines de l'Éducation en France. Paris.
6. Barnard. German Teachers and Educational Reformers.
7. Barnard. French Teachers, Schools, and Pedagogy.
8. Barnard. English Teachers, Educators, and Promoters of Education.
9. Barnard. American Teachers, Educators, and Benefactors of Education.
10. Barnard. Pestalozzi and Swiss Pedagogy.
11. Biber. Pestalozzi and his Plan of Education. London.
12. Donaldson. Lectures on the History of Education. Edinburgh.
13. Krüsi. Pestalozzi: his Life, Work, and Influence. Cincinnati.
14. Lorenz. Life of Alcuin. London.
15. Mrs. Mann. Life of Horace Mann. Boston.
16. Meiklejohn. Dr. Andrew Bell. London.
17. Morley, J. Rousseau. London.
18. Mullinger. The Schools of Charles the Great. London.
19. Quick. Essays on Educational Reformers. Cincinnati.

20. Shuttleworth. Four Periods of Public Education. London.
21. Arnold. Higher Schools and Universities of Germany. London.
22. Hart. German Universities. New York.
23. De Guimps. Histoire de Pestalozzi. Lausanne.
24. De Guimps. La Philosophie et la Pratique de l'Éducation. Paris.
25. Meunier. Lutte du Principe Clérical et de Principe Laique dans l'Enseignement. Paris.
26. Gaufrés. Claude Baduel et la Réforme des Études au XVIᵉ Siècle. Paris.
27. Bentham. Chrestomathia. London.
28. Drane. Christian Schools and Scholars. London.
29. Ascham. The Scholemaster. Notes by Mayor. London.
30. Locke. Thoughts concerning Education. Notes by Quick. Cambridge.
31. Laurie. John Amos Comenius. Boston.
32. Lancelot. Narrative of a Tour to La Grande Chartreuse. London.
33. Schimmelpenninck. Narrative of the Demolition of Port Royal. London.
34. Hamilton, Elizabeth. Letters on the Elementary Principles of Education. London.
35. Spencer. Education : Intellectual, Moral, and Physical. N. Y.
36. Rousseau, Émile. Extracts. Boston.
37. Blackie. Four Phases of Morals. N. Y.
38. Aristotle. The Politics and Economics. London.
39. Craik. The State in its Relation to Education. London.
40. Cousin. Report on the State of Public Instruction in Prussia.
41. Gill. Systems of Education. Boston.
42. Souquet. Les Ecrivains Pédagogues du XVIᵉ Siècle. Paris.
43. Mann. Lectures on Education. Boston.
44. Quintilian. Institutes of Oratory. London.
45. Plato. The Republic and the Laws. London.
46. Xenophon. The Memorabilia of Socrates. N. Y.
47. Plutarch. Morals. Boston.
48. MacAlister. Montaigne on Education. Boston.

49. Pestalozzi. Leonard and Gertrude. Boston.
50. Necker de Saussure. Éducation Progressive. Paris.
51. Cochin. Pestalozzi: sa Vie, ses Œuvres, ses Méthodes. Paris.
52. Compayré. Cours de Pédagogie. Paris.
53. Milton. Tractate on Education. Cambridge.
54. Fénelon. Fables. Paris.
55. Fénelon. The Education of a Daughter. Dublin.
56. Martin. Les Doctrines Pédagogiques des Grecs. Paris.
57. Jacotot. Enseignement Universel. Paris.
58. Adams. The Free School System of the United States. London.
59. Conrad. The German Universities for the last Fifty Years. Glasgow.
60. Capes. University Life in Ancient Athens. N. Y.
61. Mahaffy. Old Greek Education.
62. Chassiotis. L'Instruction Publique chez les Grecs. Paris.
63. Spiers. School System of the Talmud. London.
64. Simon. L'Éducation et l'Instruction des Enfants chez les Anciens Juifs. Paris.
65. Edgeworth. Practical Education. N. Y.

NOTE. — For other supplementary works, and for a more complete description of the books in the above list, consult the Bibliography of G. Stanley Hall (Boston : D. C. Heath & Co.).

INDEX.

EDUCATION.

"Thou that teachest another, teachest thou not thyself?"

FOR American Schools and American Scholarship there is no more healthful sign than the newly-awakened interest of teachers in all that pertains to successful work and personal culture. At the outset of this great and wide-spread movement in favor of better methods and worthier results, it was but natural that the practical side of education should be treated out of all proportion, while its theoretical and historical aspects should be somewhat overlooked. But if education is to become a science and teaching to be practised as an art, one means to this end is to gather and examine what has been done by those who have been engaged therein, and whose position and success have given them a right to be heard. Another and not less potent means is, to gain a clear comprehension of the psychological basis of the teacher's work, and a familiar acquaintance with the methods which rest upon correct psychological principles. As contributions of inestimable value to the history, the philosophy, and the practice of education, we take pleasure in calling the attention of teachers to our books on Education, mentioned in the following pages. It is our purpose to add from time to time such books as have contributed or may contribute so much toward the solution of educational problems as to make them indispensable to every true teacher's library.

The following good words, and also the opinions quoted under the several volumes, are an earnest of the appreciation in which the enterprise is held:—

Dr. Wm. T. Harris, *Concord, Mass.:* I do not think that you have ever printed a book on education that is not worthy to go on any teacher's reading-list, and the best list. (*March* 26, 1886.)

J. W. Stearns, *Prof. of the Science and Art of Teaching, Univ. of Wis.:* Allow me to say that the list of books which you are publishing for the use of teachers seems to me of exceptional excellence. I have watched the growth of the list with increasing pleasure, and I feel that you have done a service of great value to teachers. (*May* 26, 1886.)

Nicholas Murray Butler, *Acting Prof. of Phil., Ethics, and Psychology, Columbia College, N.Y.:* I am greatly interested in your series of pedagogical

Educational Classics.

The following books contribute so much toward the solution of educational problems as to make them indispensable to every teacher's library.

Extracts from Rousseau's Émile.

Containing the Principal Elements of Pedagogy. With an Introduction and Notes by JULES STEEG, Paris, Député de la Gironde. Translated by ELEANOR WORTHINGTON, recently of the Cook County Normal School, Ill. 5 by 7¼ inches. Cloth. 157 pp. Price by mail, 80 cts.; Introduction price, 75 cts.

" There are fifty pages of the Émile that should be bound in velvet and gold." — VOLTAIRE.

M. Jules Steeg has rendered a real service to French and American teachers by these judicious selections from Rousseau's Émile.

Émile is like an antique mirror of brass, — it reflects the features of educational humanity no less faithfully than one of more modern construction. In these few pages will be found the germ of all that is useful in present systems of education, as well as most of the ever-recurring mistakes of well-meaning zealots.

The eighteenth century translations of this wonderful book have for many readers the disadvantage of an English style long disused. It is hoped that this attempt at a new translation may at least have the merit of being in the dialect of the nineteenth century, and may thus reach a wider circle of readers.

Pestalozzi's Leonard and Gertrude.

Translated and abridged by EVA CHANNING. With an Introduction by G. STANLEY HALL, Professor of Pedagogy in Johns Hopkins University. 5 by 7¼ inches. Cloth. xii + 193 pp. Price by mail, 80 cts.; Introduction price, 75 cts.

Externally, "Leonard and Gertrude" occupies a somewhat peculiar position in literature, since it is neither precisely a story nor a pedagogical treatise. It might rather be called a realistic picture of Swiss peasant life in the last century, which, if not of absorbing interest, yet contains much that is curious and instructive concerning old manners and customs. But the moral value of the work is far more than this. In describing the measures taken to reform the corruption and raise the moral standard of the little village of Bonnal, the author expresses his views on some of the greatest social and political questions of all ages. His opinions and theories on educational topics are scattered incidentally throughout the book.

[*From Translator's Preface.*

This is a book which all good teachers should read with care; and having read it, will thank the translator for the great and discriminating labor she has spent upon the very voluminous and intractable original in converting it into the present pleasing form.

[*From Introduction by G. Stanley Hall.*

Levana ; or, The Doctrine of Education.

A translation from JEAN PAUL FREDERICH RICHTER. 5 by 7¼ inches. Cloth.   xliv + 413 pp.   Price by mail, $1.15; Introduction price, $1.00.

We add this volume to the series in the belief that it will tend to ameliorate that department of education which is most neglected and yet needs most care, — home training.

Among other topics it treats of : —

The Importance of Education.
The Spirit and Principle of Education.
To Discover and to Appreciate the Individuality of the Ideal Man.
Religious Education.
The Beginning of Education.
The Joyousness of Children.
Games of Children.
Music.
Commands, Prohibitions, Punishments.
Physical Education.
Female Education.
The Moral Education of Boys.

Development of the Desire for Intellectual Progress.
Speech and Writing.
Attention and the Power of Adaptive Combination.
Development of Wit.
Development of Reflection.
Abstraction and Self-Knowledge, together with an extra paragraph on the Powers of Action and Business.
On the Education of the Recollection — not of the Memory.
Development of the Sense of Beauty.
Classical Education.

Rosmini's Method in Education.

Translated from the Italian of ANTONIO ROSMINI SERBATI by Mrs. WILLIAM GREY, whose name has been widely known in England for many years past as a leader in the movement for the Higher Education of Women. 5 by 7¼ inches. Cloth. About 400 pp. Price by mail, $1 75; Introduction price, $1.60.

This is a work of singular interest for the educational world, and especially for all those who desire to place education on a scientific basis.

It is an admirable exposition of the method of presenting knowledge to the human mind in accordance with the natural laws of its development; and the disciples of Frœbel will find in it not only a perfectly independent confirmation, but the true psychological estimate of the principles of Frœbel's kindergarten system. We believe that this translation of the work of the great Italian thinker will prove a boon to all English-speaking lovers of true education on both sides of the Atlantic.   [*Ready in May.*]

Habit and its Importance in Education.

Translated from the German of Dr. PAUL RADESTOCK, by FANNIE A. CASPARI, Teacher of German, Girls' High School, Baltimore, Md.; with an Introduction by Dr. G. STANLEY HALL, of Johns Hopkins University. 5 by 7¼ inches. Cloth. Introduction + 115 pp. Price by mail, 70 cts.; Introduction price, 60 cts.

Prof. Radestock has devoted some of the best years of his life to practical teaching and to researches in the principles at the base of most habits. In this little book he draws freely upon the work of men like Wundt, Horwitz, and Lotze in Germany, and contemporary writers like Maudsley, H. Jackson, and the school of Spencer in England, and Ribot, Renomier, and Charcot in France.

A study of the book will impress one anew with the fact that all true education is but a building up of habits; but that, in order to have the building strong and beautiful, both physical and psychological laws should be observed. Normal School students especially will, on reading this book, find themselves confronted by some of the most fascinating phenomena of mental science, and will feel with renewed vigor what a responsible thing is this training of the human soul from the first faint dawn of the intellect and will to the full glory of manly and womanly hearts and minds.

Gill's Systems of Education.

A history and criticism of the principles, methods, organization, and moral discipline advocated by eminent educationists. By JOHN GILL, Professor of Education, Normal College, Cheltenham, England. 4¼ by 6½ inches. Cloth. viii + 312 pp. Price by mail, $1.10; Introduction price, $1.00.

School education has to become a science. One means to this end is to gather and examine what has been done by those who have been engaged therein, and whose position or success has given them a right to be heard. Others have been employed, if not *in* it, yet about it. School education at its present standpoint, is the result of many agencies, individual, social, and national, and these have been very varied, and often antagonistic. It has been a growth, to which the philosopher, the politician, the doctrinaire, and the amateur have contributed, as well as the actual workers in schools. With these it has been a course of efforts, schemes, mistakes, and failures, but sometimes of partial successes, all of which have yielded something to the fabric as it now stands. The Author's hope is that the sketch here attempted may stimulate those just starting in their profession, ever to work with the purpose of ultimately placing their art on a scientific basis.

Lectures to Kindergartners.

By ELIZABETH P. PEABODY. Published at the urgency of a large number of Kindergartners, inasmuch as Miss Peabody is no longer able to speak *viva voce*.

The first of these lectures introduced and interested the Boston public in Kindergarten education. The seven others are those which, for nine or ten successive years, Miss Peabody addressed to the training classes for Kindergartners, in Boston and other cities. They unfold the idea which, though old as Plato and Aristotle, and set forth more or less practically from Comenius to Pestalozzi, was for the first time made into an adequate system by Frœbel. The lectures begin with its natural exemplification in the nursery, followed by two lectures on how the nursery opens up into the Kindergarten through the proper use of language and conversation with children, finally developing into equipoise the child's relations to his fellows, to nature, and to God. Miss Peabody draws many illustrations from her own psychological observations of child-life.

Levana; or, the Doctrine of Education.

A Translation from JEAN PAUL FREDERICH RICHTER. 5 by 7¼ inches
Cloth. xliv + 413 pages. Price by mail, $1.35;˙Introduction price, $1.25

WE add this volume to our series of "Educational Classics" i
the belief that it will tend to ameliorate that department o
education which is most neglected and yet needs most care, — hom
training.

Among other topics, it treats of : —

The Importance of Education.
The Spirit and Principle of Education.
To Discover and to Appreciate the Individuality of the Ideal Man.
Religious Education.
The Beginning of Education.
The Joyousness of Children.
Games of Children.
Music.
Commands, Prohibitions, Punishments.
Physical Education.
Female Education.
The Moral Education of Boys.

Development of the Desire for Intel lectual Progress.
Speech and Writing.
Attention and the Power of Adaptiv Combination.
Development of Wit.
Development of Reflection.
Abstraction and Self-Knowledge, to gether with an extra paragraph o the Powers of Action and Business
On the Education of the Recollectio — not of the Memory.
Development of the Sense of Beauty
Classical Education.

A Descriptive Bibliography of Education

Arranged by topics. By G. STANLEY HALL, Professor of Psychology an
Pedagogy, Johns Hopkins University, and JOHN M. MANSFIELD. 5¼ b
7½ inches. Cloth. ∞ + ooo pages. Price by mail, $1.10. Introductio
price, $1.00.

IN his preface to this book, Dr. Hall says : —
"In the field of more strictly pedagogic literature, which is rela
tively limited, the material is yet far too great to be mastered in a life
time of the most diligent reading, and the reading time of mos
teachers is quite limited. Hence they cannot be too select in thei
choice of books. . . . The habit of reading what is beneath one'
level, whether fostered by a sense of duty, or, worst of all, by a fals
sense of the authority of things printed, is belittling, and the exac
inverse of educational.

"Teachers who will be as select in their reading as we should al best, — to say nothing of the tenth or twentieth best, and making all reasonable reservations, — may, I believe, in the time at their disposal, and now squandered on print unworthy of them, reasonably hope to master most of the best, if they confine themselves to one language and one department.

"To do this, however, not only is some hardihood of self-denial, but also some knowledge of the good and evil in pedagogic print, needed, and just this is what American teachers are at present seeking with more interest and in more ways, as I believe, than ever before. In seeking the best there is much to mislead and little to guide teachers. In the great work of designating and grouping the best, the present volume is only a hint, a first suggestion. It is, in the phrase of an educational leader to whom its writer has been chiefly indebted for suggestions during its preparation, only a foot-path roughly blazed, and by no means a finished highway, though the latter may eventually follow about this course. . . .

"In the general reading of every teacher, of whatever grade, should be included some work on the history of education, and some psychological and some hygienic literature. Every teacher should also select some department or topic, connected in many cases probably with the teaching they prefer, about which the reading should centre. In this field they would in time come to know the best that had been done or said, and themselves become more or less an authoritative centre of information for others about them, and perhaps make contributions that would render many their debtors, not only by positive additions to their knowledge, but in guiding their reading, which is one of the greatest aids one person can render another. As teachers thus gradually become specialists in some such limited sense, their influence will do more than has yet been accomplished to realize the ideal of making their work professional in a way in some degree worthy that high term, and they will be able gradually to effect a greatly needed reform in the present character of text-books, and all who would lead in public school education will slowly come to see the need of thorough and extended professional study."

N. E. Jour. of Education : Prof. G. Stanley Hall's Bibliography of Educational Literature promises to be the most valuable teacher's aid in home We know of no man who is better equipped for such service; and he has taken the time and been given all the assistance necessary for the perfection of

Monographs on Education.

MANY contributions to the theory or the practice of teaching are yearly lost to the profession, because they are embodied in articles which are too long, or too profound, or too limited as to number of interested readers, for popular magazine articles, and yet not sufficient in volume for books. We propose to publish from time to time, under the title of *Monographs on Education*, just such essays, prepared by specialists, choice in matter, practical in treatment, and of unquestionable value to teachers. Our plan is to furnish the monographs in paper covers, and at low prices. We shall continue the series as long as teachers buy freely enough to allow the publishers to recover merely the money invested.

Of this series we are now ready to announce the four following: —

Modern Petrography.

An account of the Application of the Microscope to the Study of Geology, by GEORGE HUNTINGTON WILLIAMS, of the Johns Hopkins University. 5 by 7¼ inches. Paper. 35 pages. Price by mail, 25 cents.

The Study of Latin in the Preparatory

Course. By EDWARD P. MORRIS, M.A., Professor of Latin, Williams College, Mass. 5 by 7¼ inches. Paper. oo pages. Price by mail, 25 cents.

Mathematical Teaching and its Modern

Methods. By TRUMAN HENRY SAFFORD, Ph.D., Field Memorial Professor of Astronomy in Williams College. 5 by 7¼ inches. Paper, oo pages. Price by mail, oo cents.   [*Ready in August.*

How to Teach Reading, and What to Read

In the Schools. By G. STANLEY HALL, Professor of Psychology and Pedagogy, Johns Hopkins University. 5 by 7¼ inches. Paper, oo pages. Price by mail, oo cents.   [*Ready in September.*

Methods of Teaching and Studying History.

Second Edition. Entirely recast and rewritten. Edited by G. Stanley Hall, Professor of Psychology and Pedagogy in Johns Hopkins University. 5¼ by 7½ inches. Cloth. xiv + 386 pages. Price by mail, $1.40; Introduction price, $1.30.

THIS volume contains, in the form most likely to be of direct practical utility to teachers, as well as to students and readers of history, the opinions and modes of instruction, actual or ideal, of eminent and representative specialists in each department. About half the material of the first edition has been eliminated from this second edition, and new matter substituted to an extent which somewhat enlarges the volume, and of a kind which so increases its value and utility that readers of the old edition will find this essentially a new work. The following Table of Contents will give a good idea of the plan and scope of the book : —

ON METHODS OF TEACHING HISTORY. By Professor C. K. Adams, Corne' University.

ON METHODS OF HISTORICAL STUDY AND RESEARCH IN COLUMBIA UNIVER SITY. By Professor John W. Burgess, Columbia University.

PHYSICAL GEOGRAPHY AND HISTORY.

WHY DO CHILDREN DISLIKE HISTORY? By Thomas Wentworth Higginson.

GRADATION AND THE TOPICAL METHOD OF HISTORICAL STUDY. Part I.— Historical Literature and Authorities. Part II. — Books for Collateral Reading. Part III.— School Text-Books. Supplement.

HISTORY TOPICS. By Professor W. F. Allen, Wisconsin University.

BIBLIOGRAPHY OF CHURCH HISTORY (see special index to this article). By Rev. John Alonzo Fisher, Johns Hopkins University.

The following opinions of the book will be of interest to teachers and students of history :—

Alice E. Freeman, *Pres. of Wellesley Coll., Mass.:* It· is an admirable book in every way. What these men say in regard to their methods of work is most wise, as I know by experience as a student and as a teacher. The "Seminary Method" was an inspiration to me under that eminently good teacher, Prof. C. K. Adams, and it is our method of advanced work here. (*Jan.* 16, 1884.)

George Lilley, *Pres. of Dakota Agricultural Coll., Brookings:* I wish to recommend the work to our class of normal teachers connected with the college. (*April* 12, 1886.)

Paul Frederica, *Professeur à l' Université de Gand, Ghent, Belgium:* Veuillez remercir de ma part celui ou ceux des auteurs qui ont bien voulu me faire envoyer cet intéressant ouvrage. Agréez mes salutations distingués. (*Jan.* 12, 1884.)

A. M. Sperry, *Supt. of Schools, Dodge County, Minn.:* In adopting it as a guide for the teachers of this county in teaching history in our common schools I express in the most practical way possible my opinion of its adaptation to their needs. It marks the beginning of better work in history. It will reveal to the teacher the means of awakening and guiding the historical sense in their pupils, and of giving to the study its true place as a source of pleasure and of power, not less in the common than in higher schools. (*Feb.* 21, 1884.)

Rev. S. L. Stiver, *Prin. of Bunker Hill Academy, Ill.:* It is the most complete of its kind, and clearly sets forth the best general methods of work in this important branch of science and pedagogics. The appendix, upon historical outlines and bibliography, is well worth the price in itself, and should be in the possession of every well-informed and progressive teacher of history. (*March* 8, 1884.)

S. J. Sornberger, *Teacher of History, State Normal and Training School, Cortland, N.Y.:* I am very much pleased with the book. It gives to the teacher an outlook into the field of history which without it would never have been realized. The list of works of reference is alone worth the price of the book. (*March* 17, 1884.)

Mailloux, S

8 2/19/93